SUPERFLUOUS WOMEN

Art, Feminism, and Revolution in
Twenty-First-Century Ukraine

JESSICA ZYCHOWICZ

Superfluous Women

Art, Feminism, and Revolution in Twenty-First-Century Ukraine

UNIVERSITY OF TORONTO PRESS
Toronto Buffalo London

ISBN 978-1-4875-0168-6 (cloth)
ISBN 978-1-4875-1375-7 (EPUB)
ISBN 978-1-4875-1374-0 (PDF)

Publication cataloguing information is available from Library and Archives Canada.

Publication of this book was made possible, in part, by the financial support of the Shevchenko Scientific Society of Canada.

Наукове товариство ім. Шевченка в Канаді
Shevchenko Scientific Society of Canada
Société scientifique Ševčenko du Canada

This publication was made possible in part by the financial support of the Canadian Foundation for Ukrainian Studies.

Канадська
фундація
українських
студій

Canadian Foundation
for Ukrainian Studies

Fondation canadienne
des etudes ukrainiennes

University of Toronto Press acknowledges the financial assistance to its publishing program of the Canada Council for the Arts and the Ontario Arts Council, an agency of the Government of Ontario.

Canada Council   Conseil des Arts
for the Arts   du Canada

ONTARIO ARTS COUNCIL
CONSEIL DES ARTS DE L'ONTARIO

an Ontario government agency
un organisme du gouvernement de l'Ontario

Funded by the   Financé par le
Government   gouvernement
of Canada   du Canada

This book is for
my grandmothers
who were barred from attending university
the women of my generation
and for authors and artists anywhere
made invisible for seeking a voice
but especially those in Ukraine and Poland
before our time who disappeared
despite or because of their dedication to their talent
— and for those who did not —
whose words survive in our words
so that we do not perish.

There are important moments of apprenticeship.
The first moment of writing is the School of the Dead,
and the second moment of writing is the School of Dreams.
The Third moment, the most advanced, the highest, the deepest, is the School of Roots ...
It's the book stronger than the author: the apocalyptic text,
whose brilliance upsets the scribe.
How can it be written? With the hand running.
Following the writing hand like the painter draws:
in flashes.

– Hélène Cixous, Wellek Lecture, 1990

Maidan is a School.

– Nikita Kadan, interview with the author, Kyiv, 2019

Contents

Figures

Acknowledgments

I aspire to offer to others the generous intellectual support that I have received from the institutes and many individuals who have helped me over the course of researching and writing this book. The following have been especially critical to this project: Benjamin Paloff for transforming how I understand the text; Brian Porter-Szűcs for showing me how to remain a sceptic of history; Elena Gapova for leadership on all fronts in gender studies on both sides of the Atlantic; Herbert J. Eagle for insights into the "canons" of revolution in early Soviet and East European film and literature; Michael D. Kennedy for providing me with an invaluable role model as a publicly engaged intellectual; Marysia Ostafin for holding steadfast in the face of all adversity while innovating new platforms and opportunities for the study of Eastern Europe; Marusya Bociurkiw for friendship and unwavering commitment to justice; and Geneviève Zubrzycki for lighting the torch on the idea of aesthetic revolt and paving the way for me and others in all of the above regards. I also thank Stephen Shapiro at University of Toronto Press for his editorial acumen, and three anonymous readers for their expertise as reviewers.

This project is largely owed to the many incredible artists and activists in Ukraine who lent their words and images to these pages, and generously shared with me all aspects of their lives as leaders, thinkers, and creative producers. There are too many names to mention here, so let it suffice for a few of these dedicated souls to stand in for the many who deserve recognition: Oksana Briukhovetska, Zakhar Popovych, Kateryna Ruban, Oksana Kazmina, Olha Martenyuk, Oksana Karpovych, Galka Yarmanova, Olga Plakhotnik, Maria Mayerchyk, Nadiya Parfan, Kateryna Mishchenko, Vasyl Cherepanyn, Oleksii Radynski, Yustyna Kravchuk, Mykola Ridnyi, Alina Kleytman, Nikita Kadan, Lesia Khomenko, Yevgenia Belorusets, and many others. I am especially grateful for the sharp intellect of Natalyia Tchermalykh, without whose solidarity this book may never have manifested.

I owe special thanks to the University of Michigan, especially the Copernicus Program; the Weiser Center; the Center for Russian, East European, and Eurasian Studies; International Institute; and the faculty of the Department of Slavic Languages and Literatures, especially Mikhail Krutikov, Olga Maiorova, Tatjana Aleksic, Assya Humetsky, Svitlana Rogovyk, Ewa Małachowska-Pasek, and Piotr Westwalewicz. I am grateful to have received the honour of being a Rackham Merit Fellow, to have been hosted by the Institute of Research on Women and Gender, and for support from the Institute for the Humanities, the Center for the Education of Women, and the Jean Monnet Award. I thank my friends and colleagues at Michigan: Deborah Jones, Jodi Greig, Paulina Duda, Yana Arnold-Quintana, Markian Dobczansky, Anna Whittington, Natasha McCauley, Grace Mahoney, Eugene Bondarenko, Eli Feiman, Oksana Malanchuk, Oksana Posa, and Barbara Melnik-Carson, and others. I also thank University of Michigan staff Jean McKee, Jennifer White, Rachel Facey Brichta, Julie Barnett, and Janet Crayne at Rackham Library.

I am indebted to the Munk School of Global Affairs and the Petro Jacyk Education Foundation at the University of Toronto, especially Lucan Way, Robert Austin, Peter H. Solomon Jr., Ksenya Kiezubinski, Frank Sysyn, and Marta Baziuk. I also owe thanks to my graduate students and members of Lynne Viola's history workshop. It is thanks to generous support from the University of Alberta, the Canadian Institute of Ukrainian Studies, the Canada Shevchenko Society, and the Canadian Foundation for Ukrainian Studies that I was able to complete this book. In Edmonton I am especially grateful to David R. Marples, Myrna Kostash, Volodymyr Kravchenko, John Paul-Himka, and Chrystia Chomiak. I also thank Peter A. Rolland, Vita Yakovlyeva, Joanna Dobkowska-Kubacka, Xenia Kopf, Olena Sivachenko, Oleksii Polegkyi, Oleksandr Pankieiev, Kalyna Somchynsky, and Susana Lynn. I am humbled by the support that has been generated in the writing of this book by my expanding circle of colleagues and friends in Canada.

I thank the following institutes for hosting me in residencies or talks in the development of this project: Ohio State University, University of Chicago-Illinois, the Digital Humanities Summer Institute at the University of Victoria, St. Petersburg Higher School of Economics, the Association for Women in Slavic Studies, the Danyliw Seminar in Ottawa, New York University Center for European and Mediterranean Studies, University of Arkansas History and Gender Studies, Uppsala University Institute for Russian and Eurasian Studies, and Harvard Ukrainian Research Institute.

The Fulbright Commission gave me the unparalleled opportunity of researching and teaching as a US Fulbright Scholar in Kyiv. I am thankful for the leadership of Marta Kolomayets, along with Veronica Aleksanych and Inna Barysh, and Christi Anne Hofland at America House. I also thank Pavlo Kutuev, Mark Issac, Gabriela Bulisova, Ian Bateson, Peter Bejger, Terrell Jermaine Starr, Aaron Kennet, Nina Fontana, Christopher Robinson, Sophia Farion, David Kurkovskiy, Marta Dyczok, Sandra Joy-Russell, and Hanna Söderbaum. My students and colleagues at Kyiv-Mohyla Academy also deserve recognition: Tamara Martsenyuk, Anna Osypchuk, Anastasia Riabchuk, and Mikhail Minakov. While there are many more, I thank the following institutes in Ukraine for hosting me at different points: Odesa Museum of Modern Art, PinchukArtCentre, Kyiv Polytechnic Institute, Taras Shevchenko University, Kyiv National Economics University, Kyiv National Linguistics University, Center for Urban History of East Central Europe, and others.

My gratitude extends to the following scholars for ongoing support as fellow travellers: Sarah D. Phillips, Jesse Labov, Vitaly Chernetsky, Serhy Yekelchyk, Beth Holmgren, Marian J. Rubchak, Matthew Kott, Ann-Mari Sätre, Joshua Sanborn, Mayhill E. Fowler, Sofia Dyak, Nadja Berkovich, Olga Onuch, Daniel Fedorowycz, Markian Dobczansky, Mateusz Świetlicki, Emily Channell-Justice, Jennifer J. Carroll, Serhiy Bilenky, Oleh Kotsyuba, Diana Dukhanova, Pavlo Kutuev, Sarah Zarrow, Meghann Pytka, and Angelina Lucento; and Lyn Hejinian at Berkeley for inspiring me early in life with her experience in the first cultural exchange organized by an independent avant-garde literary group in the late USSR.

Friendship has been and remains an ark in challenging times and it is thanks to Billy Williams, Kimberly Peacher, and Samantha Wilhoite for reminding me that life is for living uncommon adventures that I could have ever found the bravery to go to Ukraine in 2004, or to keep writing and pursuing the ideas in these pages. I also thank Shannon, Pavlo, Nina, and Benjamin Voytsekhovskyy; Yulia, Lesya and Ivan Zavalona; Lisa Mann; John and Tara Bawden; Jill Deaver and Brian C. Moon; Shelley Stinelli; Alexander Beringer; Jenny Lee Hurst; Dorothy Boxhorn.

Family, in all of its dimensions, is the oldest source for the conflicts and cohesion which drive narrative texts both ancient and modern. I am surrounded by colourful characters in mine, whose unconditional love, patience, and infinite jest provide me with constant inspiration: Marge Mittendorf, the Rahals, the Hanleys, the Pietrykowskis, Andrew and Lisa Zychowicz, the Mossings; Gordon Smith, Johnny Smith, and Debra and Steve Smith; Bay and Noel Jackson, Gail Nelson; Mychailo,

Natalia, Sofiya and Roman Lozynsky; Johnathon, Sasha, and Kathryn Zychowicz; my mother and father, Suzanne and John Zychowicz; and my grandparents Eugene and Mary Zychowicz and Charles and Suzanne Smith, who have each instilled in me their generation's twin gifts of resilience and invention. I thank Vasyl Lozynsky for holding steadfast. Lastly, I am most grateful for Rozalia, whose life is emerging into the world at the same time as this book.

Note on the Translation and Transliteration of Terms

The spellings of authors' and artists' names follow their own stated preferences and/or common public usage (e.g., Yevgenia v. Evgenia). The names of places in Ukraine follow standardized modern Ukrainian, unless the reference is to a different usage in the original body of work being cited (e.g., Dnipro v. Dnipropetrovsk; Kyiv v. Kiev). I have chosen to refer to the events that took place over winter 2013–14 on Kyiv's central square, or Maidan, as the Maidan Revolution of Dignity, which reflects how these events are addressed by Ukrainians themselves and by state officials. The term "Maidan Revolution" appears in my text as shorthand for this particular moment, although there have been other mass gatherings on the same site at other times in history. The convention in Cyrillic of only capitalizing the initial word of a title appears only when this is the case in the original source. All transliteration follows the Library of Congress system.

Note on the Archiving of Materials for Future Research

Many of the primary published and unpublished texts, images, and other materials from Ukraine collected through the course of writing this book are not widely available. A fond has been opened in the author's name at the Joseph A. Labadie Collection at the University of Michigan where these materials are deposited. The Labadie is located at the Special Collections Research Center in Hatcher Library and is one of the largest collections documenting the history of social protest movements and revolution from the nineteenth century to the present. Sources for this book will be maintained at the Labadie, and the collection of materials pertaining to protest in Ukraine will be ongoing.

SUPERFLUOUS WOMEN

Art, Feminism, and Revolution in Twenty-First-Century Ukraine

Introduction

Young people in Ukraine do not remember the fall of the Soviet Union. Neither do I. Each of us has found ourselves at a crossroads with no signposts: Soviet and post-Soviet, nations, revolutions, languages, day and night all mix together as though in a mosaic viewed up close. Ukraine has a tendency to disorient the uninitiated. In the poem "A Tale Begun," Wysława Szymborska hurles her voice into the vastness of this terrain, marking its expansiveness in a series of unfinished tasks of monumental proportion: "We've got to outwit the watchmen on the desert of Thor / fight our way through the sewers to Warsaw's center / gain access to King Harold the Butterpat / and wait until the downfall of Minister Fouché. / Only in Acapulco / can we begin anew." As the poem makes clear, history in all of its guises, not only those haunting postwar Europe, simply cannot be overcome: "We've run out of bandages / matches, hydraulic presses, arguments, and water." Contrasted with the extraordinary effort involved in attempting to prepare for catastrophe, outwit an enemy, or settle the score, historical change in Ukraine – as in Szymborska's poem – so often appears to us in its most profound forms through experiences that are, by any other measure, quite ordinary. Change, or our perception of what change is, to be more precise, is grasped and marked not by towering public figures or arcane notations carved out from their sweeping dramaturgies of Utopia: "We don't know whom to trust in Nineveh / what conditions the Prince-Cardinal will decree / which names Beria has still got inside his files." For the many, a generational turn is often the torque of a revolt against the few. The vast expanse of the interior of the self is not won, but recognized out of what goes undetected in the radicalism of common, everyday experience: "The world is never ready / for the birth of a child."[1]

Revolution is about self-recognition among many and visibility for the few; it is a concept of change that marks time set against death – and for the revolutionaries themselves, whether they recognize it or not, their acts and words are often the only condition left by which to sustain life in the face of overwhelming precarity. Revolution is the opposite of war. Judith Butler, in *Frames of War*, describes precariousness as a function of arbitrary state violence. For so many around the world today, not only in Ukraine, it is the devaluation and exclusion of different populations from safety and care, which people experience as a state of grieving, that ultimately come to reinforce war.[2]

Other frames – counterframes, alternative frames, double frames – appear throughout this book, which spans the years between the Orange Revolution and the Framework Agreement, the other name for the European Union Association Agreement that President Viktor Yanukovych refused to sign (even after the striking of the Anti-Discrimination Law from the document) – a decision that soon afterward catapulted Ukraine into the Revolution of Dignity. The processes leading up to and following this decision indicate the obvious logics of a state that had long viewed civic expression as unimportant. In an increasingly globalized Ukraine, where the inheritance of the Soviet past is immediate, underlying not only the infrastructure of the political system but also the everyday lives of inhabitants, studying the very idea of a civic identity offers a profound window into the construction of *frames* – material conflicts by which history is made by the few, and the chimeras that can become binding to so many. And there are yet still multitudes of histories, voices scattered in kaleidoscopic frames that, if we dare to look through alternative lenses, can rework, almost spontaneously, all the patterns we knew beforehand into unique sequences. These are the histories that I have attempted to gather for fifteen years and woven, together with Ukraine's artists, revolutionaries, and feminists, into our writings and our lives: "May delivery be easy / may our child grow and be well. / Let them be happy from time to time / and leap over abysses. / Let their heart have strength to endure / and their mind be awake and reach far. / But not so far / that it sees into the future. / Spare them / that one gift, / O powers that be."[3]

The title of this book is an ironic reference to the common sidelining of women's needs and experiences evident throughout periods of uncertainty, including postcommunism. "Superfluous women" is an allusion to "superfluous man," a term popularized by Ivan Turgenev that he applied to a character type originating in Pushkin's *Eugene Onegin*. The description first described men of status and wealth of the 1830s, men whose privilege largely prevented them from contributing to society and were too young to participate in actual revolution. The notion later gained widespread currency in Russian literature to convey the idea of a "lost" generation. This project charts works by Ukraine's youngest generation of artists and activists who actively resisted the unravelling of the reforms promised during the Orange Revolution by protesting where they believed the state viewed their particular interests to be dispensable. What follows here is an attempt to document a generation of artists and activists, many of whom, initially, were viewed much in the same way as the superfluous men: as involved with "protest for protest's sake" lacking any critical value. Only by closely reading their performances, artworks, and other cultural outpourings as texts – texts, moreover, produced by an emerging generation living out the cultural turn brought about by the Orange Revolution – do we begin to see them for the vanguard that they are.

Analysing first-hand interviews, visual art, literature, dissident manifestos, official speeches, and other materials, I demonstrate how several distinct contemporary collectives in Ukraine throughout the 2000s contested Soviet and Western connotations of feminism in the local context to draw attention to a range of human rights issues. Gender and sexuality remain in the foreground of these activists' experimentations and their appropriations of representational schemata of past canonical works from nineteenth- and twentieth-century Slavic and Soviet literature, painting, and photography. In the process, many individual artists, writers, and performers have created an emerging aesthetic that explores, through various techniques, conventions, and media, the notion of the female body as a medium of dissent. Perhaps the most globally visible and controversial of these groups from Ukraine in the 2000s was the women's topless protest group Femen, whose leader, Anna Hutsol, stated in an interview with a Kyiv-based journal in 2012, "We dream of a thousand naked women taking to the streets!"[4] But whose dreams are reflected in the dreams of a thousand women? As a researcher working in the post-Soviet space, I have encountered "feminism" as a signifier of ideological borderlines, a useful heuristic, and for lack of a better term, a "red flag" with which to index a range of debates involving theories of democracy, civil rights, economics, and violence. "The Woman Question" has never been palatable in polite society and always carries with it so many addendums, caveats, and negotiating points (red herrings) in each national, cultural, and social context in which it appears. None of its terminological clockwork or etched monuments to unknown authors readily translate – is the poet "Anon." the universal calque of non-language? How do we name *Her*?

The idea of the superfluous man that emerged from Turgenev's generation gave way to critics' later attitudes towards conformism versus nonconformism in the early twentieth century, after which Soviet socialist realism changed the predominant strain to conformism. The 1990s allowed for more radical critiques of the status quo during a time of extreme instability. Throughout these changes, different associations were ascribed to the women placed opposite nineteenth-century superfluous heroes in the prose of that era. These women were traditionally strong and aligned with ideas fostered by the Slavophiles linked to national purity and the soil. Later twentieth-century recensions, including Lyudmila Petrushevskaya's and Lyudmila Ulitskaya's heroines, contain the iconoclasm and subversiveness of Dostoevsky's Grushenka or Tolstoy's Anna Karenina. These female characters' choices do not conform to the social mores of their time, and in this failure they are spurned for harbouring intellectual proclivities deemed unseemly in women.

The women and others in this book are obviously not literary characters. The term "superfluous women" functions as a metaphor for the intellectual strains I trace across several examples of politically concerned, creative outpourings in performance, digital art, photography, painting, and poetry. Each of these works utilizes very different media and thematic content to address diverse audiences, yet all of them contain commentary on the twentieth-century experience: the artists, in their own way, also deal with the Soviet legacy of their parents' and grandparents' lives – and for some in the emerging generation – their own fading memories of a Soviet childhood. The Orange Revolution looms large across these artists' lives, as does the idea of a "transition" piloted in the 1990s, although these projections of a neat teleology or clean break between eras are conflated and interrogated, even challenged in alternative lines of continuity drawn between past, present, and future in their works.

The sensation of becoming invisible or irrelevant, a feeling of superfluity or alienation deriving from split consciousness, as in Ralph Ellison's antihero, is at the core of every struggle against the centre, every movement for recognition by the marginalized. This sensation is not the same as being a woman or a man, black or white, or any other number of identities; the resulting struggle is the capacity to define one's own ontological position within oftentimes unnameable codes that determine how power is leveraged through societies. One might say that this struggle belongs to every writer, and every revolution. But what does it mean to "fight for one's rights" if those rights are still undetermined? What does it mean to be a body threatened from an unknown source in the name of a cause that has no words yet capable of expressing its aims and contexts? These are the questions that Ukraine's two recent revolutions have brought to the forefront of my thinking about rights, gender, and that one pesky word that nobody seems to like: the perpetual placeholder, the "bad word" that slips off the page and out of the recipe, a stigma and stigmata, a dysfunctional overstatement, or just the unseemly choice of a transgressive woman – feminism.

But revolution and feminism are both words that cede into the background when we think we no longer need their frames; and yet, they are always with us and return in full force when we think we cannot quite distinguish the patterns by which we mark time, and time marks us. They signal the concept of freedom stripped down to the body and sexuality – notions that are hardly universal and come in many disguises. The narrative stripped of its rhetoric, as Joan Didion once remarked. She spoke about her own writing on the countercultural movement and civil rights struggles of the 1960s, and her coming to grips with the national chaos at the time. Her path through the storm was to create, in her words, "a verbal record," a transcription based on an intuitive pattern of the violence that she was witnessing. The result was *Play It as It Lays*. Feminism in contemporary Ukraine is equally fraught with chaos. A term that has at its core only one universally recognizable function in describing nonrecognition is in and of itself the ideal trope for ironic twists of history. The dual frames of devastation/emancipation have emerged as a simultaneous revolution and war. Feminism is just one frame, but in this book, it is the most critical of all.

The idea of the "art-activist" has come to take the place of the antihero archetype of the superfluous man in the artistic practices involving counterimages to representations of the body in post-Soviet political rhetoric. The counter frames within these images are multiple and aesthetically complex. Their complexity is further nuanced by the fact that discursive divides between East and West across the European continent abound in imaginings of the nation and notions of feminism. These terms evidence subtle codes and local etymologies that do not readily translate. I trace points of connection between those activists and artists experimenting with the grammar of prior movements, wherever these discourses come to bear upon ideas of progress, freedom, and censorship. While these groups agitate for diverse causes tied to a range of civil rights discourses, this project's central concern is the question of how protest becomes meaningful, particularly where aesthetic exchanges between activists and audiences rhetorically frame the body as an ideological site in public speech. I combine approaches from history, anthropology, literature, and art criticism to trace how these groups mediate rhetorical frames for staging public conversations around gender and power. Reading their work closely can supply critical narratives in efforts to bridge understandings of feminism in prior East-West dialogues with contestations around human rights and civic vocabularies amid revolutionary struggle.

The nonviolent gatherings on Kyiv's Maidan against the rigged presidential election in the Orange Revolution of 2004 were a mild upheaval compared to the repressions that followed and culminated in violence. A decade later, the mass demonstrations on Kyiv's Maidan in November 2013 began in response to President Yanukovych's refusal to sign an association agreement that would have moved the country closer to joining the European Union. They ended with a different meaning. Some have called what occurred a Revolution of Dignity, an observation that has since been complicated by invasion, occupation, and war. It is significant that when violence broke out on the Maidan, it was leftist student and feminist groups that first organized into emergency units that transported the wounded to churches that had been converted into hospitals; they also guarded the wounded both from the attacking police and from being kidnapped while receiving medical attention in the churches at the hands of these same volunteer first responders. Their prior activist experience and initial scepticism of the idea of a "Euromaidan" revolution lent them the objectivity and ability to act quickly and effectively in their rescue efforts.[5] What follows throughout is the largely unknown story of how Ukraine's feminists and art-activists reached this point in time, and where they are now.

The Orange Revolution

The Orange Revolution supplied a watershed for protest. Growing up in an independent Ukraine has given the nation's youngest generation direct experience of street demonstrations involving the free association of citizens. Yet Ukrainians who had hoped for democratic change in 2004 witnessed the nation's leaders squander their individual and national autonomy by repressing civil liberties in the years that followed. A national debate on "feminism" and "gender" soon emerged in the wake of that moment, symptomatic of deeper, widespread dissatisfaction with the promises for a better life that had gone unfulfilled. This sense of squandered promise may also stem from the unusual qualities that set the Orange Revolution apart from revolution in the classical sense. As Michael McFaul noted as early as 2006, "The final word ... on whether the Orange Revolution was a 'true' revolution rests with the people of Ukraine. That so many immediately adopted the phrase 'Orange Revolution' to describe the tumultuous events of the Fall of 2004 suggests that the term will stick, whether academics like it or not."[6] What McFaul does not suggest is that, perhaps, all revolutions appear "revolutionary" only in hindsight, and that the Orange Revolution had never really come to an end.

The former opposition leader Yulia Tymoshenko, who was united with Viktor Yushchenko in the Orange Revolution in 2004, served as Ukraine's prime minister from 2007 to 2010. She was ousted in the 2010 presidential election by a coalition between Yushchenko and former rival Yanukovych. In October 2011 she was incarcerated on charges of negotiating an illegal gas deal with Putin during her years as prime minister. Some commentators remarked that President Yanukovych's allies orchestrated her imprisonment in order to cut competition in Ukraine's following election cycle. In early 2013, while still imprisoned, she was charged with the 1996 murder of businessman and rival oligarch Yevhen Shcherban. She would later be released and join demonstrators on the Maidan in 2013–14, only to receive very little support from the crowds gathered on the same site where she had helped lead the Orange Revolution a decade prior. Polls revealed low popularity ratings in her campaign to run for president in the lead up to Ukraine's 2019 election cycle. Part of Yulia Tymoshenko's populist charm resided in her performance of a folk-feminine ideal in her hairstyle and her standing by Yushchenko in their joint platform, which was based on a "Return to Europe" as the "end" of transition.

The two recent revolutions in modern Ukraine are as equally fraught with cultural mythology as the official socialist-realist representations of gender and social change that proliferated throughout the USSR in the twentieth century. For women in Ukraine, 2004 was a catalyst for organizing around issues directly concerning gender, such as reproductive rights, employment, and representation in government. Sarah D. Phillips has traced a gap between women's grassroots articulations of the shape of these issues and the rhetoric of development funding programs designed to promote elites' own agendas.[7] As the ambitious reforms promised by Orange leaders dissipated in the second half of the 2000s, many women across the academic and professional sectors began to mobilize around equal representation in parliament.[8] International Women's Day, or March 8, symbolically unified the many petitions, conferences, and street demonstrations that ensued under an increasingly regressive regime. What this moment reveals is that conflicts over March 8, like conflicts over feminism, are ultimately motions on how to commemorate a past regime: which parts to inherit and which ones to reject. In the landmark study *What Was Socialism, and What Comes Next?*, Katherine Verdery attributes the particular weight that gender has in post-Soviet political rhetoric to the ways in which it was legislated under socialism. The Woman Question, like The

National Question, presented ideological risks as a vehicle for subversive counter-revolutionary views forbidden by the Politburo.[9]

In *Sex in Public*, Eric Naiman traces the heightened significance of sexuality in post-Soviet policymaking back to the year 1907. Where the young radicals of the 1860s expanded the scope of political life into the home, it was the later revival of mysticism through symbolism, Naiman writes, that intensified the examination of personal life and brought the body and sexuality into these discussions. The publication of the first instalment of Mikhail Artsybashev's novel *Sanin* in 1907 coincided with the intelligentsia's pivotal turn towards the inner life and its desires as the "lasting basis for the building of any society."[10] *Sanin* was unique because it broke from symbolism's universalization of internal life and instead "purported to offer a unified worldview that smoothly blended changes in contemporary attitudes about morality into a new sexual ethos."[11] The novel exploits women and aggrandizes male fantasies, but the protagonist triumphs over the right, in addition to "the latest – Marxist – incarnation of the 'superfluous man,'" and this triumph signifies "a rejection of the entire system of values that produced the problem of the superfluous man, a system predicated on the notion that an individual establishes his worth (or social potency) through his contribution to society. The hero's creed is the affirmation of the individual through the satisfaction of his desires."[12] The public semantics of privacy and sexual expression as the basis for individual political subjectivity would persist after the Bolshevik Revolution, "when pre-Revolutionary ideals of communality would be brought down to earth and put into practice."[13] Traces of *Sanin* and its equation of sexuality with individuality in Soviet intellectual life remain in the contemporary ideological contexts of the successor states.

In contemporary Ukraine, women were some of the first civic activists to step into the vacuum left by the Orange Revolution in Kyiv's streets, museums, libraries, and other public spaces. The word *feminism* graced their petitions, publications, and headlines – followed by debates on what the term means, or could mean, for the future. I have chosen to study controversies around the idea of feminism as a method for decoding these signs, following the line of theorists whose thinking on democracy involves an approach to politics as a philosophical object of study. In this approach, "the political" has both local implications and universal trajectories. The underlying idea remains that the tyranny of the majority can be apprehended only on hegemonic terms, meaning that democracy is always dependent upon performing its own critique and, therefore, validating future consensus. I have discovered the same to be true in my experiences researching and writing on post-communism – the political cannot be separated from performance.

In the performative notion of politics, spaces of dialogue cluster around the valuation, not the moral judgment, of art. This view requires thinking of politically engaged artists beyond the aspiration to govern. This is, ultimately, about cultivating an aesthetic critique that remains self-consciously within its own historical paradigm as an allegory of art – a work of art or a performance that turns over its own expressions, or doubly expresses. In Bakhtin's concept of parody, the language of travesty is also one that depends upon a doubling effect, or repetition. Many of the texts in this study revisit the past, in particular the late-Soviet past, to mine its cultural vaults for new meanings. The ambivalence, playfulness, and bohemianism of counterculture during the glasnost era, in particular, resurface in reminders that protest is never superficially as simple as being for or against something. The people versus state approach to cultural history is too limited for seeing deeply into how politics, art, and time inform one another. Walter Benjamin penned his theses on history during a time when ethical inquiries into politics on the European continent could not have been more exigent.[14] His claims that the aestheticization of politics could yield fascism, and that the politicization of aesthetics eventually turns to socialism are, ultimately, about the lack of validity of aesthetics and politics taken to extremes. Perhaps what we can take from his observations now is a greater vigilance in our own critiques of the theatrics of human action, and inaction, in the performance of politics.

For young people who did not grow up in the Soviet era, but can recall the Orange Revolution from high school or college, the democratic promise of that moment has largely given way to scepticism of mainstream politics, further stigmatizing feminism as a term. For a brief moment between the revolutions of 2004 and 2014, March 8 provided a powerful reference for staging demands to reorganize gender relations as a symbol of transnational women's political mobilization preceding the Bolshevik Revolution. Communist rituals embedded in the day's celebration, in contrast to the gendered restructuring of the workforce after 1991, rendered March 8 a powerful topos for activists who wanted to revisit or challenge the political immediacy of the public/private divide. In Ukraine, the day's widespread commemoration and its positioning as a "strengthened vehicle for post-socialist politics" provided emancipatory rhetoric for re-evaluating the outcomes of the Orange Revolution in the years preceding the Maidan Revolution.[15]

In post-Orange Ukraine, the term feminism was an already controversial rallying point to form alliances around highly varied issues that activists wanted to draw attention to. Some of these issues, such as access to basic services like public transport and hot water, did not appear to be conventionally feminist at all. I approach postcommunism as a nonclassical instance of postcoloniality, ascribing to the idea that national autonomy and feminism can coexist, and that the latter often productively conflates the national identities subsumed within the mainstream. Thus, I historically situate the protest texts and artefacts in my study as being not only "after" the Orange Revolution but also "after" many other critical and theoretical posts – postcommunism, postcolonialism, and postmodernism. My approach shares a common root with Vitaly Chernetsky's characterizations of Ukraine and Russia in the 1990s as paradigmatically rich with a certain "postmodern post-colonial" sensibility.[16] I extend his critique of gender as cultural quali-fier to contemporary Ukrainian cultural, media, and artistic production.

The media, commercial culture industries, and campaign technology that produced the Orange Revolution synthesized a rhetorical context specific to that particular moment. Several strands of this rhetoric were present in the performances on Kyiv's Maidan by the controversial women's protest group Femen in the years following their founding in 2008, especially in their use of regional symbols associated with the Euro-pean Union and the Russian Federation in parodies of local issues at the municipal level. I explore both local and global vantage points for view-ing how Femen – a political project contested by feminists of all stripes – manoeuvred within diverse cultural codes to advance their image within a broader protest paradigm.[17] Ukrainian anthropologists and members of the group Ofenzywa, Olga Plakhotnik and Mariya Mayerchyk, first localized Femen's street activism as a particularly post-Orange cul-tural phenomenon, linking their project to a broader generational shift: "Femen is a product of the post-Soviet system, they are out in the streets as the generation of 20-25 year olds who have grown up during the inde-pendence period ... Femen is also a post-revolutionary phenomenon in terms of the powerful opportunities for street protest that were brought on by the Orange Revolution."[18] Femen's own vision of themselves largely matched this initial assessment: "We are working to change pub-lic opinion and, in many cases, our results will not be seen today, nor tomorrow."[19] Internal to Ukraine, Femen's early public appearances cre-ated a wave of discussion that entered presses in debates on the mean-ing of feminism, equality, and women's rights that, for a time, remained severed from outside influences.

More generally, where the socialist past has been discarded as irrele-vant, or counterproductive, by Ukrainian policymakers facilitating the advent of free market shock capitalism, so too have many individu-als' positive associations with socialism – including feminism – been tossed aside. Verdery links this tendency to the rise of nationalism in the formation of statehood after communism: "Because communist parties all across Eastern Europe mostly toed the Soviet internationalist line in public, national sentiment became a form of anti-communism ... To the extent that women are seen as having benefited from socialism, as having had the socialist state as their ally, feminism becomes socialist and can be attacked as antinational."[20] Taking into account these links between feminism and socialism in the popular account of history, I argue that Ukrainian women's recent moves to reclaim March 8 are also an attempt to overhaul a system of memorialization that symbolically outlaws feminism in the name of the state, wherever the state replicates antisocialist and/or nostalgic sentiments to legitimize itself. Weaving together socialist revolutionary narratives colouring the region's modern past into their own movement, the times when feminists, such as Ofenzywa, in chapter 3, marched through the streets as a group calling for changes to the Ukrainian Civil Code, they reenacted protest as it was figured by nonviolent street demonstrations on Kyiv's Maidan in 2004. They reintroduced feminism to the public as neither Soviet nor antinational. And along with it – the will to stand on the Maidan in 2014.

"The Collective"

Several groups of artists and intellectuals in Ukraine's emerging generation are continuing to revisit and adapt the notion of the art collective to their own cultural projects.[21] These injunctions into Kyiv's public spaces comprise the foundational performance strategies of the post-Orange collectives REP (Revolutionary Experimental Space) and SOSka Group, and in their earlier years often resembled the street performances known as "happenings" in Poland towards the end of the Polish People's Republic, or Polska Rzeczpospolita Ludowa (PRL). The eighties in Poland saw the early avant-garde's ironic humour enter the narratives of large-scale public street demonstrations. The usage of street environments, pop art, public provocation, and cultural alterity shared across these periods was also reflected in the pop singers associated with the stages of the Orange Revolution.[22]

Many of the Ukrainian avant-garde groups that broke with official Soviet cultural policy during the twentieth century also practised their dissident art in small collectives that offered them some social protection from the central authorities, which largely controlled the censors. One such group in Kyiv and Kharkiv was initiated by Mykhaylo Semenko in 1914 as an alternative to Russian Cubo-Futurism (кверо-футуризм). This was the beginning of Panfuturism that would take the form of a "pan-avant-gardist" approach, "treating all revolutionary moments as a single phenomenon and a special stage in the overall artistic process."[23] The 1921 manifesto of Nova Generatsiia, by Semenko, in which he critiques his contemporaries for failing to carry forth the aims of the revolution, evidences the fervour with which the political winds were howling at that moment: "We speak of those who once 'accepted' the revolution, who digested the new hastily – of the DECADENTS who lost faith in it, because they 'accepted' its mottos, its gusto and its romance, and stumbled against its system."[24] Semenko's theory of culture involved a design of systems and subsystems driven by dynamics of construction and destruction that led to sociopolitical principles: "The process – perceived as an impersonal and external force – placed demands on the artist and not the other way around."[25] Semenko became a victim of Stalin's purges in 1937, along with other members of his generation, which was referred to as the generation of the Executed Renaissance. This story would repeat itself throughout the twentieth century.

Today his works, like many others, are adapted to political campaigns in Ukraine by different nation-building projects that seek to erase, rather than debate, the Soviet past. It is worth contrasting this tendency with another moment from the past, when the aims of artists and even the very notion of the collective itself had shifted under glasnost, as mass media and pop culture expanded within the USSR. In the period just after independence in the 1990s, radical poets in Lviv and Kyiv, for example, critiqued both the West and the emerging Russian state from within collectives based in countercultural expressions that maintained an ambivalent stance towards official representations of the nation.[26] Echoes of their voices can be heard throughout the refrains of contemporary nonconformist groups in Ukraine in both their dealings with the state and their internal debates.

Ultimately, what our reflections on these groups now can reveal to us, aside from a story about Ukraine's defection from the Soviet Union, are the early developments of what has since evolved into a lasting modus operandi for displays of collective dissent. The language experiments of the early 1920s Soviet avant-garde and the countercultural undertones of 1970s Western rock music became fused with political scepticism towards both Russian and Western imperialism. The landmark Chervona Ruta rock festival organized by the democratic opposition movement Rukh in 1991 attempted to link Ukraine's defection from the USSR to the wild characterization of the Cossack and the insubordination of punk. At the festival, the Lviv group Snake Brothers created a sensation among young Ukrainian audiences with their song "We're the Boys from Banderstadt." As William Risch writes, "For such listeners, this word, a response to the marginalization of Western Ukrainians in Lviv as 'Banderites' and 'Nazi collaborators,' explicitly rejected Soviet definitions of being Ukrainian."[27] As this example shows, the Ukrainian language itself, alongside Western styles of music, supplied artists and activists living in Lviv and Kyiv with a readily available set of unofficial terms they could use to rebel against national stereotypes. Risch notes that Snake Brothers, like many rock groups in the region at the time, began as a circle of poets.[28] The countercultural rhetoric that these past performances introduced in Ukraine through the adaptation of the poetry collective to the punk stage has accomplished a reordering of older aesthetic conventions in an innovation on the language of protest itself.

How is protest recognized? imagined? legitimized? The generation of artists that I trace here express themselves in paradoxes, like the dissidents that came before them, yet do so while opening the floodgates to ask what it means to live on the precarious crossroads between "East" and "West." Through them, we are also able to ask more nuanced questions about the desire to redefine such divides as we inherit the twentieth century, or reflect on the impetus towards social change that has touched nearly every corner of the globe in the ongoing protests throughout the 2000s from the Colour Revolutions, to the Arab Spring, Occupy, and beyond. Those years now appear strangely disjointed from the mass discontent of the late 2010s.

The aesthetic experiments by which contemporary Ukrainian collectives appropriate, invent, and attach meaning to the semantic codes that already existed in post-Soviet spaces reveal their cultural output as an artefact of how wider publics symbolically inscribe themselves into the imagined landscape of "the square." Many of the creative ties between the individuals here have continued well into the post-Maidan era, despite the onset of Putin's war with Ukraine. Only the size of the square has changed – by moving abroad or breaking apart entirely – sometimes through the rearranging of personal ties across borders, at other times in sustained exchanges of intellectual and symbolic labour; nonetheless, the shape and focus of the work persist. There is always a return to Kyiv's urban spaces as a kind of laboratory for investigating continuities with prior generations, even a refuge, if you will, from the anxiety of having to choose completely between Europe versus Russia, Soviet versus post-Soviet, or any other number of binaries. Yet their stories change as they grow older. They shift between desires to redefine the past, claim new ground, or simply break away from certain aspects of society completely.

In chapter 1 I provide a broader context for understanding these protest-performance scripts. In this context, Femen's performances exposed taboo sexualized fantasies against ethnic narratives rooted in older orientalist discourses. The satire of these performances, I argue, turned on the utopian idealization of Europe, and independence from a "bad" Russia as a cure-all for Ukraine's social ills. These ideals have largely shaped the construction of Eastern Europe in the Western imagination, and served the platforms that pro-Yushchenko elites used to portray national progress in their campaigns. Femen actively adopted the cultural rhetoric that the Orange Revolution left in its wake to a critique of the public sphere, and did so as women, which historian Marian J. Rubchak and others pointed out early on.[29] They depicted the nation from a position marginal to its foundational terms.

On the one hand, Femen's politicized representations of the female body shared ground with past conceptual artists of the 1970s–1990s who experimented with the female form for making art in attempts to depict the physical markings of power. On the other hand, Femen diverged from those earlier aesthetic experiments in their hybrid blend of genres borrowed from contemporary pop, street art, and the information marketing and branding industries. Many counternarratives emerged in performances tangential to Femen, yet employed Femen's aesthetic to signify dissent. In chapter 2 I investigate the representational strategies within these performances in the context of international mass media technologies. In particular, I focus on media marketing and the ways in which feminists have appropriated and diverged from identity categories in global feminist media art since the 1970s.

Technologies of censorship and coercion warrant greater vigilance given the disjuncture between patterns in the digital production/consumption of women's bodies and the very real material consequences of such images as they traverse different cultural contexts. During the nearly ten years they were active, Femen's visual language became instantly recognizable across the globe. They offended all sides of the political spectrum in nearly every country they visited. Conversations about the line between replicating versus overturning mainstream images of women clustered around the Femen brand. These conversations are ultimately about the commodification of protest exploded across virtual media: in particular, where depictions of liberation, repression, consumption, and production play upon viewers' relationship to the feminine stereotypes that Femen and others pantomime. I do not intend to propose a defence of their negative reception, nor do I uncritically approve of their "transgressions"; rather, I present a close analysis of the role of the mass media in Femen's project in order to contextualize the group within a broader ethical framework.

My third chapter examines street mobilization and wider contestations around the local commemorations of International Women's Day organized by Ofenzywa, the largest women's rights group to have emerged since Ukraine gained its independence in 1991. Mainstream celebrations of the day reflect the nationalist ideas exploited by the oligarchy in the 1990s, when corrupt ruling elites fought to maintain power in the Rada despite extreme economic crises. These ideas promoted a narrow vision of social progress, despite the egalitarian ideals of the Orange Revolution that some leaders set forth.[30] Nonetheless, the peaceful grassroots gatherings of the Orange Revolution did provide people with valuable experiences, and it is these peaceful gatherings that Ofenzywa re-enacted when they first marched through the streets of Kyiv. In stating that they were "reclaiming the political meaning of International Women's Day," they appropriated an international protest narrative founded in early twentieth-century women's labour organizing. Ofenzywa's manifesto and march rehearsed past transatlantic movements, framing the present as being out-of-joint with the "original" meanings of women's liberation proffered by Zetkin, Kollontai, and others as early as 1913. Borrowing the moving vectors of three bygone revolutions – the industrial women's labour movement, the Bolshevik Revolution, and the Orange Revolution – the group's collective aesthetic contrasts the utopian dreams of the past with their own critiques of society during the interrevolutionary period in 2000s Ukraine.

In Ukraine during and after the Orange Revolution, the street becomes a place for envisioning nationhood and the "people" as acting unitarily to found a democratic ethos. In this chapter I compare photography featuring women living in Kyiv tenement homes by one participant in Ofenzywa, Yevgenia Belorusets, with the aesthetic experiments of the Soviet giant of photography, Alexander Rodchenko. While the affective qualities underlying Belorusets's photos render residents' experiences more accessible to a broader audience, their political meanings are motivated by her written texts as an author and activist, transforming them into a site of public contention bearing a richly layered text about women's marginalization in the years before Maidan.

The series I focus on, *32 Gogol St.*, is named after its location in a tenement house. The artist includes interviews and writings about the protagonists in the photos on a blog associated with the project. The result is an epistolary text. The images themselves become conduits by which viewers are asked to engage with alternative meanings of what it means to feel "at home," to belong, or to become a part of communities that do not necessarily fit linear definitions of "progress" in more mainstream conditionings of post-Soviet time and space. Belorusets addresses her photos to a public that includes people who view the house at 32 Gogol Street as a symbol of failure in the social and economic pulse of the nation. She situates her photos within texts comprised of interviews with the people in them. As a result, the photos also illuminate the signifying practices involved in inhabiting the variegated structures that shape daily life. The diverse audiences that the photos apprehend convey the group's overarching gesture towards instantiating a more open and receptive public, which is also mirrored in the group's protest marches through Kyiv's cityscape.[31]

Refashioning Rodchenko's aesthetic, Belorusets's photographs express, through allegories, nostalgia for the Soviet past, an era that she is too young to remember herself. The social conflicts and fissures in the production and circulation of these photos problematize common notions of the private sphere. Many of the photos reveal the manifold dichotomizations of public and private identities that guide self-representation, and representations of the self in society – overturning the sequestering of minorities from mainstream ideas of the public. This dynamic is especially foregrounded in the series A Room of One's Own, which subverts social narratives tied to domestic spaces in depictions of gay and lesbian couples at home, exposing the ways in which the mainstream imaginaries of public and private produce and maintain gender roles. Arguing that these images estrange everyday life, a site from which all politics proceed, I illustrate how their narratives convey an alternatively gendered history of late-Soviet culture, and thus make possible important critiques of class inequality in the present.

Chapter 4 centres on two teams of curators who also organize politically, both in the symbolic meaning that they create in their work and in street protests against state enforcement of "official culture" in contemporary Ukraine. In the case of one banned exhibit, entitled *Ukrainian Body* (2011), curators deployed art objects in Kyiv-Mohyla Academy's museum space to publicly frame censorship and the marginalization of different minorities by the state. The main question in this chapter asks how art-activists in contemporary Ukraine conceive of notions of creative expression, free speech, and civic freedom. In official terms, there is no equivalence between the Western ideas of "freedom" and "independence" and the concepts of незалежнiсть and свобода (nezalezhnist'; svoboda) in the Ukrainian constitution that was adopted after the Maidan revolution of 2014. Arriving at different understandings of these terms than they commonly connote or suggest in the West, I analyse how those in my study were experimenting with these concepts in extra-judicial and unofficial contexts in the years between the two revolutions. Their installations in which they depict the self and its mediation through visual paradigms offer an alternative lens for viewing how such ideas are politicized within the ideological space of the state museum complex as Ukraine continues to reinvent itself.

The post-Soviet museum has a particularly close relationship to the state in the exhibit I focus on in this chapter, and the images of the body within it include commentary on biopolitics within activists' lived experiences in Kyiv's urban spaces. It is significant that the stolen state treasures from the private estate of ousted president Viktor Yanukovych were put on display in the National Museum after he fled Ukraine for Moscow. The exhibit I focus on here, *Disputed Territory* (Spirna teryto-ria/ Spornaya terytorya), took place in the same museum in Kyiv in the summer 2013 and was organized as part of a trans-European avant-garde event named Draftsmen's Congress (Konhres rysuvalnykiv). The artists who took part are distinct in their concern with art practice as public gathering. They have been described as part of a Third Avant-Garde in Russia and Ukraine.[32] But this term is insufficient; it overlooks the specificity of Ukraine, and the peculiarities in the nature of dissidence at the heart of artists' lives there today.

Between the two revolutions there was a critical shift in the idea of the square (Maidan) – a shift that also signified a broader change in concepts of democracy in post-Soviet Ukraine among what I call the *interrevolutionary generation*. Freer and more open uses of public space by youth and minorities, and the decentralization of state institutions that produce culture (museums, media, universities) moved to the forefront of artists' long-standing concerns with censorship. A colourful civic life emerged in which self-proclaimed feminists and dissidents of all stripes achieved important gains in the search for freer and better lives for all. I describe how "the body" became and has continued to function as the central organizing mechanism in this new civic vocabulary for activists and their art after the Orange Revolution. The nude female body in particular, but also the alternatively gendered body, became the primary site for protests around causes that have gone well beyond those traditionally tied to women's or gender rights, such as equal access to housing and tolerance for religious diversity.

Humour is a weapon in the hands of a dissident. The difficult legacies that members of contemporary art collectives continue to face in navigating Ukraine's recent "decommunization laws" – as a form of censorship – reveal the barbs in what it means to fight against inheriting the oppressive Soviet policies towards "official" versus "dissident" artists. The idea of censorship versus freedom of expression in the art-activists' own productions and writings testifies against the terrifying legacies of the Soviet past. Provocative, erotic, deliberately "pornographic" images, along with open debate about Leninism, cults of personality, the GULAG, and neo-Nazism manoeuvre cleverly between direct citation of the state's targeting of the 1920s avant-garde, or Executed Renaissance, and the dismantling of archetypes, ruins, and ideological traps from the Soviet era that still haunt the present. I decode how artists utilize the body as a medium of dissent to make statements about official state institutions in their positioning of themselves in public spaces in Ukraine, and in media dealing with Ukraine. Here you will find the "bad myths" (ch. 5) of the twentieth century set against the social pathologies of authoritarianism in the twenty-first. It is the interrevolutionary generation in Ukraine that can, like no other, give the world the gift of laughing and crying at the same time – to keep us from taking ourselves too seriously. This is the gift of a future free from despots and their iron fists.

All of the works created by the protagonists in this story are shaped by stylistic devices, narrative affects, social affinities, and grammar that I associate with prior samizdat, underground, or nonconformist texts. Yet I am less interested in documenting these inherited forms than I am in exploring the generational turn both *towards* and *away* from the Soviet past in the activation of these forms. The political statements issued by the groups in this study are marginal, yet they are symbolically rich as they are situated at the intersection of two revolutions layered over their parents' and grandparents' memories of 1991 and 1917. Alienation of the individual appears here in my investigations of how images mediate society. Art-deployed-as-protest in my thinking comes to signify social resistance differently among authors, participants, and audiences in the intricate displays and rituals of nationhood among the post-Soviet successor states.

The internet emerged as an important stage for extending the sense of the square after the protests on Kyiv's Maidan in 2014. The final chapter continues into the post-revolutionary period, with emphasis on first-hand follow-up observations and interviews conducted over the course of a year living in Ukraine (2017–18), and ongoing, extended research visits to different regions in 2019. Utilizing aesthetic forms from the early twentieth-century Modernists to depict revolution and war, the intellectuals and artists of the emerging generation have introduced new variations into the historical narrative of Ukraine's two recent revolutions and conflict with Russia. The works I focus on here are in and of themselves unique sites for posing several questions about freedom of expression in these collectives' experimental appropriations of urban spaces and monuments, and their adaptations of different artistic languages to the surfaces that shape the intersection of information and rights in the twenty-first century.

Methodology

How does one inherit concepts of the past in conflict with the varied public(s) that one inhabits? To answer this question, I continually return to the tropes of an artist and an activist, and the role of the intellectual in society, along with the valuation of art: should it have social meaning at all? To better understand the technologies of censorship, networks, and media shaping Ukraine today means constantly shifting the frame: making visible the invisible practices that maintain the centre and margin points is the origin for imagining alternatives to a failed state. Many of the authors and performers whose narratives appear within my own have unleashed debates around the very terms upon which speech is legitimized. The meanings generated through each of these examples are protest "texts" that challenge the gender paradigms in more conventional histories. Throughout this project, I have attempted to identify the scripts and artefacts of dissent across many texts: reading them closely and within the context of their authors' own times and places, their own lived experiences, and their own words.

Each chapter of this book illustrates how artists and intellectuals employ creative media (visual, performance, literary, digital) to contest the enduring cultural mythologies that shape public discourse, especially wherever those discourses come to bear upon the body in imaginings of the nation and notions of progress. Chapter 1 supplies a local history of public dissent and examines parody in performances by Femen, the controversial women's protest group of the 2000s. Chapter 2 traces the role of medium and message in the global media production of protest by analysing the body in digital environments. Chapter 3 explores the work of one photographer from the feminist group Ofenzywa as a critical representation of everyday life among tenement residents and LGBTQ couples in Kyiv. Chapter 4 focuses on the art collectives REP and HudRada in the context of the state and its changing relationship with public institutions for culture and education. This study thus offers a transnational critique of how the politics of self-expression, censorship, and protest come to be inscribed in civic vocabularies that translate unevenly and shift over time.

The final chapter examines works by artists from the Visual Culture Research Center (VCRC), SOSka Group, and Izolyatsia, updating the political and cultural landscape through to the late 2010s based upon over a year of first-hand participation, interviews, and observation. Utilizing forms from the early twentieth-century avant-garde, Kyiv's contemporary generation of authors, intellectuals, and artists continue to introduce new variations into the historical narrative of

Ukraine's two recent revolutions and conflict with Russia. These aesthetic experiments can be viewed as a method for reclaiming political creativity from a postrevolutionary patrimonial state that seeks to regulate and divide, rather than facilitate, public debates about the past as Ukraine works to reinvent itself after the Maidan Revolution of Dignity.

My conclusions in this book are based on fifteen years of studying and travelling to Ukraine, and over eight years of research on this specific project. During the span of 2011–18 I met regularly with curators, painters, artists, editors, and writers from the contemporary art groups HudRada, REP, Shilo, VCRC, Izolyatsia, and several others. In 2018–19 I followed up with individuals from all of these groups in formal and informal settings, finding that we shared a profound sense of disorientation stemming from an uncertain future that now marks our generation around the world – a sense of the uncanny as a unifying narrative thread. And despite the fact that some of the specifically feminist platforms featured in the first half of this book had dissolved by 2019, most individuals had remained committed to their artistic practices. I also compiled extensive primary material, including original interviews, paintings, photography, poetry, essays, manifestos, news reports, blogs and social media sites, official speeches, and first-hand observations of performances by artists and activists from Kraków, Warsaw, Kyiv, Kharkiv, Lviv, and St. Petersburg.

In 2011 I met with the founders of the controversial women's group Femen and soon after, Pussy Riot. Both of these groups were at the time signs of dissent in a much broader, indeed global, constellation of public discourse and scholarly debate. I first conducted interviews with Femen leader Anna Hutsol in Kyiv in 2011, as well as former Femen member Angelina Diash, also in Kyiv, in the summer of 2013; I interviewed the founder of Femen Canada, Neda Topoloski, in Montreal in 2016. I met with Nadezhda Tolokonnikova and Maria Alyokhina of Pussy Riot in Ann Arbor during their visit to the University of Michigan campus in the fall of 2014 and communicated with individuals tangential to their group who broke from them for reasons I discuss in this book. I have conducted other, ongoing interviews in 2016, 2017, and 2018 with feminist and LGBTQ activists from Ofenzywa and the NGOs Krona, Insight, Igliyo, and the Kharkiv Gender Museum, in addition to Ukrainian feminist scholars at Kyiv-Mohyla Academy, Kharkiv Center for Gender Studies, and feminist activists unaffiliated with any of these groups. In 2018 I spent a full year living in Ukraine as a US Fulbright Scholar in the sociology department at Kyiv-Mohyla Academy where I taught visual culture and gender studies. Throughout 2018 I attended many events, formal and informal, with contemporary artists and authors in the collectives featured in chapters 3, 4, and 5. I was also invited to speak about human rights at several universities, organizations, and institutions throughout the country. Major media sources that I have consistently examined over the course of travelling to, studying, and researching Ukraine (2004–19) include the *New York Times*, *Washington Post*, BBC, *The Atlantic*, *Foreign Affairs Magazine*, Radio Free Europe, *Huffington Post*, *The Guardian*, *Christian Science Monitor*, *Kyiv Post*, Hromadske TV, *Euromaidan Press*, Kanal 1+1, *Ukrainian Pravda*, *Moscow Times*, *Pravda*, *Izvestia*, *Correspondent*, *Le Monde Diplomatique*, and *Der Spiegel*, among many others.

When I began drafting this project in 2010, nude protest was first beginning to appear en masse around the world. One of my challenges in writing this book has been balancing and updating my text's scholarly insights against constant flux in the polity, civic life, media, and art production in Ukraine. I witnessed a boom in performance art-activism studies after 2011 that dealt mostly with artists embroiled in high-profile legal cases, for example, with Russia after Pussy Riot (e.g., works by Janet E. Johnson, Valerie Sperling, Elena Gapova). There is no comparable study on Ukraine, perhaps because during those years there were no serious legal repercussions for actions by Femen and other art-activists inside Ukraine. Yet the absence of punishment or legal scandal does not mean that the Ukrainian works are without consequence. Quite the opposite, I believe this book points out that we could stand to learn even more from their unique positioning in the years between the Orange Revolution and the Revolution of Dignity – when the territories between the European Union and the Russian Federation experienced massive struggles against oppressive rule. The collectives featured here, while largely on the margins of society, illuminate in bold and interesting ways the centrality of those struggles to international discourse on democracy.

The Ukrainian context after the Orange Revolution merits a unique set of conceptual tools. In anglophone countries, the question often asked in more recent literature on performance art-activism is, Should art be political at all? Why or why not? Does performance art achieve autonomy from politics more than other forms of art do? Yet in the Ukrainian context, these questions do not readily apply. The stakes are completely different. Artists who consider themselves to be civic activists in Kyiv cannot be understood apart from the Soviet legacies that they are challenging, questioning, and citing in their works.

The unique conceptual tools that are introduced and developed throughout this book are also my point of departure for my use of the word "transnational." The current situation in post-Soviet Ukraine demands that we cultivate new civic vocabularies for understanding protest. I have pulled my theoretical frameworks less from US and UK performance art-activism: instead, viewing the art as in situ, I refer to foundational theorists, including those working on postcommunism intersecting with globalization (e.g., Claire Bishop, Piotr Piotrowski, Gregory Sholette). I have also chosen theoretical frameworks from key sources in media theory because the internet is where Ukraine's twenty-first-century art-activists are engaging globally (e.g., Anne Balsamo, Marshall McLuhan, Anikó Imre, Ariella Azoulay, Guy Debord).

The voices I am in dialogue with in Ukraine are, in many ways, my peers. Through dialogue we are engaging, but also challenging and redefining for ourselves, the feminism and activism in transatlantic contexts of the 1990s. This observation brings up a vital point, and while my text makes many references to the feminists of this period through the formal presentation of key works and their intellectual relevance to current circumstances, the connections are also deeper and intuitive. In fact, much of this manuscript was developed under the personal guidance and friendship of those selfsame groundbreaking feminist scholars and activists (from Ukraine, but also Belarus, Poland, Russia, New York, Detroit, Toronto) who have worked together transnationally in conferences, anthologies, and political actions in order to pave the way for my generation.

Throughout the decade and a half covered in this project, the most consistent concern voiced in my interviews with feminists has pivoted on how Ukraine's women's rights movement would be received by Western audiences unfamiliar with the post-Soviet context. My respondents' supportive concerns have been a welcome reminder of the value of self-reflexivity in participatory research on political rights, and a vivid illustration that my own position as a fourth-generation citizen born in the United States shapes my approach to the question of feminism in its local articulations. Working on this project from Canada as a Postdoctoral Scholar in Toronto and in Edmonton, and as a Fulbright Scholar at Kyiv-Mohyla in 2018, has also impacted my perceptions of myself as a researcher.

One of my strategies for navigating cultural difference has been a strong sensitivity to language on multiple levels. I work in Ukrainian, Russian, and Polish. Throughout my text I have chosen to priviledge the language of the activists' own voices, translating interviews and other documents into English. In the course of writing this book I took on additional projects, including the translation of publications produced by many of the artists and activists featured here, such as the book of essays *Ukrainian Night* by Katia Mishchenko of VCRC and poetry by

Taras Fedirko for the 2014 special issue of *Prostory* called "Documenting Maidan," as well as the ongoing translation and proofreading of collectives' and artists' websites, promotional materials, gallery texts, and other documents. I have also worked collaboratively with artists and curators featured in this book by contributing research and writing to artists' books, exhibits, and publications; conceptualizing and consulting on the production of projects; mentoring younger artists on pathways for research; fundraising for residencies and educational programs; building contacts between international human rights NGOs in Ukraine and leaders in the art world; speaking alongside artists in public diplomacy programs sponsored by the US Embassy in Kyiv; and serving in a curatorial capacity by designing, fundraising, and hosting international platforms featuring dialogue between Ukrainian artists and scholars based in Canada and the United States.

The ethical imperative of doing research at a time of global austerity and professional precarity in both academia and the art world has meant recognizing my own limited resources and also strategizing with my counterparts in order to maximize the shrinking budgets for cultural production in Ukraine, especially during the Russia-Ukraine conflict. This has meant working as an advocate for the artistic communities that I am increasingly a part of, with many of the activities described here happening in parallel, and sometimes intersecting, with the writing of this book. Throughout, I have worked to build and sustain research relationships by establishing reciprocity with my peers in nonhierarchical structures of communication and knowledge exchange. My own creative capacities have expanded as a result of this critical approach to the intellectual fields of aesthetics, language, gender, and political theory. And my community-centred focus continues to emerge and evolve the more I am able to work in these capacities.

Another component of my methodology stems from the literature by anthropologists and sociologists working on gender in postcommunism. Concerns about Western receptions of post-Soviet feminism correlate with the observations of prior scholars about the impact of international NGOs on local Ukrainian activists in the 1990s.[33] Large NGOs, mostly funded by the European Union, continue to support the majority of research and social projects on the basis of predefined notions of "gender" and "women" in Ukraine. Differentiation, described by Sarah D. Phillips, is highly dependent on rhetoric and shapes the funding structures of social projects in Ukraine. This is a process by which activists develop ways of articulating needs in order to argue for, advocate, and validate causes; the state then prioritizes sociopolitical issues within a shifting distribution of needs across varied populations.

With this dynamic in mind, it may be worth remembering that while some of the activists in Phillips's study, conducted in the 1990s and early 2000s, were able to position themselves as agents of differentiation, other projects lost funding within a shifting social and economic stratification that privileged Western donors' predefined discourses of need. These privileged discourses were those that tended to table more localized articulations of need in favour of projects that more directly resonated with the priorities of Western funding agencies. In a very immediate sense, although none of the activist figures or cultural leaders in this book have chosen the pathway of formally entering politics, all have successfully introduced new dimensions to the potential impacts of activism based on more locally scaled definitions of need in the funding of initiatives.

Nearly all of the people in the communities in Ukraine that I have become a part of as a researcher, most notably those from the groups Ofenzywa, the Visual Culture Research Center, and HudRada, continue to productively challenge the critical, creative edge of my work as a chronicler and discursive translator. My participatory observation of the impacts of two revolutions, and the decade between them, while living and working between continents mirrors, in many ways, my colleagues' own movements between the European Union and Ukraine. Grassroots groups in the 2000s such as the feminist Ofenzywa and the first LGBTQ organization, Insight, and their members' stories are a critical page in Ukraine's history. Few others have lived through what they have lived through, and few can shed new light on our generation's search for a time and a place where safety and care are a given, and *human dignity* is no longer a demand.

Over the past decade, my Ukrainian colleagues' lives have taken many different routes. The spaces of our communication have become increasingly virtual. Yet I believe that what has kept a core cluster of writers, researchers, and visionaries of my generation intellectually bound, both across borders and to others who have walked these paths before us, is our shared commitment to human rights in the ways in which we choose to live our lives, and in the conviction that a revolution is a frontrunner of better things to come.

Chapter One

Performing Protest: Sexual Dissent Reinvented

The world at once present and absent which the spectacle
makes visible is the world of the commodity
dominating all that is lived.
The world of the commodity is thus shown for *what it is,*
because its movement is identical to the estrangement of men
among themselves
and in relation to their global product.

— Guy Debord, Society of the Spectacle, 1967

The economy in both the narrow and the broad sense
that is in place in our societies
thus requires that women lend themselves to alienation in consumption,
and to exchanges in which they do not participate,
and that men be exempt from being used and circulated
like commodities.

— Luce Irigaray, "Women on the Market," 1978

I. Introduction

In 2008 four young Ukrainians named Anna Hutsol, Inna Shevchenko, Oksana Shachko, and Roman Zviazsky living in the city of Khmelnytskyi formed a feminist protest group. They settled on a theme – anti-sex tourism; a name – Femen; and a method – nude street demonstrations. Anna Hutsol would serve as their chief ideologue: her background in marketing would not be lost on the group. While interviewing Hutsol, just before Ukraine's twentieth anniversary of independence in 2011, I would encounter her sense of conviction at close range: "Nothing will change if women remain timid and quiet in Ukraine. In principle, our ideas, our protests, are full of ideology and philosophy: a philosophy of life. Men who are looking for something like a show or a cabaret can go see those, but we're doing something else, we're involved in protest."[1] Hutsol and I had arranged to meet at Café Kupidon, a café in an underground brick cellar often frequented by the city's writers and intellectuals. The location of the cafe in downtown Kyiv was near Maidan Nezalezhnosti (Independence Square) where nearly 300,000 Ukrainians camped in tents for weeks in the darkest months of winter in order to protest an unfair election.

As I enter the café, I notice an older man sitting in the corner, hunched over several newspapers and a cigarette. Hutsol later told me that he is from the Ukrainian diaspora and is one of the group's main donors. Newspaper clippings, memorabilia, and photographs of Femen line the walls. Expats and locals mingle and smoke together. A small library of used books is tucked into the corner. A few other Femen activists in the café are busy at work writing and editing online, some are chatting with a journalist. Three or four laptops grace the room's sticky wooden pub tables. Hutsol is still recovering from a cold she caught on the group's recent trip to Odesa – a trip taken partly to plan future demonstrations in nearby Turkey, and partly to increase press coverage. Despite her cold, she is chain smoking and typing furiously. Recognizing me from Facebook before I am able to spot her myself, she rises to greet me in a very welcoming fashion. I learn from her that the café owner is a fan of Femen's and has dedicated his space to their ongoing meetings, endless writing, and strategizing. We sit and talk for nearly an hour. Despite her cough, or perhaps because of it, Hutsol alternates swigs of beer with sips of a thick green syrup, a pine-flavoured liquid called "basalm" that I recognize as a common cold remedy sold at the local bazaar. Hutsol's intense dedication to maintaining her group is apparent; she continues to sift through stacks of papers, photos, and blog posts as we sit and talk.

Femen is the most visible and most controversial activist group to have emerged in the history of Ukraine's independence. Founded in 2008, the group gained notoriety worldwide for topless protests that once featured mostly street theatre, but now primarily consist of five-minute flash-mob performances circulated online. The group's website lists twelve active members and over four hundred non-active members, mostly women in their twenties and thirties. Their performative political stance "against all dictatorship and religion" has provided them with rhetorical strategies through which to attach their image to news stories on causes indirectly related to women's rights.[2] Although Femen's original stated aim was to bring greater awareness to the impacts of the widespread phenomenon of sex tourism in Ukraine, the performances now target a broad range of issues. Even early on in the group's formation, members "protested" commemorations of the Chernobyl disaster, Ukrainian government responses to the swine flu epidemic, and municipal water shutdowns in Kyiv.

One only need utter Femen's name to incite debate. The group's blend of sugary pop art with overt images of sexual violence has made their style nearly synonymous with scandal. There is nothing moderate in Femen's approach. They yell shocking slogans, paint their torsos in the colours of various national flags, and poke fun at the church. In recent years, Femen activists have appeared more often abroad than on the streets of Ukraine, yet many of their actions can be aesthetically traced back to the moment of the Orange Revolution. These connections are most apparent where Femen's topless protests desacralize the religious and folk symbols that political elites once employed to legitimize their campaigns. Even in Femen's later work, iconic references to local politicians abound: one activist wears Yulia Tymoshenko's thick braids, another holds up a picture of Putin, a third wears Belarusian President Lukashenka's moustache. Since their founding, Femen has remained sarcastic, even cynical, in their characterizations of a parsimonious parliament. Beyond the starkly opposite reactions that the group's performances have incited – ranging from outrage to fandom – the symbols that designate Femen's now highly recognizable, controversial image speak volumes about a prior moment when Ukraine's future seemed open to more positive possibilities. The scope and ferocity of the controversies that Femen's topless protests unleashed – first locally, then globally – provided a flashpoint for much deeper anxieties about national independence, gender identity, and sexual liberation – issues that transnational feminist scholars have debated since the fall of the Soviet Union in 1991.[3]

In my early interview with Hutsol, she let me know that she does not often collaborate with other members of the feminist activist community in Kyiv. Hutsol explained this gap between herself and other feminists by distinguishing a separate "academic feminism," explicitly distancing herself from the academy.[4] On the surface, Hutsol's position would seem to work at cross-purposes with local feminists who could become potential allies of her group. Yet underlying her statement are deeper political and social divides around the idea of feminism in the postcommunist context. In their article for the academic journal *Krytyka*, Olga Plakhotnik and Mariya Mayerchyk localized Femen's street activism as a particularly post-Orange cultural phenomenon, linking Hutsol's project to a broader generational shift.[5] Plakhotnik and Mayerchyk explained the group's hyper glamorous, sexualized image as a response to local, negative connotations of feminism and its Soviet connections: "Several critiques of Femen activists' strategies could be made. Stylistically, they are not readily changing the stereotypes of post-Soviet glam femininity, but rather appropriate these types, using them for their marketing potential without problematizing them or challenging any actual assessment of women in society, though they are giving weight to these types."[6] Taking into account that Plakhotnik and Mayerchyk remain sceptical of Femen as a political project, it should also be noted that a broader debate among Ukrainian feminists of all stripes at the time provided an important vantage point for thinking about how Femen manoeuvres within the diverse cultural codes driving their public image in an unprecedented media paradigm.[7] Grounding Femen in the Ukrainian context, this chapter aims to set the stage for studying the group's campaign and what it can reveal about the synthesis of local political experience, mass publicity, and creative forms of dissent.

The idea of dissent, dissidence, and what it means to become a dissident carries unique weight in Soviet history. Femen's spontaneous street shows contain strains of the absurdist, interactive performances known as "happenings" that took place in the region during the last two decades of the twentieth century. The eighties in Poland and Ukraine saw the avant-garde's hyperbole, surrealism, and ironic humour enter the narratives of large-scale public street demonstrations. Some aspects of Femen's performances reflect these earlier styles of street activism, but do so by producing their own mythos of popularity. Added to the more ambiguous, whimsical atmosphere of street protests of the past, in Femen we also find scathing attacks on a wider range of topical issues and a darker sense of sarcasm, their bare breasts and oblique overtures to feminism. In this chapter, I look at the processes of branding and commodification driving Femen's parodies, in particular, where their depictions of liberation, repression, consumption, and production play upon the viewer's relationship to the feminine stereotypes that the group pantomimes in real and virtual public spaces. I argue that Femen's topless spectacles employ the language of marketing and branding in ways that highlight and amplify the accumulation, value, profit, and exchange of women as symbolic capital within the larger economy of entertainment and politics.

There are historic links in Femen's development connected with the discursive environment and ideological design of the Colour Revolutions. Femen's protests challenge these inflections within a pop idiom that predates the Orange Revolution, and they appropriate these styles for their own mythmaking of themselves as dissidents. Verka Serduchka and Ruslana, two major pop singers whose Eurovision entries in 2004 and 2007 marked key moments when gender and a renewed affiliation with Europe converged within a pop idiom in a significant way, manoeuvred between their Western audiences' individualist notions of freedom and a distinctly Ukrainian, Romantic lyricism that guided the songs, slogans, and speeches of the Orange Revolution. The cultural hybridity of these past pop singers' stage marketing underpins Femen's own protest brand, especially in their earliest parodies on Kyiv's Maidan.

If we narrow our focus to the central figure – the prostitute – in Femen's "protests against sex tourism," we can see how the archetype structures the cultural semantics of their performances, in particular, when the group appropriates and exploits a mass media context.[8] Scholarship on sexuality in the Soviet era can also illuminate where Femen's protest narrative deploys associations of the prostitute figure with enterprise, transformation, autonomy, and criminality that have featured in stereotypes of Slavic women at different points in history.

Femen's stagings mixed civic symbols with violent imagery that went against the grain of more mainstream media scripts about national independence and social development in Ukraine. Their prostitute caricatures played upon the campaigns of the Orange Revolution and the idea of having to choose between a utopian "Europe" versus independence from a "primitive" Russia as the answer to Ukraine's social and economic issues. There are no roles, names, or consistent characters in Femen's appearances. Critiques of Habermas's public sphere, including Michael Warner's work, can help articulate Femen in terms of the global language of the mass media, and show how the group manipulates the cultural dialectics of desire, consumption, and appropriation in structuring a mass audience. Femen's brand architecture, blending of real with virtual spaces, and body rhetoric involve multiple, often conflicting, venues for participatory public(s). Femen's sign-systems and the growing, virtual culture market in which the group functions emerged within what both Teodor Adorno and Chantal Mouffe have observed in the close relationship between art and commodification processes.

Giving attention to different receptions of Femen by a range of audiences, I have chosen to focus on aspects of the group's performances that capture some of the paradoxes within late-Soviet and postcommunist cultures viewed through a postcolonial lens.[9] Luce Irigaray's seminal essay on exchange value and the female body, "Women on the Market," underlies my thinking here.[10] I suggest that Femen's performances unfold on three intersecting planes: as a wry retrospective or spectacle of the Orange Revolution; as a parody of the branding of the nation by elites to simulate experiences of national belonging; and as a pun on feminism itself that, like their controversial displays of the female body, problematizes the East/West cultural assumptions that often script media coverage about Ukraine in global discourse.

I pose the following questions: Could Femen be thought of as a retranslation of the Orange Revolution and the pop sensations of that period, specifically in the latter's projection of domestic protest into an ideation of Europe? Do the group's humorous and offensive protests commodify women along with the campaigns they attach themselves to? How does Femen's marketing of themselves as "New Amazons" affect their reception? What was it that became so compelling about these scandalous women? World media did not lose interest in the group. How was it that such an enormous audience – of critics, fans, opponents, police, scholars, politicians, and passersby – could not look away? What passes, versus what gets passed over, as legitimate public behaviour in the period leading up to the events on Maidan in 2013–14 reveals a very different story of local protest culture with roots in the late Soviet period. How do Femen's staged acts, as public displays of the female body, manifest much deeper cultural fissures around nation and gender in Ukraine?

II. Protest after 2004: Beyond Orange

Who Is Femen?

In the years after they formed in 2008, Femen activists staged several parodies of sex work on Kyiv's Maidan Nezalezhnosti (Independence Square) where thousands of peaceful demonstrators had camped in winter to protest an unfair election in 2004 – the same site of the Maidan Revolution that would occur one decade later in the winter of 2013–14. Many of these initial protests took the form of theatrical, topless plays featuring tongue-in-cheek commentaries on any number of issues. Their public appearances usually included ironic references to politicians from the street protests and populist campaigns that members recalled from the Orange Revolution, which took place during their younger years. For example, Femen members dressed up as Yulia Tymoshenko during her trial in 2011, and staged a spoof talk show cleverly named "PMS: Post-Maidan Syndrome." In another protest, they mocked Putin by stealing the symbolic ballot box that he presented in Moscow before his re-election. While the majority of the group's actions in Kyiv took place on the Maidan, other significant sites in Kyiv included parliament (Verkhovna Rada); SBU headquarters; Pechersk Court; Turkish, Russian, Georgian, Saudi Arabian, and Polish embassies; Kyiv polling stations; the Cabinet of Ministers; the Ministry of Health; the statue of Lenin on Khreschatyk; the private residence of the Ambassador of India; Olympic Stadium; and Kyiv-Boryspil International Airport. The group briefly acquired an office in Kyiv in 2011. From September 2008 to 2012, in their most active years, Femen staged approximately fifty-five street protests in Ukraine.[11]

Femen's leader, Anna Hutsol, like many of Femen's members, is from Ukraine's middle class and uses Russian and Ukrainian interchangeably. She has worked in marketing and also received training from a US Department of State leadership program. During the Orange Revolution she was involved with the democratic youth movements PORA and Young Rukh. In 2009 Anna Hutsol reported to newspapers that she would run for office someday and that she would create "the largest all-women party in Europe."[12] She seemed less ambitious in my interview with her three years later, stating that she was disappointed with Yanukovych's ascendancy to the presidency and the increasing restrictions on protestors: "Since protesting has become more difficult in Ukraine, we need to fight harder to prove that women can protest here."[13]

After Viktor Yanukovych entered office, Ukraine's political climate became increasingly conservative. At that time Femen activists faced several short jail terms, though they were usually held in custody only for a few hours or days and maintained a relatively benign relationship with local police. In fact, images of smiling policemen standing by and then calmly cuffing Femen activists became a consistent backdrop in the photos and videos of the group that were published online, on television, and in world newspapers.[14] For a time, the multiple arrests and prompt release of Femen activists bolstered the group's public visibility, rather than posing any real physical threat or state barrier to further street protest. These minor arrests also aided Femen's media output by facilitating their own framing of themselves as resisting an oppressive regime.

In this regard, Femen's tactics mirror prior movements in the region that also used street performance to push the boundaries of "minor hooliganism" as a criminal charge.[15] Although the Orange Revolution was a watershed for protest, Femen's parodies are, in form, rooted in the street protests staged by artists and activists during glasnost. These earlier street actions pivoted on humorous responses to the pressures of a restrictive public sphere. Many of these prior groups' humorous tactics served to make police appear harmless before a generalized public and, in the process, to air very real public fears around state authority.[16] They often featured absurd props, odd caricatures, oblique references to critical social issues, and surrealist overtures to party slogans. Femen adapted the lighthearted theatrics of these antecedents to their own takes on the economic flux and political upheaval of the 2000s.

Throughout the Yanukovych years, Femen faced more serious encounters with police both at home and abroad. In early 2011, three Femen members were kidnapped and taken to a forest after a demonstration in central Minsk in which members parodied Lukashenka's repressive policies on the steps of parliament by wearing his signature moustache and epaulettes.[17] The following year, the group faced more criminal charges, including defamation of public property for cutting down a cross in central Kyiv allegedly erected in honour of Stalin's victims. In the summer of 2013, the group's office in Paris was burned. Shortly thereafter three members, including Hutsol, were attacked and beaten on the streets of Kyiv. No suspects were arrested and no one publicly claimed responsibility for these attacks. These increasingly threatening encounters with police and unknown assailants coincided with a radicalization of Femen's image and an overall reduction in the frequency of the group's protests in real time.

Femen immediately adapted to the rise of internet use in Ukraine, documenting all of their activities on two blogs. In 2010 Femen streamlined their virtual identity by adding Facebook, Twitter, and a website to their online presence. The group has been blocked for nudity on some sites: Facebook suspended Femen's account early on, but only temporarily, and the group's livejournal.com blog in Russian switched to read-only in 2012. Paintings, drawings, and popular graphics by Femen member Oksana Shachko, in concert with outside artists' works, became indispensable to the media forums through which Femen performed their movement. An extensive collection of cartoons, glamour ads, leaflets, and other cultural artefacts comprises an archive of Femen's nearly decade-long history.[18] Over time, the group's increasing contact with the media outlets reporting on their street activities melded with the group's virtual design as members switched their operations to five-minute-or-shorter protests that they could capture on social media. Femen's overall design necessitates looking more closely at the idea of politics that the group ascribes to.

Staging Transgression – Initial Critical Receptions

Femen's first protest took place on the former site of the Orange Revolution, Maidan Nezalezhnosti (Independence Square), in 2008. It was designed, in participants' words, as a protest "against sex tourism and all forms of oppression against women in Ukraine."[19] Imagery from this first protest entailed an anachronistic, sardonic retelling of the nation's past. In one socialist-realist style poster associated with the campaign, a young woman carried an orange banner with the slogan "Ukraine Is Not a Brothel!" A wintry Kyiv cityscape framed the lower corners of the drawing. Such details juxtaposed the "official optimism" that Soviet propaganda art projected onto the proletarian revolution with the freewheeling sentiments of the Maidan in 2004. In a later protest near the same site, on Ukraine's Independence Day, the group dressed up as serf women in orange skirts and pretended to harvest the landscape of intricately manicured flowerbeds not far from the parliament buildings. The overall performance was a reference to repressive regimes, and to earlier dissident actions that mocked official, socialist-realist propaganda. In figure 1.1, overtures to "The Woman Question" by Soviet ideologues hover below the semantics of the protest in the scythes in the women's hands, as the police rush to arrest them in the background: all details in the image work to expose the identity categories that are imposed on women in the nation-building processes of revolution.

Feminist critiques of Soviet women's emancipation argue that early Soviet labour policies failed to address the domestic sphere, and thus created a lasting "double burden" in which the majority of women had to take on the brunt of the work both at home and in the factory. The gap between the original Soviet propaganda image, and the Femen version, juxtaposes women's duty to the state with the actual impact of revolution on women: the message that Ukraine is not a brothel includes the idea that women are often the first ones forced to repeat history. Read as a homology between the Bolshevik and Orange Revolutions, the overall image could be said to draw up a past in which national "progress" was twice imagined, but never fulfilled: once by the "transition" in 1991, and again by the revolution in 2004. The message appears even more eerie in hindsight given what would take place on the Maidan a decade later.

Early on in their formation, Femen members' public statements reflected a more general attempt to relate the emotional impact of the Orange Revolution, which had faded under Yanukovych, to a broader mix of audiences. Hutsol went so far as to state, "We are the children of the Orange Revolution."[20] Given today's context of "fake news," her statements at the time appear even more vanguard in her claiming to an online Russian paper that Femen was part of a larger "information war."[21] Yet Hutsol and other members of Femen were unreliable witnesses to their own role in such a "war," as they would often change their position on key issues and made no actual, lasting political demands. In interviews Hutsol pitched Femen's campaign differently for domestic and foreign audiences, although she consistently argued for

Figure 1.1. Femen protest on Ukrainian Independence Day, Kyiv, 24 August 2011. Costumed as nineteenth-century serfs, members swing sickles across the manicured garden not far from Ukraine's Offices of Parliament on Hrushchevskoho Street (the street was renamed Heroes of the Heavenly Hundred / Heroyiv Nebesnoyi Sotni after the Maidan Revolution of Dignity in 2013–14). Photo shared with permission by Tomasz Grzyb.

Ukraine's place in a modernizing world. This fixation on modernity reflects movements for national independence across the post-Soviet context, in which "becoming modern" is often paramount to being perceived as an equal by the West.

In addition to her middle-class background and her willingness to use both Russian and Ukrainian in public, Hutsol differs from the Orange elites in several important respects. In particular, she openly discusses and even attacks the oligarchical class structure for corroding democracy. Her position on Russia's massive anti-Putin demonstrations, for example, conveys both distance from Putin and solidarity with the citizens of the Russian Federation. Civil liberties take priority over national borders in her opinion on Putin, which contains a sense of residual anger at Ukraine's corrupt elections in 2004. In my interviews with feminist scholars and activists in Ukraine, Poland, and Russia over time, nearly all emphasized change over stagnation. They are not alone. Chantal Mouffe has described the global protests of 2011 as a rearrangement of the very terms of protest itself, as "a diversity of spaces" in a struggle "to create a different form of articulation among public spaces."[22] Femen is no doubt part of the broad arc of changes that led to the global protests of 2011, and yet the group's origins in Ukraine distinguish members in important ways.

Initial receptions of Femen by Ukrainian feminists were mixed. Marian J. Rubchak placed Femen at the forefront of a broad shift in national politics.[23] Her analysis builds on consensus among scholars who write on postcommunist discourse that, in reinventing the categories for thinking about gender in the early 1990s, women vacillated between identifying with an amended Soviet worker-mother ideal and emulations of a commercialized, Western femininity pushed to the point of "absurd expressions of an illusory sense of Western panache."[24] In Ukraine, pre-Soviet folk images that had formed the basis of Soviet nationality policies continued to shape nation-building well into the independence period.[25] The search for "a lasting symbol of Ukrainian cultural identity" parallels similar searches by subjugated nations with histories of occupation and foreign rule, including nearby Poland. In Rubchak's early analysis of Femen, the group is a political counterweight to the traditionalist sentiment capitalized on by an oligarchic class of policymakers.[26] She discusses two performances in particular, one in 2008 and one in 2010, that were staged in front of the parliament building to direct the attention of cabinet members and voters to the "dirty nature of Ukrainian politics." She reads the red boots and flower wreaths of Femen's early protests – the latter a trademark of the group's style – as appropriations of a repressed, alternative local lore with subversive popular connotations. In folklore these symbols often signified a woman's single status and were associated with hidden feminine power.[27]

The ascent of "a new women's movement" in Rubchak's analyses dovetailed with other Ukrainian feminist critics' initial receptions of Femen. Some compared the group's style to a localized 1990s nouveau riche feminine ideal. Many have linked this style to women's shifting roles as economic producers/reproducers at the time and their efforts to distance themselves from the Soviet past. Aspects of Femen's camp and glamour mirror such emulations of the Western "bourgeois" housewife. Early on, Olga Plakhotnik described Femen as a rhetorical outcome of neoliberalism: "Ultimately, evidence would necessitate that this kind of popular feminism would manifest in such images of young blondes, whose gender has been so brutally styled, invented, and trampled upon by postcommunist misogyny."[28] Many of these early assessments provided valuable accounts of Femen within broader historical contexts. Rubchak suggested that the group was at the "vanguard for momentous change" in a new wave of emerging activists galvanized by the critical failure of the Orange Revolution and "an administration tending toward a police state."[29] A closer look at the group's design and marginal political position can widen our view of the broad resentment, fears, and desires that were boiling beneath the surface in Ukrainian society in that critical decade between two revolutions.

To begin to understand digital protest necessitates shifting attention away from the state as representational entity towards media technologies and globalization, and the roles that these factors play in structuring messages about rights and freedoms. Scholars have stressed the emerging links between citizenship and electronic media in mediating national imaginaries. In the seminal study *Reproducing Gender*, Susan Gal and Gail Kligman wrote as early as 1998 that, under socialism, "social actors reacted as much to the representations of themselves in official communications as to the often unforeseen consequences of state policies."[30] They discuss how capitalist media since 1989 have changed official discourse, claiming that, despite the illusion of more openness, certain issues remained undiscussed and "the disjuncture between such public discourses and ordinary practices" merits close analysis in order to understand change in the region.[31] Femen's early preoccupations with Ukraine's national past, layered over their controversial claims to feminism, render the group a unique site for exploring the tensions around official, mass, and popular culture that have emerged in postcommunism.

Soviet Precursors – Happenings

Absurdist street performances were just as overtly politicized in Eastern Europe as in the West; they persisted throughout the 1970s–1990s along the tailwind of a vibrant avant-garde scene, and continued to dominate public art and protest throughout the postcommunist period. Describing "happenings" in New York City in the late sixties, Richard Schechner linked the relationship between performance and politics to a process of staking new ground for making claims. He formulated his ideas in *The Drama Review* (TDR), where the genre was then being debated:

> The political actions of young radicals are sometimes hard to distinguish from guerrilla theatre. Putting the lemon pie in Colonel Akst's face or

even taking a building and demanding amnesty are not "real" acts. They are authentic and meaningful. They trail consequences. But they are also self-contained (as art is) and make-believe. They lack the finality of, say, an armed attack. Radical actions are often codes – compact messages falling somewhere between war and speech. They stake out a new area not mapped by either traditional politics or aesthetics.[32]

This quotation is useful for understanding the notion of politics in Femen's aesthetic in two ways. The first is historical. As part of the descriptive foundation of new theatre movements in New York City in the 1960s, the performances described in *TDR* travelled to Central Europe during perestroika in the 1980s where they took on more overt political tones as critiques of postwar decadence. The spontaneous and interactive nature of performances by avant-gardists like Zero and Vienna Group would also come to influence street demonstrations in Poland in the 1980s by Wrocław's Pomarańczowa Alternatywa. Padraic Kenney has pointed out how Major Frydrych and his followers in Wrocław, Poland, would exploit "the politics of everyday problems" in absurd demonstrations that made participation easier by reducing the risk of engaging in them, and thus, "offered the sublime as a defense against fear."[33] Kenney cites a happening on 15 October 1987 in which participants held signs that read "RIP Toilet Paper and Sanitary Pads" and "Who Is Afraid of Toilet Paper?" in reference to chronic goods shortages within the People's Republic of Poland.[34] Obviously, with much graver problems to worry about, the humour in slogans like these provided participants with a collective moment to diffuse deeper fears and concerns, while also giving them the chance to practice social mobilization with relatively little risk to the freedoms that they enjoyed in their day-to-day lives (see figure 1.2).

Young Ukrainian self-styled punks, "hippies" (sixty-eighters), and pacifists in Lviv soon followed in the footsteps of their Polish counterparts. In September 1987, a student named Oleh Olisevych formed Doviria (Trust) in opposition to the Soviets.[35] These Polish-Ukrainian exchanges led to ongoing contacts between the two countries and helped to found Lviv's dissident culture in the 1990s, which was marked by a thriving rock music and poetry scene. The rock opera *Chrysler Imperial*, staged at the Vy-Vykh festivals in Lviv in 1990 and 1992, was loosely based on works from the Bu-Ba-Bu group of writers, who solidified a new absurdist aesthetic in Ukrainian arts and letters.[36]

Thousands of people gathered in Lviv for both festivals. The playful marches, costumes, and general buffoonery contributed to the event's atmosphere and could be considered Ukraine's first large-scale happening. The opera debuted in the Lviv Opera House and featured a long-eared troll who warned the audience about the dawning of a new age called "The Chrysler Imperial" – a sarcastic allegory for the Western capitalists who had come to "save" Ukraine through neoliberal shock reforms.[37] The staging culminated in an actual American Chrysler automobile driving onto the stage. The opera's ironic, acrid narrative and its bold suspicions of both capitalism and communism crystallized a style of political humour that would soon gain momentum throughout the arts during Ukraine's shift to a market economy.

The absurdist humour, spoofs of popular celebrities, pranks, and caricatures of authority figures that marked the style of these groups can be traced in Femen's public appearances well into the 2000s.[38] Activists acted out scenes without any standard dialogue, linear plots, or definitive characters in street demonstrations with "a shifting, nondefinitive relationship between piece and audience."[39] In this way, Femen's style reflected the same "nonmatrixed" structure of happenings that past activists in the region had adopted in their street demonstrations – with one key distinction. While Femen would never issue any concrete political demands, the group's performances always contained two consistent referents: women and the state.

Despite the outward differences between Femen and Ukrainian and Polish dissidents of the 1980s, their preoccupations with the "dangers of swapping one mass culture (Soviet) for another (Western pop culture)" remained in Femen's scepticism towards the ideologies they attacked.[40] Figure 1.2 features Major Frydrych (Marek Krukowski) staging a mock funeral for toilet paper. Frydrych's protest scenario presupposed two different audiences: the Polish masses who "mourn" the loss of accessible goods, versus the state – an absent, even Godlike, presence presiding over economic regulation, life, and death. Early Femen protests in Ukraine utilized similar strategies. In one protest in Kyiv in 2011 called "Stable as a Cemetery!" an activist stood topless in a cemetery in a scene mirroring Pomarańczowa Alternatywa in setting and stance. The activist held a cardboard sign above her head in English, as would become the norm for Femen; it read, "Stable Is Poor." Anna Hutsol posted this photo on Femen's blog, with commentary comparing the cemetery to President Yanukovych's austerity measures and their impact on daily life in Ukraine.

The official marble Soviet graves framing the Femen activist portrayed a gap between the people and the state. The flower garland on the activist's head recalls the bohemianism of glasnost and its musicians and artists who incorporated Western countercultural styles of the era into their own innovations on Soviet kitsch.[41] The people in this

Figure 1.2. Action by Pomarańczowa Alternatywa: "Who Is Afraid of Toilet Paper?" Wrocław, Poland. October 1987. Photo of Major Frydrych (Marek Krukowski) holding an Obituary of Toilet Paper and Sanitary Napkins. NAF Dementi, IPN Collection. Courtesy of Orange Alternative Museum.

portrayal are the "poor," while the state, as the main addressee of the image, consists of a well-funded elite that has lost very little in the shift from communism to capitalism. The wealthy will live and be buried with the same grandeur that they have always lived and been buried. Stability in the image marks the continuation of a corrupt status quo – total stagnation that ultimately leads to death.

Thus, early on, Femen invited audiences to see Yanukovych's regime as having already failed. The activists depicted a stable economy – once also a Soviet promise –as a cynical compromise designed by elites to ensure their personal status at the expense of the people. The makeshift funeral for the "dead" Soviet past also suggests that Ukraine has come to a stalemate with the promises of capitalism. This inter- pretation is consistent with Femen's overall indifference to real politics and suspicion towards elites. Femen blurs sexual relations – the most fundamental and oldest metaphor for human exploitation – with the sophisticated mechanisms of the state. The plots in Femen's protests usually follow a pattern in which elites in turn betray the state and its people to Ukraine's more powerful neighbours.

So, what is Femen's feminism? Femen's protests cross-reference signs (ethnic, civic, and otherwise) at the intersections of nation and gender. The group's constant deferral of signs encompasses some of the ongoing problems with seeking a postmodern feminist theoretical model for a rights-based social movement – challenges that have been discussed in the past by feminist critics in other contexts.[42] Seyla Benhabib has squared the tension between the idea of feminism and postmodern epistemes of representation by describing the former as "the political outcome of a subject-position immersed in language."[43] But Femen's "language" is built from already controversial national symbols couched in the taboo around sex tourism in Ukraine's mainstream public, a discussion that remains despite the crimes stemming from an unregulated prostitution sector with soaring rates of illegal trafficking in narcotics and labourers. The impacts of these issues on Ukraine's GDP will only grow more acute with the overall increase in displaced people due to the onset of Putin's war in the east, and the nation's expanded role as a transit zone after the successful signing of the European Union Association Agreement.

Ukrainian history is filled with bold women, which is why Femen quickly became a symbolic site for airing anger in a much longer trajectory of local women's contestations around citizenship and rights. Vitaly Chernetsky has observed that "similarly to the discourse on postcoloniality, and perhaps to an even greater degree, articulations of gender concerns and feminist interventions [have come] to occupy in Ukrainian culture a position of prominence unmatched in most neighbouring countries, Russia among them."[44] Chernetsky highlights Ukraine as part of the former "Second World," a space marked by a unique postcolonial condition, and proposes that feminist literary representations challenge this condition. He refers to Ukrainian feminist and public intellectual Oksana Zabuzhko's book *Fieldwork in Ukrainian Sex* as only one example within this tradition.[45]

Femen's cemetery image also points to the lives lost and trauma caused by keeping silent about the conditions that can force women in poverty to seek sex work as a means of survival. Gayatri Chakravorty Spivak has grounded the politics of public trauma in demarcations of female sexuality within patriarchal power systems.[46] Femen echoes the postcolonial strains in the feminist intellectual tradition established by earlier figures like Zabuzhko. The female activist's cynical poster "stable is poor" references the Orange past as a polity divided by elites playing pro-Ukrainian and pro-Russian sentiments against one another. In this ghost image of the faded "ideals of the Maidan" of 2004, stasis has returned to the once vibrant search for democracy. The cemetery protest is essentially a public funeral staging of the Orange Revolution.

Design of the Colour Revolutions

Many younger generations cite the Orange Revolution as a turning point in their lives, recalling the early 2000s with both inspiration and great disappointment.[47] In addition to personal experience, there are practical connections between Femen's founding and the ideological design of the colour revolutions. The Serbian-based political consulting group CANVAS (Center for Applied Non-Violent Actions and Strategies) was instrumental in coordinating the slogans, platforms, and imagery of the many youth movements involved in the rallies and events around the electoral failures that sparked each of the revolutions in Georgia, Ukraine, and Kyrgyzstan.[48] Georgia's Velvet Revolution (known abroad as the Rose Revolution) contributed to the aesthetic course of the revolutions that followed. Paul Manning traces how a popular cartoon series functioned to create spaces for debate in the student-led campaigns and protests that initially sparked Georgia's revolution. He describes the cartoons as a tactic that students used to detach themselves from any formal party affiliation, calling their performances a "visual spectacle" of "the dynamics between rhetoric and metarhetoric, between opposing metarhetorics (and their associated logics of reception), and between rhetorics and the representational economies in which they operate."[49] Though Manning points out how the symbols through which "the Georgia of Roses" came to signify a peaceful rebellion, as opposed to Georgia's violent protests in 1989, ultimately, there was nothing new to this strategy. Students in Georgia, like Femen, poked fun at authority to unravel fears around peaceful public protest much in the same way that Frydrych, Bu-Ba-Bu, and others parodied authority under glasnost.[50]

Underlying Femen's parodies of the figures, slogans, and images associated with the Orange Revolution's mainstream party politics is a countercultural legacy of music, humour, street theatrics, and underground publishing (samizdat) with roots in the transatlantic exchanges of the 1960s. The group's cynical, and often offensive, pokes at the Orange Revolution, however, included critiques of the media spectacles that produce mainstream politics for mass consumers and audiences.

What was unique about the dissident culture of the colour revolutions was its production: the branding of pop celebrities who stood in for revolutionaries on mainstream stages.[51] The visual language in Femen descends from the same political architecture that encompassed the slogans, imagery, songs, and celebrity figures that served to imagine an Orange moment of unity. Femen's beginnings as a parodic retrospective of the now-faded "ideals of the Maidan," as the aims of the revolution were popularly referred to, grew from an Orange ico-nography that was popularized through multimedia concerts, songs, television commercials, fashion, and more. For example, their mock reality TV show "PMS: Post-Maidan Syndrome" featured members asking random passersby in the street to undress "for the country" in a talk-show format about future directions the nation could take. The playful tone of Femen's early activities exposed the rhetorical mecha-nisms of the Orange moment by putting the places and slogans of those years into sharp relief with the repression of street activism under Yanu-kovych. Femen's cartoonish celebrity aspects stood as much in contrast with, for example, the faceless activists in the youth group Rukh who blockaded the streets of Kyiv, as with the women and other feminists who opposed them. Viewing the "kitch" in Femen as the by-product of Orange campaign design, we can begin to read the group for deeper meaning in the production of political subjectivities through media.

Hutsol has described her group's topless strategy as a litmus for civil liberties: "The reaction to a nude protest is a measure of freedom in a country: we were not arrested in Switzerland, but we were almost killed in Belarus."[52] The political spectrum Hutsol presupposes here, with Belarus counterbalanced by Switzerland, positions Femen in a relativist notion of state repression. This reasoning is ideologically rooted in an Orange past. In the Orange Revolution, Yanukovych's Russian-leaning party stood in sharp contrast to Yushchenko's pro-European platform, as both leaders formed their bases from a highly bilingual population. Femen's manifesto and its overstatement to "fight against all forms of oppression" echoes the popular sentiments that historian Serhy Yekelchyk ascribes to the stage character Verka Serduchka: "Verka's language-mixing persona became a runaway hit, in part because surzhyk [the mixing of Russian and Ukrainian] was a marker of lower class and low culture, both things that the character clearly parodied early on. Yet, as Laada Bilaniuk notes perceptively, there was also a larger cul-tural context of the Ukrainian state gradually imposing linguistic purity on the society in which the mixture or situational use of Ukrainian and Russian was the long-established norm."[53] As Michael McFaul notes, when Kuchma declared Yanukovych the winner of the November elec-tion, Yushchenko answered by holding his own swearing-in ceremony in the Ukrainian Rada. For a brief moment, Ukraine had two sovereigns claiming the same territory – a circumstance that he and other political theorists list as a classical example of revolution. His assessments reflect Ukraine's bilingual sociolinguistic context: "In contrast to interpreta-tions that split protesters as being for or against the 'civilizations' that these two leaders apparently stood for, in actuality, very few harboured any East/West leanings; most people simply wanted a fair transfer of power."[54] Historian Andrew Wilson, looking back in 2009 at the Orange Revolution, wrote, "Political and cultural elites may be switching to Ukrainian, but little has changed on the ground, where not only have patterns of language use barely shifted, but there is also widespread support for some formal means of recognizing the status of the Russian language in Ukraine."[55] In my own observations living and working in the country in 2018, bilingual patterns, including Polish in western Ukraine, continue to feature in everyday informal encounters with culture, art, and media throughout the country's diverse regions.

Scholars have drawn parallels between 2004 and 1991, describing the immediate situation in both cases as a democratic breakthrough.[56] Yet perhaps what made the Orange Revolution truly unique was the consistency in the branding of its campaigns. The longer-term outcomes of the Orange Revolution for shaping dialogue about civil rights in Ukraine, as a relatively new nation state, had far more impact than Yushchenko's term in office and the eventual unravelling of his promised reforms. Femen members' own identifications of themselves within the legacy of the Orange Revolution, on one level, reflected an attempt to legitimize the right to peaceful protest. Hutsol's conceptualization of her group and her own self-identification with feminism changed often, but her and others' positive associations with the Orange Revolution remained consistent over time. Femen has had very little direct impact on policy, yet the group's ongoing activities throughout the decade between Ukraine's two revolutions, however ridiculous those displays were, served as a kind of litmus on Maidan vis-à-vis the Orange Revolution and the democratic ethos that that moment stood for.

Formed in 2008, Femen appeared after the "official" story of the Orange Revolution had taken shape. Scholars tend to mark 2006, when Yushchenko introduced his former rival Yanukovych to the Supreme Rada as the nation's new prime minister, as the end of the revolution.[57] When I interviewed Hutsol in the summer of 2011, just days after Yulia Tymoshenko had been put on trial for brokering a covert gas deal with Putin, she was ambivalent about the street protests taking place around the trial.[58] She told me that the next day Femen would ambush the crowds near the courthouse dressed in McDonald's uniforms to drive home the idea that in Ukraine's justice system, freedom is bought and sold like fast food. Topless activists would yell "Free Cashier!" ("Vilna Kasa!") from atop one of the many minivans (martshrutkas) parked along the streets in rows to serve as makeshift barricades.

Observing the protests in downtown Kyiv around the trial over the full course of a week, I noted that, although hundreds of demonstrators had gathered at the courthouse, they were organized into neat camps of rival parties. Most were middle-aged and reflected the older Yushchenko versus Yanukovych split from 2004. One woman I spoke with in the crowd told me that most demonstrators were being paid for their efforts. From the opposite side of the street, where I stood among curious passersby, the scene was set for Hutsol's "Vilna Kasa!" A sudden burst of nude women atop one of the parked vans, their screams, and immediate arrest made the orchestrated nature of the other protests all the more obvious. It was hard not to laugh at the police officers, who seemed confused and slightly embarrassed at having to utilize their training on such an oddball "threat." The whole situation remapped in physical space where the public imaginary around what is "possible," not necessarily expected or even legible as protest, is shaped by what is permissible to think, say, and do in public spaces.[59] The act ricocheted online.

III. Archetype and Caricature: The Prostitute

What sets Femen apart and has made their demonstrations highly controversial is not just their nudity, but also their performance of a specific kind of nudity – the kind that is bought and sold. Narrowing in on the prostitute figure in Femen's protests, we can better read the discursive context. The prostitute archetype drives Femen's protests about women becoming "nationalized sex products" (Hutsol's description of sex tourism). Campy, violent, and in-your-face jabs convert the sales product into something unpalatable: the naked woman for sale becomes just a naked body when its exchange value is emptied of its symbolic content. The economics of the exchange leave their mark as visible trace: the Femen girls come after-the-act, in which the body is shown as the outcome of economic violence acted out upon it by human agents.

Femen's prostitute as antiheroine is the central protagonist in an aesthetic that takes shape as a parody of cultural transformation in the postcommunist period. The figure of the prostitute in Slavic letters is associated with sex and capitalist enterprise, criminality, imperialism, tourism, secret knowledge, and autonomy. Representationally, such characters often contain traces of where commodification begets commodification in an absurdist theatre of political history. Socialist-realist heroines, post-Soviet stereotypes of the "sexual revolution," and much older narratives of sexual conquest are contrasted with their Western counterparts: high-fashion models used to project consumer desire onto products. Femen's spectacle pivots on the myths underpinning East-West cultural relations, the gender stereotypes within them, and public shifts in the idea of women's emancipation over time.

The prostitute archetype is rooted in discourse involving imperial sexual conquest. Many features of the archetype function to convey notions of autonomy that are intimately bound up with shifting anxieties over relations with the West at various points in Ukraine's history. In post-Soviet contexts, the prostitute appears as an entrepreneur and mediator between the Soviet past and the emerging capitalist economy. Earlier notions of serf women sold to foreigners, Amazonian libertines, and Dostoevskian "holy fool" peasant outcasts all deal in allegories of collective subjugation/emancipation. Femen is inscribed on these selfsame political surfaces. Three main narratives can be seen in their design, each serving in different ways to sublimate anxieties about national upheaval and cultural belonging, including those that elites in the Orange Revolution had set out to resolve.[60]

Capitalism and the USSR – The Natasha

The symbolism of the prostitute in the shift from communism to post-communism functioned as an allegory for the influx of capitalism. Literary scholar Larisa Lisyutkina describes how nineteenth-century Russian depictions of the prostitute contained aspects of her opposite, the saint: "In the image of the prostitute, Russian culture found a convenient opportunity to combine both deifying and disparaging attitudes towards women. In the works of Dostoevsky and Tolstoy, the prostitute-saviour is poeticized and presented as the female equivalent of Christ."[61] Lisyutkina goes on to contrast this older image with later constructions of the prostitute as the "pioneer of the market economy."[62] She grounds this shift in changing social relations: "The age of the transition to a free market in post-communist Russia may be graphically symbolized by the grotesque marriage of the hard-currency 'intourist girl' to the foreign businessman."[63] In the Soviet era, prostitution was a crime. Many sex workers, including women working in positions not directly involving sex, such as the well-known "intourist girl," were also often suspected of smuggling capitalist propaganda and aiding their foreign clients in gathering intelligence about the USSR.

In an image of an early Femen demonstration, members of the group pose as prostitutes holding mock campaign posters featuring the five major electoral parties of the Orange Revolution. Here, Femen appropriates stereotypes from the 1990s "sexual revolution" to defang the enterprise of party politics.[64] The resulting image functions in two main ways. On one level, it is a parody of contemporary sex tourism:

contextually, many such images Femen posts on their blog circulate on the internet with English captions next to ads for Ukrainian escorts, marriage services, and other services automatically generated by cookies that link the word "Ukraine" to "sex." On another level, it is a parody of parliamentary politics, pointing to where holding office is still mostly a male endeavour, and where sexist rhetoric is folded into official discourse. Each sign bears the same slogan: "Choose me!" This is a reference to a popular Soviet song from the 1980s.[65] Femen's sarcasm targets the promised happiness that was betrayed by postcommunist restructuring and the redistribution of wealth during that period. Part of the irony in the image is that, throughout much of the post-Soviet period, revealing fashion choices were a way for women to distance themselves from the conservatism of Soviet dress codes. Ads for escorts, such as those Femen's style of dress parodies here, are now ubiquitous in Ukraine and are a main feature in both state and private sector efforts at building tourism in the country. Members of Parliament and other public officials have even gone so far as to publicly note Ukraine's long-standing tradition as a purveyor of fine women.[66]

The carnivalesque presidential campaigns in Femen's early mock-demonstrations on Kyiv's Maidan depicted power in abstract form, suspended above the boundaries between the public and private spheres that regulate monetary and sexual exchanges elsewhere in society. Luce Irigaray argues that the value of women's bodies is derived from their exchange in economic relations between men in the patriarchal structuring of society. The value of the prostitute is extracted from her "use value" as an economic object in a male-dominated public sphere: "The qualities of her body have 'value' only because they have already been appropriated by a man, and because they serve as the locus of relations – hidden ones – between men. Prostitution amounts to usage that is exchanged."[67] The version of Ukraine's political system in Femen's images is one based upon liminal economic transactions. Parodying the red-light district in broad daylight, the activists in the photo put the average viewer of the image in the position of the sex client: the Western tourist cruising an avenue to purchase Ukrainian sex, the nouveau riche politician looking for a good time, or, in a more heterodox reading, the voter whose only available choices are candidates pandering to the crowd for a profit. Blending the plight of the prostitute with that of the politician, the image conflates consumer desire with the electoral process, and the electoral process with sex tourism and corruption. The image implies that women, like voters, are not valued beyond their exchange in a system of profit and self-enterprise.

Enlightenment Fashionings of "The East" – The Amazon

The Amazonian plays upon older stereotypes of Slavic women embedded in Western myths about an Eastern frontier. The figure of the Amazon is featured in the photograph of activist Inna Shevchenko taken by a French photographer, Guillaume Herbaut, in October 2011 for the French fashion magazine *Stiletto* (see figure 1.3). The photograph, which received second place in the prestigious World Press Photo Contest of 2012, originally appeared in a longer feature titled "Dans l'intimité des Amazones" composed from individual portraits of five different Femen activists posed in front of a set of apartment blocs in a residential section of Kyiv.[68] The dialogue between French photographer and Ukrainian activist takes place in several different temporal frames. Inna Shevchenko wears a garland of black and pink roses and is poised in a stance Femen often uses: one arm raised overhead brandishing a fist. Her exposed torso reveals a tattoo of a rose garland similar to the one she is wearing. The photo is set in a field of late October grass with several large, grey apartment blocs rising beneath a steely sky. The warrior princess image calls to mind Ukraine's Eurovision star Ruslana's leather-clad stage persona from 2004. At the same time, Ruslana was a pop star and thus stood for all of the individualism associated with such performers in the West, while Femen's illicit nudity provoked audiences to think about collective "refutation[s] of the Orientalist stereotype."[69] The widespread online circulation of the image propelled the figure of the Amazon into a new salient site in which power relations are exposed vis-à-vis the "wild frontier woman" at the Eastern edge of "civilization."[70]

Time is marked in the photograph by the posing of the nude female in a contradictory subject/object relationship with the camera lens – the all-seeing eye within a modern paradigm of mass-produced images. Shevchenko's stance in this photograph also reflects Soviet socialist-realist depictions of female Soviet workers and heroines of the "Great Patriotic War."[71] Her tanned skin, determined expression, and raised fist stand between the viewer and blocs of apartments on a field that could be likened to the steppe. The activist's nudity is all the more out of place set against stock images of the Soviet past: a row of grey Soviet apartments, a field of grain – and the iconic peasant flower garland. Shevchenko's blue jeans and tattoo further contrast with this backdrop as more general signs for Western counterculture. The overall effect of these underlying anachronisms in the photo create tensions that work to convey the arbitrariness with which norms are assigned to the female body – and the nation – in fashioning modernity.

Figure 1.3. *The New Amazons*. World Press Photo 2012. © Guillaume Herbaut / INSTITUTE.

In this sense Ukraine is positioned within a specific concept of modernity rooted in the Enlightenment. The image of the Amazon has appeared in constructions of Eastern Europe dating to Voltaire's forays eastward in his rumoured romance with the notorious patron of French culture, Catherine the Great. Larry Wolff has written about this exchange as only one example within a much broader intellectual trend that located a proximate European Other as foil to the rise of the Enlightenment in Western Europe. Narratives of dominion over Eastern Europe became couched in sexual fantasy. Wolff writes, "Travelers from Western Europe in the eighteenth century perpetrated and advanced a sort of conquest as they travelled. Casanova, his century's most celebrated general in sexual conquest, had already tasted the aphrodisiac power of mastery and fantasy that gave even sex a special character in Eastern Europe."[72] Depictions of sexuality in the rise of a split between East/West Europe continued to propagate with Enlightenment authors' images of the token slave girl in eighteenth- and nineteenth-century narratives detailing crusades into "Ubi Leones," land of lions, or *no man's land*.[73] The sexual undertones in this photograph, as elsewhere in Femen, are a pastiche of prior moments involving Western European sexual conquest.

Casanova's idealizations of an indentured concubine foreground another, later voyeuristic journey eastward by a major figure in the history of European sexuality: Leopold von Sacher-Masoch. In Masoch's semi-autobiographical novel, *Venus in Furs*, a young German nobleman named Severin living in the Galician city of Lviv makes a sexual agreement with a local Ruthenian woman named Wanda Dunajew. Although she submits to the terms of the contract, Wanda embodies in appearance and manner the wild image that Masoch held of Carpathian women, retaining an inherent ruthlessness that the author compares to ancient Venus. Wanda is a caricature of the deity mapped onto an image of Slavic barbarity surpassed by the "civilized" West. She constantly demonstrates her understanding of power with bold quips, such as "I have a real talent for despotism" and "everyone knows and feels how closely sexual love and cruelty are related."[74] Despite this posturing, her authority only goes so far in that it serves as a mirror of Western imperialism. Tyranny, possession, and the will to rule are only outwardly applied to Wanda, who dutifully acts out her part in fulfilment of the contract she signed in which she pledged to punish Severin daily (based on the actual contract Masoch carried out between himself and his mistress, Fanny Pistor).

In truth, although he submits to his mistress daily, the German nobleman remains in possession of his Slavic harem girl, whom he indexes alongside other women from the East: "all the women who the pages of history have recorded as lustful, beautiful and violent; women like Libussa, Lucretia Borgia, Agnes of Hungary, Queen Margot, Isabeau, the Sultana Roxolane, the Russian Czarinas of last century ..."[75] Masoch, like Casanova, equates sexual desire with an orientalizing claim that imagines Eastern Europe as captive to the West by way of sexual fantasy. The layering of empowered warriors over "captive" prostitutes in Femen's performances blurs the civilizational power dynamics between East and West assumed in these older sexual exchanges. The result is an off-the-cuff humour driven by metaphors for sexual conquest and subjugation in more contemporary political contexts.

The differentiation of a particularly *Slavic* female sexuality in Femen's performances situates an aesthetics that dates to fin-de-siècle tropes and the beginnings of the market for mass-produced copies of fine art. Perhaps no other person singlehandedly defined visual representations of Slavic women at the time for Western audiences than the Czech artist Alphonse Mucha, founder of the Art Nouveau movement, which spread largely through his work in advertising. Mucha's portraits of goddesses, muses, and mistresses graced everything from the World's Fair to architectural wonders in Prague, Paris, New York, Chicago, and San Francisco, theatre posters featuring Sandra Bernhardt as Medea, and Job brand cigarette ads. Mucha's modernist renderings of the muse were exotic, defiant, and subaltern all at the same time, combining the gentleman's theatre bill with the escort ad. Nearly all of his depictions of Slavic women, in particular, combined the figures of the virginal, empowered warrior with the divine goddess, layered over a libertine sexuality in harmony with the natural world. The prostitute archetype in his works is compared to the figure of the ancient muse, but stylized in a fiercer way in his images of Slavic women, despite the traces of imperial conquest underlying their harem costumes, gilt props, and opiate gazes. By contrast, Mucha portrayed Parisian women as haughty and ephemeral, wistfully looking beyond the frame in classical poses that differ from the bold, direct, and confrontational stares of his Slavic models.[76]

Figure 1.4 is an advertisement for an art sale of mass-produced images of Mucha's works at his Paris studio, Salon des Cent. Thorns, jewels, and flowers make up the three rings around the heart in the painting. The artist often used these three symbols to stand for Slovaks, Bohemians, and Moravians, respectively, each mired in political movements taking place at the time pushing for autonomy from the Austro-Hungarian Empire (these movements would become more significant to Mucha later in life, after the end of the First World War).

The three rings of thorns, jewels, and flowers reappear in Mucha's works where he features Slavic heroines, saints, and peasants, most often in coronation scenes, war, or other moments of divine intervention. His cycle *Epic of the Slavs* (1911–28) is the most well known and widely debated example of this Pan-Slavism, and likely precisely because of these deeply embedded resistance narratives. In essence, Mucha's portrayals of East European women, distinct from his images of French women, were some of the earliest iconographs that popularized the links between the Slavic folk flower garland and widespread resistance to officialdom. What is especially important about this Mucha image is that the garland appears twice: once worn by Slavic women in his photographic prototypes for the painting, and then again in the

Figure 1.4. Poster advertising the *Salon des Cent* Mucha Exhibition, 1897 (colour lithograph). By Alphonse Marie Mucha (1860–1939). Shared with permission from the Mucha Trust / Bridgeman Images.

final rendering. It is an image of revolt within the image itself, which is extracted from the subaltern.

Later uses of the garland repeat a similar mirroring effect that turns back on the viewer. The most proximate and well known example of

Figure 1.5. Film still from *Sedmikrásky* (Daisies), Věra Chytilová, 1966. Shared with permission of the Czech National Film Archive Collection (NFA) and © State Cinematography Fund (SFK).

this from the twentieth century is by Věra Chytilová of the May '68 generation of Czech New Wave filmmakers in her film *Sedmikrásky* (Daisies). This work draws out the older revolutionary iconicity of the garland imagery ahead of the gaze of the protestor – the idea of "resistance" here is marked by the accumulated symbolic value of the garland worn by two anarchist-feminist provocateurs whose staging by Chytilová contains, at its core, a brutal critique of the conservatism and nationalism of postwar Czech society (figure 1.5).

Time is marked in the film by two amateur actresses (originally models) contrasted with aging men who display their allegiance to the patriarchy by either worshipping or admonishing the two young women for their unruly behaviour. In this way, the two women are always posing in a contradictory subject/object relationship with the camera lens – the all-seeing eye within a modern paradigm of mass-produced images. Chytilová's stance on the war appears only in the opening and closing sequences of the film, each featuring actual footage of bombs dropping over Europe, set to the sound of a loud typewriter, as if set to dismantle the propaganda regime. Like Femen, Chytilová consciously worked in a feminist vein, and so takes direct aim at the socialist-realist depictions of female Soviet workers and heroines of the "Great Patriotic War," as it was named within the USSR.[77] The actresses' behaviours appear all the more out of place set against stock images of the Czech past: a row of grey apartments, a field of grain – and the iconic peasant flower garland – indexed here with more radical, anarchist qualities. Other elements in the backdrop involving more general signs for Western counterculture stand for Chytilova's '68 affinities and clash with the postwar repression of discourse about the war. These underlying anachronisms in the film create tensions that convey the arbitrariness with which norms are assigned to the female body – and the nation – in fashioning modernity.

In the early twentieth century the figure of the peasant, and pastoralism more broadly, were portrayed as backwards and démodé by urban avant-gardists across Europe preoccupied with industrial modernization. Later on, however, the figure re-emerged in Soviet propaganda and its celebratory socialist-realist portrayals of the factory worker. At this time Kyiv was becoming one of the main centres for film and graphic art production within the USSR. Paradoxically, where the peasant had once been central to lyrical notions of the nation in Romanticism, the figure suddenly gained new traction as a symbol of "modern progress" in building the revolution.

The Ukrainian avant-gardists of the twenties and thirties closely associated themselves with a modernization campaign that rejected the Romanticism underpinning nineteenth-century ideas of the nation (on balance with the rest of Europe in the rise of nations after the end of serfdom in 1863). Fierce debates ensued between opposing groups of writers on the definition and direction of cultural "progress." The poet Mykola Khvylovy, first a member of the Ukrainian Communist Party CP(B)U organization Hart, later founded VAPLITE in 1925 (Vilna Akademiia Proletarskoi Literatury – The Free Academy of Proletarian Literature), which served as a powerful platform for his critiques. He disagreed with Rosa Luxemburg and her Ukrainian supporters Iurii Piatakov and Evgeniia Bosh, who claimed that the world transformations then occurring were successfully dissolving national boundaries; by contrast, he put forward that any conclusion to the search for a more revolutionary, more progressive internationalism had yet to be achieved.[78] Writers from the Young Muse (Moloda Muza) poetry movement, including Ostap Lytsky, Bohdan Lepky, Vasyl Pachovsky, Petro Karmansky, Mykhaylo Yatskiv, and others united in trying to develop cultural platforms to account for the uniqueness of the Ukrainian language in the Soviet project's claim to internationalism. While Soviet modernization projects quite literally eclipsed the Ukrainian modernists (many were shot or forced into exile), the latter's ideas re-emerged among Ukrainian postmodernists in the 1990s who sought to avoid "the obligation to serve the nation."[79] This idea often surfaced in their critiques of President Leonid Kuchma's neoliberal policies. Members of this later generation share their predecessors' irreverence: they use playful language, laud the absurd, and are suspicious towards authority.

Where the idea of Eastern Europe turns on imaginings of a "femininized, sexualized East" by a "modernized rationalist West," by contrast, early- to mid-twentieth-century Pan-Slavism, the imaginings of the '68 postwar intra-European generation, and arguably, early Ukrainianization policies, each, in one way or another, complicated deeper patterns of colonial conquest. These forms and their recensions came into direct conflict with later developments in modernism and its origins in masculinist notions of linear progress, fuelling the now more widely recognized aesthetic contradiction at its centre as one of proto-fascism versus internationalism.

Femen's parody is rooted in modernism's origins in masculinist notions of linear progress. Femen's Amazon figure troubles the idea of "progress" articulated in the Orange Revolution, which was filled with folkloric images rooted in pastoralized and highly individualistic feminine ideals, humorously manifested in the phenomenon of Yulia Tymoshenko's braids (popularly compared to Princess Leia's hairstyle). For readers attuned to these forms, the outcomes play on borderlines between East/West that are symptomatic of conquest, the fetishization of medium, and rejection of the colonizer, which, in this context, is always synonymous with sexual dominance.

Romanticism and Taras Shevchenko – The Serf

The Ukrainian serf woman emerged as an important figure in Marxist-Leninist rhetoric framing women's labour in the shift from peasantry to communism. One of the earliest advancements of The Woman Question in socialist ideology arose through Nikolai Chernyshevsky's novel *What Is to Be Done?* in which a female protagonist dreams of a utopian society where she is able to work alongside men in building a futurist state. Chernyshevsky's novel was published in 1863, just after the emancipation of serfs, and later became a classical Soviet reference in building the case for a female proletariat. The novel raised interest in the issue of serfdom and also helped to pave the way for women's authorship. Ethnographies of serf women in Ukraine collected by Mariya Vilinska (pseudonym Marko Vovchok) were highly regarded by both Taras Shevchenko and Ivan Turgenev – the latter translated and published her work in 1859.[80] Assya Humesky has described how Vilinska made numerous trips to the villages around Chernihiv, Poltava, Kyiv, and Nemyriv to collect local songs, legends, and proverbs.[81] Humesky claims that Vilinska was one of the first writers to adapt the "positive traits" given to women in the oral folklore that she had collected to the depiction of serf women on the written page. Vilinska's depictions of resilient serf women in local folk culture would later become folded into the underpinnings of the rhetoric that more broadly framed women's labour in the Soviet Union. The socialist turn would then come to shape gender roles based on allegiance to the emerging Soviet state, ahead of the Ukrainian national idea.

The contrast between defiance and subjugation in many of the images associated with Femen mirrors Mucha's visualizations of Slavic femininity. The animal pelt rug in Mucha's photography experiments, for example, cues the nineteenth-century travelogue and its voyeuristic associations of Slavic femaleness with unbridled sexuality. Yet the years intervening between Mucha and Femen are significant. As a new and relatively expensive technology, photography was not commonly used in advertising during Mucha's lifetime, and certainly not in its ubiquitous uses today. Femen photos often appear as though almost lifted from a glossy graphic menu, the kind seen posted outside a seedy building to sell everything from cheap Chinese food to Xerox copies to sex-on-demand. This framing plays on the same post-Soviet "Natasha" stereotypes as in the mock-up election protest discussed earlier.

This variegated regional past of voyeurism and sexual conquest, met with resistance, can be clearly discerned in a photograph of Femen member Alexandra Shevchenko taken by a freelance Polish photographer named Agnieszka Rayss and given the descriptive title *Sascha from Femen*.[82] The overall composition is subdued and minimalist. The topless activist is its main subject: a leopard print blanket is visible on a bed behind her, a prop often included in the background of escort ads. In this particular example, animal print carries the obvious symbolism of ferocity and independence that women turning away from the regimentation of Soviet workers' dress sought in the 1990s sexual revolution (animal print textiles in Eastern Europe gained popularity towards the end of the Soviet era). Fake fur also carries a less obvious meaning in that it communicates a synthetic quality, and thus also a certain amount of distance from agricultural peasant labour and village life. In both cases, although for different reasons, the animal pelt in the Femen image, as in Mucha's work, is a status symbol. At the same time, Femen's characteristic flower garland has been replaced with a snowflake headdress wrought in the style of a traditional East Slavic crown evoking the headpieces worn by waitresses and barmaids in some provincial Soviet restaurants in the 1950s–1970s. This type of headdress is also sometimes associated in the popular imagination with "Snizhynka" (Snow Maiden), the female companion to "Did Moroz" (Grandfather Frost), two characters invented by the Soviets to replace St. Nicholas in celebration of an atheist New Year. These two characters are sometimes jokingly referred to in pop culture as a euphemism for the coupling of an aging Soviet president with his infantilized people.

In figure 1.6, the icon painted by Femen co-founder Oksana Shachko in 2016, not long before she committed suicide in 2018, features a scene arranged according to the ecclesiastical laws governing icon painting dating to the tenth century in Kyivan Rus'.[83] Femen's and Mucha's folk flower crown, which the latter employed to signify feminine agency in his works about Slavdom, but not his advertisements (he used other crowns in them), is here doubled as a halo. The overall scene points to the table where one angel extends her hand in the sign for peace over an ashtray placed next to open bottles. Evocative links surface here around the idea of emancipation of serfs juxtaposed with Soviet discourse on class emancipation – yet the transgressive woman is clearly the strongest motif, and consistent with Femen's overall message that women's rights and freedoms over their own bodies constitute an ancient and ever-present battle. These angels could just as easily be prostitutes, or workers taking a short smoke break; or perhaps, even in both of these guises they might also be recognized as thinking people simply discussing the news of the day in free association on the public square. Certainly, they are the artist's portrait of Femen. The contrasts between sainthood, transgression, and paganism – both in the flower crown and in the tarot card Three of Cups – further signify the bonds of feminine fraternité. As one of the final images she gave the world before ending her life, it can be understood as an autobiography composed in Ukrainian iconographic visual language. In my reading, the icon, like Femen itself, is an allegory for deeper collective memories of subjugation in Ukraine.

A series of poetry readings entitled Naked Rhymes (Holi rymy) took place on Femen's blog in the summer of 2011. The series was inspired by lines from "Young Masters, If You Only Knew" (Якби ви знали, паничні), a section of the Ukrainian epic poem Kobzar, by the national poet Taras Shevchenko. The first video features Aleksandra

Figure 1.6. *Untitled* (*St. Trinity*) icon painting by Oksana Shachko, co-founder of Femen, 2016. Courtesy of the Family Estate of Oksana Shachko.

Shevchenko, who wears the lines on her torso in the form of a tattoo, reading the entire poem of which her tattoo is a fragment. She is seated on a brass sculpture of the national monument to Taras Shevchenko. Her tone is sharp, angry. Tattoos in the Slavic context visually mark subversion in a manner that differs from tattoos in the West in the complex sign systems associated with them.[84] The language of tattoos in Slavic history grew in parallel to the language of the prison, and was always one of subversion because a tattoo assumed ownership over the body. Prison tattoos throughout the Soviet period contained codes that conveyed information about male inmates' status within criminal hierarchies, their prison terms and crimes, and even their sexual preferences. Female prisoners also had tattoos, although they carried a different set of meanings.[85] The divergent connotations of the pastoral peasant maiden and the tattooed prisoner converge in the prostitute archetype underlying Inna Shevchenko's and Aleksandra Shevchenko's performances: their tattoos become a type of serf's brand, and also a company logo; in both cases, the mark denotes a privatized body in the exchange of women as capital.

Aleksandra Shevchenko's tattoo is from "Young Masters, If You Only Knew" (Якби ви знали, паничні), a section of the Ukrainian epic poem *Kobzar*, by the national poet Taras Shevchenko. Throughout, the poet admonishes the nation's writers for painting the villages of Ukraine in idyllic tones, failing to convey the abject poverty within. The poem begins:

Young masters, if you only knew	Якби ви знали, паничі,
How people weep there all life through,	Де люде плачуть живучи,
You'd not compose your rhapsodies,	То ви б елегій не творили
And God for nothing you'd not praise,	Та марне Бога б не хвалили,
Nor mock our tears by twisting truth.	На наші сльози сміючись.
That tranquil cottage in the grove	За що, не знаю, називають
You call a paradise – I know.	Хатину в гаї тихим раєм.

The lines on Aleksandra Shevchenko's torso are from the section in which the poet addresses women in serfdom:

And you my sisters! Fortune has	А сестри! Сестри! Горе вам,
Reserved for you the cruelest fate!	Мої голубки молодії,
What is the purpose of your life?	Для кого в світі живете?
Your youth in service slipped away,	Ви в наймах виросли чужії,
Your locks in servitude turn grey,	У наймах коси побіліють,
In drudgery, sisters, you will die!	У наймах, сестри, й умрете![86]

In the original version of the poem, the repetition of the phrase "у наймах," approximated as "in service," "in drudgery," or "in exploitation," underscores the poet's admonishing tone. Shevchenko's direct personal address to his "sisters" comes as an aside in his angry condemnation of the alienated writers who overlooked the wretchedness of bondage and slavery in their pastoral portraits of the villages scattered throughout the countryside near Kyiv. The women that Shevchenko invokes here are presented as serving unworthy masters who have conquered Ukraine. They stand in contrast to the poet's "brothers" who have "slaved on the estate / And then, conscripted, marched away!"[87] Aleksandra Shevchenko's literary tattoo speaks to the bondage of women on several levels. Bearing the same surname as the poet, the activist doubles the author's persona, and her addressees, as conveyed by the poem, are not the women who suffer from their fate, but the men who fail to see their suffering.

A former serf himself, Shevchenko grounded the Ukrainian national project in the end of serfdom. The poet's lyrical, Romantic verse idealized the serfs and later persisted as a typology tied to the idea of "narodnost'" or nationality/people in the Ukrainian national imagination. The emancipated serf paralleled the nation. Differing from Oushakov's formula of "orthodoxy, autocracy, and narodnost," in Shevchenko's writings, the narodnost also implied distinction from Asia, Poland, and Russia. In the video of the reading, the activist's distracting nudity and vengeful expression suggest that she has taken up the authority of the poet and is now staring at the men he had originally attacked in his poem. The activist counters the poet's pastoralizing ideals in a satire targeting the idea of a benevolent Europe.

In writing about gender in Taras Shevchenko's works, Humesky notes how, like Gogol, Shevchenko portrays his Cossack maidens as extensions of the natural environment. They are straightforward, organic: "Love of the Cossack for his maiden is depicted as 'sincere,' as natural as their surroundings."[88] Humesky discusses the role the nation plays in Shevchenko's verse, pointing out how national virtue replaces erotic desire in the positive attributes he gives women. She writes, "Shevchenko expressed his admiration for the beauty of the female body ... the characteristic traits of feminine beauty which were praised by the people (narod) ... Other poets have portrayed women as their ideal of beauty, as the object and cause for their feelings of love, thanking them or cursing them as they saw fit. For Shevchenko 'woman' was also his ideal, but of a spiritual order."[89]

Like other Romantic writers across Europe at the time, Shevchenko appealed to an imagined ethnic ideal in his figurations of the nation. Humesky refers to the "narod," here translated as "people," in describing the diverse populations that Shevchenko's portraits of women attempted to unify in the author's appeals to a "spiritual order" common among East Orthodox worshippers living in the lands stretching from the Donbas to the Carpathians. The author Shevchenko angrily laments the Cossack maidens he believed served foreign men at the behest of the intellectuals who failed to represent them. This idea takes on new meaning as commentary on the modern sex industry when transposed onto Femen's protest narrative. Romantic appeals to the folk nation are diffused by the production and circulation of references to Shevchenko in a mass-media environment, and the publicity around the images that drive that industry.

The passionate address in the lines "What is the purpose of your life? / Your youth in service slipped away" draws, on one level, an intertextual parallel between the writer Shevchenko's posturing towards serf women who were sold abroad and Femen's similar outbursts "against sex tourism in Ukraine." On another level, Shevchenko's tattoo subverts the poem's nationalist Romanticism in her nude manifestation of the men (and serf women) who were once "conscripted away." The final line of Shevchenko's tattoo delivers a warning: "In drudgery sisters, you will die!" Mucha was attacked by the critics of his day for his work *Slav Epic*, which he considered his magnum opus, but in which others saw tokenism towards serf women. This tendency and its persistence are perhaps indicative of the struggle inherent to any search for a language of feminist resistance. What resonates most here is that same search, but within national contexts that are not traditionally considered in postcolonial terms, even though they display a long history of subjugation between different peoples based on ethnic and other differences.[90]

Stereotypes of women as prostitutes, sinners, and saints can be observed in dominant gender categories across many cultures. Femen's references to the national poet of Ukraine, however, draw upon a wider trend in Ukrainian feminist writing in tension with folk romanticism that exposes the social risks of such anachronism in the public narratives promoted by Ukrainian leaders in the 2000s. In contemporary Ukrainian feminist literature, as others have observed, there is an overabundance of national allegory. For example, in Shevchenko's *Shevchenkiv mif Ukrainy: sproba filosofs'koho analizu* (Myth of Ukraine: An attempt at a philosophical analysis), Oksana Zabuzhko dismantles the processes whereby Taras Shevchenko's monolithic status as Ukraine's national poet has been employed to serve contradictory ends in state-building projects, at the risk of silencing other perspectives. Zabuzhko's works often appeal to an unnamable feminine order that precedes the nation state. These appeals share a broader common ground at the level of language as well. Vitaly Chernetsky has brought Gayatri Chakravorty Spivak into conversation with the Ukrainian canon, pointing to parallels in her experiences of anti-imperial resistance in India, and her views that in the constant struggle to be heard as an Indian woman globally, constructions of a mute, subaltern woman must be vigilantly averted.[91]

IV. The Mass Subject and the Public Sphere

Pop Culture Contexts: Chervona Ruta, Ruslana, Serduchka

While Femen adopts much of Ukraine's pop rhetoric of the mid-2000s in their combination of nineteenth-century folk with modern civic symbols, Femen's spectacle also presupposes a more global, mass public conditioned by the internet and its capacities in constructing a mass consumer.[92] Michael Warner has critiqued the roles of self-abstraction, identification, and desire in the mass discourse of contemporary news media technologies, arguing that disparities arise between subjects in the individual apprehension of the self within a mass-public context. This is because the mass public engineered by contemporary news media depends on the individual's self-negation.[93] Access to the mass public, like Habermas's bourgeois public, remains unequal, a dynamic Warner terms "minoritizing logic."[94] The mass media thus premises itself on an invisible, abstract body based on a hegemonic, white, male subject descended from older notions of Habermas's bourgeois public sphere. In contrast to earlier mass-print culture, the contemporary mass media pivots on more visual displays of many different bodies to elicit emotional responses from the viewer. Warner notes that "to be public in the West means to have an iconicity, and this is true equally of Muammar Qaddafi and of Karen Carpenter."[95] In contemporary displays of corporeality, desire drives the mass subject's search to reconstitute a body from within the abstract, metalanguage of media publicity and its "public" mass body.

Femen puts on display a violent comedy that at once feeds the mass subject's desire for corporeality in the mass public, but also unravels the parameters in which the popular is performed in the mass media. Femen resembles Rancière's critique of gallery art: "In the end, the *dispositif* feeds off the very equivalence between parody *as* critique and the parody *of* critique ... unfortunately, however, it has become increasingly clear that this mode of manifestation is also that of the commodity itself."[96] But the commodity, unlike the mass public that Femen presupposes, can differentiate its subject.[97] Femen's performances differentiate the private consumer-subject that a prostitute – presenting herself as a commodity – would assume towards a client.

Guy Debord's idea of the public sphere with the rise of television is perhaps most relevant for tracing changes in social subjectivities with the rise of new media technologies. He argued that the spectacle created by the media image (film) is an alien commodity. Warner claims that mass media differs from commodities because a commodity can differentiate its subject, whereas media only *mediates* between subjects. Femen pantomimes the dynamics of commodification in a mass-media context. They use camp and violence in taboo public acts that both visually feed and undercut the abstract, male, mass audience presupposed by the mass media and its scripts for displaying female sexuality.

In the "erotics of a mass imaginary," the minority subject – and every subject is minoritized to some degree – finds itself in an especially asymmetrical relationship to the media because "the mass subject cannot have a body except the body it witnesses"[98] The individual desires to identify with an abstract, collective body by witnessing the visual display of bodies onscreen and in print. This tendency manifests in the mass media's fixation on corporeality through disaster, camp, and vulgar modes of expression. Disaster is popular because "it is a way of making mass subjectivity available, and it tells us something about the desirability of that mass subject ... In the genres of mass-imaginary transitivism, we might say, a public is thinking about itself and its media."[99] Feeding this desire to subjectively identify with a collective public, the mass media also fetishizes political figures (who produce the myth of their own popularity) by shaping the discourse of publicity itself as "the rhetorical conditions under which the popular can be performed."[100] Iconic for their topless street demonstrations both in Ukraine and abroad, Femen occupies the space of the pop celebrity miming a politician's performance in mass media.

In Femen, one can easily observe vulgar expressions of femininity. These expressions put on display what is forbidden from the mass subject; they reveal the very "minoritizing logic" of the mass public sphere on which viewers depend in constructing the realities they inhabit. Warner discusses 1980s urban graffiti as a kind of "counterpublicity" to the mass media: a personal trademark that can be spread quickly across a nearly anonymous landscape.[101] Although Femen activists differ from graffiti artists in many respects, both share a staging of their own popularity set against the status quo. Replicating their own style and trademark across cyberspace and mass media, Femen produced platforms for enacting the idea that they were growing incredibly popular, even while closely managing the status and shape of that popularity.[102]

Anna Hutsol has experience in the entertainment industry and explained her group's strategy in terms of mass marketing: "I think that if you can sell cookies using one method, then why not use the same method to push for social causes? I don't see anything bad in this."[103] This statement begs the question as to whether the body can ever translate a clear message in a mass context, where the abstract media body "claim[s] an imaginary uniqueness promised in commodities, but canceled in the public sphere proper."[104] Femen's politics, read not as a movement in the classical sense, but as a controversial trace within public discourse, show where patterns in media consumption underscore the "imaginary uniqueness promised in commodities."[105] Their image mimics a political campaign, revealing the commodification processes in the gender and branding schemes at the core of all nation building.

Anachronism

Femen's early humorous street theatre capitalized on a particular, nationally inflected rhetoric that has shaped Ukraine's pop industry over the past decade. The Chervona Ruta music festival that took place in 1989 after the inaugural congress of the youth pro-independence movement Rukh, and again in 1991, eight days before the dissolution of the Soviet regime, set a precedent for popular displays of national identity. The festival took place in Zaporizhyia, the historic seat of the Cossack host. Performers appropriated the freedom-loving figure of the Cossack and its anachronistic qualities to draft a myth about independence and survival, and to legitimize Ukraine's newly won independence as a modern nation state.[106]

Catherine Wanner has written about the Chervona Ruta festival as a site for uncovering a Ukrainianness in order to challenge the dominance of Soviet ideology in public discourse.[107] Western-style rock music, already established as a language of dissent in the Soviet Union, became the lingua franca of the festival. Religion also played a role as Orthodox priests dressed in black robes opened the night with a ceremony in the centre of the stadium. Attempting to recover a "lost" identity, participants placed pre-eminence on the Cossack to reorient Kyivan Rus' as a western frontier to mollify public anxieties by airing the Soviet past.[108] The alternative cultural memories that festival organizers worked to achieve provided a lasting conceptualization of national autonomy. The liminal national rhetoric they instantiated through pop, based in nostalgic images of folk culture, eventually fused with the official language of the state.[109]

Many Ukrainian pop music celebrities adopted similar projections of national identity later on, during the Orange Revolution. Where Chervona Ruta's Cossacks had once "uncovered" Ukraine's lost history beyond its Soviet one, during the Orange Revolution, pop stars preached a "true Ukraine" founded in a mythical tribal history, whose democratic potentials had been suppressed over time. These performances complemented political elites' accommodating signals to the European Union at the time, as pop artists depicted individualism, progress, and freedom differently for domestic versus Western audiences. The indigenous Carpathian style adopted by the pop singer Ruslana in her song "Wild Dances!," for which she won the Eurovision contest in 2004, was, for the general listener, according to literary scholar Marko Pavlyshyn, "a proclamation of solidarity with the prevailing values, beliefs, and practices of the civilizationally dominant West. It is a claim to belong to a modern global community conceptualized as Western in its fundamental features."[110] For domestic audiences, Pavlyshyn notes, the song approvingly distanced folk culture from "sharovarshchyna," an ossified notion of folk life once common in socialist depictions of national culture. Ruslana's images of the Carpathians rested on a fusion of Hutsul instruments, leather costumes, and live wolves in an eroticized rendering of a "wild" frontier. Among domestic audiences this glamourized portrayal of western Ukrainian folkways passed muster, in part, as a familiar tale about overcoming hardship rooted in nineteenth-century Romantic depictions of peasant life.[111]

Ruslana's blending of nineteenth-century Carpathian folk culture with the Amazon myth predates Femen's combination of these two archetypes. The Amazon woman, like the Cossack, emerged within a constellation of nationally inflected pop performance in Ukraine that Femen has since adopted as a liminal protest site. Unlike Ruslana, whose warrior image preserved a utopian notion of Europe for Orange demonstrators, Femen's topless prostitutes underline the utopian optimism of that dream. Ruslana's caricature of folk life differs from Femen's in that hers is devoid of any specific references to actual events or contemporary political figures.[112] This ahistorical quality lent her a degree of palatable popularity that Femen could not achieve in their design and positioning of themselves as an oppositional movement. Where pop stars associated with the Orange Revolution once reflected the heightened euphoria of that moment, seeking to merge Ukraine "with others in the culturally heterogeneous contemporary world," by contrast, Femen's protests later on appear much more cynical, even Orwellian.

Cultural Hybridity

Blending glamour with the grotesque, Femen's style turns on black humour, self-deprecatory satire, and the not-quite-deliberate faux pas. The hyperbole and camp in Femen's performances also have antecedents in the singer Verka Serduchka's experimental stage identities. Serduchka rose to fame quickly during the late 1990s and early 2000s as part of a broader fascination with transgender performance as a mainstream genre in Ukraine. What set Serduchka apart from other stars' gender crossings was his creative use of "surzhyk," a mix of Ukrainian and Russian often spoken in villages. Cultural historian Serhy Yekelchyk has argued that Serduchka's irreverent humour purged the fetishization of an "authentic" Ukraine in the mid-2000s by presenting audiences with "a carnivalesque, liberating take on the very real cultural and political tensions caused by the imposition of political correctness."[113] He notes how the singer's use of the vernacular voice in audacious skits about daily life in post-Soviet Ukraine expressed a freedom to be oneself in public, in contrast to the Ukrainian state's fixation on official language.

An important difference between the public receptions of Serduchka, versus Femen, is the controversy that *never arose* around the former's stage persona as a transgendered citizen. The polarization of Russia and Europe that features in Serduchka's humour functions as a superficial posturing by political elites, which reflects the way that many Ukrainians who identify with both of these cultures experience such divisive moves in their everyday lives. For most Ukrainian audiences, gender identity was less important than Serduchka's national hybridity.[114] Like Femen's protests, Serduchka's liminal gender identifications countered nation-building projects throughout the 2000s that equated modernization with Europeanization. Serduchka assumes a wide gap between the popular voices of her characters and the officialdom of post-Soviet statehood. The widespread acceptance, even fetishization, of Serduchka's blending of genders and languages mapped her bodily hybridity onto a national hybridity that many mainstream consumers could identify with. These language affinities and blending have remained consistent in everyday encounters, despite raging debates about language at the policy level, including a bill in October 2017 to prevent the use of Russian in universities or academic institutions.

A controversy finally *did* arise around Serduchka, and pushed her career to a breaking point, when the hybridity ended. Protests erupted in Ukraine following her 2007 Eurovision performance in which she sang in English, "I want to see ... Russia goodbye!," lyrics that are relatively mild compared with Femen's overtly anti-Putin sentiments. The "low" humour in Femen shares the roots of this controversy that ended Serduchka's popularity. Yet humour has its limitations, especially at the scale of a mass audience. Both Femen's and Serduchka's clearly political statements, even if their pro-Ukraine stance *was* popular among their audiences, perhaps gave the impression that they were becoming too closely allied with elites themselves – no longer capable of connecting with "the people" regardless of their language choices. The mix of Russian and Ukrainian, or surzhyk, associated with village life and the urban working classes remains a familiar and uncontroversial point of identity for huge swaths of the population. Common to many border zones where cultural contact is the norm, the creolization of language generates its own standard. It is precisely this lively spoken mix of Ukrainian and Russian – which has developed its own lines of continuity throughout Ukraine's highly distinct regional cultures, interlinked through familial ties – that continues to unify the form and syntax of an instantly recognizable local humour, despite the upheaval and confusion brought on by Putin's war between Russia and Ukraine in 2014.

Femen's performances employed popular forms, but they were not popular in Ukraine. They were dark and hard to digest as a radical counter-image of the optimism of the Orange Revolution. The notion of "becoming European" in Yushchenko and Tymoshenko's joint campaign relied on a hopeful imaginary ideal, beyond the nation. As in the pop performances at the Chervona Ruta festival, both leaders argued for a "return" to Europe as a cure-all for Ukraine's domestic ills. A utopian, outside imaginary became central to imagining a reformed Ukrainian parliament. By contrast, Ruslana and Serduchka staged national belonging in the pop idiom most familiar at the time, grounded in the 1990s Chervona Ruta festival and its anachronistic Cossacks: oriented towards "the idea of Europe" – away from everything Soviet, towards a fluid and diverse notion of Ukrainianess internal to its borders. Both artists projected positive, yet amorphous, ideas of a "wild" and "hybrid" Ukraine as the baseline sentiment for Orange demonstrators' aspirational statements about joining the West.

This sentiment reappears in Femen, but as a parody that depends upon the mechanisms of the mass media. Unlike Ruslana's warrior-princess body, or Serduchka's transgendered "surzhk" body, both of which offered positive national fantasies to hopeful demonstrators on the Orange Maidan, Femen put on display a vulgarized body, what Michael Warner terms a "disaster discourse body," for an alienated mass subject.[115] The "minoritizing logic" of this effect, to borrow Warner's term, is a function of gender in Femen's nude sketches on the already politically saturated space of the Maidan. Differing from Ruslana's erotic fantasy of Ukraine as an untamed wilderness, Femen's constant deferral of signs evades any consistent message about the violence that they put on display. Optimistic visions of Europe do not appear in Femen; rather, given the group's mass context, the world of a Femen performance is thoroughly dystopic.

Between 2008 and 2014, Femen members became global celebrities. One might say that, initially, they were airing anxiety in Ukraine around collective identities of all kinds, mapped onto gender and sexuality. Their early protests interrupted media around politicians' scripting of an equal partnership that Orange elites had signalled to Europe. Unlike Ruslana and Serduchka, who both managed their public images across two contexts – an Orange Ukraine projected into European space, versus Western consumers' fantasies of an Eastern frontier – Femen, by contrast, cynically jabbed at these fantasies.

What do these jabs mean for the rest of us beyond Ukraine? With the rise of social media, the state becomes less representational. This outcome requires new inquiries into the public sphere in different cultural contexts. Jacques Rancière wrote in his tenth thesis that "the essential work of politics is the configuration of its own space. It is to make the world of its subjects and its operations seen. The essence of politics is the manifestation of dissensus as the presence of two worlds in one."[116] In Femen, the satire on "Europe" and "Ukraine" is united by an economic relationship in which it is not clear who controls whom. Images of the prostitute are always unwelcome on the public square. Femen's spectacle of sex work became so provocative not just because of their nudity, but because it activated deeper taboos: forbidden scripts of behaviour that call to mind certain modes of consumption at the point where East/West cultural stereotypes meet.

V. East/West Cultural Stereotypes: A Parody of Media Consumption

Mobilizations around the actual issues at stake in the sex industry – issues that Femen lays claim to – persist in conversations around the group. These conversations, in turn, are mediated by the sale and consumption of mass media reports on Femen, whose protests morph relative to the group's publicity within the logic of a variable market. It is the sexual consumption involved in creating commodities out of the female body that underlies Femen's images, more than the images themselves, that is arguably the most shocking.

In 2013 it was a Femen image, discussed in more detail later in this chapter, that would take centre stage at the World Press Photo Contest. The Femen photo was rapidly reproduced countless times across mass media outlets. By contrast, few journalists paid attention to the winning World Press Photo in 2012 that preceded the one of Femen activist Inna Shevchenko only one year prior. As shown in figure 1.7, the first photo *also* featured a prostitute, but went almost unnoticed by both feminists and the mainstream public within and beyond Ukraine. This other image is one that clearly shows the brutal marks of abuse, struggle, and survival against all odds and stands in stark contrast to Femen's staged, abstract caricatures of sex work. The image is a realist portrait of another young woman, also Ukrainian, from the town of Kryvyi Rih near

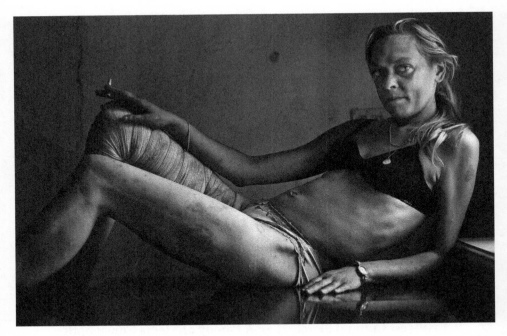

Figure 1.7. *Maria from Kryvyi Rih*, by Brent Stirton. World Press Photo
Contemporary Issues, 1st Prize, 2012. Shared with permission of Getty Images.

the city Dnipropetrovsk in the southeastern industrial mining region of
the country.[117] She is roughly the same age as Shevchenko.

Bruised, emaciated, and scarred by drug abuse, the woman's grim
appearance leaves little to the imagination about the lack of available
social assistance in the region, despite extremely high rates of intra-
venous drug use and a soaring HIV/AIDS epidemic. This photo of
an actual prostitute went nearly unnoticed in subsequent reports on
Femen. This image's silent position in the constellation of mass media
that surrounded Femen, and later, Pussy Riot's trial in Russia, begs
the question: can protest cast as pop performance generate meaning
beyond the producer/consumer relationship?

Femen and the mass media outlets reporting on the group maintained a symbiotic relationship for nearly a decade. After their Euro-
Cup tour, Femen members increased the scope, frequency, and online
component of their protests, switching to five-minute flash-mob photo
opportunities, professional studio sessions, and extensive blog entries.
Streamlining their online presence, the group began to address a more

international audience while taking advantage of the rise of internet use in Ukraine. This change also provided a way to evade the increasingly repressive environment for public gatherings under Yanukovych. In 2011 a young photographer from Australia, Kitty Green, travelled with the group to Belarus where she was arrested along with two other Femen members for publicly ridiculing Lukashenka.[118] The length of Femen's public appearances began to shrink in disproportion to the group's fame. The vast online photo archives on Femen's two blogs (their Russian blog on livejournal.com was switched to read-only in 2012) aided their increasingly virtual format within an image-saturated environment.

To a large degree, Femen's tactics resemble those of the fashion industry. Journalists were informed of the time and location of a Femen action well in advance, and editors played a role in the management and invention of new scenarios. The industry took notice. German journalist Alice Schwarzer, founder of the feminist magazine *EMMA*, reported to *DerSpeigel*: "I recently saw that the women from Femen posed completely naked for the magazine *Elle*. That's one of those slip-ups. Now they have to be careful that the boomerang doesn't fly back and they become objectified."[119] The "boomerang" in Schwarzer's comment alludes to Femen's critics, who target the group's statements as undermining the nude images of themselves that they manufacture. There are certainly issues with the duality in Femen's claiming to protest against the objectification of women through advertisement. And yet, the fashion and entertainment industry's failure to fully assimilate Femen is also complicated by the fact that the group's parodies of sexual conquest also fall upon the Western consumer.

The prostitute, by definition, is always excluded from debate, seen as "tainted" – an outsider, a noncitizen. On this level, Femen's performances are always about a corrupt public sphere, and thus do not possess the correct formula to become popular either at home or in the West. Ruslana and Serduchka did gain Western audiences because their images pivoted on an Orange Ukraine projected into European space that played up to Western consumers' fantasies of individual freedom on the Eastern frontier. Femen's design, by contrast, rejects both of these fantasies: the parody turns on the mutual dependence of East and West.

These allegorical dimensions emerge clearly in Femen's witchy, naked siren dashes across diplomatic events. In 2009 the group greeted Putin's visit to Kyiv with banners featuring the name of his former mistress that read "Ukraine is not Alina!" ("Ukraina ni Alina!"). The slogan can be read as a challenge to stereotypes of Ukraine's subservience to Russia stemming from Moscow's former hegemony within the USSR.

Femen activists also made themselves known to Hilary Clinton in 2011 – screaming topless across the Kyiv Boryspil airport, they warned her not to overlook women in her meeting with Yanukovych. Later that week they poked fun at Yulia Tymoshenko by styling their hair in thick braids and parading in front of Kyiv's courthouse while pretending to devour dollar bills.

Although their humour has long targeted dignitaries and other functionaries of the state, only in the later years of the Yanukovych regime did Femen activists face higher legal penalties for defacement, public disturbance, and attempts to interfere with national security measures. In January 2012, four members of the group were facing a four-year jail sentence for their protest on the balcony of the Indian ambassador to Ukraine in downtown Kyiv. In that protest Femen activists wore flowing silk garments, bindhis, and henna tattoos combined with traditional Ukrainian garlands and red wooden necklaces. They carried signs that read "We are not prostitutes!" to protest against the Indian government's decision to raise restrictions on transit visas of Ukrainian women travelling to India on the grounds doing so would reduce rates of prostitution. In each of these manoeuvres, Femen sarcastically depicted Ukrainian women as politically disenfranchised by the assumptions drawn without their voices in regard to sex work. Whether or not we agree with their radical approach, the effect of Femen's interjections drew attention to the overall lack of debate on the issue. As comparative case studies on policies in other nations have shown, such silence on sex work can invite all kinds of manipulation by self-interested stakeholders working at cross-purposes to women's choices over their own bodies, health, and safety.

In the preparations for Ukraine and Poland's joint hosting of the 2012 EuroCup soccer championship, Femen activists achieved another means of attention: they desacralized the branded symbols associated with the event to spotlight it as a catalyst for the dark undercurrents of the sex industry. They targeted the messages in ads featuring Ukraine as a destination for sex tourists ("sexpats").[120] These media stunts interrupted the utopian scripting of the equal partnership that elites were signalling to Europe at the time.[121] Hutsol cited remarks by President Viktor Yanukovych, who, in commenting on the soccer championship's slogan "Switch on Ukraine," bragged to international audiences that "In order to switch on Ukraine, it is enough to see it by your own eyes when the chestnut trees start to blossom, when it gets warmer and the women in Ukrainian cities start undressing. To see such beauty is marvelous!"[122] In response, Femen hit the road, launching a "EuroTour" across ten nations. While all of their stunts incorporated symbols specific to the country in which they appeared, each of their "shows" pitted stereotypes of the nationalism displayed by European soccer fans against a cynical caricature of Ukraine as a dangerous sexual playground.

The logo for the EuroCup branded Ukraine and Poland as cartoon "twins," providing an all-too convenient target for critiquing the asymmetries in Ukraine's relationship with the European Union. In Warsaw, two Femen members dressed up as the Polish and Ukrainian hooligan twins "Vladek" and "Vladko" and invited journalists to film them at a press conference on the sidelines of an official championship in a live performance of the mascots screwing, fighting, and drinking beer. To members' satisfaction, Femen earned themselves angry audiences. Many refused to accept that the protest had anything to do with the EU-Ukraine relationship, even though the stunt was part of calling attention to a range of local corrupt business practices going well beyond sex tourism alone.

Femen's capers catapulted the group into fame.[123] By attaching their brand to the marketing of the soccer championship, Femen dramatically increased their online visibility. The rise in their earned media attention, even where negative, served to unleash the elephant in the room – the corrupt underworld of business ventures in the sex work industries back home in Kyiv. Performance based, Femen's controversial stunts broke the widespread taboo against openly discussing the social issues and legal battles surrounding red-light districts in cities around the world, not only in Kyiv and Warsaw. Similar graft and labour exploitation would come to light in the International Olympic Committee's dealings with Moscow during the Sochi Olympics two years later, in winter 2014, at the height of the Maidan Revolution. As civilians died on the square, and President Viktor Yanukovych fled the country, several Olympic competitors from Ukraine would stand down from the competition in protest, while Putin looked on impassively. As Femen pushed farther into European spaces, their references to Ukraine would largely disappear. Rhetorically, the East/West stereotypes they attacked would remain in bold in the templates underlying their design as a virtual production for global presses and social media networks.

VI. Conclusion: Double Parody

As in the happenings that took place in the region in the 1980s, in the years after the Orange Revolution, Femen poked fun at authority by lampooning national politics in public street performances. The body rhetoric in their stagings maps figurations of the prostitute archetype and its associations onto deeper fears and fantasies assumed within much older East/West exchanges. The group's early performances on Kyiv's Maidan employed these stereotypes in irreverent, deconstructed scenarios couched in the same pop idiom as the Orange Revolution. Caricatures of nouveau riche glamour, peasant serfs from folklore, and legends of Amazonian warriors are all present in their appearances. Local and international associations with the prostitute as a sign for transgression differ, but share a common fear of contamination, as well as taboos around women's autonomy undermining the patriarchal order. These connotations arise in pictures of Femen activists calibrated for the logic of the mass media. The result is an open text that confuses and blindsides viewers with profanity, a profanity that is not easy to locate because it is also about the dual nature of the subjugation and idealization of feminine ideals in the capitalist marketplace. The result is a simulacrum that turns back on itself in parodic gestures within those selfsame media mechanisms and their internal ordering of erotic identification, alienation, and consumption.

Early Femen's body rhetoric appropriated celebrity styles from Ukrainian pop culture that expressed national autonomy through breaking from Russia and the Soviet past. The group's initial performances in Kyiv blended irony with authentic political comment in ways that drew out the discordant representations of the national past, and thus, anachronistic qualities of the "ideals of the Maidan" proffered by elites in the Orange Revolution. By putting themselves on display as prostitutes on the public square – the site of democratic debate from which the prostitute is always excluded – Femen activitists elicited outright rejections that exposed the limits to sensibility, tolerance, and public action among local audiences in the 2000s. Manufacturing both a physical performance and a media phenomenon of significant scope and frequency, the group's presence allowed for the airing of a good deal of anger at the shortfalls of the Orange Revolution and the failure of leaders to connect with people in the years that followed. Femen members themselves were targets of this anger, especially where they pitted pro-European and pro-Russian sentiments against one another, thus losing a shot at any authentic following in Ukraine. Ironically, oligarchs utilize similar scripts to consolidate their power bases in a bilingual population. Femen's puns were a spectacle of Ukrainian elites at a specific moment in time, and yet, one in which their activism would slowly come to descend into the same spectacle, as a parody of themselves. How could it not? Femen's caricatures of the nation projected onto the prostitute archetype are an allegory for the exchange of women in economic relations between men. At their core, Femen is a picture of anxieties about capitalist relations with the West over time.

The transferral of the red-light district onto Kyiv's central square, a site saturated with ideological meaning, unearthed the most immediately available social taboo – sex work – by which to criticize the "faded ideals of the Maidan" throughout the 2000s, a common phrase that would soon be evacuated of any romance or nostalgia in the violence that culminated on the Maidan during the winter of 2013–14. Morphing relative to the laws of the media photograph, the structure and design of Femen would soon play a role in rearranging the compass for global protest in the digital age. What Femen did not know is that they had already invented the seeds of their own demise.

Chapter Two

An Anatomy of Activism: Virtual Body Rhetoric in Digital Protest Texts

Sexuality remained central to fears about the future of the revolution.
— Eric Naiman, *Sex in Public*:
The Incarnation of Early Soviet Ideology, 1997

Grammar is politics by other means.
— Donna J. Haraway, Simians,
Cyborgs, and Women: The Reinvention of Nature, 1985

I. Introduction

Kyiv 2011. I am standing in the location of Femen's headquarters at the time: a brick cellar bar named Café Kupidon, not far from Maidan Nezalezhnosti (Independence Square). Before interviewing members of the group, I ask if I might take a photograph of a bulletin board coated in a collage of news clippings and other memorabilia that they have collected to commemorate their protests up to that point. The resulting image, figure 2.1, turns out to be a photograph of many photographs. Its temporal locus – the disjointed years between the Orange Revolution of 2004 and the Maidan Revolution of 2014 – puts on display the logic of a phenomenon that is, in itself, a mirror of global media; specifically, the mechanisms of its media design and transformation within the scripts for protest specified by the unwritten laws that make culture into commodities. My found portrait of Femen is now, in some ways, more descriptive in capturing the dynamic that the group has come to embody than are the vast online archives of pictures of the actual bodies of the women in the group. The more I look, the more I ask: Where is the locus of the "real" Femen protest – in the hyperreal photograph of a live-action street "flesh-mob," or in the media reproduction

Figure 2.1. Media wall, Femen headquarters, 2011, Kyiv. Photo by the author.

of the protest and its consumption? Is the medium of the message in the sound of the blackbird singing, or just after?

Conversations on the politics of public nudity expanded in the wake of the global protests of 2011.[1] Economic upheaval and new media technologies created a key juncture in activism that resembled the onset of the sex wars in the 1970s in North America, when feminists converged upon strategies for critiquing the design of the protest message itself. Organizing into collectives, they appropriated the broadcasting technologies developed in mass media during the Vietnam War to their own specialized media techniques aimed at diverting audiences' attention away from sexist advertising and negative images of women, towards debates about social violence and women's rights then raging in the streets and courts.[2] Many of these debates addressed the rise of pornography industries in the context of access to women's health services in the United States.

Of course, there are important formulaic differences between these earlier media activists and Femen. Femen's proclaimed stance against all forms of prostitution was conservative by legal measures in Canada and the European Union, even as the group openly challenged censorship laws in their nudity (they have been blocked on Facebook and other social media sites). Sex-positive arguments in support of the legalization of prostitution in Western countries tend to be allied with the traditional left in shying away from tighter regulations on media that could create an increase in cases of censorship. The conservative feminist viewpoint is epitomized in the figure of Catharine MacKinnon and her push for broader legal definitions of what constitutes pornography. These earlier feminist lines of argument have changed dramatically in the globalized information markets of the twenty-first century. This distinction elicits important questions about how protest is mediated and legitimized, not only in Femen's original post-Soviet context, but also in the group's virtual communications and the global reporting and exchange of views about rights that emerged through the Femen phenomenon.

The affordances of social media have resulted in more widely dispersed, informal streams of communication, creating what might be called an "off" media culture that positions itself against the mainstream. Visual icons, sardonic humour, and provocative statements feature widely in this culture, which varies only slightly across national contexts. Recent research into aesthetics and politics explores the idea of art-activism and the subversive potential of this new media structure. Shifts in the public/private divide driven by new communication mediums brought on by social media reveal a preoccupation with *space* and its uses in media-driven protests. The resonance between Femen and other nude protest groups worldwide in 2011 put the role of the body in resistance narratives at the centre of public transformation. Femen's parodic scenes undermined assumptions about "post-Soviet life" in a visual language that translated differently across national contexts. Analysing the group's mistranslation, in particular their controversial body image, can reveal much about the evolving strategies that activists have employed in order to transpose real and virtual spaces in dissent with one another and with the status quo.

In many ways, both stylistically and in their virtual format, Femen failed to actively assimilate to the conventions of feminist protest that have come before them. Since their founding, Femen's ubiquity – at first on Ukraine's streets and newspapers, then abroad, and finally, almost completely online – has served, in many ways, to produce through media memes the illusion of a worldwide presence. Although the group maintained a toehold in international media for over a decade, the slogans and themes of their activities were broad and lacked any specific political demands. The group's debut protest, "Ukraine Is Not a Brothel!," set the tone for later initiatives with similarly hyperbolic slogans such as "Happy Dependence Day Ukraine!," "KGB Euro," and "Sex Bomb." Nonetheless, the globalization of Femen manifested a wide-ranging conversation about feminism in which their topless performances became a key flashpoint for deeper conflicts, solidarities, and anxieties about gender, sexual liberation, and national belonging. The digital medium shaped Femen's design: morphing with the venues and conventions of internet media culture, the group expanded the edges of what protest could look like.

The "political" in the Femen phenomenon can be traced in their circulation, particularly their reception by other protest groups outside of Ukraine that adopted their aesthetic. The explosion of nude protest as a global phenomenon in 2010–11 lent Femen's project wider publicity. The Canadian feminist group Slutwalks, with whom Hutsol collaborated on a project at one point, adopted a similar protest method by stripping down in the streets to draw attention to domestic violence.[3] Other activists followed suit – attaching all sorts of signs, slogans, and symbols to their exposed bodies in actions broadcast on TV and computer screens: a nude man in New York joined the Occupy Movement and his image went viral; fans of Chinese artist Ai WeiWei posted nude photos of themselves online; a young Egyptian woman named Aliaa Magda Elmahdy associating herself with Femen posted a nude photo of herself and announced her action on Twitter.[4] In the midst of this sudden surge in nude demonstrations around the globe, Femen's style remained as widely featured in online circles and international media outlets as it had been at the time of the group's formation. Their visibility increased, bringing the "New Amazons," as the group began calling themselves, into greater and greater contact with international media outlets.[5]

Studying the images and counter images produced through the flurry of protest in the early 2010s can provide a lens into the evolving critical relationship between media technologies and the public sphere.[6] In Ukraine's post-Soviet context, where others have pointed out that neoliberal discourses have overlooked women in the shift to a market economy, it is exigent that transnational feminisms continue to take into account the full range of possible meanings of alternatives that do not fit familiar, linear narratives of progress, including those that may be problematic for other reasons.[7] The scripts, costumes, and site-specific locations in which Femen activists displayed their bodies in real time are illustrative of media apparatuses that shape how different publics are imagined.

While during the initial years of Femen's existence their parodies carved out plots from an Orange past in the political foibles, stunts, and facades they staged on the streets of Kyiv, the group's later religious iconography troubled many observers as a picture of feminist struggle. Their aesthetic shift after going abroad, as a media protest, was also symptomatic of deeper cultural memories of the Iraq War and the media imagery and stereotypes of Islam that have since become paradigmatic of news reports from the mid-late 2000s. The digital text of the Femen phenomenon was, in many ways, an outcome of the dichotomous language of suffering/salvation in depictions of military intervention in the Middle East, arguably throughout the modern era, but especially during the decade of the group's existence.

Scholars of democracy in comparative contexts have long debated the role of representation in mediating dialogue around freedom of speech. Especially important over the past twenty years has been a critical examination of the entrenchment of East-West discursive divides in the postcommunist context. This distinction is important for viewing how Femen gained media traction. Locally, Femen's performances constituted a deeply sardonic, tongue-in-cheek spoof on the protests that had taken place during the Orange Revolution, when elites had set forth claims to resolve issues but soon abandoned their plans for reform. Femen's global performances also contained cross-referenced signs, hyperbolic slogans, and vague gestures towards nonspecific issues that served to air generalized anger and grief. Over the course of their existence, throughout the Yanukovych presidency, the polysemic nature of Femen afforded them the ability to maintain a steady presence throughout major international media networks. This media fetish merits closer academic attention as an instance of local struggles around civil rights in Ukraine that would continue to have global impact.[8]

A virtual economy of image and cultural commodity arose through the street protests following the Arab Spring and the Colour Revolutions. Through the digital circulation of Femen as a sign for protest, a visual body language formed in which one can trace highly varied, sometimes contradictory, statements about gender, sexuality, subjugation, and power. The circulation of Femen's aesthetic – its rejection, appropriation, and contestation – by followers and opponents worldwide instantiated a broad-ranging debate about the virtual display of protest, a debate that reveals deeper patterns in the central role of digital media in translating concepts of civil rights and democracy across national borders. What do the rhetorical conventions deployed in digital texts by Femen and others reveal about this role and its impacts on society, the state, and international relations?

II. Internationalization: The State and Pussy Riot

With Femen's move abroad in 2012, they became an internationally recognized sign for dissent. At the same time, the group's performances remained devoid of any actual political demands. Femen had no constituency, and their actions, for the most part, no longer took place on the streets. By any conventional understanding of political agency the group remained largely innocuous, even as their topless displays continued to draw more and more of the world's attention. As Femen catapulted into world presses, they continued to manage the status and shape of their popularity. Ukrainian gender scholars Olga Plakhotnik and Mariya Mayerchyk observed that "the measure of a successful Femen action is a popular action. Popularity, for Femen, is publicity that draws attention to social issues; for them, this is the way out of obscurity."[9] Going abroad, Femen activists adopted a system resembling a franchise by streamlining their social media presence and merchandising. Their Ukrainian folk flower garlands, red boots, and blue-and-yellow logo came to serve as templates through which they rotated civic symbols from other national contexts.

The internationalization of Femen's campaign proceeded in three main phases after the group's initial forays into the European Union on their "EuroTour" campaign, organized to bring attention to an expected surge in prostitution connected with the EuroCup 2012. The first phase occurred after the women's protest music group, Pussy Riot, performed their "Punk Prayer" concert against Putin's regime in Moscow's Cathedral of Christ the Saviour on 21 February 2012.[10] The location and the lyrics of Pussy Riot's protest song "Mother of God, Drive Putin Away" borrowed the exact same locus and slogan of Femen's topless protest in front of Christ the Saviour one year earlier, on 9 December 2011, in which several Femen members wore peasant costume pants made of burlap and held posters reading "God Chase Away the King!" and "God Rid Us of the Tsar!"

From October 2011 to January 2015 Femen staged approximately sixty street actions outside of Ukraine.[11] They appeared at events of global prominence including the G8 leaders' summit, meetings at the Vatican, and court hearings in Quebec regarding the public display of religious symbols. Countries where Femen's core members or women affiliated with the group staged protest-performances included Belarus, Russia,

Poland, France, Germany, Italy, Bulgaria, Switzerland, Spain, Portugal, Turkey, Tunisia, Brazil, India, and Canada. The themes of Femen's international protests included sexual harassment policies at the EuroCup, freedom of the press and censorship, the Olympic committee's stance on Islamic law, the wearing of the veil, human trafficking, and the Catholic Church's stance on gay marriage. Members' increasingly radical actions landed several of them in jail, lead to near-fatal kidnappings in Belarus, and put many of them on trial, which also had the effect of increasing their publicity.

On the day of the verdict in Pussy Riot's subsequent trial for "hooliganism motivated by religious hatred," Femen activist Inna Shevchenko cut down a large wooden cross in central Kyiv that she incorrectly stated was constructed by the Ukrainian Greek Catholic Church on public land in order to memorialize victims of Stalin's policies.[12] She claimed that her act was in solidarity with Pussy Riot against their sentence of two years in prison; Pussy Riot denied any connection, as their member Maria Alyokhina stated, "We may share the same immediate appearances and general stance against authoritarianism, but we look at feminism differently, especially in our actions. We have never stripped and never will. The recent action in cutting down the cross, unfortunately, does not create any feeling of solidarity."[13] Where Pussy Riot's action aimed to symbolically unravel the unification of church and state in Russia, Femen's material desecration of the cross as a symbol of victims of the state discursively diffused the act across three signifiers: the nation, an abstract female body performed by Shevchenko standing in the position of the cross that she destroyed, and the absent Soviet victims of Stalin's purges that the orginal cross was stated to have represented.

The role of religion in state affairs also appeared in a Femen protest against clericalism several months earlier, when they occupied the Saint Sophia bell tower in Kyiv in April 2012. Global reporters seized upon the fact that the cross had been erected in honour of victims of Stalin, but were too quick to remark that it had been erected by religious groups disconnected from the state and church authorities. Local feminist activists on the left, not associated with Femen, warned against diffusing the main point of the protest being against clericalism, claiming that the cross had been a gift to the City of Kyiv. Criticized by feminists and the public, Shevchenko responded in an interview with Euro Radio's Liavon Malinovsky that she was unaware of the specific history of the cross as an anti-Stalinist symbol, redirecting her otherwise misaligned act into a general statement about authoritarianism in post-Soviet Ukraine: "The main fact is that the same thing we fought against 50 years ago is happening again."[14]

Unlike Pussy Riot's dramatic trial and prison term, Femen's destruction of a religious monument failed to focus public attention on state power in its local forms. Despite Pussy Riot's public statement that they had no intention of destroying any images of the Orthodox Church and felt no solidarity with Femen, the latter pressed forward with a "Free Riot" media campaign. A wave of copycat cross-fellings continued over a span of months across the region. Femen's desecration of religious iconography continued to incite debate about the (in)effectiveness of the group's claims, with critics pointing to the potential harm of destructive imagery on positive dialogue concerning civil rights. Solidarity between the groups never arose, despite the fact that they shared many of the same tactics, ideas, and locales.

Pussy Riot's imprisonment earned the group a modicum of legitimacy among many circles in the West that Femen would never come to know, marked by formal statements of support from US officials, invited public talks, benefit concerts with Madonna and other stars, collaborations with Amnesty International, record deals, and in one brilliant twist on art-as-reality, or realpolitik – a cameo on their stated favourite American TV series *House of Cards*, featuring Tolokonnikova and Alyokhina as themselves snidely pouring champagne on an actor playing Putin at a fictional state dinner.

The systematic purging and affirmation of authority in the Pussy Riot trial, as opposed to Femen's act, signified the three women's bodies differently. Both actions aimed to target and criticize the role of the church in state decisions, but the women themselves became the sacrificial bodies in the media surrounding their performances. The same dramaturgy played out through opposite means: Femen overexposed their bodies, while Pussy Riot performed fully clothed and masked; the latter's concealment supplied distance from the taboos in Femen's formula. In all instances, the women transformed their bodies into both objects of violence and sites of resistance.

It is important to note that Femen was the first to perform a protest on the same site as Pussy Riot. Femen members have been critiqued for commodifying themselves, while Pussy Riot, despite their commercialization, received a harsher response from their own members than they did in the global media. What this tells us is that audiences worldwide were more willing to accept the corporatization of feminist protest in the case of Pussy Riot members who fed into the neoliberal sale of their brand, whereas Femen's performance of nudity simply could not be assimilated into the capitalist marketplace in the same way.

The feminist question on nudity in mass media now appears more radical by degree: the erasure of Femen's first transgression at the site of Pussy Riot's famous "Punk Prayer" maps onto asymmetrical perceptions of Russian dissidents versus Ukrainian dissidents. The latter struggle to be seen and heard as equally legitimate. From the perspective of artistic and political communication, the two members of Pussy Riot lost an early opportunity to publicly disagree with Femen in a way that could have linked both groups' pro-Ukrainian and anti-war media statements later on.[15] Femen member Oksana Shachko, interviewed in December 2017 by the Parisian art journal *Crash*, comments,

> I knew some of the girls personally, because when we made an action in 2012 in Russia against Putin, I was in prison for three weeks. Pussy Riot contacted me and we were supposed to meet as activists. It was before they became well-known. People started noticing them when they took action in a church and got arrested three months later because of it. What's funny is that when they were doing their performance in the church, their slogans said, "Virgin Mary, drive away Putin." One month before, we were protesting as FEMEN in front of the same church with the slogan, "May God drive away Putin." I like to think they were inspired.[16]

Elsewhere, she talks about fleeing threats from secret services in Ukraine in 2014, the war, gaining refugee status in France, and her disappointment in individuals there whom she felt only joined Femen because they wanted to "be photographed in the press and had nothing better to do with their lives." Looking back, she says, "I don't feel sad or depressed anymore because I can see that this kind of phenomena that we have with the women of FEMEN and Pussy Riot, this kind of political art was very strong in post-Soviet countries in the last five years, but none of us are active anymore." She speaks about gains made by feminists, but also, disappointment: "The power is still the same and even worse. It's war in Ukraine, they kill people very easily. In the last year, fifteen activists or people who dissent in general have died." She goes on for awhile longer, then turns her focus on her decision to enrol in the Beaux Arts School in order to return to her love for icon painting. The interview is by 22Visconti Gallery, where she presented paintings in the exhibitions *Surface Sans Cible* and *Talking about a Revolution*. She would commit suicide seven months later.

What Femen's and Pussy Riot's performances share are strong examples of the female body as a highly contentious, violent site for building and dismantling state ideologies. Nadezhda Tolokonnikova, Maria Alyokhina, and Yekaterina Samutsevich, the three women in the Pussy Riot case, were subjected to ongoing state and public rituals around their punishment. Anthropologist Anya Bernstein elaborates on the dynamics of the trial in the ways in which it served to mediate between official and imagined publics: "The sovereign power sacrifices Pussy Riot to the *narod*, the opposition sacrifices them to the government, and the *narod* performs an apotropaic sacrifice while longing for a sublime sovereign power."[17] The connotation of "narod," meaning both nation and people, while also containing the mythic quality of each of these concepts, functioned on the level of collective sacrifice in the Pussy Riot case. Where Pussy Riot's "Punk Prayer" concentrated general anger at a defective regime, Shevchenko's act diffused that anger through an individual instance of transgression against the Ukrainian state as surrogate for "all religion and patriarchy." The different power dynamics in these two acts rendered the second less threatening to any actual political hierarchy in its over-the-top overtures to authority. Indeed, far lighter punishment was inflicted on Femen than on Pussy Riot. Nonetheless, after the cross incident, Inna Shevchenko was forced to emigrate. She relocated to France, where she would later receive amnesty.[18] Rhetorically, neither Femen's nor Pussy Riot's actions were, in practice, directed at God or Christianity: they were both public, symbolic acts targeted at the state and *its* appropriation of Judeo-Christian symbols.

Both Femen's and Pussy Riot's interjections into public spaces strike to the core the democratic idea that state symbols *should* be publicly contested and debated – an idea shared by a wide range of movements throughout the post-Soviet region. The cross itself was given to the City of Kyiv at the time of the Orange Revolution, connecting its symbolism with a specific moment in Ukraine's history.[19] People at the time aired their social anger towards an unjust election and helped to shape a lasting civic, public culture of debate by openly demonstrating the future directions they wanted their country to take. Femen formed four years later, when it had become clear that the ideals promoted during the Orange Revolution had been sold out by infighting elites concerned with maintaining their individual economic bases. Had the cross, which was constructed by a private group in 2005 "to Stalinist repression," been planned and constructed through an open and public process of memorializing the past, it would have facilitated a more democratic ethic in the present.

Although Femen's tactics missed their mark in instantiating any lasting ethic of measured discussion around monuments in Ukraine, as the debates around decommunization and the removal of Lenin statues, or Ленінопад (Lenin-falls) after the Maidan Revolution would make painfully clear, they did provoke a debate over the state-religion bond in Ukraine similar to the one in Russia that raged after Pussy Riot's "Punk Prayer."[20] Given past struggles over the usage of the cross by the Ukrainian state, it is surprising that more critical inquiries into the nature of memorialization within Ukraine had not been raised earlier. Both Femen and Pussy Riot drew attention to the closed doors behind which so many decisions about public space continue to be made in Ukraine and Russia. Although the two groups would not unite in any substantial way beyond, perhaps, in the imaginations of their more distant audiences, both of their acts were radical and valuable, if equally nascent, as local statements about memorialization and who gets included/excluded in the construction of national history.

Femen moved farther into European media spaces on the heels of the Pussy Riot Affair. This began the second major phase of their global push. In the summer of 2012, the group shifted their operational epicentre from Café Kupidon in downtown Kyiv to a run-down theatre in the northern Paris Goutte d'Or neighbourhood, where they changed their ideological positioning. Slogans painted directly on their torsos in black warpaint featured heavily in their new image. This new design first appeared in a demonstration with the Parisian Egyptian activist Safea Lebdi in front of the Eiffel Tower in August 2012 against the inclusion of nations practising sharia law in the Olympic Games.[21] As a direct outcome of this event, the group collaborated for a short time with Iranian-born activist Maryam Namazie and Safea Lebdi, although both split with the group later on. In late 2012 fierce public backlash erupted in response to Femen's depictions of Islam and their targeting of the mandatory wearing of the veil and sharia law.

By now, Femen's new aesthetic had nearly completely severed them from their original Ukrainian context and gained them many global opponents. The exclusion of a plurality of women's voices from Femen's marketing of protest both lost the group credibility among feminists of all stripes and challenged the brand's purchase on the media. Nonetheless, as Femen's image grew ever more radical, their group's number of followers on social media grew exponentially, expanding their rhetorical ability to enter global news streams on any number of topics.

The third phase of Femen's saga began in summer of 2013. In late August, Femen's Paris headquarters were burned by an unidentified arsonist. The group posted online that in Kyiv the Ukrainian Secret Services (SBU) had increased monitoring around their activities. A few weeks later, Anna Hutsol, Alexandra Shevchenko, and Roman Zviazsky were physically assaulted and beaten on the streets by unknown men they claimed were connected with state security services. Yanukovych's decision to begin the process of EU Association in November 2013 had long coincided with an overall increase in the domestic monitoring and targeting of protest in Ukraine. The group then announced plans to cease all activity in Ukraine.[22] The high level of violence directed at Femen only served to further position the group within global mass media.

Virtual and Real Spaces

Femen often modified the physical spaces of their protests within the frames of their photos as though they were tagging information in virtual space. This tactic afforded them early on the ability to attach to diverse media stories. As a result, their aesthetic became a polysemic sign for dissent within the rhetoric of news media.[23] One particular example perfectly exposes the civilizational discourses around the prostitute discussed in chapter 1. A female nude on the revolutionary square has long been associated in Western art with democracy in the figure of the Marianne. In July 2013, French president François Hollande unveiled a drawing of Inna Shevchenko, created by artist Olivier Ciappa, as the annual Marianne image for French stamps. The selection sparked controversy not only among French feminists, but the wider public as well.[24] The stamp's design mixed signifiers for liberalism that are usually opposed: the Western Enlightenment of the French Revolution versus the Orientalized Eastern maiden liberated from her Eastern captors. This image was a challenge to Femen's audiences – supporters and opponents alike; it threw into question the group's broader protests pitted against sexual conquest in its historical specificity and revolutionary associations.

In Western culture markets, both Femen and Pussy Riot emerged within the legacy that drives a much a larger media economy tied both to the history of the Cold War Soviet dissident and to more contemporary locales for civil disobedience. In our information paradigm, in which the accrual of capital through the economy of images and text online rapidly transverses national borders, Femen's directing attention to themselves in a particularly unorthodox "feminist" manner, through sex appeal in mass media, was, in many ways, a rhetorical publicity game strategized against those civilizational messages. Brett Lunceford has analysed the rhetoric of the body and its deployment across four distinct case studies of nude activist groups in the United States in the 2000s. Emphasizing the viewer in the transaction between performer and audience, he writes, "While naked, it is more difficult to manage one's projected identity. The naked body is left at the mercy of others for interpretation."[25] Lunceford cites Laura Verdi: "Thanks to technology, the physical body has been liberated from the power of the social body: the former has been deified in order to make the latter a symbolic object of undisputed media power."[26] Femen's performances ran the interpretive risk of objectification in the erotic charges that accompanied their posing topless in the stances of models for glossy cover photos. But how much of this risk was unique to Femen? What about the paradoxes in the idea of a "celebrity activist," or the question of "fame" in Soviet and post-Soviet dissidence? Is this not always a double-edged sword for conveying struggle?

On a mass scale, the cultural registers that structure desire in pictures of nude bodies are intertwined with the same social attitudes that shape state policies on sex. Eric Naiman has observed in the Soviet case, but also more generally, that "sex, in particular, presents problems for utopian mentalities," citing Althusser's definition of ideology as an "overdetermination of the real by the imaginary and of the imaginary by the real" to explain how sex creates obstacles for absolutist thinking.[27] The rhetoric of nudity and its scripts for producing female celebrities into subjects of an imagined social body are carefully managed and often culturally determined. In the West, female nudity is a basic requirement for maintaining celebrity status – in tabloid exposé, accidentally leaked porn videos, onstage foibles or blunders – and perhaps has been so thoroughly commodified as to be nearly invisible in its displays upholding the status quo. The amateurish quality of Femen's outpourings contains a verisimilitude that reaches across these genres in its depictions of the sex-power myth in entertainment and politics. Their protest performances resemble the genre of reality television, in which audiences are provoked to question how much of the production is staged, versus spontaneous and therefore "authentic."

Dystopian themes moved to the centre of Central European art in the wake of totalitarianism and war in the twentieth century. The Viennese Actionists employed blood and ritual in horror scenes that attempted to depict violent histories acted out upon humans. Hermann Nitsch's public re-enactment of a crucifixion put the cross in the context of a past war, but also brought Central European performance art into conversation with global counterculture amid the international oil crises of the 1970s. Women Actionists such as VALIE EXPORT exposed their bodies to confront what some described as lingering Nazi ideologies in Austrian society. Dynamism in EXPORT's work problematizes the centre/margin in her photos. Women's live bodies stand in as sculptures in urban zones, troubling the regulation of space and the dichotomies in renderings of the female nude as virgin/whore. Her guerilla public performances gained worldwide attention and sparked a national campaign against her. Carolee Schneeman later adapted these militaristic and ritualized images of violence in her own work in New York City in experiments around how language comes to bear upon women's lived experiences, opportunities, and political subjectivities. In the late 1970s, second-wave feminists alongside her in many Western contexts sought to communicate the psychosocial gendered effects on individuals of systems of regulation, abortion legislation, the criminalization of rape, welfare laws, fair hiring practices, urban segregation, and more. These artists often deployed the figure of the nude body to varying effects to critique the standardization of labour, reproduction, and other social impacts of the nuclear family ideal.

These prior twentieth century visual languages appear in Femen and Pussy Riot in ways that transgress twenty-first century politics in post-Soviet Ukraine and Russia by targeting gender norms.[28] Their literal and figurative explosions of themselves into the "theatres" of post-totalitarian architecture, monuments, and churches in Moscow, Kyiv, and elsewhere contrast the mortality of the body and physical trauma with the sublime nature of grand historical narratives. Eric Naiman, mentioned elsewhere in this book, has pointed out how the Bolshevik and NEP era utopian literary and historical texts that became foundational to the state each fetishized narratives about sex: the collective body, castration, penetration, trauma, and other visceral themes served a common interpretive thread about the role of the individual within society.[29] Femen has incorporated raw meat, gas masks, fake blood, animal bones, chainsaws, and other props into their appearances. The Actionist threads in their disaster scenarios tugged at the chains in the destructive rhetoric of the state under Yanukovych and Putin, their propaganda media apparatuses, and the intimidation tactics used to stifle dissent. Where VALIE EXPORT and others of her generation once installed themselves into the built environment, Femen and Pussy Riot posed in place of the crosses, altars, and other deities that they invoked in their own image through their lyrics and slogans – calibrated for the global flow of information.

III. The Body and the Information Commodity

In Femen and Pussy Riot, as in stagings by other feminist performance artists before them, the body appears as both a material and an ideological form. In March 2012 three members of Femen travelled to Istanbul, where they dressed up as victims of acid attacks by painting fake scars on their skin. The protest was the first time in which Femen performed as Muslim women. Carrying signs that said "Death to Barbarians," they yelled statements such as "Asian cocktails" and named the protest after sulfuric acid, "H2SO4." They reported on their blog that they were protesting violence against women in "all totalitarian regimes."[30] The protest's religious iconography and location near Istanbul's central mosque earned the group a night in jail, forced deportation, and suspended transit visas.

Days after the event, Femen posted a series of black-and-white photographs on their blog showing the three activists involved in the protest in their full costumes. Two things set this series of photos apart from Femen's past photo campaigns. The first is a photo showing Aleksandra Shevchenko wearing a hijab, completely covered except for her scar-painted face. The second are images of Aleksandra and her sister Inna applying and removing their fake scars.

The photos generalize conflict in the Middle East by indexing patriarchy in Turkey with a picture that more closely resembles Iran. Shevchenko's scarred face estranges the surrealism of civilian violence within the "theatres" of war. The colour tones and camera angle replicate early mid-twentieth-century documentary photography and its claims to authenticate the past. In the street protest that took place after the photo was taken, Femen's slogans linked acid attacks to an inherently Asiatic patriarchy, implicating viewers in a voyeuristic visual system, one that provoked audiences and authorities to immediately reject Femen. The group was arrested and deported from Turkey. Although Femen activists did not change the colour of their skin in this protest nor have they done so elsewhere, the privilege they gave *Europeanness* was clearly displayed in both their slogans attacking Asia and their visual communication to audiences through media produced behind the scenes of their protests that they were able to maintain the choice to remove their scars – for them, violence remained a performance.

One of the central aims in this chapter is to trace a broader ethical context concerned with media stereotypes and their (mis)translations across cultural paradigms. In 2011 the photo that won the World Press Photo Contest featured a Yemeni woman holding a wounded man in her arms, an image that is both emotionally difficult to look at, and yet generic, given that similar images appeared in a number of media streams during the height of the Iraq war, the same period in which Femen was founded. Arguably, the group's statements on Islam result from an overidentification with the subject position of Muslim women; this overidentification both amplifies and undercuts the appropriative display of women to frame war in a media-saturated environment.

In the wake of the protest, the "backstage" photo of Shevchenko completely veiled and wearing the (temporary) scars of another's suffering, taken by a Turkish photographer, was posted online to Femen's blog beneath the other media photos of the group protesting on the square. The verisimilitude created by the "fake" pseudo-documentary photo dislocates viewers from the first protest that took place in real time, and from its physical space. The contrast between the exposed Femen activist in the street, and the fully covered body in the second photo, is

Figure 2.2. *Sana'a, Yemen*, by Samuel Aranda. 55th Annual International World Press Photo of the Year, 2011. Panos Pictures.

striking. The street protest is easy to reject offhand because of the way the activists use their slim, white female bodies to project internalized Western fears about the Other. This particular protest became a prototype for Femen's later aesthetic shift that would raise the level of anger directed at them, and at their commentary on tropes of violence in the Muslim world, to a new intensity within Western media.

In the now famous World Press photo, a woman holds her wounded son in her arms in a mosque used as a field hospital by demonstrators against the rule of President Ali Abdullah Saleh during clashes in Sanaa, Yemen, on 15 October 2011 (figure 2.2).[31] The photographer, Samuel Aranda, took the photo while working on assignment for the *New York Times*. Another distressing irony in the Femen portrait is that feminist demonstrators in the Ukrainian feminist group Ofenzywa, unaffiliated with Femen, would organize field hospitals in churches during the clashes on Maidan against Viktor Yanukovych's regime two years later.[32]

The Femen photo provokes one to recoil from the imitation of another's suffering. Audiences are poised to question the mediation of the gaze in moving between the two shots. The tension between the two photos emerges in virtual space, further compounded by their circulation together with thousands of other photos in networks of images associated with the impact of war on human life. What are the specific elements that make these photos resemble similar images published in the *New York Times*, *National Geographic*, and a host of other journals throughout the 2000s? Alienating viewers from the site of the violence performed on actual women's bodies during the Iraq war, the photograph makes visible the conditions and media mechanisms by which the black veil has become a symbol of suffering. The offence in the Femen photo is a critical offence.

Islam would continue to figure in Femen's statements and protest actions long after this physical insertion of themselves directly into the Muslim world. The full range of critique of their actions, including by Muslim women in conflict with Femen after their move abroad to Paris, and former members criticisms of Inna Shevchenko's leadership during the group's residency in an abandoned theatre, and her close association with the satiric French journal *Charlie Hebdo*, has been well documented.[33] After *Charlie Hebdo* was attacked by a terrorist group linked to Al-Qaeda in January 2015, the authorities in Paris retaliated by raiding private residences belonging to Muslim individuals throughout the city. While the journal is known for depicting inflammatory caricatures that have offended Muslim populations, anti-Muslim demonstrations ensued in the wake of the attacks.

At the time of the raids in Paris, I was working on this book as a postdoctoral scholar in Toronto, where I was renting an apartment on the Danforth not far from the mosque in the east end, which enjoys a large community of recent immigrants from Muslim countries. The night of the raids in Paris my apartment was broken into and ransacked by an unknown source while I was on campus; upon returning home, it was my Muslim neighbours and landlord who kindly assisted me by calling the local police, providing their knowledge as witnesses, and driving me to a colleague's home. I have yet to confirm the source of the intrusion, but in the years following this instance I would experience more "coincidences" in the digital sphere, including the hacking of my accounts on dates corresponding to media events in the public exposure of feminist actions and voices. These phenomena are not new. At the same time, I have since made efforts to cultivate among peers, colleagues, family, and friends a renewed vigilance around emerging technologies in the interest of reducing harm to researchers and securing our voices from practices of censorship in all forms, especially where very real external threats can lead to spirals of internal self-doubt.

Figure 2.3. *Untitled* (*Virgin in burqa*) icon painting by Oksana Shachko, co-founder of Femen, 2016. Courtesy of the Family Estate of Oksana Shachko.

The women in Femen and Pussy Riot have spoken out about the stresses that they have faced as highly visible targets, many choosing anonymity or exit strategies to protect themselves. There have also been tragic casualties in the backlash against feminists after Trump's election and the inauguration of regressive regimes throughout the world. Not long before her death by suicide in 2018, one of the founding members of Femen, Oksana Shachko, created a painting of an icon (figure 2.3). The image is a powerful gesture of empathy. It appears to be a mirror of the now well-known, winning photograph of the World Press Photo Contest for 2011, which depicted a Yemeni woman and her son shouldering the burden of an authoritarian regime.[34] The symmetry is profound, and could be read as an offering that invites women living in distant times and places to reflect on solidarity and expressions of love in times of struggle.

The alterity of these layered aesthetics through the repetition of the same image, on one level, points to the fact that identity categories are in themselves reductive and the outcomes unpredictable when digital surfaces move across real-time contexts. In May 2013 a trial was held in Tunisia involving a young woman associated with Femen named Amina Tyler for posting nude photos of herself on Twitter. Femen activists protested topless outside the central courthouse in Tunis. The event went nearly unnoticed. By this point, it had become clear that Femen's "sextremism," discussed below, had severed them from their original Ukrainian context and gained them many opponents, even while their increasingly radical rhetoric expanded their ability to enter global media streams on any number of topics. A Facebook group called Muslim Women Against Femen formed. Femen had suddenly come to an impasse in their purchase on the media.

On the one hand, the affinities Femen assumed throughout the 2000s with Muslim minorities by adopting the position of "suffering" under the veil satirized Western mass media images of the same tenor in a metanarrative on post-Iraq war reportage. Yet on the other hand, their sextremist image played into the selfsame ideologies about "rescuing" Muslim women that Femen attempted to unravel. The group's depictions of Muslim women's struggles lost them credibility in the eyes of journalists who reported on counter-demonstrations by women in dissent with the group's anti-religious rhetoric. The situation proved that in terms of realpolitics, the language of the Femen brand was neither calibrated nor subtle enough to avoid the backlash caused by possibly unintended interpretations. Meanwhile, Femen's radical alterity within and among a much wider range of protests of the era pointed to the conflicted deployment of the media apparatus. The true source of resistance, read in this way, is anger at the reductivism in the production of world news as a spectacle of locally meaningful protest.

After moving abroad to Paris, Femen members continued their marketing campaign with increasingly radical depictions of physical violence and anti-religious sentiment that they termed "sextremism." Slogans painted directly on the body in black warpaint became key to this new image, in addition to an overall shift in the language, stances, and public image of themselves as a military squadron of women training at their "feminist camp" for a style of protest they referred to as "an information war."[35] Anger, militarism, Second World War–era political symbols, blood, and poses borrowed from hardcore porn all met in streamlined advertisements that could have been lifted from the pages of a corporate marketing manual.

And while Femen's politics would continue to play out as a virtual happening within a complex web of dissenting voices, their image would also become more deeply intertwined with the same media surfaces that silence women in the public sphere. In hindsight, we are now able to see Femen's appearances in news reports throughout the 2000s as a satire on the bleaker aspects of war journalism. Unlike Pussy Riot, whose trajectory was fuelled by the US State Department and other Western governments' grievances around Putinism, Femen could not earn such credentials, arguably because their image contained more explicit references to Western patriarchy and hegemony. Instead, Femen's unravelling took place as the group's aesthetic collapsed into a parody of their own activism. With the invention of "sextremism," Femen had exceeded itself.

Feminist Media Performance

After Femen's move abroad, the nationally inflected pop rhetoric from the Orange Revolution receded from their design. Scholars increasingly vocalized their concerns about Femen's topless images being posed for the male gaze, noting where the transmission of a social message through female nudity risks being lost on the consumer.[36] An important international exchange of information channelled through the Femen brand and its mass-media venues as a platform for debate on the conflicted meaning of feminism. Femen had staked their public persona on an idea with largely negative connotations in the postcommunist context as an imposed term, because of its dual etymological roots in Soviet ideology and Western thought. Along with this, their performances also revealed much about the translation of civic terms between ideas of East and West, specifically in viewing what passes as "acceptable" or legitimate political activity in each case, versus what is taken for having no social worth simply because it appears unintelligible or even ridiculous on the surface.

Organizing around the social effects of popular imagery, twentieth-century feminist media activists in the West developed techniques that attempted to avert audiences' attention from collective mythology, trivialized clichés, and accrued negative connotations regarding women and violence. In one example, entitled *In Mourning and in Rage* (Los Angeles 1977), roughly ten women from the group Ariadne Social Art Network completely covered themselves in black cloth and stood in a row in front of the Los Angeles Civic Center in order to undermine "images of mourners as old, powerless women" in response to a rape case then under consideration (figure 2.4).[37] An important difference between these early media actions and Femen is the emergence of social media networks and their ability to diffuse and refract messages across vast geographical and cultural boundaries. This difference elicits new inquiries into how message and medium function. The controversy Femen ignited, and the deployment of their aesthetic by oppositional groups, were symptomatic of deeper global tensions that are, arguably, still very much ongoing in the broad unravelling of the US-Russia relationship through investigations into election meddling and charges of conspiracy.

Femen's hyper-emotive displays appeared spontaneous both online and in real time. Anna Munster's idea of "digital embodiment" can be useful for thinking about how the engineering of digital "protest" aims to disrupt the familiar codes that produce consumer-audiences cued by commodity, image, and news technology.[38] Productive critiques of Femen must account for the commodification of the female body in the group's design, and also the processes at work in the technologies Femen employed, given the role of digital information in signifying bodily experience. This signification could be considered in light of Donna Haraway's initial queries into the theoretical links between gender and machines, virtuality, and the material conditions of information culture in her pathbreaking 1985 text, "A Cyborg Manifesto: Science, Technology, and Socialist-Feminism in the Late Twentieth Century."[39] Such an approach foregrounds the sensorial means by which we inhabit and interpret meanings and patterns in text, whether in digital or analogue mediums. The contradiction in Femen's reception collapses any attempt to "read" a critical narrative into their project, seek in their actions a stable genre, or account for their intentions as artists or activists. What we can gain here, however, is an alternative understanding of how political algorithms are deployed in different media cultures to build networks, undermine opponents, and provoke or silence individual viewpoints.

The preoccupation with *violence* underlying Femen's online visual texts is cast within the same frame as the scripts that underlie other news images. Either completely covering or stripping the body bare make it easier to point to the binaries in the codes in which visual narratives in popular news images operate. Femen activists' scrawling of

Figure 2.4. Performance by Suzanne Lacy and Leslie Labowitz, *In Mourning and in Rage*, 1977, City Hall, Los Angeles. Photo by Maria Karras. Shared with permission of the artists.

black text directly on their bodies collapses the newsprint text completely into the visual image. The outlandish and alienating offence in the protest slogans of Femen's first Paris protest, where they debuted their body texts such as "Muslim Women Let's Get Naked" and "Naked War," parried with the written text of news reportage and familiar headlines depicting the West's relationship with Middle Eastern nations over the past decade. The visual text remains in the realm of parody. By contrast, the written text is sarcastic and points to the reductive processes that underlie major news stories in their commoditization and transmission of complex issues into tiny bits of information that can be consumed rapidly.

Rather than conveying a unified message, Femen's media stunts collapsed the border between politics and art, thereby momentarily subordinating the public sphere to its own doctrines. Polish art critic Piotr Piotrowski has termed this tendency in postwar Poland, Ukraine, and Russia "agoraphilia," describing a certain anxiety, even fetishization, around the borderline between art and politics, action and thought, the actual and the imagined. In these instances, an artist acts upon a deeper desire to shape public life: "to perform critical and design functions for the sake of and within the social space."[40] In this sense, street protest entails a rich history in the former Eastern Bloc and post-Soviet regions, where art and artistic communities have often functioned as a haven for reinventing the very idea of a dissident culture.

Femen involves both commoditization and protest processes. Their design nearly completely subjects the text to the image by modifying it into "bad" text: offensive and ridiculous slogans, misspelled words, and unclear referents expunge credibility from the text within the image. This in turn complicates Femen's potential for gaining any actual constituency. The tabloid is juxtaposed with feature documentary to elicit a highly marketable media product, but one that lacks any external references to its actual context. The extremism in "sextremism" falls apart as a movement or a "Naked Jihad!" based in a terminology that, in any truly critical assessment of its meanings, could only be considered as blatantly racist. Rather, the more lasting shock in the extremism of Femen's "sextremism" is that, in actuality, they did not really invent it themselves. What emerges in the circulation of their images of news text written on their exposed flesh is the news, not themselves. The irony here is most apparent when considering Femen over time and across outlets: news media circulated reports on the group as an actual protest movement even while online audiences, in printed text below these images, posted denunciations of the idea that Femen could ever represent any actual public interest. Thus, these audiences position themselves in a dissenting relationship with the same news scripts that the Femen sextremist image interpolates.

In this way, the misspelled, hyperbolic, warpaint text scrawled on Femen members' torsos put on display the crude reductionism in information commoditization. Like jesters, they point at the tropes underlying our media consumption, and how this consumption shapes public life. The extreme tropes underlying major news images are more often than not wholly subsumed by text, oftentimes diluted through overstimulation in the visual scripts that circulate alongside them online in everything from pop-up advertisements to pornography. In this sense, Femen is more visual than textual. They can be understood as an experiment that exposes some media mechanisms through flesh, but that cannot fully address the impact of those news stories on actual bodies, a fact that both gives Femen's virtual body rhetoric media traction and elicits troubling images upon which feminists of multiple stripes have converged in their critiques. Given Ukraine's recent statehood, economic infrastructure heavily linked to the Russian Federation, conflict in the Donbas, language debates, and the annexation of Crimea, Ukraine remains a space of lingering hegemonies, a space that often goes undisclosed in the public sphere but nonetheless continues to exert psychological and political pressure on the daily lives of citizens.[41]

Insofar as Femen layers national and religious references over pleas for women's rights, their protest aesthetic collapses cultural difference and overly universalizes patriarchial systems. This transversal of cultural difference structurally resembles Homi K. Bhabha's idea that in postmodernity "extraterritorial and cross-cultural initiations" happen in "interstitial" spaces that estrange, dislocate, and relocate cultural struggles for self-recognition – a process he calls "the unhomely."[42] He refers to the "hybridity of the history of sexuality and race" to illustrate how "social differences are not simply given to experience through an already authenticated cultural tradition; they are the signs of the emergence of community envisaged as a project – at once a vision and a construction – that takes you 'beyond' yourself in order to return, in a spirit of revision and reconstruction, to the political conditions of the present."[43] These conditions manifest through questioning cultural borders and how membership is determined. For feminism, these conditions are also about patriarchy as it shapes the negotiation of public/private divides.[44] The central claim here is that struggles over public/private domains hold universal value for feminists, and that feminism is in itself a cultural axis capable of unifying and refracting postcolonial culture(s) as they come into contact with one another. This ambivalence generates multiple textual and subversive possibilities.

Intersectional feminist critiques based in postcolonial theory and critiques of the public sphere continue to grapple with how, in practice, marginalized groups who view each other from within subordinated histories often negotiate affinities that blur race, gender, class, and other categories counterintuitive to how they are constructed by the mainstream.[45] Ukrainian scholar Larisa Lisyutkina situated Femen early on as a struggle over the collective national body: "The antinational aspects of Femen's performances are marked by parodic folkloric garlands that do not refer to the commercial or the glamorous as objects of social criticism, but to the imagined, collective national body."[46] In Lisyutkina's analysis, Femen's juxtaposition of Iranian culture with "parodic folkloric [Ukrainian] garlands" was a double entendre on Ukrainian nationalism in which the underlying definitions of East/West are deliberated upon and left open. Lisyutkina has also described Femen's references to Islam as a device designed to shock domestic audiences out of apathy.

Where Lisyutkina points to a generalized notion of women's oppression, not to Iran, as the true referential subject in Femen's performances, she describes protest as a transhistorical site through which colonized subjects come to recognize themselves and each other as marginal subjects. The assumptions here are that Iranian and Ukrainian women both inhabit postcolonial subject positions, even if gender difference cannot be universalized across cultures. If we were to assume any ready affinity between Femen's protests and Muslim women's own struggles, this could easily be interpreted as overly victimizing Muslim women as passive subjects who would somehow benefit from a representative Ukrainian demonstration of women's rights. Lisyutkina does not go so far as to make this claim. Anna Hutsol's early comments seem to confirm Lisyutkina's observations in this regard: Hutsol overidentifies with Muslim women in her interest in the Muslim world as a point of reference, or comparison, for illustrating duplicity within Euro-Atlantic self-idealizations of civil liberties.

These observations necessitate a closer look at the civilizational messages of the post-Orange period. Intellectuals were some of the very first to cast doubt on Ukraine's autonomy after observing the unravelling of the Yushchenko-Tymoshenko coalition from 2005 to 2007. Best known for publicizing a feminist, postcolonial perspective in Ukraine is the writer Oksana Zabuzhko, a key figure in Ukraine's Orange Revolution.[47] She writes that many political issues framed in terms of women's issues are actually symptoms of Ukraine's greater struggle in learning how to inherit the bleaker sides of its communist history, which she calls "a system of social lies extending to the point of mental rape affecting both men and women."[48] The imprint of national history on the colonial subject's psyche takes on even more violent tones in Zabuzhko's writings about the Orange Revolution in *Let My People Go*. Femen's public spectacles, however inarticulate they appear in the public imagination, are constructed from the same language of systemic oppression. But perhaps Femen assumes too much.

Overidentification

Femen's public spectacles appeared as experiments at finding affinities between themselves and other marginalized groups in overstatements that exposed systemic forms of oppression. As a mass media experiment, these obfuscations blurred with the missionizing rhetoric of the West during the Iraq war. Because Femen is so ridiculous, their dystopic messages are removed from political realism, and their overtures to patriarchy begin to pun on consumers of mass media and the imagery of suffering Muslim women employed within it.

The group's crude depictions of an Islamic Other are rooted in some of their earliest protests. The first public appearances in which Femen referenced a nation other than Ukraine took place on 21 September 2008 in front of the Turkish embassy in Kyiv. A dozen Femen members dressed up as nurses in smudged makeup and pink high heels and paraded in front of the Turkish embassy with slogans targeting "sexpats." In an interview following the protest, Anna Hutsol stated, "Foreign men should simply stay out of Ukraine if they cannot restrain themselves."[49] The tinge of xenophobia in Femen's singling out of Turkish men was treated causally by the press and, naturally, provoked sharp disapproval and scepticism among a wide range of audiences in Ukraine.[50] On 11 November 2010, five Femen members tore off their shirts at a Ukrainian-Iranian cultural event at Kyiv's Ukrainian House cultural centre, shouting "don't Kill Women!" They stated their act was in response to the trial of Sakineh Mohammadi-Ashtiani, an Iranian woman in Tehran sentenced to death by stoning whose case had gone global. The event was sponsored by the Iranian embassy and included dignitaries from both countries. Referencing the same case later that week, fully dressed Femen activists gathered once more in front of the Iranian embassy. While holding up banners with similar slogans, they prostrated themselves on the ground in imitation of Islamic prayer.[51]

In a demonstration on 16 June 2011, topless Femen protesters donned hijabs beneath Slavic flower garland headdresses and circled the Saudi Arabian embassy in cars, holding up slogans such as "Let's Drive!" Femen's blog post that day listed the protest as being "in solidarity" with Saudi women in protest against the Saudi regime's ban on women's driver's licences.[52] Yet the posters read like a laundry list of stereotypes associated more with Western imperialist attitudes towards the Middle East: "No Men's' Dictatorship!" "Cars for Women, Camels for Men!" "Wild Morals!" One poster even featured commentary suggesting the impotency of the petro-state alongside a cartoon of a phallus dripping into the word "OIL."[53] The posters were in a mix of English and Russian, expanding Femen's audiences to digital networks on different sides of the media circuit. Within this matrix of shifting signifiers, as elsewhere, the most consistent messages appeared to take aim at discourses that link modernization to Europeanization.

Semantically, this protest imagery equated patriarchy with power, and power with petro politics. It included references to Ukraine's own geopolitics. Mounting a critique of the oil industry from within Ukraine – the main transit country for Russian natural gas into the European Union and a key supplier of raw iron ore and coal to Moscow – Femen's act could be read as an affront to the Ukrainian parliament's proposals at the time to sell off natural resources to foreign corporations. Connecting the dots between oil, automobiles, and women's rights in Femen's off-putting version of civilian struggle also adds up to a picture of corruption. The group's references to the fuel economy mirrored popular anger in Ukraine at the time over oligarchs' monopolization of all public assets, including heavy industry, and the squandering of the nation's natural resources for personal gain.

Thus, Femen's explicit demonstrations – in both their local and digital forms – are symptomatic of women's subjugation in a particular post-Iraq historical order and its shaping of race and gender. Identity categories function loosely in Femen's protests and are grounded in ontologies of oppression anchored in the connections that they draw between themselves and sex tourism. The development of the group's aesthetic, over time, reveals a blurring of race and gender.

Debates among scholars of media over how Femen's nude performances can easily blend into mainstream entertainment parallel critiques in a larger body of scholarship on the stage performance of ethnic identities. Correspondences between racial masquerades, political upheaval, and social emancipation/subjugation were also present in the blurred intersections of race and gender in cabaret and burlesque throughout Europe during the twentieth century.[54] The limits to such genres as agentive sites for social resistance have been addressed in multiple volumes on how their stagings as popular comedy troubled their reception. Similarly, Audre Lorde's famous words that one cannot "dismantle the master's house with the tools of the master" could be applied to the way Femen uses the tools of mainstream media to criticize the commodification of women as sex products.[55] In Femen's case, the "tools of the master" become the language of global corporate marketing that panders to mainstream consumerist appetites, a language deeply implicated in the naked female torso that Femen employs to stake their claims to their own subjugation. Arguably, when read as a satire on the global sex industry cast in the language of that very industry itself, Femen's performances start to echo an earlier era in their Orientalist exoticism. These layers aggravate deeply embedded anxieties in Ukraine about national belonging on the European continent.

Within racial crossovers onstage, on the whole we find negotiations of gender and sexuality that almost always take place in frameworks dealing with primitivism and the nation.[56] Femen's performance as "feminist" prostitutes – an archetype always linked to sexual primitivism – can be traced to early- to mid-twentieth-century European discourses embodied in the widespread theatre stagings of the harem figure of Salome: "Primitivism evolved into myth, often referred to as Orientalism, with the common thread being the symbolically sexualized representation of the nonwhite body ... the perception of the prostitute 'merged with the perception of the black' and this perception created the 'commonplace' notion that the so-called primitive black woman 'was associated with unbridled sexuality.'"[57] Femen adapts the figure of the prostitute's culturally specific and complex sexual associations to a generalized, racialized marginality that they claim to overturn. Yet Femen's caricatures, while inverting some of the primitivism assigned to female sexuality more generally, also absorb all aspects of these narratives, including the position of the colonizer, in the affiliations that Femen's performances *overassume* between themselves and Muslim women "against patriarchy."

And while Femen does not perform colour, they do employ racial tropes. Annemarie Bean suggests the term "race change" as a point of departure for examining transgressions of gender that parallel the performance of colour on the stage.[58] Unlike the concept of "passing," which usually means "passing for white," a "race change" encompasses a more socially expansive "traversing of racial boundaries, racial imitation or impersonation, cross-racial mimicry or mutability."[59] Femen's "cross-racial mimicry, or mutability" circulates in a composite of race and gender that is "white" in colour, but blurs ethnic and national identifications by referencing violence and sexual primitivism through the figure of the prostitute.

The mutability of civic, national, and ethnic stereotypes in Femen's provocative rhetoric retains some of the undercurrents of the older Soviet operative term "narodnost" used to describe the nation-state.[60] Alaina Lemon has pointed out in her work on Roma performance in Russia that the Soviet deployment of the term "narodnost" (ethnicity/peoplehood) differed only slightly from the term "natsional'nost'" (nationality/ ethnicity). She notes that while neither term expressly meant "race," both terms included concepts tied to race: "However firmly the Soviet state declared itself against racism, it purged neither racial discrimination nor racial categories."[61] Femen's approximation of "cross-racial mimicry" within the frame of a feminist protest (as they define their own project) is a "race change" that highlights a Ukrainian identity inclusive of an Other within the bounds of the "commodity fetishization" of femaleness.[62] As Ukrainian feminists have pointed out, this kind of parody in Femen's work affords the possibility of replicating ethnic stereotypes.[63] The crude airing of sexual and racial stereotypes in public that Femen engages in collapses the boundaries between criticism and entertainment.

The affinities that Femen members draw between themselves and other minority subject positions produces what W.J.T. Mitchell has

termed "a surplus of meaning" in which there is no clear path of identification for the spectator, as multiple referents between images overlap. The outcome is not entirely dissimilar from sexploitation films
of the 1970s, developed out of the genre of *blaxploitation*. In the end,
the spectator is impinged upon to question the validity of the performance: "the unreliability of the narrator to keep all the referents of the
story straight reveals cracks in the system, because exploitative systems cannot allow for a story about being exploited."[64] The story is
about the medium.

IV. Rhetorical Scripts

Genre – Dystopian Satire

Femen's performances portray a non-specific totalitarian dystopia
in which national experience is depicted as a byproduct of historical
trauma. For example, after the earthquake in Japan in March 2011, Femen members dressed up as Japanese male warriors and then documented themselves performing martial initiation ceremonies in a
tearoom and on the streets of Kyiv. They carried over-the-top slogans
addressing the victims of the earthquake: one banner read "Praise to
Those Who Defeated the Dragon!" (хвала победившим дракона!). In
a cross-referencing of signs on their blog they rendered this performance as a film poster linking the aftermath of the earthquake to the
twenty-fifth anniversary of the Chernobyl disaster taking place that
same year. The connection extended to the short film that Femen members produced of themselves exploring the Chernobyl disaster zone in
gasmasks and flower headdresses. At one point in the performance,
they carried a banner with the Japanese flag superimposed onto the
Ukrainian flag; another banner contained both flags within the group's
Cyrillic icon "Ф," and a third featured a death's head. The juxtaposition of the Ukrainian and Japanese flags compared the Chernobyl
accident to the horror of the bombing of Nagasaki and Hiroshima. Gasmasks double the link, and are placed next to the former symbol of the
Nazi party: a skull-and-cross bones that is *also* the international sign
for poison.

The location of the activists' bodies in real time in the protest is
important. Putting their bodies at risk at the *actual site* of a past nuclear meltdown, the image provokes questions about the present and
its political stakes for human life (figure 2.5). The protest is set within
Ukraine: it is ultimately about Ukraine, and the Ukrainian flag is given
precedence. The overall message is anti-war in the depiction of its

Figure 2.5. Femen Chernobyl Protest. March 2011, Ukraine. Shared by permission of the photographer Matteo Ferrari.

consequences: the possibility of poisoning, fascism, meltdown, and piracy, repeated in text on signs posted to a fence behind the women: Контроль (STOP) and Небезпека (DANGER). The mixture of national flags, locations, disaster, and memory politics in the frame of a nude sex tourism advertisement – the Femen brand features as well – diverts viewers' attention in several directions.

By putting their actual bodies at risk, Femen differs from protest body art from the second half of the twentieth century. Members' depictions of disaster and sexual subjugation are rooted in their other protests against the persistent corruption and economic inequality that defined the Yanukovych period. While it holds true that Femen rarely made any actual political demands, early on Anna Hutsol responded to accusations of xenophobia levelled against her with concern for the rise of far-right nationalist groups in Ukraine, openly blaming their prevalence on an increasingly oppressive Ukrainian parliament.[65] Moving between actual sites and virtual settings, the group portrayed a dystopic totalitarianism in which patriarchy and annihilation are one and the same.

Femen's overtures to totalitarianism point to the futility of extremist thinking precisely *because* they are so over-the-top. They publicly air fanaticism through ridicule. In some ways, this transgression of *all* discourse that can be traced to the state is the same type of strategy employed in earlier happenings that claimed to be "antipolitical" and sought to deconstruct communist rhetoric. Satirical jabs at Western hegemony and manifesto-like calls for international unity against absolutism can be seen in the futurist strains of the 1990s Ukrainian avant-garde. These strains echo in Femen's appeals to feminist solidarity; their mutual affects compare the differences between political regimes of the twentieth century, in order to carry over forms by which to dissent from the lasting horrors of war and its technology in the twenty-first.

Yet parody is a complicated genre for mounting a critique precisely because its reception is so unstable. In both the Iranian and the Saudi protests, Femen visually embodied Muslim women's subject position in a language of blurred race/gender and national regimes. Femen's equation of the hijab with Ukrainian nationalism confuses the cultural inflections in different systems of patriarchy, assuming that repression and religious devotion are automatic synonyms, thus taking for granted that for many women this is not the case. In my interview with Hutsol, she conveyed her view on the ability to reveal the female body in public as the ultimate litmus for women's rights: "Some say we are selling ourselves. Some say a woman's body should be cloaked and hidden, revealed in private for men only. We say that both of these attitudes limit our freedom. The greatest risk, for us in Ukraine, is silence and apathy."[66] Hutsol's position rejects both conservative and left critiques of Femen's nudity from groups within Ukraine. On the one hand, her equation between exposure and freedom of expression is overly totalizing in assuming to speak for actual conditions that could be better voiced by Muslim women themselves. It has been argued that by extrapolating too far out of the Ukrainian context, Femen's performances risked turning the hijab into an itinerant symbol of oppression. On the other hand, this interpretation overlooks the full range of symbolic stakes at issue. Arguably of equal concern is the second addressee of Femen's satire in the diversion of our attention to what already commands so much attention: Western media and its fetishization of a "suffering" Middle East.

In today's globalized public sphere, social and cultural difference should not be treated as essential concepts, but as organizing metaphors in symbolic plays on meaning. The media scripts in Femen's cultural outpourings unfold digitally around globally symbolic cultural borders, like the veil, that through public signifying processes, come to be associatively seen as a civilizational metonyms, absorbing all sorts of contradictory meanings. Homi K. Bhabha describes globalization as "a rejection of instrumentalist histories and a transnational and translational sense of the hybridity of imagined communities."[67] Femen could be described as an "insurgent act of cultural translation" situated within a contact zone where "the intersubjective and collective experiences of *nationness*, community interest, or cultural value are negotiated."[68] The offensive nature of Femen's performances makes explicit a range of post-Iraq imagery and taboos in the mechanisms of mass media as it mediates the emotional registers along cultural fault lines.

In their shift abroad, Femen's marketing of themselves as "sextremists" alienated them from many audiences. Controversy around this new image ensued in several counter-demonstrations by the two French groups Les Antigonnes and Hommen, The Krasnals! in Poland, and Muslim Women Against Femen in North Africa. Each of these groups co-opted Femen's aesthetic to construct messages of disagreement with the group and their references to religion. Many openly targeted the legitimacy of Femen's feminism. Questions arose as to how dissent is validated as protest.

In these online culture wars over Femen's "sextremism," a visual body language developed and came to be instantly recognizable as shorthand for feminism in debates over its authenticity. This language was characterized by the following device: graffiti-style black text scribbled on a nude torso; this language formed the basis of experiments around the interaction of real and virtual spaces as public sites in which political subjectivities are formed and enacted. Audiences attached a range of meanings to the digital surfaces on which this style of text appeared by appropriating, mirroring, or adapting its full range of grammatical expressions to their own political statements. Thus, the controversy around "sextremism" exposed deep rifts in what is considered appropriate/inappropriate behaviour in vocabularies of resistance, as they evolve with trends in the information economy. The most disturbing irony of Femen, then, very well may be that they themselves did not invent the extremism underlying "sextremism." Rather, their references to Islam unleashed wider anger around the more coded displays of Orientalist rhetoric that had already become so familiar as to appear almost invisible in a post-Iraq era.

Semblance and Rebellion

What can the Femen phenomenon teach us about dissent and the mass media apparatus that shapes how citizens imagine and practice national identity? Media scholar Anikó Imre discusses postcommunist Hungarian media contexts, stressing the link between citizenship and information markets as an experimental cultural site. Imre examines feminist media collectives in seeking a more critical model for the contemporary public sphere, grounded in the context of new media. In her work on the Labrisz Lesbian Film Collective in Budapest, Imre underlines the limitations that formal, representational critiques of the nation pose for the politics of Eastern European feminisms.[69] Invisibility and apathy feature as symptoms of wider insufficiencies in public discourse. The idea that Ukrainian women have greater battles to fight than women in the West also guided Anna Hutsol's early justifications for Femen's radical nude technique: "I think that strong women cannot remain quiet and timid in Ukraine. I've been to Europe and I've seen how calmly the women protest there. Here the situation is different, women have to be louder, bolder."[70] On one level, Hutsol's statement is an extension of her group's activities in illustrating ownership over their basic right to protest. On another level, the group's visibility through online media shares with Pussy Riot, Imre, and opposition groups much deeper cultural anxieties around European belonging, isolationism, the East, and postcommunism.[71]

Oftentimes, Femen activists painted icons and slogans borrowed from commercial brands on their bodies. For example, in April 2010 Femen responded to censorship from Google by painting the company's copyrighted logo onto their naked breasts and circulating the resulting image throughout the internet. A sign, unlike an icon, which always has a relationship based on resemblance with the object it signifies, has an indirect relationship with the object it represents. By painting Google onto their bare skin, Femen produced dissonance between the sign "Google" and its indexical signification. By changing the sign's context, Femen re-indexed the Google symbol's original meaning as a copyrighted logo for a search engine into a signifier for the commodification of the female body. This image entails a struggle with representation, with being not-quite, yet still containing residuals of the signified. Teodor Adorno wrote, "Art is yet in this process where it comes to resemble realia, it assimilates itself to that reification against which it protests: Today *engagement* inescapably becomes aesthetic concession."[72] Following this, by painting brand names on bare skin, Femen conflates ownership over the body with ownership over the brand; in effect, interrogating the ideologies that have accumulated within the brand through its circulation. It is worth noting that Google, unlike automobiles or lipstick, is a neutrally gendered product. In this instance, by painting a gender-neutral icon onto their breasts, Femen produced dissonance between the body and its commodification in social commentary on profit and enterprise. Without naming one cause or political platform, Femen's topless spectacles put on display the accumulation, value, profit, and exchange of women as symbolic capital in a larger economy of politics and media entertainment.

Writing on art and industry, Adorno remarked that cultural hegemony claims its field of influence through material shored up in capital flows. Art is also illusory. In *Semblance and Expression* Adorno claims that the classical opposition between art and reality is the main theme in all cultural artefacts. He writes, "Clearly the immanent semblance character of artworks cannot be freed from some degree of external imitation of reality, however latent, and therefore cannot be freed from illusion either."[73] The argument that art always suffers from a degree of both imitation and illusion – that all art involves some element of camouflage – describes the paradox in Femen's attempt to transcend the reification of the female body through bodily expression. Their painting of certain brands, usually involving two round "OO" shapes on their breasts, displaces advertisement with all sorts of associations ranging from humour, to erotica, to farcical plays on materialist appropriations of power, to many other frames for showing the hidden meanings in the linkage between ad and ideology.

In this critical reading of Femen's happenings, it is easy to find many subversive statements about branding as a modern, global language. In another example, activists employed the word Facebook in response to the company's decision to block nudity on their page. The uneasy relationship between replicating and eluding advertisement can also be traced in the Femen brand itself. Femen's professionally designed, custom logo is ironic – an image of two breasts cast as a Cyrillic "Ф" (Фемен/ Femen) filled in with the colours of the Ukrainian flag.

As a brand, Femen is positioned in a contradictory relationship with earlier feminist theory on women and capitalism where scholars have noted, along the lines of Luce Irigaray, that women are symbolically exchanged within circuits of use and exchange value, depending on their social status.[74] Scholars have stressed the emerging links between citizenship and electronic media in mediating postsocialist national imaginaries.[75] Imre, in her work in the Hungarian context, has noted that digital media has become a generative component of national culture by liberating minority voices.[76] Imre's search for a more critical model of the contemporary public sphere is useful for engaging a flexible notion of "the political" to account for Femen's formation and ongoing activities as a media performance.[77] The focus here is on the affective identifications that drive ideological frameworks.

The dissonant codes in Femen's aesthetic can be viewed as speech acts in a visual vocabulary that parries with commercial media as it shapes a global public sphere. Contradictory codes drive this sphere. Femen manipulates the symbolic contexts within which icons and signs appear. They encode multiple layers of meaning in each sign that they incorporate into their work, oftentimes creating new significations by cross-referencing the original referents of two or more distinct signs. In many cases, Femen achieves this semiotic play within the bounds of the language of global corporate branding.

Femen's body language thus walks a fine line between highlighting, versus replicating, the sources of women's subjugation that they seek to expose. Given the complex etymology of feminism as a term in Femen's part of the world, where women's rights at times were seen as the province of the bourgeois, generating this kind of attention is arguably the most provocative layer of their protest. The group's visual language mimics the mechanisms of their own objectification and the commodification of oppositional politics, both indulging and parodying the notion that all branding consists of a pornographic reduction of human desire into effective ad campaigns. The pun falls not only on the sex tourist, but on the consumer as well.

V. Representation and Circulation

Exposure and Desire – Mediating the Gaze

Twentieth-century female "anti-artists" associated with the conceptualist movements in Western and Soviet cultures experimented with the body as a surface for art. Many focused on sexual liberation over political correctness in their approach, provoking audiences to think about the body as a vessel for exploring social limits.[78] Intertwined with the Actionists' later works, the conceptualist and nonconformist movements also interrogated assumptions about the body that structure culture, behaviour, and social norms. In her 1975 series, *Art Must Be Beautiful, Artist Must Be Beautiful*, Marina Abramović deconstructs how art is valued by breaking with the social conventions that order acceptable feminine behaviour.[79] As shown in figure 2.6, she documents herself in a violent outburst while nude from the waist up, brushing her hair in front of the camera lens, which stands in for an invisible mirror. The overall effect is of a stop-motion camera capturing the artist fighting with her own image. Instead of composing herself into a picture-ready face for public consumption, the artist and her art split the subject across several frames: her pent-up tension is released as motion. The multiple shots also mirror investigative photos from a sequential police lineup, further suggesting that the artist is directly confronting a system of norms that are not only prescribed, but also violently reinforced.

The sequencing of text and movement across frames became a popular convention in 1970s feminist art and was borrowed from the theory of montage in film. The idea was that explicit emotional material would enable viewers to see their social circumstances in new ways. Feminists wanted to draw attention to subjugating images of women used to organize desire in the cultural and media marketplace, and yet, at the same time, their experiments were also subversive in another way. As in the different liminal roles as go-between that the prostitute played in the twentieth century, the sexual entertainment layer of a growing porn media industry remained one of the most prevalent and reliable channels for the exchange of currency and information across the Berlin Wall.

In 1972, Polish artist Natalia LL in her most well known work, *Sztuka konsumpcyjna* (Consumer Art), parodied "the money shot" of hardcore porn in campy poses with a banana (figure 2.7). In April 2019, the video was removed from the National Museum in Warsaw, sparking widespread street and online protests against censorship. The director of the museum soon after capitulated and restored the video to the collection, but only for a short time, having scheduled a complete redesign of the museum's modern art collection on the heels of Poland's elected conservative government and its newly appointed Ministry of Culture's slashing funds to the European Solidarity Centre, a separate museum in the city dedicated to teaching the history of Polish resistance movements.[80] It is likely that the ongoing targeting of artists associated with the long history of Poland's democratic opposition to authoritarianism, not only Natalia LL, but hundreds of others like her, will spark more protests. The irony of the situation is that this is also the fastest route to new feminist art!

Figure 2.6. *Art Must Be Beautiful, Artist Must Be Beautiful*, one-hour performance by Marina Abramović. Charlottenburg Art Festival, Copenhagen, Denmark, 1975. © Marina Abramović. Courtesy of the Marina Abramović Archives.

Revisiting these earlier examples from the twentieth century, we can find in them new relevance for viewing how social media is rearranging sexual and gender relations through the online sex industry in the twenty-first. At the core of Femen there is a glamorous, heavily made-up feminine image that echoes fashion magazines. Their leader Anna Hutsol describes their style as a "fun, fresh feminism" to fend off apathy among young women.[81] They project slim, white female

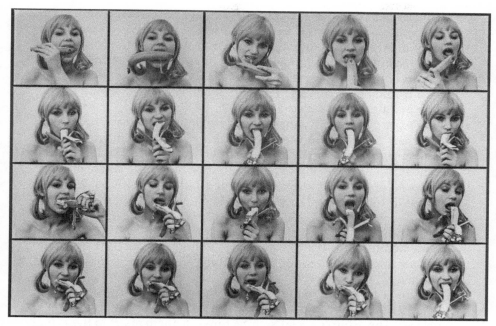

Figure 2.7. *Sztuka konsumpcyjna* (Consumer Art), by Natalia LL, 1973.
Courtesy of Natalia LL Archive (ZW Foundation).

bodies into international media spaces as their foundational body image, treading on the risk of repeating stereotypes. Femen claims to use
the body to "invert" sexism or "reclaim" breasts as a political symbol,
yet this is complicated by the fact that feminism *as an idea* does not
readily translate. It has been argued that digital images of bodies can
flatten the differences between cultures in the media circulation of femaleness – but this deserves closer attention.

Three points set Femen apart from 1970s feminist media performance
experiments, all due to their digital context: (1) the position of their
actual bodies in real time can more easily facilitate communication
between individuals in disparate locations; (2) the performed char-
acter(s) and design juxtapose news headlines with the conventions
of internet meme culture; and (3) the virtual body/avatar allows for
(re)identification by individuals and populations in mapping out
sociopolitical contexts. Femen paints on their actual bodies, but also
the "digital body" in projecting themselves into media as avatars. If
we think of them as a conceptualization of the social body, then the
patriarchy is the central (absent) protagonist in their narrative. As

individuals in different geographical locations act in accordance with the same aesthetic script, they plot a landscape of virtual similarity across highly varied cultural systems in real-time. Yet participants in their disparate locations traverse very different actual spaces of freedom and unfreedom, defined by national borders, class, race, gender, and any number of aspects of identity that determine one's subject position in different power structures.

For example, the individuals shown in figure 2.8 in each frame map onto their own bodies discourses that are *about* feminism, and also about negotiating subject positions within local/global circuits of digital media. Viewers are invited to assume that in the movement between frames all of the women involved share similar experiences. This may be true in some sense; however, the difference between those experiences is downplayed. Captions such as "Bodymessengers against Putin!" posted alongside the virtual composites facilitate the flattening of cross-cultural experience that actors within internet media can manipulate and exploit to simulate common experience, similarity, and symmetry.[82]

In this regard, Femen differs from prior feminist body artists, such as VALIE EXPORT, in their use of space due to their virtual media surfaces. The group's social architecture sets them apart in their dual flows across both social media and physical platforms, and on the level of the individual and the group. Marxist-oriented theorists continue to ask whether artistic practices can play a critical role in advanced capitalist societies, where identities are always formed in process, and culture is regulated by industry. What Femen does share with earlier feminist body artists is a vigilance towards the central role that labour and reproductive rights play in dividing the private and public spheres – one of the most ideologically consistent and controversial focal points in both the Soviet and post-Soviet eras.[83] Insurgent within social media advertising space, Femen's images bring into view the striated, hegemonic field of politics driving the *uncritical* economy of images that produce, circulate, and sell politics to consumers.

Image / Counter Image

The exact opposite of an image is the same image, only in reverse. Femen's acts ignited several copycat protests – some adopted the group's iconicity in order to critique them. In one example, several months after Femen's foray into Warsaw, a Polish art group from Łódź named The Krasnals! posed as actual prostitutes disgruntled

Figure 2.8. Femen, *Bodymessengers against Putin! Body Text Part 1*, 2014.
Courtesy of Femen.

with Femen for "stealing their business away."[84] Named after Mayer
Frydrych's orange dwarves (Krasnoludki) of Pomarańczowa Alternatywa, discussed in chapter 1, the group had already established
themselves in Poland's art world. Media outlets picked up on the
story and reported the event as though it were an actual protest (the
group concealed their hoax). Members taped slogans like "Poland
Welcomes You!" and "I Love Poznań" to their backs, mimicking the
saccharine, supplicatory tone of Femen's slogans. Dressing in orange workers' overalls, The Krasnals! replaced Femen's caricatures
of prostitution with an alternative image of unionized sex work. In
The Krasnals Contra Femen, workers "relax" on the job, their cigarettes
suggesting insubordination towards mainstream modes of productivity in an overall gutter punk noir aesthetic. The phallus prop in The
Krasnals! mock-up also mirrored the surreal patriarchal imagery of a
Femen-style protest.

The Krasnals! state on their blog that they are "focused on exposing the mechanisms of consumer society."[85] This statement fits with
the nonconformism associated with the styles of music, dress, and lifestyles of punk, which carries with it a level of authenticity in the coding
of dissidence over the course of its social and technical development
into several subgenres. The overtly crass aesthetics of class-based dissidence among British youth in the 1970s that gave birth to punk soon

gave way to its corporatization in selling the idea of an underground to later generations of consumers.

Dick Hebdige argues that the class and race politics in the punk and ska music scenes of 1970s London were a microcosm of broader social relations in the UK that emerged out of the mixing of races and classes in the circular migration throughout the Atlantic at the time. His landmark study *Subculture: The Meaning of Style* helped define the Birmingham School of Culture and remains a founding contribution in the field of cultural studies. To a good degree punk has now become cliché in the global cultural marketplace, despite its connotations with antiauthoritarianism. Here it is employed to illustrate by contrast where Femen's notoriety is itself embedded in the media they critique.

In The Krasnals! protest imagery, unlike in Femen's, there is a privileging of gender difference over gender equality, engaging feminist theory that attempts to make room for alternative sexualities beyond male/female binaries.[86] For example, the performance of lesbian identity in The Krasnals! media stunt downplays the hyperfeminine ideal in Femen's foundational image, while drawing out those elements of Femen that satirize the ideal by assuming negligence towards the male gaze. A few of the Krasnals' images feature women performing sexual acts on each other in postures that mirror the overt stances, expressions, and forthright verbiage of mainstream pornography. Masking their identities with balaclavas and holding posters with anarchic symbols drawn into slogans such as "Parade of Difference" (Parada Różności), The Krasnals! can be understood as a kind of double parody.

This double parody depends on the gap between the original and the copy. Neither Femen's protest nor The Krasnals!' counter protest was designed for a gallery, and neither has appeared in a museum exhibit.[87] Both the image and the counter image in this exchange played with the language of news reporting in cartoonish humour without attempting to actually represent segments of society, make any concrete demands, or pursue a stake in the systems of power in which both groups' critiques of sexual exchange are already embedded. The Krasnals! counter image draws attention to the locus of constituency versus consumer in the branding of protest by identifying themselves with Femen's headlining campaign "Ukraine Is NOT a Brothel!," a campaign that is ironic, and therefore cannot be representative. The dissonance or "slippage" between image and word in The Krasnals! copy protest played upon the language of Femen's brand and its limited applicability to actual sociopolitical struggles. Again, the media itself is both the medium and the message.

The Krasnals! staged an important critique of Femen's anti-prostitution stance. By appropriating Femen's highly visible brand calibrated for mass media, The Krasnals! disrupted Femen's protest narrative where it negatively defines sex work as harmful towards women.[88] In other words, the counter image created the rare opportunity to publicly interject commentary in support of sex work (making a sex-positive statement) – an often underanalysed stance in feminist discourse.[89]

Femen's rhetoric of inequality, unlike The Krasnals! rhetoric of gender difference, is entrenched in figurations of the prostitute primarily as a metaphor for East-West relations. Femen has referenced Chernobyl, the DAVOS World Economic Forum, Ukrainian pension reform, and a range of other gender-neutral issues in their hyperbolic slogans.[90] Both protests are ad-hoc, humorous jabs at national symbols and sex work: transposing the official mainstream with a powerfully consistent taboo. Sex work rarely enters public discourse in either country, despite the fervent policy debates during and after Ukraine's two revolutions, as well as the ubiquity of unregulated sex tourism and human trafficking throughout the region.

Other artists and activists continue to engage with these issues on a local level, less driven by mass media. The artist Oksana Briukhovetska in her essay "What in Me Is Feminist?" gives examples of artworks in the Ukrainian context that she curated in an exhibit in Kyiv in November-December 2015 in a Polish-Ukrainian collaborative project aimed at revealing a range of strong, creative women artists. Like the Krasnals!, Briukhovetska is informed by intersectional and difference feminist theory, and leverages harsh critique on Femen in a valid and critical comment that makes clear to audiences that there are other feminist artists not working in media who are deserving of worldwide attention: "Ukrainian feminism is not Femen." She also writes, "The [patriarchial image of a woman] which Ukrainian women artists both recognize, and refuse to recognize in themselves, pushes them to look for new forms of identity, new forms of reflection on their own gender, new images of 'a different' woman. In any case, the main feature of this other 'different' woman is nothing other than feminism."[91]

In the years since the end of the Maidan Revolution, local initiatives in Ukraine have persevered in drawing attention to women's and gender issues through ongoing marches, courses, exhibits, events, and other gatherings.[92] And there are new challenges. In late 2018, Briukhovetska, after installing her work, I Am Ukrainian, featuring several posters dedicated to the theme of destigmatizing Ukrainian migrant labour, experienced a backlash from both Polish and Ukrainian mainstream audiences, in which some claimed that representing the working classes, even featured alongside images of Lesia Ukrainka, was "disrespectful

Figure 2.9. Poster from the series *I Am Ukrainian*, by Oksana Briukhovetska, for the *Warsaw Under Construction* exhibit (Warszawa w Budowie), 2017. Courtesy of the artist.

to the representation of Ukrainian society" (figure 2.9).[93] This is only one of many examples that continue to bring into sharp focus the fact that the protests, creative productions, and debates featured throughout this book are still ongoing.

The visual language in The Krasnals!'s counter images, Femen's performances, and Briukhovetska's artworks, as well as Bruikhovetska's critical leadership as the co-founder of the Visual Culture Research Center (VCRC), are rooted in the same foundation of critique: sharp scepticism of the ideological traps of utopian thinking not only about gender, but any number of issues, that only a childhood forged under postcommunism could detect and deploy. For example, the rhetoric of reform pertaining to "gender equality" that has come to define more mainstream discourse in Ukraine about economic transition has also overlooked a great deal of potential for aiding local women's own experiences, aims, and preferences with regard to the regulation of the sex trade and other forms of labour.

Looking back at the 2000s at Femen, The Krasnals!, and Briukhovet-ska, including her founding of VCRC, a critical cultural centre the importance to Ukraine of which will be stressed later in this book, we can see how, although in highly divergent ways, each of these groups satirize nationalism and media markets as factors that can amplify, muf-fle, and distort more immediate concerns. And yet, nearly a decade on since their explosion onto the streets and museums of Eastern Europe, it is very clear that each of these artists (and many more!) have played a critical role in opening up important spaces for dialogue. Two of the most consistent outcomes of their work are (1) increased awareness of the critical impacts of branding and transmission of protest by the mass media, and (2) greater vigilance around how the mainstreaming of po-litical causes into consumer markets can produce silence around issues, such as sex work legislation.

A new wave of activists and artists in Ukraine are now taking on these challenges, despite the rise of the far-right and a surge in author-itarianism. For example, the protest by FemSolution at Kyiv-Mohyla in 2017 against sexual harassment was initially met with suppression by the university authorities, but the group later succeeded in securing a policy on campus to protect students, in part due to solidarity with older generations, who helped get the story into trusted post-Maidan media circuits like Hromadske.[94] Artists of the youngest generation are also finding mentors to help them take these issues on in ways that pro-mote self-preservation and safety, while still creating visibility. Artists play a vital role in this sense, and newer waves of feminists each con-tinue to pioneer and develop an aesthetics of their own that speaks to local audiences in playful, humorous, and inventive visual languages. The artist Alina Kleytman (figure 2.10) is one of the most prominent figures among young feminist artists working in Ukraine today, having a large online following and a list of experimental public projects and people's choice awards to her name. Her sardonic humour in probing and exposing women's inner fears and insecurities, along with her puns on sexist stereotypes of women, including the hegemonic undertones in the Western consumption of Slavic sexuality, draws upon the artists of the 1970s in new ways that resonate with her generation today.

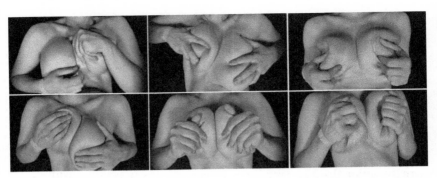

Figure 2.10. Alina Kleytman, *I'm the Worst. I Cannot Do Anything. My Thoughts Are the Worst Thoughts. I'm the Old Fat Girl. Look at Me*. Old Fat Girl series. Multichannel video, 2019. Shared by permission of the artist.

VI. Critical Receptions: "Dissidence" East/West

Femen's shock tactics have offended all sides of the political spectrum. Initial debates about Femen by Ukrainian feminist scholars in late 2011 and early 2012 contextualized Femen's performances in the shift from Soviet to post-Soviet regimes.[95] Some scholars underlined Femen's value in bringing visibility to important concerns about sex tourism but described the group as a political coalition alien to other feminist projects in Ukraine.[96] Others classified the group as a pop movement completely devoid of any ready social application, while at the same time remaining ambivalent about the value of the group's puns on local stereotypes as a way of airing the very idea of feminism for their audiences.[97] Some pointed to the group as a site in which the antagonism between official versus popular voices in the media in the post-Soviet context suddenly became more apparent. My ongoing interviews with feminist scholars and activists in Ukraine from 2009 to 2018 reveal huge shifts of opinion not only on Femen after their move abroad, but also on feminism as a term during and after the revolution on Maidan in 2013–14. I will discuss some of these broader changes in more detail later on. Overall, the consensus among Ukrainian scholars on Femen over time moved sharply in the direction of viewing the group as carnivalesque performers without any local ties.[98]

In the summer of 2013 an anti-gay, far-right group of men calling themselves Hommen staged a Femen-style protest against same-sex marriage in the streets of Paris. It became clear that Femen's stylistic formula could be co-opted from positions of extreme social intolerance, thus revealing a concerning fact about how digital networks function.

Language codes projected across vast populations, spread over great distances, may split off local political meanings from their speakers, thus limiting one's control over the intended message and reducing the ability to maintain a clear position on any single issue.[99] In an article for the industry journal *Art Ukraine*, Ukrainian critic and feminist scholar Nataliya Tchermalykh describes her encounter with Femen abroad:

> Among the thousands of demonstrators standing up for LGBT rights in Paris I was surprised to hear: "Ukrainian Women Fear Nothing!" These words were coming from Femen activists. In France, the group was at the forefront of the movement that culminated in the legalization of same sex marriage at the constitutional level. I confess – I often criticize Femen. Our political orientation could not be more different, but there, in Paris, my immediate impression was that Femen was speaking on my behalf. I was, in all honesty, really pleased to see Ukrainian flower wreaths with their characteristically colorful ribbons in conjunction with the slogan "In Gay We Trust!" scrawled on Femen's bare chests – both pleased and saddened at the same time. Last May, during Kyiv's first gay parade, we might have done well by a little of their courage; but Femen was not there with us. I suppose that this fact, too, is already just another page in history.[100]

Here Tchermalykh contextualizes the group in a larger story about dismantling the effects of institutional censorship and other factors limiting artists' creative licence in Ukraine. What stands out most in this anecdote is that Femen abandoned participation in actual initiatives by civic activists in Ukraine early on, even while, conceptually, Femen's *misbehaviour* provided a backdrop for debates local and global, not all directly tied to feminism, that continued to circulate.[101]

Perhaps it should be less surprising then to discover that the disavowal of Femen by international critics has served to expose inequalities in who gets legitimized –that is, who is "allowed" to speak for women and carry the mantle of feminism. Put another way, the anger in the wake of Femen's acts has radicalized digital networks of sceptics and activists, many of whom have taken to task the limits and definitions of feminism on their own terms. Agata Pyzik analyses Femen in her work on post-Soviet culture entitled *Poor but Sexy* (after the mayor of Berlin's ad campaigns for the city, aimed at Western tourism). She contextualizes Femen's linking of Islam with oppressive patriarchy as an instance of misrecognition and miscommunication in a much longer story of complex East-West cultural relations: "It seems a typical case of mutual misunderstanding, with each side blind to each other's concerns: Femen doesn't see racism behind their calling patriarchy 'Arab,' and the Western pro-underprivileged women-of-color feminists see in Femen only the distasteful theatre of naked boobs, which overlooks their needs, not seeing how they remain blind to the postcommunist reality Femen represent."[102] Femen's (mis)identification of women's own agency within Islam reproduces a well-intentioned, Pyzik seems to suggest, but impoverished message of suspicion of Western suprema-cism. A supporting critique here is that if Femen performs as "rescuing" Muslim women (and who would not feel offended by such rhetoric?), it is also because the digital media networks of the West, in rhetoric about democratizing the Arab world, have created the conditions for this critique.

This is not to lend Femen a free pass for their transgressions, but to sound a chord of apprehension around global inequalities and the mul-tiple ethical contexts that debates about Femen's "feminism" represent. Perhaps, for the misunderstanding that Pyzik notes to become clear on all sides, Femen would need to open dialogue with their opponents, and thus break the "fourth wall" of their media spectacle. A possibly more lasting lesson to be gained from Femen, as well as Pussy Riot, is how both groups reveal citizenship as a function of media. What are the risks and opportunities of digital networks and their uneven spread through populations with varied levels of access to technology? The cyber war, election meddling, and propaganda trolls unleashed by the Kremlin in the years following the 2013–14 Maidan Revolution of Dignity in Ukraine have made this question even more pressing.

VII. Conclusion

Understanding protest today necessitates shifting attention away from the state as representational entity towards media technologies, globalization, and the roles that these factors play in advancing and manipulating messages about rights and freedoms. Scholars have stressed the complex outcomes between citizenship and electronic me-dia in mediating postsocialist democracies. Digital media have become a generative component of national culture by liberating minority voices. I agree with the political dimension of creative expression that Mouffe inscribes in the artistic process. She writes, "Critical art is art that foments dissensus, that makes visible what the dominant consen-sus tends to obscure and obliterate."[103] This concept of art-as-activism raises several questions as to the kinds of representations – both wel-come and untoward – that critical art is able to foster, and the social implications of a brand like Femen.

Activists I have spoken with in Ukraine concerned with gender issues are ambivalent as to whether Femen has contributed to ameliorating

Ukrainian women's daily lives, though they unanimously state that the group made a lasting impression in world news. Sociologist Tamara Martsenyuk found that social tolerance towards gender minorities actually decreased in Ukraine, in proportion to an increase in visibility around LGBTQ and pro-women's rights groups in the period after the Orange Revolution.[104] The debates about marriage and reproductive policy that served as target issues in the lead-up to Yanukovych's second term likely contributed to this situation as well. In 2013 protests erupted on both the left and the right around the legislation of an anti-gay propaganda law. Artists and intellectuals came under fire in Ukraine, with increasing shutdowns and targeting of museum exhibits featuring LGBTQ and feminist themes.

Some women's initiatives on policy in these years were less polarized than the individuals in the groups organizing them, and so their impact served a more immediate function of generating new intellectual and institutional forums for renewing the idea of feminism. In 2009, Oksana Kis drafted a letter to reduce the stigmatization of women's hiring and employment practices in the professional, business, education, and government sectors.[105] Mobilizations around International Women's Day by the Kyiv-based feminist group Ofenzywa, discussed in chapter 3, also put pressure on unfair labour practices. In the city of Kharkiv, the Museum of Women's History and Gender Movements pioneered efforts to create new archival databases in the historiography of women's experiences in the twentieth century with the aim of partnering with researchers, activists, and social workers.[106] Since the Maidan Revolution, the alliances, projects, and ambitions of the people in these groups have folded and rearranged into new directions, and have become more expansive in their resources and networks.

In July 2013, I met with former Femen member Angelina Diash in Kyiv. Diash is a university student, a theatre performer, an actress, and a writer. She is from Khmelnytsky, the same city as Anna Hutsol, and was recruited there by members Inna and Sasha Shevchenko in 2009. Diash is African-Ukrainian and informed me that she experiences constant harassment by local police and passersby for the colour of her skin: "The situation is especially difficult because Ukrainian is my native language. I was born here."[107] When I asked her why she decided to join Femen, she replied, "I saw a chance to fight racism, to find justice for women because they should be equal to men, and a community." Femen provided Diash with a sheltered space for engaging in politics, but that space was limited: "Everyone would sit around trying to decide what an action would look like and then Anna Hutsol would create it her way." In late 2011 she left Femen: "I didn't believe in the direction the group was moving in. There were too many girls involved without any interest in feminism or women's rights, social justice, or antiracism – issues I care about and wanted to change, but my voice wasn't heard. Sometimes girls would just show up at events thinking they might earn some money or make a few professional contacts with journalists." Diash expressed the sentiment that Femen filled a time and a place in her life when she needed to escape the "constant psychological pressure" she faces as a racial minority in Ukraine.

Diash is ambivalent about whether her time with Femen was a positive experience: "I learned a lot. I became braver – unafraid to go into the streets. At the same time, you know, sometimes I think that they needed me more than I needed them." In our conversation, I learned that she was referring to the tokenism displayed towards minorities in the media. Her comment illustrates a much broader problem in the marketing of rights-based protest for media consumption that Femen could also be said to be responding to by breaking the "rules" prescribed for nudity among celebrities and juxtaposing them with the "acceptable" terms upon which the West legitimizes and markets narratives of post-Soviet dissidence. After leaving the group, Diash became involved with a government campaign to increase sensitivity around racism, and she continues to this day working on discrimination issues. Her personal narrative is a powerful testament to her own agency: she was able to successfully manoeuvre her life opportunities by joining Femen, strengthening her individual convictions further by eventually choosing to leave the group in order to apply the skills she gained there to new experiences in other venues.

To remain critical of transnational articulations of race and gender in the face of the corporate flow of information ahead of us, we need to think twice when looking back at where Femen screams to their audiences that no one is listening. The risk of not listening, of overlooking individual voices, seems the greatest. Tchermalykh, writing only months before the demonstrations on Kyiv's Maidan, stated,

Has the neoconservative [Soviet] ethical regime already reached its aesthetic culmination, or is it still in formation? And, insofar as we on many levels still remain unaware of this process, how often do we unknowingly retranslate its moral precepts, returning back to the times when, on these territories, self-censorship was as notorious as working "for the drawer," or having collective discussions about "oblique morals" in the workplace. The Ukrainian response, as Femen has shown, is that, at best, if you protest something the "wrong way" here, the whole world may learn something from you, but then your voice will remain forever tossed out from your native land ... In Ukraine, as always, things are unclear. The situation is characterized by constant uncertainty, our political landscape being comprised as it is of multiple and conflicting vectors of intention.[108]

The body image in Femen's design certainly deserves critique. And yet, the constellation of media surrounding Femen could instantiate more critical analyses of the tropes they parody, specifically where these parodies point to pre-existing media representations that prescribe what dissidence *should* or could look like within post-Soviet and other contexts.

In twenty years, it may come to pass that Femen is remembered less as a *message* about the predicament of actual women living under a specific regime, than for their adaptive reinvention of dissent to a virtual language enacted within digital environments. They have asked us to look at them, and we've looked.

Femen's appropriation of signs plays upon conventional pop culture by airing audiences' fantasies and fears in satires on the mass media and its internal logics of erotic identification, alienation, and consumption. There are certainly many problems in thinking about Femen as a viable political movement, not the least of which includes the group's original stated aim to "eradicate sex tourism," a position that ignores the possible benefits of regulation and supports the illusion that sex work is eradicable in the first place.[109] Known to change their stance often, depending on the media interviewing them, Femen members' opinions were likely to morph into something else as soon as a new critique emerged. Their simulacrum of an actual protest reveals how dissidence itself has become a commodity in the contemporary political environment driven by images, icons, and mass information.

While Femen expanded to a broader range of body types in 2010, they remained unpopular in Ukraine and were still viewed with scepticism abroad.[110] The group's shift to a "sextremist" image in 2012 and their internationalization in virtual space entered them into global debates over the meaning of the term feminism. Audiences began to replicate, reject, and mock Femen's aesthetic online. The term "cultural hybridity," which Homi K. Bhabha uses to describe the cross-cultural borrowings that emerge in moments of radical political transformation, could be applied to the fierce backlash that played out against Femen's depictions of violence and explicit statements on the sex industry.

The moment Femen activists adopted an image of themselves associated with Islam, they took on a central position in global media. The group created a controversial framework for their digital text by appropriating media rhetoric in the reportage on Western intervention in the Middle East. Femen's controversial imagery of Muslim women points to the Orientalist passivity attributed to photos of Middle Eastern women that proliferated in mainstream Western media in the 2000s. This imagery has radicalized women into a debate: rethinking and questioning the racism and sexism that underscore the more subtle, mainstream images of Muslim culture in news media. Below the surface of Femen's overidentification with Muslim women, particularly where the group depicts Islam as inherently repressive, are deeper media tropes from which those depictions derive. As actual women with actual bodies themselves – the politics of image / counter image having material effects – this dynamic demonstrates to online and also proximate real-time audiences alike the relative degrees to which tolerance for public speech has continually shifted downward, even counterintuitively so, with the consolidation of mass media conglomerates over the past decade.

Femen's false sense of universalism risks inviting interpretations of the group as reinforcing the stereotypes they aim to lampoon. Their strategy certainly deserves critique. And yet it would be a grave mistake for critics to completely overlook the deeper messages in Femen's parody. Dismissing the group's members outright as naïve and silly reinforces the subjugating categories that replicate patterns of condescension by Western critics, and thus only perpetuates the traps that are so antithetical to transnational dialogue about gender. The colonial gaze that falls upon those regions that were once, not so long ago, referred to as "the Second World" is still pervasive within the stories circulated within consumer media that produce dissidents for Western audiences. Perhaps it is wise to look past Femen's smoke and mirrors to consider them for what they are offstage – young women. The twin risks to the free flow of information and creative debate may be of greater long-term impact than Femen's perceived downsides. They are worth our attention.[111]

Paying close attention to Femen's calibration within digital networks can help parse the rhetorical limits and risks that feminists undergo when making a protest out of their own bodies, and reveal the condescension towards "non-Western" societies so pervasive in the marketing and production of protest for mass media. This is not to say that we – as feminists, scholars, activists, consumers, or simply curious passersby – should refrain from dismissing Femen for their failures in addressing the actual needs of real women, or their lack of willingness to collaborate with those outside their group. Rather, the ethical contexts of our observations might benefit from casting a warier eye towards the deeper discourses that might be evoked, silenced, or reinforced in the *form of our dismissal*, whatever our stance.

Kyiv's city square is no longer a stage for offensive parodies, but a globally contested crucible. I return to my photograph of the Femen phenomenon: it is more newsprint than flesh, its paper clippings a relic of a past that marks the edge of only one of many outcomes; its multiple languages symptomatic of deeper conditions – the mutual stereotyping that can occur, all too often, at a cultural crossroads.

Chapter Three

The Image Is the Frame: Photography and the Feminist Collective Ofenzywa

Politics is not, as it was for Hannah Arendt,
the field where human freedom is unfurled.
The modern world, the world of war, the developing world,
the underground world of death that acts upon us
do not have the civilized splendor of the Greek City State.

– Julia Kristeva, *Black Sun*, 1989

... the stories and legends that haunt urban space like superfluous or additional inhabitants.

– Michel de Certeau, "Walking in the City,"
The Practice of Everyday Life, 1980

I. Introduction

On 8 March 2011 roughly thirty young people gathered on Kyiv's main thoroughfare carrying banners featuring a raised fist on a purple background. The ages of members of the group ranged from early twenties to mid-thirties. Nearly all of them were women. They had come to gather around a set of ideas echoing the demands that Clara Zetkin had first set forth for women's labour when she announced the first International Women's Day in Copenhagen in 1910.[1] The intellectual feminist collective Ofenzywa was founded by gender scholars from Kyiv-Mohyla Academy and Kharkiv University. Ofenzywa was the largest feminist organization to have appeared in Ukraine since the fall of the Soviet Union, and their members – who mostly consisted of non-profit workers, writers, academics, and artists – would play instrumental roles in the events that took place on Kyiv's Maidan over the winter of 2013–14. Although the group split into two separate factions during their critical involvement on the Maidan, and has since not reunited, their ongoing work is an important page in the history of women's activism across the region.

By the time that Ofenzywa had formed in 2010, Ukraine's shift to capitalism and the promise that democracy would follow – reinforced by elites in the Orange Revolution – had substantially dissolved and would continue to cave beneath scepticism of popular stories of national progress circulated during the Yanukovych years. With close ties to Russia cultivated through a long career inside the criminal and patron-client networks of the Donbas region, Viktor Yanukovych, in ascending to the presidency in 2010, co-opted the Soviet past in concert with Putin-style demagoguery. Emerging from liberal opposition networks, Ofenzywa stated in their Mission Statement of 2012 that their primary aim was to reclaim the transnational origins of International Women's Day as a "celebration of women's right to vote and work professionally."[2] Their collective formation around March 8 as self-proclaimed feminists, in particular, reveals local gender epistemologies in conflict with the term's negative connotation in both its official Soviet and Ukrainian parliamentary usages. Thus, the creative output of Ofenzywa's former members, in both their projects past and present, can provide valuable insight into various shifts in discourse on labour, class, and reproduction in post-Soviet contexts. Adopting the revolutionary language proffered by women of their grandmothers' generation, Ofenzywa's cultural output can be considered an unofficial archive from which we might reconstruct a more continuous history of local women's experiences. As Ukraine seeks to reinvent itself after the Maidan Revolution, these experiences can provide an invaluable alternative to populist narratives of national progress that overlook the negative impact of rising social inequalities rooted in widespread kleptocracy, the feminization of poverty, and exploitative labour practices.

In this chapter, I zero in on several close readings of two series of images by former Ofenzywa member and photographer Yevgenia Belorusets: one featuring residents of Kyiv tenement housing, and the other of local gay and lesbian couples' everyday lives. I explore in detail the political contexts for thinking about these photos as part of a broader rhetoric of dissent, discussing, in particular, how Ofenzywa interpolates a collective identity through the genre of the manifesto, adapting the action-oriented conventions of the early Soviet avant-garde on the role of art in society to their own critiques of the post-Soviet condition. In Belorusets's work there is a self-conscious, even quotidian quality to the photos in their fixation on the vulgarity of daily life. It is precisely because of this fetishization of everyday life, this sense of ordinariness transposed against the background of revolution, that the photos can convey a sense of witnessing human interaction, or disclosing the present condition of living badly/well in one's own home, nation, skin, and so forth.

The ways in which subjects in these photos inhabit times and spaces largely rendered obsolete by the rest of society suggest empathy on the part of the author to the frightening ease with which history can become the exclusive province of the few. Symptomatic of the historical mobilizations around travelling terms like "feminism," the photos illuminate where larger ideological borderlines in contestations around gender saturate daily experience in Ukraine.

To localize what I mean by "the everyday" in Belorusets's photos, I turn to cultural theorist Svetlana Boym's notion of "common places" in late-Soviet life and their centrality to myths about community, the public, and the modern citizen that have dominated the imaginations of those who experienced life under Soviet rule.[3] Born in the 1980s, Belorusets to a large degree can only approach the "common place," living memories of the Soviet past second-hand, filtered through the memories of Ukraine's older generations. I have chosen to focus on the places where memory works on the physical landscapes that Belorusets frames, creating out of them commentary on how individuals inhabit time differently, and how these anachronisms, or incongruent chronologies, inflect political subjectivity. I trace where the photographer inserts herself into the project as its narrator in order to unfold various dialogues out of the images themselves. Documenting changes in her perception of Self/Other, as her experiment progresses, the surrounding environment and all in it are subverted by the lens, which is the only constant. The banal and seemingly quotidian details in these photos are the grammar of a broader conflict over access to Ukraine's public spaces in tumultuous times.

The history of "everyday life" is itself culturally specific. Intertwined with nineteenth-century writings on urban space, including the concepts of public space and the private sphere, the concept of "byt" (быт), derived from Roman Jakobson's literary theory of the everyday evolved into character portraits and landscapes quite distinct from Benjamin's flâneur. Yet in both theorists' approaches to time, space, and language, the idea of public space originated in the individual subject's positioning of themselves vis-à-vis the crowd or the mob. Michel de Certeau's wanderings through the city in *The Practice of Everyday Life*, Henri Lefebvre's *Critique of Everyday Life*, and countless depictions of

the daily grind in Russian letters, whether of the experiences of bu-
reaucrats or prisoners, all pivot on the idea that the inevitable conflict
in lived day-to-day experience can regenerate the self, and thus also
transform society.

Ofenzywa members activate history by reviving and revising locally
familiar visual and narrative forms that have, throughout Ukraine's
twentieth century, been employed by a range of actors to signify protest and revolution. The manifesto, the march, the camera, and the
photograph – even the art collective itself – have each functioned in
both the early- and late-Soviet periods as vehicles for social commentary by subversive artists, some of whom were employed by the state,
sentenced to death, or both.

In this chapter I focus on two of Belorusets's series: *32 Gogol St.* and
A Room of One's Own. The first features residents in a dilapidated public
housing unit in central Kyiv. The second is organized around different framings of home through portraits of lesbian, gay, bisexual, and
transgender couples in domestic settings. Formally, I trace Belorusets's
work to the Soviet giant of photography, Alexander Rodchenko. Not
unlike her predecessor, Belorusets pursues the documentary properties of photography to social ends. The sometimes opaque or invisible
processes involved in making and viewing photos are foregrounded
in both artists' work as social documentary. In their texts and images,
the enterprise of photography itself becomes a series of asymmetrical
negotiations between artist, subject, and audience. I explore alternate
concepts of "the political" following on the ideas of Chantal Mouffe's
agonistics and Michael Warner's counterpublics. My particular interest
rests with how Belorusets extends the visual experiments developed in
Kyiv by the early twentieth-century Soviet avant-garde to contemporary contexts of decay, obsolescence, and transgression in her photos.
This composite language allows us to widen our framework inside revolutionary Kyiv (2004–14) by viewing "The Woman Question" through
shifting timeframes across the spaces of one city.

The inclusion of gender and sexual minorities into Ofenzywa's cultural output, and Belorusets's framings of home and domesticity yields
the opportunity for a profound critique of the private sphere. I show
how the photos index non-normative timeframes, discussing, for example, how her photos of a gay Orthodox priest performing the sacrament in a Kyiv apartment map "geographies of resistance" that are
asymmetrical to mainstream naturalizations of space.[4] As we sat in her
kitchen sipping tea in 2018 talking about events that had intervened
since that project, she reminded me of the struggle that artists working
with themes like hers face in finding spaces and venues for speaking

and sharing work. Later, when I shared parts of this chapter with her, she commented on "geographies of resistance," writing in an email that "it is very important to know that I visited Makyivka – now in occupied Donetsk Oblast – to find and photograph the priest. He lived in very dangerous and conservative surroundings, where it was maybe even lethal for him to live an openly gay life. Today this couple no longer lives in Ukraine."[5] Looking back now, in 2020, at the violence unleashed by the state against demonstrators on the Maidan in 2013–14, and the ensuing Russia-Ukraine conflict, Belorusets's description of the lethal threat surrounding her protagonist when she photographed him, nearly a decade ago, brings into sharp relief both the universality of his experience of social discrimination and its immediacy for a significant proportion of the population in Ukraine – and the world – today.

Belorusets's photos present people living their daily lives outside the representational economy in the mainstream production of citizenship. The photos in both series address many challenges of the post-Soviet era, some made more acute during the Yanukovych years, but do so by investigating how to inherit the Soviet past while still accounting for Ukrainian experiences of poverty and social marginalization beyond "the losers of the transition" often referred to in the parlance of more conventional histories.

In contrast to the performances discussed in chapters 1 and 2, I trace a very different framing of protest in the manifestos and photographs included here. These texts approximate a collective voice, a voice that ultimately estranges individual consciousness from daily life. By adopting the rhetoric and aesthetics of the early labour movement and the Soviet avant-garde as a *feminist* collective, Ofenzywa refashioned an earlier mode of political speech against the backdrop of modern Ukraine's official history, which states that the "transition" of the 1990s supplied a clean break from the Soviet era.

Insofar as memory is also lived, the Soviet past is still inhabited in different generations' uneven experiences of time and space. The act of making and displaying visually ethnographic photographs – as sites of social interpretation and educational practice – can come to trouble public/private divides. This is especially the case wherever discourse on production/reproduction reinforces gender binaries through the organization of space into two spheres. This troubling of the divide in Ukraine can kindle more egalitarian concepts of everyday life by increasing access to the public sphere. The built environment in Ukraine's cities is saturated with the Soviet past, as are the memories of its citizens. Rethinking such spaces will necessarily involve processes of open debate in order to ensure a democratic future, against the totalitarian impulse towards erasure, such as the legislation on "decommunization" introduced with the unilateral removal of Lenin statues and other monuments from public spaces in the initial years following the Maidan Revolution.

II. The Many Faces of March 8: The State and "The Woman Question"

Kyiv was herald to its own vanguard of women thinkers and activists in the early twentieth century. To a large extent, official discourse based in Engels' theory of the family had declared that "The Woman Question" had been solved by the emancipation of women from the home and into the factory. Of course, this was not the case in practice. Women in the region would continue to particularize labour issues specific to gender throughout the twentieth century.[6] Offering a more globalized version of women's labour history and suffrage that predates the Bolshevik Revolution, International Women's Day provides an alternative origin story beyond the development of feminism as a specifically Soviet or Western project. The day's transatlantic beginnings provided contemporary activists in Ofenzywa with a narrative for constructing more continuous histories of local Ukrainian women's experiences beyond the conventional "transition" periodization.

In the early twentieth century, International Women's Day provided a conduit through which modern gender roles were understood to be inextricable from class politics. This class orientation contributed to solidarities between women of the working and middle classes because, in practice, those roles did not conform to the emerging Bolshevik ideology, which had declared "The Woman Question" solved. The first Women's Day demonstrations in the region took place in Kyiv and St. Petersburg in 1914. The wife of Vladimir Ilyich Lenin, Nadezhda Krupskaya, subscribed to Zetkin's ideas that women should consider their interests first and foremost in economic terms. She wrote in the inaugural issue of the magazine *Rabotnitsa* (The woman worker): "Women's issues have a totally different character in the working environment than in the bourgeois one. It is not a struggle against men for equality; but a struggle alongside men against general lawlessness, against the conditions exploiting people's labor, and a class struggle for the victory of which the unity of all working people is required."[7] This statement was Krupskaya's response to the tragic fire at the Triangle Shirtwaist Factory in New York in 1911 – the event that sparked a larger women's movement in the United States. The fraught birth of unionism in Western factories inspired Emma Goldman and others to look to the USSR; it was the Marxist notion of international friendship that globalized feminism as an idea by defining women's rights in terms of class.[8] This crystalized an important, if often underanalysed, transnational path for later feminist activism energized by fervent discussion between Washington and Kyiv, as American suffragists consulted with women's organizations abroad that had already gained access to the ballot box.

Ofenzywa's rallying around International Women's Day, by citing the moment when Zetkin, Krupskaya, and Goldman attempted to universalize women's rights, highlighted the patriarchal discourses that underpin political subjectivity. Wherein systems of authority represent the discursive constructions by which the category "woman" becomes representative, this is because "it is through representation that collective political subjects are created, and they do not exist beforehand."[9] Gender is as much a part of constitutive publics as any other marker of identity. Thus, for a feminist political statement to have any leverage in systems that are inherently unequal, it must become visible by gaining traction in what has been termed "conflictual" processes.[10] Transposing the rhetoric of women's activism from the industrial labour movement onto their own group, Ofenzywa adopted an internationally recognizable idiom by which to gain legitimacy as a minority public among and in conflict with other publics. But the question still remains: what was being recovered/uncovered by Ofenzywa in their framing of post-Soviet women's rights?

Ofenzywa's collective formation around March 8, and their particular investment in feminism, stemmed from local gender epistemologies in conflict with the term's negative connotation in its official meanings. Historian Oksana Kis foregrounded Ofenzywa in her timeline of the "feminist upheaval" over International Women's Day in Ukraine as "the first time in the history of modern Ukraine that the general public was exposed to words like 'feminism,' 'feminist,' and the like in a public setting ... allow[ing] people to see Ukrainian feminists who contrasted greatly with their rather demonized public image."[11] She begins her overview of the controversy with an open letter to President Yushchenko in 2009. Kis herself drafted the document along with twenty other women leaders. The letter responded to Yushchenko's "political sexism" in his 2008 public address on International Women's Day, when he spoke to Ukrainian women "as little more than lovers, mothers, and housewives, instead of full-fledged members of society."[12] In this instance, Yushchenko followed a ritualized gesture that he inherited from Soviet celebrations of the day, praising women and thus enacting a script for public oratory that also, ironically, played to older conservative audiences' distance from social organizing around women's rights. Kis's article displayed the weakened social contract in her anger at his commemoration of women's passivity on a state holiday with origins in a supranational, albeit feminist alliance.[13]

The following year, NGOs throughout Ukraine composed another letter informing managers and leaders in politics and industry on the political origins of International Women's Day "to prevent them from continuing ... [a patronizing] Soviet-style celebration."[14] This second letter cited international monitoring groups and national legislation impacting gender rights in Ukraine. The letter was published online and gained over a hundred signatories from leaders in business and academia.[15] The critical mass of women who joined Ofenzywa in gathering around the day pointed to an even deeper problem: widespread frustration over the outcomes of Ukraine's Orange Revolution and the ideals (of which there were many) that promised to improve women's lives by putting Ukraine on the path to EU Association.

Insofar as state institutions can claim to be democratic, it is only in their capacity to prevent minority voices from being totally neutralized by more powerful segments of society.[16] In Ukraine, the narrative of "transition" attempts to overlook and silence the Soviet experiment as an actually lived and remembered period that only officially ended in 1991. The ways in which individuals view themselves as citizens are intimately intertwined with that period of time. The state's failure to take this into account also emerged in its inability to respond in any representative capacity to the protests on Kyiv's Maidan in 2014. Ofenzywa's prior demands to "reclaim" International Women's Day were direct attacks against Yanukovych's public oratory and its silencing overture to a communist past that, for all intents and purposes, his rhetoric falsely suggests never existed – or, at least, a past that existed differently for women than for men.

What makes Viktor Yushchenko's comments on International Women's Day particularly notable is that his demeaning remarks are not unique to his leadership alone. Kis' splits off the origins of International Women's Day from its later, Soviet-style celebrations in Ukraine, noting how the day first "entered Soviet mythology" as an official state holiday by decree of the Supreme Council of the USSR on 8 May 1965, the twentieth anniversary of the end of the Second World War.[17] The day soon descended into a token celebration of an essentialized femininity, resulting in several conflicting public opinions on the meaning of March 8 in post-Soviet Ukraine.[18] Kis contrasts the "original meaning" of the day with politicians' appropriations of its commercial popularity to gain votes. Ukrainian politicians continue to doubly disempower women by relegating their "essential nature" to an imagined idyllic realm beyond the provenance of representative democracy altogether – off "somewhere in an unnamed site *a-priori* to the state's appropriation of the day."[19] Extremely low numbers of women in state positions (less than 18 per cent) contributed to the anger leading up to the Maidan protests in 2014, which were ultimately not about the EU Association Agreement but the disparities pervasive throughout every fibre of life in Ukraine. Thus, the exclusion of women from the public sphere served to both delegitimize the civic category of "woman" and to entrench the feminization of the private sphere. Given that the very concept of the private sphere emerged from the bourgeois classes of the Western European industrial revolution in the eighteenth and nineteenth centuries, there is a good dose of irony in post-Soviet leaders' melding of Soviet oratory with condescending references to International Women's Day.

French feminist Simone de Beauvoir penned *Second Sex* during the reconstruction of social and political life that took place across Europe in the postwar period. Although she has since been criticized for collapsing gender into sexuality, her text is still useful for understanding "woman" as a categorical subject in history. Beauvoir contrasts the legal rights of women in the USSR with those in Western Europe. She cites the Comintern on the legalization of abortion and free childcare as laudable state responses to the notion of "woman" as an oppressed subcategory of the proletariat. Yet she only permits this line of argument to go so far. Unlike the proletariat itself, which at the time was a relatively recent ideological concept, the social and political category of woman has always existed. Moreover, she notes, the social tensions arising from the public/private divides that classically oppress this category were never really resolved in the Soviet experiment. She leaves her thoughts on the issue unfinished: "Strictly subordinated to the state like all workers, strictly bound to the home, but having access to political life and to the dignity conferred by productive labor, the Russian woman is in a singular condition which would repay the close study that circumstances unfortunately prevent me from undertaking."[20] Where Kis contextualizes a search for and recovery of older meanings as part of a larger effort to restore the "broken connections between the Ukrainian and international history of women's emancipation," she picks up where Beauvoir left off, and does so by describing a renaissance of feminist street activism and petitions concerning March 8 in the years after the Orange Revolution.

By contrast, Ofenzywa situated their movement vis-à-vis calls for the massive restructuring of family, work, and leisure, mirroring events dating to the turn of the twentieth century. The group's orientation towards this earlier moment of social upheaval drew a parallel between the hollow emancipation proclaimed by the Soviets and the false statements of progress under Yanukovych, when the group formed. This admixture of timeframes marks "the double burden" in which women's entering the factories in the postwar era failed to achieve equality between the sexes in shared forms of domestic labour, but only served to increase their overall workload.[21] By publicizing the labour rights of women, including the woman intellectual as a special kind of labourer, Ofenzywa foregrounded the daily work that women do as a primary ideological site, and, in particular, the asymmetry of power relations between genders as one that pervades every corner of society, and has survived every regime change in Ukraine.

Henri Lefebvre links ideology and its apprehension to a dialectics of the everyday.[22] Although he wrote *Critique of Everyday Life* in the postwar era, Lefebvre's notion of power reflected in everyday life is current with many post-Foucauldian thinkers. He writes, "Everyday life is profoundly related to all activities, and encompasses them with all their differences and their conflicts; it is their meeting place, their bond, their common ground."[23] In my interactions with Ofenzywa members during the years leading up to the Maidan Revolution of 2013, I observed that the everyday is also latent with transformative and transgressive potential through which women's identities as workers, consumers, and reproducers are constituted, often in conflict with their idealized representation.

After their 2012 march, Ofenzyva hosted a public "feminist art workshop" in Kyiv's Visual Culture Research Center (VCRC). The event included several art projects. The artist Yevgenia Belorusets served in two roles as a curator and photographer – she invited participants to choose an object representing their gender and write a short piece explaining their choice. Each person then posed with their object in a process involving dialogue with the camera as well as individual self-descriptions of their identities. Belorusets later curated the photographs into an online series featured on Ofenzyva's social media platforms.[24]

Participants took an abstract approach to the project. The artist Alina Kopytsa declared herself a minimalist and went nude while standing in front of a wall painted by the artist Vova Vorotniov in the colour blue – the signature mark inherited from the Soviet era that still designates "official" public spaces in Ukraine, such as schools, hospitals, and prisons. By baring herself against a wall marked by institutional power, and then documenting her act, the activist in the photo refused to behave in the ways that the mark was originally devised to function in the regulation of citizens' bodies. In these images, the wall becomes a signifier for the dissonance inherent in the overlap between public institutions and privatized bodies, in effect, pointing to how this overlap functions as a resource for silencing dissent and creating the appearance of consensus. Contrasting the blue wall (one of the most ubiquitous visible ghosts of Soviet biopolitics) with a naked female body, this activist resignifies the mark from its ideological basis in a pre-existing state to a set of material meanings antithetical to the total freedom of bodies in space and time.[25] The dissonance between the activist's body and the wall's regulatory purpose points to the continuous regulation of bodies by a Soviet (and then post-Soviet) marker of hegemonic state power.[26]

This kind of visual insubordination mirrored Ofenzyva's broader style of protest. Their cultural output throws into question the seemingly ordinary surfaces of everyday spaces. Nearly all of the creative acts inspired by the feminist workshop, including the meditation on the blue wall, can be read as pushing against the erasure of difference subsumed in both the socialist and capitalist projects as hegemonic, all-pervasive scripts for living and working.[27] In this sense, much of Ofenzywa's cultural output aimed to throw into question the seemingly ordinary surfaces of everyday spaces. In doing so, their practice reflected upon spaces' central function within the conditioning of the self as the origin from which all politics proceed.

In November 2018, Belorusets recreated the photo event from the feminist workshop in 2012 entitled *Ya i Ona* for a larger exhibit that I participated in as an author, invited and encouraged by the feminist art-activists featured in this chapter.[28] The exhibit, entitled *A Space of One's Own* (*Свій простір*), was held in Kyiv in November 2018.[29] Ofenzywa's original 2012 invitation to participants in the feminist workshop was featured as part of the installation of *Ya i Ona*, reflecting Belorusets's individual artistic collaborations within the wider context of critical feminist activism. It is important to note that the first feminist workshop, curated by Ofenzywa member Nataliya Tchermalykh, was the last event of the Visual Culture Research Center in Kyiv-Mohyla Academy in 2012. In fact, the workshop only took place because VCRC was allowed to reopen temporarily. The exhibit *Ukrainian Body*, curated by feminist artist and co-founder of VCRC, Oksana Briukhovetska, along with curators Serhiy Klymko and Lesia Kulchinska, had been shut down by the university for showing nudity and same-sex couples. When Nataliya Tchermalykh and other participants in the feminist workshop dared to raise the question of censorship, VCRC was closed and banned from Kyiv-Mohyla Academy permanently. After this, Belorusets invited Nataliya Tchermalykh to curate the photo series discussed in this chapter, called *A Room of One's Own*, about the everyday lives of LGBTQ couples. A description of these events in

Yevgenia Belorusets's own words can be found in a text accompanying the exhibit that she created in 2018 specifically for *A Space of One's Own* reflecting on this history.[30] This more recent installation explored the Ukrainian social construct of femininity by inviting participants from the public to contribute their descriptive objects and personal stories to a renewed, swiftly changing space.

Social transformation always involves transformations of the self. As each of the pieces in the 2018 exhibit revealed – from Oksana Pavlenko's iconic *Long Live March 8!* (1930–31) to Kharkiv avant-garde artist Alina Kleytman's spoken text in *Old Fat Girl* (2017) – The Woman Question dating back to 1917 remains one not of location inside/outside the metaphorical room of one's own, but of speech. The space of one's own in the exhibit is between author/subject/audience: it appears in the approximation of a common language shaped within and against representations of the category of "woman" as a political tool, a mentality, or another condition of being. Figures 3.1, 3.2, and 3.3 are examples of the repetition of the blue wall, nudity, and repurposed objects contrasted with the outward objectification of the human body in other contexts, by signifying gendered subjectivities as plural and self-initiated.

During Woolf's lifetime, labour protections for women in industrialization, voting rights, and birth control had not yet been achieved in the West. Her famous statement that "a woman must have money and a room of her own if she is to write fiction" has since been received by feminist literary and cultural theorists Julia Kristeva, Luce Irigaray, Hélène Cixous, and others as an epitome of "écriture féminine" – a breakthrough in the search for a language by which to express non-normative gender experience. Woolf hypothesized that in order to break free from a patriarchal society, women writers should create an *Outsiders' Society* through which they would then transform their unique position on the margins into a source of power – thus creating a truly a feminist critique. Although in practice Woolf never created such a group, she did live an unconventional and brilliant life.

The 2018 exhibit *A Space of One's Own* reflected upon women's organizing in the 2000s in the context of the early twentieth century. The artworks I observed by my peers, friends, and avant-garde women before our time reminds us that what is brought into view can initiate the most central changes in our lives. Bringing women's history into greater visibility is the essential work of any author or artist who dares to express herself on the page or canvas. But what if the space of one's own were completely transparent? What if it were constructed within a glass house? How does artistic production – the recontextualization of

Figures 3.1, 3.2, 3.3. (*Continued*)

Figures 3.1, 3.2, 3.3. *Ya i Ona* (Me and her), by Yevgenia Belorusets, Kyiv, 1 March 2012, VCRC. Shared with permission of the artist.

boundaries between private/public, everyday materials, and multiple framings and perspectives – open up new vocabularies for constructing ourselves and the worlds we inhabit?

Milan Kundera included the term "transparency" among his sixty-five keywords in *Art of the Novel*. He comments on its popularity in journalism, defining it as "the exposure of individual lives to public view," containing residues of the nineteenth-century philosophical obsession with the metaphor of the glass house: "an old utopian idea and at the same time one of the most horrifying aspects of modern life."[31] In Ukraine the glass house projects easily onto the walls of the museums it contains. The root source of fear common to all texts that feature the terror of the glass house among authors ranging from Dostoevsky (whom Woolf admired), to Walter Benjamin, and later Foucault, is the possibility of actually having to live inside of it. The zone between public and private that the glass house came to represent was grounded in the fact that contained in its very envisioning were the blueprints for both the first shopping mall and the prison surveillance complex. Freedom, like the public square that signifies the citizen with a voice, is both a process of achieving the space of one's own *and the ability to leave it at will*.

Woolf's *A Room of One's Own*, as a compass in the hands of Kyiv feminist activists over the past decade, serves to remind us that, in its global manifestations, feminism is both transnational practice and action: an anti-architecture, an open square, and a warning against impulses that try to reduce "woman" – the most consistent *outsider* of any room – into a tiny or even invisible bacterium or specimen for display under glass – a Kafkaesque insect, or a prisoner's dilemma.

The feminist knows that the way into the room is also the way out. In *Ya i Ona*, "She" is also "We." It is significant that the first Women's Day occurred in response to the protection of the lives of textile factory workers. Fair wages, hiring equality, and workforce safety were at the centre of Ofenzyva's organizing and continue to be major areas of focus for activists in Ukraine today, especially concerning migrant labour.

The photo, video, and sculptural work entitled *Second Hand*, by artist Zhanna Kadyrova, which was included in the 2018 exhibit, could be interpreted as the outcome of the failure to fully account for this history. Where multinational employers and states no longer respond to the basic material needs of workers, society falls into disrepair, as expressed through the repurposing of tiles from overlooked buildings in the Chernobyl zone. In fact, it was the first appearance of unions in Western factories that inspired Emma Goldman and others to look for inspiration to the women who had marched in St. Petersburg in 1914, before the advent of the USSR; this transnational organizing around class interests and workers' rights first solidified and globalized the idea of women's rights. An important path of activism formed between Washington and Kyiv as American suffragists consulted with women's organizations operating to help rebuild Soviet territories between the wars– women who had already gained access to the ballot box.

When I first met with Ofenzywa members in 2011 and agreed to translate their manifesto into English, the marches of the Orange Revolution had long ago ended and the banners had faded. Yet Ofenzywa's texts immediately suggested to me that a door had remained open: that the tents, the slogans, the songs, and the camaraderie that arose through the gatherings on the Orange Maidan in 2004, despite its leaders eventually dissolving all hope, had introduced a new discourse of protest that made possible several years onward a peaceful critique of the revolution. If only the outcome had been different in the violent clashes on the Maidan in 2014 – events that would end Ofenzywa as a group, even as they continued to work together amid the crowd.

During the demonstrations on the Maidan in 2013–14, Ofenzywa activists were sceptical of the mass gatherings as pro-European.

However, they joined with other groups such as the student union Direct Action (Priama Diia) in nonviolent resistance and to debate the conflicting demands emerging on the Maidan, especially in mass media. After casualties began to mount, members put into motion their knowledge, skills, and contacts in social organizing to run medical aid centres, guard the wounded, and assist independent presses and international journalists to counter misinformation campaigns. The group soon underwent a formal split into a two-part coalition that was, to a large degree, the outcome of irreconcilable views on how to address the marginalization of women amid the violence taking place on the Maidan. The ideas driving the split partially arose from how to interpret their mission statement: whether the legacies of socialism are compatible with neoliberalism or incongruent for a feminist movement.[32]

The two factions of Ofenzywa grew further apart as a broader women's movement formed on the Maidan in late 2013. Yet despite deep disagreement over how to address sexism amid the course of events, especially with regard to the role of militancy in feminism, and whether or not to join the defence units against attacks from state riot police, in practice the two factions worked together, putting their own bodies on the line in rescue efforts that saved lives.[33] In December 2013 Ofenzywa called a meeting and held a vote in which it was decided to end the group.[34] Although the group did not formally retain their network in name, members would continue to work together even years after the demonstrations – forming a continuous, alternative history of feminist activism.

III. Rhetorical Contexts

Ofenzywa's Manifesto

Under the aegis of feminism, Ofenzywa kept alive the practice of peaceful protest, despite receding civil liberties in the short period of their existence. They were able to accomplish this by appropriating the language of revolution in terms that preceded the Ukrainian state itself. Their manifesto reads: "We call for the return of International Women's Day to its content in women's solidarity in the struggle for our political rights. May the demand for equal opportunity and our struggle against discrimination sound with a loud voice in Ukraine – especially by the state, which formulates, but does not realize, women's full potential. United and together we will celebrate a century of women's struggles for our rights!"[35]

Women's struggle is always a struggle to speak as political subjects. Ofenzywa's manifesto does not lay claim to one unified demand; even as it served to instantiate a collective voice, it borrows from old forms to signify a coming revolution. The inclusive "we" in this quote, a hallmark of the manifesto genre, suggests that after "a century of women's struggles" neither communism nor the promises of the free market have achieved "equal opportunity" for women. Rhetorically, this founding document substitutes Zetkin's battle for safe working conditions in industrial factories with a more ambiguous fight "against discrimination." Ofenzywa's underlying message here targets government elites, who "formulate, but do not realize" anything, as the ultimate barrier to reaching women's "full potential." Yushchenko's botched election being the main throttle for the Orange Revolution, Ofenzywa was not alone in their dissatisfaction; and yet, feminism itself was at the time already silenced within post-Orange nation-building projects in its popular associative links as an outdated Soviet propaganda term. By interrogating feminism at the edge of Orange ideology, the group had embarked on a profound path of activism that would eventually put them at the very centre of events on the Maidan in 2013–14.

In both of Ofenzywa's founding texts – the manifesto and the mission statement – the group likens the hope for a better quality of life that people experienced at the time of the Orange Revolution to the twin "ideological illusions" of the Soviet state and the economic shock of Ukraine's initial years of independence. Their manifesto reads,

We recall that on March 8, 1917 in Petrograd thousands of seamstresses and textile workers took part in mass demonstrations, strikes, and hunger strikes; thereby launching the October Revolution. The Soviet state soon transformed their struggles into ideological illusion. Hollow declarations of gender equality forced Soviet women into difficult work whereby they had to raise children and care for a family at the same time. Since then, the oppression of women in the modern world has changed its face, but not its content. Neoliberalism – capitalism of the twentieth century – has created many new forms for the exploitation of women. At the same time, cultural globalization has opened up to us a world of information, and with it, an understanding of our position and the opportunity to change it.[36]

Where the October Revolution gave women the double burden of caring for family and working outside the home, neoliberalism, by contrast, has introduced "new forms for the exploitation of women." The language of socialist revolution has been replaced with the language of self-invention in thinking through the possibility of an "opportunity to change."[37] This subtle shift leaves room for viewing patriarchy as a function of everyday life, as well as a descriptive space for the inclusion of more than two genders (a concept foreign to Marx and Engels) as a sine qua non of protesting for antidiscrimination.

The "world of information" and "cultural globalization" mentioned here become instruments of a broader enlightenment of Ukraine's emerging generation of women seeking "an understanding of [their] position." Knowledge (expressed in language) begets politics, as the "labor of representing" comes to define political struggle. Pierre Bourdieu has linked self-knowledge to the symbolic power expressed in language as a transformative and inherently political social site, where "knowledge of the social world and, more precisely, the categories which make it possible, are the stakes *par excellence* of the political struggle, a struggle which is inseparably theoretical and practical, over the power of preserving or transforming the social world by preserving or transforming the categories of perception of that world."[38] Knowledge is valued as greater awareness of one's own experience, but this value also depends on achieving a vantage point from which to transform it.[39]

Looking back, from the other side of 2014, Ofenzywa's texts are a zoom lens frame on the local grammar of revolt itself. The genre of the manifesto has a unique history in post-Soviet literary and artistic cultures. The conviction that words and art are consequential for building society defined the broader ideological currents in the early Soviet period. The founding manifestos of the visual art and literary journal *LEF*, published in 1923–5 and 1927–9, became prototypical of the genre. The journal's editors, formalist critic Osip Brik and futurist poet Vladimir Mayakovsky, stated that the mission of the journal was to develop leftist art in the ideological service of building communism. In the 1923 manifesto, "What Does Lef Fight For?" the editors summarized their struggle to build a futurist, communist art during and just after the Bolshevik Revolution.[40] Formally, Ofenzywa ascribed to a similar philosophy of art rooted in the local leftist history of the trans-avant-garde: intellectuals in both eras assumed that ideas precede the material world, that aesthetics can determine and even change reality, and that language is a form of social and political action.[41] Yet unlike in the mostly male circles of the early avant-garde, Ofenzywa's feminist language is intertwined with the "absent element" of the political subject described by Julia Kristeva, in which women's negative subjectivity in public discourse resembles that of an author in a text.[42]

The Politics of "Everyday Life"

There are key differences between *LEF*'s manifesto and Ofenzywa's politics. The latter does not make pretence to any unifying aim, any "true path to the impending future," a position from which the early futurist avant-gardists often spoke and wrote.[43] Ofenzywa's manifesto does not imply linear progress; rather, they call for a total break with "normative assumptions about gender." Whereas *LEF* depicts the future in their utopian aim "to create a united front to blow up old junk, to fight for the integration of a new culture," in Ofenzywa's manifesto, the future has already arrived as "a world of information."[44] At the same time, this is a world that sounds a lot like the past. The "hollow declarations" and "illusions" that Ofenzywa discredited parallel the diction of early Soviet manifestos and their anti-bourgeois statements in attempting to relieve the proletarian struggle of its "old junk." This is because the "bourgeois" illusions of past manifestos are mapped onto a critique of patriarchy and leaders who have "changed [the] face [of women's oppression], but not its content."

Unlike the early Soviet collectives that produced culture according to state policies on social reform, Ofenzywa disarms the Orange "ideals of the Maidan" in a feminist critique that combines the revolutionary aesthetics of the Bolsheviks with the neoliberal era – to reveal limits in the language of "progress" taken to extremes (which would come crashing down on the Maidan in 2014).[45] Ofenzywa's manifesto, to local ears attuned to the form, also plays on the nationalist sentiments of these two eras. They introduce a productive critique of nationalism by invoking the emphasis on national autonomy in the Orange Revolution by way of a brief window of time (1917–21), when Ukraine gained its first footing as a nation state against both the Bolsheviks and the Whites. The result is a critique of nation-building from the vantage point of women reaching an "understanding of [their] position." By situating ideology in this way, Ofenzywa demonstrates how politics are symptomatic of everyday life, which becomes the primary vehicle for a critique of the regime.

Ofenzywa named the week-long film festival that preceded their march in 2012 *Woman with a Movie Camera*, after Dzyga Vertov's *Man with a Movie Camera*. Although Vertov made his films in circumstances that served the interests of the state, his technical inventiveness defined the avant-garde according to an aesthetics that would eventually come to be viewed as visual shorthand for revolution in the public imagination. Vertov thought the camera could function as an all-seeing eye that would reveal truths about everyday life by greatly augmenting the ways the senses take in and make sense of the world. It is this shorthand in particular that Ofenzywa adopted in their own critiques of declining civil liberties.

The two photo series by Belorusets included here arose from her individual artistic practice, which remains independent and local, sometimes leading to curatorial collaborations. For example, she invited Nataliya Tchermalykh, then a member of Ofenzywa, to curate the series *A Room of One's Own*. A parallel exhibit also took place in 2012, entitled *Ukrainian Body*, curated by feminist artist and founder of VCRC collective, Oksana Briukhovetska, who brought together activists and artists from two closely related art collectives, discussed in more detail in chapter 4.

On a symbolic level, we might read these images within "a certain 'globalization of resistance'" that Vitaly Chernetsky notes in authors' works during the radical economic flux of the 1990s.[46] These photographs were also shown in London. By conflating the attitudes of author/subject/audience, the project approximates a common language shaped within and against representations of the category of post-Soviet as a political tool or mentality. The images depart from the universalism of the early avant-garde, exposing through detail the passage of time since the 1920s and revealing interesting gaps in the "authenticity" of realism as a genre.

The environments in these photos, when considered within their local contexts, ultimately shift interpretation towards a particularly Ukrainian experience.[47] Where Rodchenko once employed the principles of architecture to signify the future, Belorusets's citation of his style in Kyiv bridges her generation's daily experiences with the memories of their mothers and grandmothers. Insofar as social transformation always involves transformations of the self, the photos put on display the multiple affective registers by which individuals imagine themselves to be part of a collective public.

IV. Time in the Photo Series *32 Gogol St.*

Form and Subjectivity

Belorusets's photo project *32 Gogol St.* is named after its main subject, a dilapidated public housing unit in the historic centre of Kyiv where residents were living in cramped, communal quarters commissioned by the state.[48] One critical outcome of this photo project, its circulation in exhibits abroad, and protests concerning the site by closely associated artists and activists was the resettlement of the residents into separate apartments in 2017.

The series includes hundreds of black-and-white photos of the house's inhabitants living their daily lives: doing chores, sleeping, smoking, getting a haircut, and laughing together around the kitchen table. The inhabitants are from multiple generations, including pensioners and middle-aged individuals with low incomes. There are buoyant moments in the series: a woman playing piano, a daughter hugging her mother, a boy laughing. In one photo a woman and her daughter sit before a mirror readying the young woman's image. In another, a young man shown in silhouette stands smoking in a darkened hall as the rain pelts down through the roof. We learn in an accompanying text that he is deathly afraid of cameras and wants to be sure "that only he will know that he is the one in the photo." The photos' rich emotional tapestries reflect the way they were made: taken over a period of three years, Belorusets spent substantial time visiting the house, getting to know the residents intimately for the sole purpose of the project. Even the building itself is intertwined in her characterizations of their lives.

Time in the photos becomes symbolic of deeper ruptures between the artist and the residents. Belorusets writes on the blog accompanying her project that "the inhabitants' situation becomes the subject of conversation: landscapes guide relationships between people while their self-identification emerges in 'floating signifiers' of the past and an uncertain future."[49] The building's deterioration under the weight of time also takes on significance as a metaphor for the unnamable, human neglect that has brought the house to ruin. The visible traces of the violence that time and nature have wrought on its fixtures, railings, and appliances testify to outsiders' fears of the people living there, outsiders who cannot, and need not, fully explain why.

Belorusets writes on her blog about how she learned about the house at 32 Gogol Street. In May 2007 a large group of young leftist activists staged a protest called "Capture Your Home!" in front of the house in support of residents' ongoing appeals to city authorities to renovate the building. Belorusets explains the significance of the protest's slogan through the theory of defamiliarization: "Capturing your own home could be understood as estrangement, which, according to Viktor Shklovsky, displays a thing, creating a unique perception of the object, creating a vision of its *not-recognition*."[50] Here Belorusets likens her own sense of alienation produced by her lens and her outsider status in the house to the "unusual form" of the protest. The building becomes a device in the mimetic textual frames she writes, inviting polyvalent interpretations of the photos' meaning.[51] Defamiliarization foregrounds her camera's role in mediating experience, redirecting her audience's gaze towards the production of the images themselves through interviews, direct quotations, and thick description. Audiences are encouraged to think about the processes surrounding the photos as instances of social rehabilitation. Both the camera lens and the protest slogan gesture towards the right to a home; both capture not property, but perspective.

The residents had mixed reactions to the protest and the photographs. One resident advised Belorusets not to publicize her work: "I don't think you should let anyone see your photos of our lives here, activists have already protested on our behalf and for what? People only laugh at us at work now, nothing more." Belorusets notes the hidden affective aspect to the woman's complaint, writing, "This woman really wanted people to see, but was ashamed." Elsewhere, Belorusets notes a different response to her presence in the house:

> One resident who had been living in the house awhile told me: "I love this room, it's large and spacious. We've gotten used to living here and probably would live here the rest of our lives if the walls weren't so damp. This house is old, but you get used to it, tethered to it, not like in a new home. You see this crack on the wall? I've been looking at it for years. It's like a drawing on the wall I hadn't seen before because, although I could see it, at the same time I couldn't see it. I want to see more, you know, but alone I can't see and perhaps this is because I don't want to see. I now know that I want to learn to see things differently, for example, that which you see."[52]

This resident's description of her personal, everyday experience most likely stems not only from the class divides between herself and Belorusets, but from sharing her home with an outsider, and an acute awareness of the camera held by an artist linked to a protest demonstration.

Belorusets's texts suggest that images can introduce new ways of seeing a situation, in this case, how residents view themselves in relation to the house and its symbolism in Ukrainian society. She elaborates on the relationships that arose between herself and the some of the residents while viewing her photos with them. In the process, she establishes herself as an active participant within her own frame by designating how power is leveraged beyond it:

> After three years of relating with residents I began to understand why the protest was the only one and why, despite its unusual form of asserting one's rights, the residents decided to carry it out. "Capture Your Home" was based on a dynamics of power and its response; it was a revolt against the personification, enslavement, and devastation of everyday life through territorial means of social and economic exile.[53]

Here Belorusets uses the language of abjection to draw out the opposite valuation of the ruined house as a home, characterizing its inhabited spaces as the outcome of social and cultural exile.[54] As Vertov wrote, "Not 'filming life unawares' for the sake of the 'unaware,' but in order to show people without masks ... to read their thoughts, laid bare by the camera."[55] Traversing "the devastation of everyday life through territorial means," Belorusets aligns her audience with the unfamiliar, disorienting feeling of "social and economic exile" that, ultimately, I believe she sets out to document *in herself and her own relationship to the camera*, its subjects, and their individual ways of seeing their living situation as at once familiar and foreign.

Scholars have long noted photography's uniqueness as a medium of expression for its capacity to combine nature and artifice by imparting images with accidental and deliberate qualities that change their overall composition. Distinct from other genres, the documentary photograph retains singular status in public institutions and surveillance technologies as a medium of disclosure by which "truths" about a situation or circumstance may be conveyed. Walter Benjamin linked authentic experience to the artistic production made possible by the camera as an instrument of class relations. He claimed that with the capacity to reproduce images by printing them came their fetishization as manmade objects through their circulation in a capitalist system. With the advent of photography, in particular, he believed that "the representation of human beings by means of an apparatus [had] made possible a highly productive use of the human being's self-alienation."[56] This, in turn, he claimed, alienated the masses from authentic art. As a committed Marxist, Benjamin, like Vertov, called for the expropriation of film capital by the proletariat, which shaped his social valuation of the medium.[57]

Faith in technology and its "interpenetration of reality with equipment" for Benjamin, like the futurists, could serve to both accelerate and ameliorate economic exploitation.[58] In his synopsis of art's relationship to history, Benjamin claimed that art is always political, and the belief that any art can be practised purely "for art's sake" is specious vanity so blinding it can yield fascism.[59] Writing from Central Europe in 1936, on the eve of the Second World War, when Stalinism and fascism were both palpable threats, Benjamin's response to the situation was to urge that "the most important function of film is to establish equilibrium between human beings and the apparatus. Film achieves this goal not only in terms of man's presentation of himself to the camera but also in terms of his representation of his environment by means of this apparatus."[60] Among the Marxist references in which Belorusets's work is situated, her camera's claim to "the political" can be discerned in her renderings of commonplace, everyday details, not to mention the negation of what lies beyond her frame, in "a vast and unsuspected field of action."[61]

Belorusets generalizes the political situation surrounding *32 Gogol St.* to the broader post-Soviet condition. She writes that the house represents "just one of numerous cases of violations of a basic human right to housing and adequate living conditions." She notes that communal services like gas, electricity, and water are in chronic shortage, and that this transgression of basic rights motivates her documentary. She effectually elevates her photos' representative "field of action" to housing shortages across all the former territories of the USSR.[62] Many of the interviews in the project draw out where a sense of decline overwhelms processes of remembering. A tenant recalls better times: "After the Soviet period the house wasn't in perfect condition, but the overwhelming sense of shame was not there." Maria Todorova, in writing about nostalgia and postcommunism, underlines dignity as the main counterweight in a loss of social cohesion:

> [Nostalgia] is not only the longing for security, stability, and prosperity. There is also the feeling of loss for a very specific form of sociability, and of vulgarization of cultural life. Above all, there is a desire among those who have lived through communism, even when they have opposed it or were indifferent to its ideology, to invest their lives with meaning and dignity, not to be thought of, remembered, or bemoaned as losers or "slaves."[63]

Belorusets, by retelling older residents' longing for a past way of life, conveys a past that she never experienced, but which appears better, or at least more secure, than the present economic problems facing "millions of post-Soviet citizens."

Like International Women's Day, this temporal juxtaposition lends continuity to a post-Orange generation's search for dignity in their re-evaluation of Ukrainian history. She writes,

> For Irina and Svitlana, photography became a way of turning the ordinary and everyday into exceptional instances, allowing them to experience their own personal history in foreign contexts ... Photography became a pretext to get rid of commonplace understandings of the situation, even to go beyond a sense of reality and weave into the fabric of the image a secondary meaning, beyond the usual boundaries of experience.

Such "exceptional instances" reinscribe residents' personal histories in active terms. The "vast and unsuspected field of action" that Benjamin once attributed to photography resurfaces in Belorusets's probing of consciousness and the latent memories that can illuminate in a landscape what may go unseen to others.

Figures 3.4 and 3.5 are side-by-side images by Yevgenia Belorusets and Alexander Rodchenko. The photographs are strikingly similar in

Figure 3.5. *Fire Escape*, by Alexander Rodchenko, 1925. Archive of the Pushkin State Museum of Fine Arts, Moscow.

Figure 3.4. *32 Gogol St.* series, by Yevgenia Belorusets, 2011. Shared with permission of the artist.

their usage of depth of field, angular perspective, and geometric shapes. Rodchenko's image of a worker climbing up a fire escape attached to a brick skyscraper conveys movement and strength; his image's clean lines and dizzying, though even, proportions are unified in the directional motion they convey, as well as their negative space and colour saturation. Yevgenia Belorusets's image also depicts the exterior fire escape of an urban building. The lines of the stone façade framing the window in her photograph echo the rails of the ladder in Rodchenko's image in a similar upward-facing arrow or "A" shape; however, in Belorusets's image, time has corroded the building's exterior. The dynamic shape of the metal ladder in Rodchenko's photo, in Belorusets's appears more like a softly handwritten A than a typeset or lithographic one. The filtered lighting in Belorusets's photo also makes for blunted contrasts between objects contained within the image; a slight mistiness suggests memory or muted emotion. Natural elements creep in at the edges: sunlight, trees, a plant growing out of the rain gutter. The square shape of the defunct balcony and the nearby walls reflecting light to the left and bottom of the frame also give the viewer the impression of being boxed in. Where the futurist Rodchenko projected into his image the swiftness, ingenuity, and muscle of the communist future, Belorusets's image conveys the passage of time differently. In her picture the balcony remains out of reach – defunct and deserted. The revolution is over. Rodchenko's image is a vision of the future. Belorusets's is a memory of the past.

Ruin, Materialism, Memory

Belorusets's photos in this series tell a cyclical story of decline through the material residue of time. The depiction of the communal Soviet interior is likened to the inner lives of the older generation of women who feature heavily as the main subject in the series. The soft-focus lens, grainy resolution, and the material objects that surround the people within these photos impart a dreamlike quality that suggests we are looking at a sequence of memories. Given the age of the author, however, these are not Belorusets's own memories of the Soviet past, but visual approximations of the memories of her subjects and stories inscribed within the built environment.

The communal apartment emerged as an artistic topos in Russia in film and art in the late 1920s. Svetlana Boym traces how plot developments often followed the adventures of beds, sofas, and chairs in comedy sketches mocking various social gaffes (e.g., *No. 3 Meshchanskaya St. / Bed and Sofa*, directed by Abram Room, 1927). This trend gave way to preoccupations and fetishes with domestic material things in the 1950s resulting from postwar shortages. It wasn't until the 1970s, however, that the communal apartment fully took on shape as a lasting topos for "the nostalgic site of the conceptual artists' own totalitarian childhood."[64] The scenes within Belorusets's photos capture both nostalgia for a bygone era and contemporary private uses of a once Soviet, communal space that the ideologies reflected in its original design could never have predicted.

Unlike in prior twentieth-century conceptualizations of the communal apartment, Belorusets's inability to access the Soviet past as a lived memory is a central theme in the photos' navigation between public and private space. It is this inability to remember that produces a sense of alienation in the photos. Ironically, the inability to remember is also what bridges the distances between their author and the people in them. In Belorusets's contemporary rendering of the communal Soviet dwelling, it is also the house of *another* in the attempt to approximate a shared memory of the past. Ultimately, Belorusets's images highlight where she remains a stranger to her protagonists' living memories of the Soviet past by interpolating and imagining that past through cues embedded within the built environment. The self's alienation takes shape as a search for mutual recognition between the author and the house's aging inhabitants, despite the generational gap between them and the fact that their subjective experiences of this former Soviet space unequivocally differ. I argue that the aesthetic of these photos filters the memories of a disappearing generation through adaptations of Rodchenko's constructivism to different depictions of time. There is a search for historical continuity between different generations in Belorusets's photos that also conveys, in many ways, a search for home. Moreover, this is a search for a home built from a common language embedded in day-to-day existence, a search that is itself a familiar one because it always also entails the search for a home in language itself. In my close readings of Belorusets's visual texts, what her photos ultimately convey is nostalgia for another's nostalgia.

In the photo of a former Soviet communal kitchen (figure 3.6), twentieth-century kitsch meets utilitarianism: cartoon characters like the popular Russian cartoon character, Cheburashka, ceramic salt-and-pepper shaker dwarves, giant dented tin pots and pans, and thick jam jars that cracked at some point and have since been repaired line the shelves in the background. Boym writes that the word "kitsch" did not enter the Russian language until the 1970s, when it was used to describe a special subgenre of books in Western mass culture.[65] The word's meaning stood in contrast to the idea of "byt," theorized by Roman Jakobson as a mode of signifying an idea of the everyday that is untranslatable into other languages because it also acknowledges the

Figure 3.6. *32 Gogol St.*, by Yevgenia Belorusets, 2011. Shared with permission of the artist.

possibility of a radical subjective alterity to the everyday.[66] Jakobson also analysed the relative significations within realism as "an artistic trend, which aims at conveying reality as closely as possible and strives for maximum verisimilitude."[67] Emphasizing realism as a genre that strives for both/either/or, the author's and the viewer's believing a depiction to be true to life, Jakobson contends that it also leaves room for ambiguity in the codes it cites and synthesizes. His theory asserts that new realism(s) interrupt prior artistic movements and their claim to the real; he quips, "Those who speak of artistic realism continually sin against it."[68] The inclusion of the carefully arranged personal items on shelves in a cabinet in the background creates a parallel between the woman's life and the author's representation of her subject; the photograph is Belorusets's perception of her elder's memories of the communist past through a double framing of the external world, and the world of the apartment.

From its beginnings in the 1920s the communal apartment, Boym writes, "remain[ed] the site of personal pride, a display of one's externalized interior and of the desire for individuation."[69] For example, one of the most common features that can still be seen in nearly every home and office in post-Soviet contexts is a simple curio cabinet, usually made of wood, with glass doors called a *shafa* (шафа), like the one depicted in figure 3.6. The shafa has survived every refashioning of the communal proletarian home in the successive leadership regimes of the twentieth century. Boym discusses at length the individualizing capacities of these tiny portals within the communal apartment, referring to them as a resident's "interface with the world."[70] The glass cabinet could be said to have functioned in the past as individualizing and buffering an all-pervasive Soviet control that Boym ominously names as a "zone" in which there is no script, and therefore no knowledge, for thinking oneself living between public and private lives.[71] However, twenty years on from the publication of Boym's book, the glass cabinet takes on a slightly different shape. With the disappearance of the "zone," other interfaces between public and private have arisen in the cabinet's place. The elderly woman in figure 3.6 inhabits her surroundings through memories that only she herself can translate into meaning. The many random items that she has preserved in the cabinet behind her are her own artefacts of "byt" that we encounter as floating signifiers of the past, but also, of memory as a kind of privatized past mediated by Belorusets's frame in the present. Emotional exchanges bring viewers close to the subjects within the photographs, while the formal aesthetic qualities collapse time and distance (figures 3.7 and 3.8).

The publicizing of private life here takes on additional significance as a site for understanding women's particular relationship to the communal apartment and the shifts in that relationship over time. While visually approximating the memories of late-Soviet life held by women a generation older than herself, Belorusets also inscribes her autobiography into the history of the house. As residents share memories with her, she filters her compassion for their experiences through her own presence in the house as an activist. The crowded shelves and nightstands boast not of abundance, but of shoring up items out of need and possibly out of habits acquired during other periods of shortage. Boym makes passing reference to an "aesthetics of survival" in describing what I can only describe in awe and wonder as the *junk gardens* of commodities within Soviet communal living quarters, writing that "there, the artifact is a personal souvenir and a souvenir of privacy itself; it is an object displaced from a common into an individual history."[72] Belorusets's photos become an artefact of their present.

The saucers, magnets, and teapots belonging to the woman labouring over her culinary chores are brought into public view by the camera.

Figure 3.7. *Varvara Stepanova (I Have to Submit the Paper Tomorrow)*, by Alexander Rodchenko, 1925. Archive of the Pushkin State Museum of Fine Arts, Moscow.

Necessity and survival foreground figure 3.6: not only in the placement of the curio cabinet next to a refrigerator in the privatization of this room by the working woman, but also in the fact she is a woman, working alone. Unlike past representations of the communal apartment,

Figure 3.8. *32 Gogol St.*, by Yegvenia Belorusets, 2011. Shared with permission of the artist.

there is nothing in this photo to indicate she is cooking for relatives or, for that matter, fellow comrades.[73] Also missing from this kitchen are the communal kitchen gatherings of trusted close friends that became popular in the 1960s and changed the kitchen space into one signified as "unofficial, though not antiofficial," in which "collective bonds of affection and friendship constituted its ideology."[74] What do remain, however, are the objects from many different pasts: each a sign for the private memories that go unsignified within the photo. Time is out-of-joint in the microcosms contained in these material traces of living memories. The photographer's lens cannot fully capture the cultural iconicity of the apartment where it is individualized by the woman's private possessions, each of their unique symbolic meanings left open for interpretation. Discursive markers of Soviet/post-Soviet life dissolve (figure 3.9).

The distancing effect that these photos accomplish in text and image suspends a split between the practices of everyday living "in public" practised within institutionalized spaces beyond the home, versus

Figure 3.9. *Varvara Stepanova with a Cigarette*, by Alexander Rodchenko, 1924. Archive of The Pushkin State Museum of Fine Arts, Moscow.

the "private" life and the personal identity this concept assumes. In one example, Belorusets accomplishes this in drawing attention to the social alienation residents feel at being denied public services and disregarded by society. Ambulances almost always fail to respond to residents' calls: "Seemingly simple and convenient, she [Natalia, a resident] is ready to accept the situation for what it appears to be in the context of the imposed, fleeting social norms that sustain it – this causes deep pain and makes you want to relieve her of this."[75] Here Belorusets shares the pain the resident feels, but is aware of her own limited ability to understand and therefore more deeply empathize with the resident. Belorusets defers to the camera as her translator and describes for her audiences the process of attempting to bridge this limit, to see another person's way of seeing. This double remove transfers her potential audience's gaze back and forth between both sides of the lens. The result is a verbal-visual montage that disassociates viewers from the familiar visual paradigms that constrain them, as in Shklovsky's theory of estrangement. In another post, Belorusets elevates the disintegrating residential interiors of 32 Gogol Street to a generalized poverty that "millions of post-Soviet citizens share," if not in actual lived experience, then in the imaginary collective memory of the past that space can foster.

V. *32 Gogol St.* as Allegory

Spatial Textures – The Soviet Communal Apartment versus the Post-Soviet Tenement Home

Many of the objects depicted in the photo series have an anthropomorphic quality, as in the pair of standard-issue Soviet "Elekta" stoves shown in figure 3.10. The arrangement of the two stoves side-by-side, the dust, and the magazine cutouts of a female model's head and a bouquet of flowers taped to the wall tell a story of consumerism and changing gender roles in the postcommunist era. As one sifts through images like these, it gradually becomes clear that below the surface of material decay lies a submerged rendering of memory bound up in objects that have been repurposed or carried over from their original contexts to sustain a new environment. In Soviet communal kitchens these two stoves would have been shared by two families living in the same apartment. This division reveals the temporary quality to the architecture of mass housing: it was thought to be more economic for each family to pay for their own gas consumption, as each would be on their way to more permanent housing. Once a temporary fixture in the service of the revolution, the two Soviet stoves in this photo now stand in homage to a contemporary absence. The cut-out fashion image suggests a bourgeois housewife in contrast with the two stoves side-by-side, which reflect a bygone time when multiple women would have cooked meals alongside one another in this formerly communal kitchen. The fact that the bourgeois and Soviet elements are both depicted as absence in the photo can be read as symptomatic of the total desertion of these formerly communal, now crumbling, spaces by the nouveau riche, whose preferences and expectations with regard to domestic life changed dramatically in the transition to a market economy.

Figure 3.10. *32 Gogol St.*, by Yevgenia Belorusets, 2011. Shared with permission of the artist.

Thus, the photo activates a critique of the feminization of the kitchen through the woman-as-homemaker ideal in both the Soviet and post-Soviet periods, constructing a utilitarian, ambiguous person-at-home in its place. Anachronistic life worlds begin to emerge through the defunct, Soviet-era objects and tools crowding these crumbling interiors. Many questions are left unanswered: Why did someone tack up these magazine cut-outs in the first place? In another image: why are there seven bottles of shampoo and paint next to the bathtub, half of them empty? The camera frame decontextualizes scenes of the house in an excavation of ordinariness and its hidden ideologies. Because the building's decay contrasts with the vitality of its inhabitants, the photos leave room for narrativizing the things in them as artefacts of everyday life in a survival against negative odds, or more simply, the fulfilment of day-to-day needs as they are invented and produced by shifting definitions of the private sphere and domesticity. Michel de Certeau describes a kind of subversive re-commoditization as the politics of "a social activity at play with the order that contains it."[76] This envisioning of everyday practice is tactical and based on indicating the invisible identities of a place and a technique of "reappropriating the product-system [and] ways created by consumers [who] have as their goal a therapeutics for deteriorating social relations."[77]

Ruin in Belorusets's photos serves as a backdrop for illuminating the human protagonists within them. The focus on minute details and emotive gestures suggests an archaeological study of the ways human memory simultaneously salvages and degrades the past. Walter Benjamin, writing on ruin, remarked that "allegories are in the realm of thought what ruins are in the realm of things."[78] The detritus of modern life documented in these photos is still in use, marked by the effort and care of human hands that have shaped a home out of the Soviet past, despite the massive state restructuring that took place in the 1990s – a home created not out of heroism, but in the same way that "millions of other post-Soviet citizens" hidden "in invisible tenement dwellings on unmarked city maps" have also done.[79]

Where in the Soviet era citizens were settled, often forcibly, into standard-issue living quarters, the residents at 32 Gogol St. are doubly blocked from state welfare and the benefits of privatization in the post-Soviet context. Belorusets writes that the house was declared condemned as early as 1988.[80] Although Kyiv's housing code states that under these circumstances residents should be given apartments elsewhere within the city limits, residents' petitions for decent housing were long left unmet. While some residents managed to leave the house by permit, many remained because they could not afford other housing.

In my conversations with Yevgenia Belorusets in 2018, I would learn that the residents of 32 Gogol St. had been rehabilitated to other sites, partly as a direct outcome of the pressure that her photo series put on local authorities. Looking back on the project, she noted,

> The residents of the building on Gogol Street fought for 32 years for the opportunity to leave the nearly-condemned structure for housing that would not leave them in such life-threatening conditions. After numerous lawsuits, newspaper articles, and ongoing communications with journalists, which increased after the opening of my exhibition in Kyiv, and then again in 2016 – 2017, all residents were offered apartments on the outskirts of Kyiv.
>
> The fact remains that, during my work on the project, many residents tried to leave the house – yet only those who, thanks to their relatives, were able to move to another dwelling could successfully leave. In 2016 and 2017, according to the residents, an investor appeared who wished to rebuild the house and use the valuable land in the center of Kyiv. In reply the Kyiv city authorities made an offer for resettlement, which was accepted by residents and the families who had spent years living in the house. Now the house on Gogol 32 stands dilapadated and empty.[81]

No signs of renovation or construction are underway.[82]

Framing the house as a microcosm of economic fallout would seem, at first, to strip its inhabitants of agency. Yet depicting the house as a kind of lost world also chips away at the idea held by the rest of society that the residents of 32 Gogol Street are somehow extraordinary; that they are the poor unfortunates, or victims of bad luck. The loss itself is revealed to be an illusion. The gulf between Belorusets's and her elders' memories of the past appears larger than the gulf between the residents and the public reinforced by the walls of their dwelling. The exigency with which Belorusets witnesses these social divides implies a search for terms adequate to the inheritance of that world, not as a static vision of the past, but as memory inscribed in material life and its vital role in shaping the present.

In figure 3.11, Rodchenko depicts Varvara Stepanova in 1924 wearing a dress in a print that she designed at Moscow's first textile printing factory. Belorusets's image of a woman reading in a makeshift chair mirrors the original in composition (figure 3.12). The approximate age of the woman in the latter image disrupts the sequencing of time. If the woman in the first photo were roughly twenty, then the woman in the second would be sixty in the early 1970s, in which case the fabric of her dress should match the fashion of that era. Yet, the broken-down interior and the leopard print faux fur curtains in Belorusets's image cue that this is a contemporary scene. The temporal dissonance amplifies the ghostlike quality to the disjuncture between how the woman in the second image visually embodies the past and how viewers see her: the book in her hands also raises questions as to how she remembers her own past, and how she sees her surroundings.

The spatial text of the photos depicts an alternate or hidden world. Rhetorically, we might then conclude that this world is actually quite ordinary, in fact, so common to everyday experience in post-Soviet contexts that it is nearly invisible. Audiences are invited to question the cognitive and affective means by which spatial environments come to shape politics. Are these inhabitants really so different from the rest of post-Soviet society? Getting a haircut, rolling out dough for varenyky or pierogies, and collecting kitsch souvenirs for the shafa all fold easily into experiences that are sometimes culturally specific, and sometimes just a part of life – even boring.

Attempting to represent the ordinary can liberate the limit of its circumscribed expressions.[83] Thus, these photos enact what Michel de Certeau calls "antidiscipline" by disrupting the language (visual and verbal) systems of common experience in post-Soviet public representations of home.[84] Writing on ordinary culture, he contends that "we are subject to, but not identified with, ordinary language ... it encompasses every discourse, even if human experiences cannot be reduced to what

Figure 3.11. *Varvara Stepanova in a Dress Produced from Fabric Dye-Printed with Her Drawings*, by Alexander Rodchenko, 1924. Archive of The Pushkin State Museum of Fine Arts, Moscow.

Figure 3.12. *32 Gogol St.*, by Yevgenia Belorusets, 2011. Shared with permission of the artist.

it can say about them"; thus an inevitable "foreignness-at-home" pervades any language of common experience.[85] Throughout this series, the images push against discourses that silence alternatives to seeing the house as just a house, and the people in it as simple unfortunates.

The photos present memory by activating the Soviet past within a certain legibility of place. The ruins of the past in the traces of the material world, taken in by the senses, are as alien to the individual as the ideological meanings that pervade common language. In several places Belorusets's written text collapses into her visual narrative, and vice versa. The result is a dialectic resembling what Certeau has described as "a certain strangeness" of the everyday.[86] The photos thus evoke memory precisely because of their ambiguity and strangeness, suggesting, rather than prescribing, the stories that people tell themselves in order to make sense of their individual place in time. In the post-Soviet context, this is also about retelling several versions of the same story: The Revolution, The War, The Fall.

By contrast, everyday life, even in the alternative navigations of time and space that Certeau explores, is most often experienced as a "grind unfolding," especially in the master historical narratives of social and cultural decline dominating public life after 1991.[87] Photography, as an artificial aesthetic language, can throw these discursive representations of "reality" into relief. Its documentary claim to represent "authentic" experience always already includes a negotiation between Self/Other in order to reveal a truth or falsehood of some kind. The presentation of a single moment in time specific to the medium can thus allow for a singular narrative about the everyday by illustrating the gaps in time in which an individual's experience comes into conflict with the visual paradigms that constrain it. For example, in figure 3.13, a triple-framing effect involving the camera lens, a mirror, and a window, a mother is shown adjusting the light for her daughter, whom we view brushing her hair in front of the mirror. The composition of the photos reflects Rodchenko's use of light and shadow (figure 3.14), but differs in that subjects are often depicted in ways that emphasize how they create their own environments.

In 2010, the same year in which *32 Gogol St.* was exhibited in the United Kingdom, three books of photography featuring the abandoned buildings of the city of Detroit were published in the United States. The absence of people in the Detroit photos soon sparked debates among critics who challenged the ethics behind representing the city's defunct factories and empty blocks as the epitome of civilizational decline. The many photos of Detroit that were published during this period mainly focused only on the exterior of buildings that served as metonyms for the city's population. The popular fetishization of the post-industrial landscape by

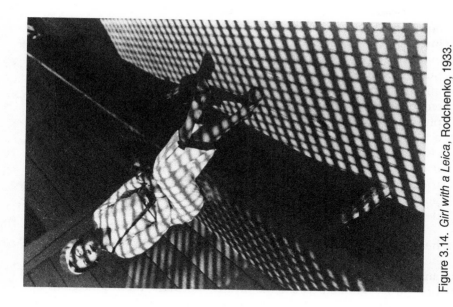

Figure 3.14. *Girl with a Leica*, Rodchenko, 1933. Archive of The Pushkin State Museum of Fine Arts, Moscow.

Figure 3.13. *32 Gogol' St.*, by Yevgenia Belorusets, 2011. Shared with permission of the artist.

outsiders directly contradicted the lived experiences of the city's approximate 670,000 inhabitants, who are actually quite vibrant and alive with
innovation – the exact opposite of decay. Belorusets's work, by contrast,
puts the body at the centre of her landscapes. This is in keeping with feminist postmodernist thinkers who insist that the speaking subject always
embodies the contexts of power from which they speak.[88] Belorusets's
physical landscapes are interwoven with a story about what it is like to
actually inhabit them. She weaves a narrative that puts women at the
centre of Ukraine's story by reversing the invisibility, nonexistence, and
irrelevancy ascribed to a marginalized demographic. Innocence, joy, and
friendship – experiences often disassociated from, or simply denied, the
poor in popular depictions of poverty – are here foregrounded as an undeniable part of childhood, family, and relations among neighbours.

In figure 3.15, an older woman stands next to a Soviet-era water
heater, or колонка (kolonka). The new dials and metal sheeting on the
heater and the water dripping down its sides indicate that the appli-
ance is still in use. Units like this one are still commonly used in many
homes in Ukraine because families do not have the resources to up-
grade to a modern unit. For the most part, residents in former Soviet
bloc apartments rely on the original equipment that was installed in the
building. Quite dangerous to operate, water heaters like this one often
explode and cause fires, or leak poisonous carbon monoxide. Here, the
photograph does not disclose whether the woman standing next to it
maintains this kolonka, or if it is a communal water heater. The mirror
balanced above the sink connected to the heater indicates a bathroom
setting. Light frames the woman's face from a bulb just beyond the
photo's upper right corner, and her hand holds the door to the room
just ajar enough to see a poster with the word "basketball" in Cyrillic
printed above a blurry picture. The woman is wearing an indoor robe
and her expression is tired and somewhat wary. Overall, the composition leaves viewers wondering what to make of this odd encounter –
are we in a public or a private space? Are we being intrusive, are we
welcome, or both? These ambivalences underlying the photo imply a
blurring of class and property relations. It is a stark contrast to the laws
of Soviet photography, where the visual depiction of the boundaries
between public and private was not up for debate, but carefully manipulated in order to project the ideological vanquishing of the bourgeois
private sphere on the road to a bright communist future.

Belorusets's use of architecture and portrait, and her focus on the
everyday, also resemble in line and form the work of the twentieth-
century Soviet giant Alexander Rodchenko. Yet time divides the two.
Rodchenko's long, vertical ladders and dizzying skyscrapers, once

Figure 3.15. *32 Gogol St.*, by Yevgenia Belorusets, 2011. Shared with permission of the artist.

calculated to project the progressive, linear vector of the Soviet future, have in Belorusets's work been replaced with a relic of that future. Rodchenko's photo, shown in figure 3.16, features an elderly woman peering through a pair of spectacles. The woman wears what looks like a wedding band on her right little finger and has on a scarf made of good quality cloth. She appears to be in deep concentration, although there is nothing in the photo to indicate that she is distressed. Her historical circumstances are revealed through one positive outcome of Soviet policy towards women evident here: she is educated enough to read.

In Belorusets's photo, on the other hand, we see the material aftermath of the twentieth century in the meagre living circumstances of a woman of similar age. It appears as though this woman has only just managed to provide for herself by invention, creatively sustaining her basic needs in what was supposed to be "temporary" infrastructure supplied by the Soviet state in the resettlement of the peasant proletariat into urban apartment blocs. Belorusets's photo offers further comment on the arbitrariness of time in the way the door being held open by the woman splits the image apart. Like Dzyga Vertov's side-by-side screens, the split creates dissonance between the narrative of the building, versus the woman's narrative of her life within it. As parallels of one another,

Figure 3.16. *Portrait of Mother*, Alexander Rodchenko, 1924. Archive of The Pushkin State Museum of Fine Arts, Moscow.

the kolonka becomes anthropomorphized next to the woman – its hulking shoulders and knobs-for-eyes begin to resemble a robot of sorts. The creaky and dented water heater, still an important part of everyday life in contemporary Ukraine, now appears out of place next to the woman, whom we know is not a Soviet citizen but is visually likened to the technological apparatus beside her that was once devised to produce the ideal Soviet citizen by projecting the ideals of the revolution onto the physicality of the built environment. Of course, actual appropriations of the environment in lived experience strayed widely from these ideals.

Ontology and Representation – Civil Imagination

Official state power and its representation can also contain subversive sites. Some have argued that photos can promote alternative imaginings of citizenship. Ariella Azoulay has described how participants in a photo interact with a camera in an "event" that destabilizes social relations and enables citizens to imagine each other differently.[89] She terms this combination of event with interpretive visual practice "civil imagination."[90] Civil discourse, she asserts, takes shape in photography by "[suspending] the point of view of governmental power and the nationalist characteristics that enable it to divide the governed from one another and to set its factions against one another."[91] Azoulay's thinking here makes possible the claim that the photograph itself can help further conceal, as well as reveal, the "truths" through which people imagine themselves as citizens in relation to the state. In this view, one way citizenship is enacted is in making and interpreting images, especially images that explicitly bridge and/or create divides between the governed.

Photography's indexical qualities can also be co-opted from within the social relationships that images mediate.[92] The affective qualities generated by the aesthetics of an image from a surveillance camera, for example, influence ethical judgments about the circumstances of the image, even though the leverage of power within those circumstances cannot determine the interpretation of the image in advance. Thus, the ontological property of photography by necessity requires interpretations that differentiate art and its relativity of judgments of taste from moral or ethical judgments about power.

This distinction makes possible a clearer discussion of the consumption of images as dialectical sites where the very divisions between public and private are construed in material practice. Belorusets's role as an activist changes her relationship to her photographs and their interpretive scope. The sovereign power of Yanukovych's oppressive state apparatus comes through in these images as an outside force, beyond the walls of 32 Gogol Street, that nevertheless still shapes the day-to-day activities of its inhabitants. In my conversations with her in 2018 about the project, about Maidan, and about her work more generally, she stressed the "repressing potential of poverty, where the people affected lack any instrument by which to see the repression. The situation is viewed by themselves and society as their own failure. And even now, after Yanukovych is gone, the problem is still the same – unsolved."[93]

Unlike in Azoulay's study, where she examines the ways in which state power is evident in pictures of refugees taken under the auspices of the state of Israel, in Belorusets's photos the Yanukovych regime is present as a largely invisible pressure. At the same time, in post-Maidan Ukraine, social inequality in Ukraine continues to increase. Belorusets emphasizes that attitudes towards poverty in Ukrainian society have not improved. A generalized fear of poverty has been *internalized* by society. The social context of the photos is stable over time: the social divides illustrated are nonspecific to any regime, serving to silence civic life and stifle minority rights throughout Ukraine. The project engages a "civil imagination" by visually impinging on viewers' expectations of what the state can, or should, do for its citizens. Instead of looking at the photos as outcomes, or proof, of realities experienced in the lives of the people in them as iconic examples of poverty in post-Soviet contexts, these photographs make more visible the daily practices that go beyond the coded logic of the regime. This latter interpretation is arguably the more democratic one in its yielding a vocabulary about everyday life that gives agency to participants in the photos and their own ways of culling meaning from their environment. Although Belorusets's privilege as the photographer is undeniable, she weaves an autocritical narrative by documenting her own experience of daily life in the house as she produces the images. Thus, the photos do more than document a circumstance – they become the circumstance.

In one photo a woman sits on a makeshift bed. Medicine is laid out on a chair serving as a bedside table. Tires and other materials have been collected and neatly stacked around the room. On its own, this photo tells a story of a woman who likely spends most of her time in this one room, judging by the careful positioning of the medicine and the arrangement of the bulky items behind her. We learn from Belorusets's blog entry featuring this image that the woman is terminally ill and relies on her son as a primary caregiver. Belorusets describes how she and the residents mediated difference:

> I began to feel that participating in the photo project had become for ... [the residents] a chess move, deflecting from view the infinite complexity of their daily lives. They took the metaposition of observers, ridding from themselves the surgical pain of a direct view of their lives ... I sensed the peculiarities of photography as a medium and how it allows the evasion of any one particular viewpoint: it was like I was pushed ... out of referential visibility, like I was transforming individual persons through formulas

somewhere between the characters' own receptions of their everyday lives and the receptions of their unknown audiences.[94]

In Belorusets's descriptive accounts of her camera's technology, it aids transcription, viewership, and authorship, but also overwhelms the relationship between herself and others. Employing written text to position herself behind the camera as a participant in the photo, Belorusets verbally relinquishes her agency over what the camera visually transcribes. She invites her audiences to critique the daily practices within which she is embedded as a participant in the circumstances of the photos. This metanarration redirects the gaze of the audience, inviting audiences to find affinities with the protagonists in the photos by looking past, in Belorusets's words, "the surgical pain" of physical and mental humiliation that subjects "deflect" when engaging with the camera.

Thus, the camera remains a part of the sequencing of the narrative, a force and trace acting on the photo. Several scenes like the one described above capture solitary moments that provide subject, artist, and viewer with access to special knowledge that cannot reliably go beyond the lens. This framing problematizes the documentary claim to "truth" in different representations of home, versus being at home, that point to how physical landscapes leverage social inequalities. The mediation of individuals' receptions of their own lives, versus the representation and reception of their lives for and by audiences, expands the "civil" capacity of the photograph by revealing how the house has become an oppressive symbol within the "disciplinary spaces" of the city.[95] The walls of the house at 32 Gogol Street are thus characterized here as visible, everyday reminders that manifest class and other social differences. By attempting to synthesize and make visible social marginalization, the photos become a counterweight to the totalitarian tendencies of the Ukrainian state at the time, which are only aggravated by what de Certeau describes as "the stories and legends that haunt urban space like superfluous or additional inhabitants."[96] On one level, the series is a visual map of the ways in which power is leveraged through Kyiv's buildings and the relationship of actual spaces to civic belonging.

In figures 3.17 and 3.18, one by Belorusets and the other by Rodchenko, the everyday experiences of bathing and the Soviet idea of exercise training are presented in private and in public, both within the social dynamics of gender. Both photographers frame their subject with a tilted lens that estranges viewers from the image.

The result inconveniences conventional readings of the photos, but does so by similar aesthetic means which convey the historical distance

Figure 3.17. *Jogging on the Roof, Student Campus in Lefortovo*, by Alexander Rodchenko, 1932. Archive of The Pushkin State Museum of Fine Arts, Moscow.

between the two images and their different frames around the spatial production of social subjectivities.

In the photo by Rodchenko, a young woman stands near a rooftop swimming pool and appears to be looking across the pool at three young men sunbathing on the concrete platform. This anonymous woman's stance and tilted head convey confidence and an air of curiosity at the lounging men she observes. The bright sunlight in the photo and the relaxed postures of its subjects convey an overall mood of leisure and good health – an ideal day off for a hardworking Soviet citizen. We see the men by the pool from the same angle as the woman's perspective, thus the position of the camera behind her omits any facial cues for our interpretation of the protagonist's facial expression. It is not clear whether we are supposed to identify with the woman or the men. This omission leaves open several possible backstories to explain the photo's

Figure 3.18. *32 Gogol St.*, by Yevgenia Belorusets, 2011. Shared with permission of the artist.

suggestive undertones. The optical effect of the slanting lines moving from the upper left corner of the photo direct the audience's gaze across the entire surface of the pool. There is an industrial scene on the horizon and a large metal pipe feeding into the pool where all the angled lines intersect. This dynamism revolving around the engineering of the landscape conveys that this rooftop oasis is indeed the product of the technological wonders of Soviet construction – the people enjoying its miracles have a bright future to look forward to.

In Belorusets's photo, by contrast, we see a young woman taking a shower in an enclosed room. Clutter surrounds her: several towels, instead of a curtain, are draped over the circular rod hovering over the now antique bathtub she stands in. Bottles, brushes, kitchen plates, and other items are haphazardly strewn about the room. Upon closer examination, a refrigerator and kitchen table in the foreground indicate that this former communal bathroom has been converted into a private single-room apartment. The woman's wincing expression suggests that she lacks the resources for storing or accessing a supply of hot water. While the photo, like Rodchenko's, includes sexual undertones, the framing of the overall image is more attenuated to the material landscape. The box framing of the room and the distance of the lens from the woman's body reveal a panorama of items that tell a story about her everyday routines. This space's original Soviet design would have functioned as part of a grander scheme of communal living arrangements. Where the room was once designed to produce an experience of home for the prototypical proletarian citizen, the woman has repurposed it to act as a single apartment. Here is a woman who is too young, just as the house is too old, to embody the socialist revolutionary ideals that the material environment around her once signified. There is an embryonic quality to her grasping the shower's water source attached to the wall. Her nakedness, rather than a spectacle arranged for the camera, appears a natural part of everyday life. Furthermore, her pose suggests an origin myth in which the figuration of "home" is revealed to be just an invention of time.

Unlike Rodchenko's buoyant images of young Soviets encountering a future full of dizzying possibilities, in Belorusets's photo of the showering woman, the camera fetishizes material sustenance over opportunity and leisure. Rodchenko's image portrays a performance of gender through flirtation, maintaining a division between two genders. The dominance of the industrial motif in the construction of a Soviet future defines the woman by her reproductive value to the proletariat. By contrast, Belorusets's image comments on the feminization of poverty. The woman's utilitarian repurposing of a Soviet communal space complicates the domestic qualities that are commonly attributed to women in the gendered divides around the tasks, motions, and endless chores of daily routine. Appropriating the material detritus of a communist future that never arrived, the woman has attained a level of autonomy through her own creativity, despite the economic chaos of the post-Soviet period and the failing social services under Yanukovych. The communal apartment is thus re-represented in Belorusets's project as an ongoing experiment in which the boundaries between public and private are flexible, despite the manipulation of this boundary by a corrupt state and its projection into daily life.

Belorusets writes of frequently being warned by passersby not to go into the building at 32 Gogol Street. She describes the condescending attitudes towards poverty that she encounters: "The majority of these passersby rely on the ideas they are socialized to believe in, mystical even, that poverty befalls those deserving it and people should stay at an arm's length from the poor." Belorusets and sociologist Anastasiya Riabchuk, an expert on socioeconomic inequality, both published articles in a 2010 issue of the journal *Spilne'* dedicated to the theme of the "criminalization of social problems," including poverty. This edition of the journal also featured Belorusets's photographs on the theme of the destruction of an open air marketplace frequented by those in need.[97] Riabchuk republished her article in English in an anthology in 2012; she explores the wider impact of poverty on masculinity: "Homeless and other marginalized people also challenge the expectations of hegemonic masculinity and reveal contradictions between ideology, real life experience, and self-perceptions, pointing to structural rather than individual causes of homelessness and failed masculinities in post-Soviet Ukraine."[98]

Here, Belorusets accomplishes a similar message; she plays with the language of science to counter the "mystical" fear of poverty in the social stigma surrounding the building as a class boundary. In linking social science to art, Belorusets adopts the conventions of Rodchenko's generation and the early avant-garde's representations of daily life. Doubling back on an earlier era, Belorusets's style strays from the intervening period, rejecting socialist realism and its didacticism in one major respect: unlike in Soviet renderings of progressive time, Belorusets's compositions depict daily struggles anachronistically. Her characters are out of step with the swift pace of capitalism; rather, they are heroic only in their ability to survive the extreme inequalities resulting from economic flux.

Thus, Belorusets's work overturns entrenched cultural myths about poverty and postcommunism. She shows where past promises of prosperity and freedom during the neoliberal era and its culmination in the Orange Revolution (and later Maidan Revolution) have failed a very palpable segment of the population. Those who suffered the most in lost opportunities during the transition to a market economy were women.[99] Her subject matter thus visually challenges the phrase "losers of the transition" used in economic policy to describe citizens who needed to rely on state assistance after 1991. Where this phrase has come to normalize the marginalization of women in public discourse, Belorusets's camera pushes against its limits. Her photos point to where the state's differentiation of needs overlooks and reinforces segmented experiences of everyday life.[100] As an experiment in optics and politics, these photos portray how the built environment conditions sociocultural practices. Alternative uses of the environments within them appear, revealing where ideas about home and everyday life can come to reinforce the symbolic divides in society, especially those that constrain civic life by reinforcing binary gender roles and stigmatizing the poor.

At the same time, I do not want to give an overly prescriptive analysis of the role of art in society. While Belorusets formally cites the early avant-garde, her politics are a radical departure from the aesthetic requisitioning of time and space by the state.[101] The interwoven, sometimes conflicting, ontologies in Belorusets's photos deconstruct past visual paradigms to move away from the historical determinism of the fall of the USSR and transition period. The dialectical relationship between art and politics in her text is also mediated by broader feminist conversations in Ukrainian public life; in part instantiated by Ofenzywa, but also spurned on by a decrease in civil liberties under Yanukovych. Her work dovetails with the group's search for continuity in local women's history, wherever feminism comes to describe women's experiences uncategorically, underscoring practices in resilience as commonplace as they are political.

VI. Depictions of Home: *A Room of One's Own*

Citizenship and the Private Sphere

Belorusets also deploys her camera within domestic spaces in the series *A Room of One's Own*. The series has been exhibited three times, twice in Ukraine as part of exhibits organized by the Visual Culture Research Center, discussed in the next chapter, and once in the Russian Federation as part of a queer festival in St. Petersburg.[102] The series features individual colour portraits of approximately twenty different gay and lesbian families in domestic settings. Roughly 40 photos out of 120 stills comprise the full exhibit. In my interview with the curator of the project, Natalia Tchermalykh, she described the selection process as a collaborative effort between herself and the artist:

> When we were selecting works we were trying to alternate the plastic visions people have of themselves generally, with somehow even more dynamic shots of daily life …While installing the project in a gallery space, Zhenya [Yevgenia] and I decided to alternate larger photos with smaller ones, and to display them in an unsystematic way; we wanted to convey that sexual orientation is not fixed. We also wanted to offer to the spectator the idea of the changeable body, which is in itself expressive of a political position.[103]

Russian critic Nadiya Plungian has remarked on the movement between frames in the series as the disclosure of the everyday, linked to a politics of oppression specific to Ukraine. She describes the project as "a repressed, closed portrait" of the LGBTQ experience capturing the "poor humility of daily life (byt), the unfolding of monotony, a typical space, but one where only the photograph is able to go in order to capture, fixate, and present its image to the viewer." She asks, "But to go where; to leave which world behind? *Is there a second Ukrainian reality?*"[104]

During the course of our conversation, Tchermalykh discussed the problem of normativity in national terms. In Ukraine, the divisions between private/public are connected with other social stigmas, even as they remain primary to the repression of human and civil rights:

> There was one shot we didn't include of a woman giving an injection of hormones to her partner. Although we did include it in the first exhibit [*Ukrainian Body*], we decided after that show not to include any sexualized photos. This is because, in Ukraine, the "normalized" vision of LGBT politics is often limited to sexual practices only. Here you often have the identification and sexualization of either gay men or lesbians as living together for reasons of sex only.[105]

The popular discourse aligning homosexuality with crime and drug use was at once a key rhetorical posture of the Yanukovych regime and a holdover from the Soviet period. Although Ukraine was the first successor state to decriminalize homosexuality, homophobia and highly normative views among the general population continued to influence policies on sexuality. Everything from city planning to reproductive health care descends from these attitudes, which serve to perpetuate and reinforce still widely held public perceptions of the only acceptable partnerships as male-female units.

By referencing same-sex partners as *families* in the curatorial texts accompanying the exhibit, the display counterbalances audiences' social paranoia around intrusions into the private sphere as a function of upholding public propriety. Early into his term, Yanukovych created a bill to introduce a law modelled on Russia's criminalization of "homosexual propaganda." He also oversaw the striking of the Anti-Discrimination Law from the EU Association Agreement in 2013, a change that was condoned by the European Union even before the demonstrations on the Maidan. Thus, temporarily borrowing the discourse of the family in order to subvert charges of deviance officially ascribed to same-sex couples carries special potency in Ukraine, where ecclesiastical and state priorities are largely bound to the same discourses.

Figure 3.19 features two men named Roman and Dennis. In a text accompanying the images, Belorusets writes that Roman Zuyev, the man wearing an Orthodox cassock, is the founder of the Church of LGBT Christians, "the only church in Ukraine which accepts members of any denomination, regardless of their sexual orientation." The church has no official place of worship, and so believers meet in private apartments. We learn from the blog that Roman supports himself as a taxi driver. It is possible that he might be able to afford a middle-class

Figure 3.19. *A Room of One's Own*, by Yevgenia Belorusets, 2012. Shared with permission of the artist.

lifestyle, although there is no information about whether he owns the apartment in which the photo was taken. In two other images of Roman, he is shown preparing the sacrament, possibly for an audience of followers gathered beyond the frame. The tilted angle of the lens in the photos gives the room an elongated shape, making Roman appear even taller. The drapes behind him, and the Eucharist laid out on the coffee table in the foreground, transform the space into an altar. The second image of Roman, taken from above, reveals the ornate golden cross and chalice, which are also on the table in the third picture. There is not enough information in the photos or accompanying text to convey how or why Roman decided to begin his church, whether the Ukrainian Patriarch ordained him, or he has ordained himself.

The cultural specifics of the Orthodox Church and apartment ownership in Ukraine are two very different spaces that wield wide influence in governing public versus private forms of behaviour. In public discourse and popular imaginings of the nation, these two settings function as opposite metaphors for the mysterious versus the trivial, the arcane and the profane, and the soul versus the body. Each of these concepts functions differently to produce the norms by which citizens imagine each other. In Henri Lefebvre's analysis of French democracy during the mid-twentieth century, "the externality of the citizen in relation to his own everyday life becomes of necessity projected outside of himself: in models, in fanaticisms, in idolizations, in fetishisms."[106] The environment of the photo suspends the official representations of the self, including the divine self. Roman's performing the role of a priest in an average modern Ukrainian apartment discloses religion as "a part of life practice, not its determinant."[107] By conveying what seems to be mysterious or exceptional as being in actuality quite banal, the photo brings into relief the mythic quality of everyday life itself. The norms that go unnoticed in day-to-day life, including those driven by assumptions around what constitutes the private sphere, and who "deserves" to access the public sphere, are revealed as political constructs largely driven by regulations stemming from church and state, which, in Ukraine, lack a full range of mechanisms to ensure participatory involvement in their legal impacts on civil society.

At the same time, a critique of everyday life can never be absolute or completely direct. Lefebvre argues that engagement in politics is made possible through the citizen's "reorientation to daily life," positing that this reorientation involves a process of "disalienation from politics" that can only happen when members of society join together in relationships that fulfil their social needs.[108] Abstracting the citizen's private life legitimizes an imagined public, which is always based in an idealized version of reality, which, for Lefebvre, is the basis for citizens' mutual blindness to each other. This is the main cognitive block in accessing a direct critique, and therefore transformation, of everyday life. The point remains salient that the abstract citizen is also a part of everyday life: "He becomes *for himself* an unreal appearance; but at the same time, by an absolute contradiction, the political fiction sanctions the *private* man, *qua* selfish individual with personal interest, as the supreme reality. This division assigns reality to egoism and abstract form to the citizen."[109] Although Lefebvre does not address the double alienation that minorities face, his emphasis on social need is valuable for conceptualizing politics in these photos as rooted beyond a simple narrative of state versus society.

Alienation in Belorusets's photo series extends from an experience of citizenship that differs from Lefebvre's theory of the abstracted life of the "private citizen." This is because, in Soviet life, privacy was ideologically erased along with the everyday life of the bourgeoisie. Plungian critiques the Soviet-style interiors of A Room of One's Own in light of the discourses of state patrimonialism and citizen dependency commonly attributed to the Soviet regime:

> Belorusets' perspective illuminates a desire to highlight the ambivalence, anxiety, and strangeness of everyday life (byt). The protagonists in her series live, work, meet and spend time in the foreignness of the self, in the interiors of another epoch. Each of these "rooms" are saturated in the disintegrating flair of the Soviet era: a recognizable record player from the seventies, a small wooden figurine on top of the T.V., a broken door, paneled walls, and lace curtains on the windows. But Belorusets saw no possibility of leaving the familial home, or the inner strength to turn toward another terrain and another consciousness. The effort to found a new family falls into the sad impasse of obedience and fear.[110]

Tchermalykh describes the photos as ironic portraits of the present set against the backdrop of the communal apartment of the past, where the Bolshevik ideologies that such architectural forms were designed to project come into conflict with the actual uses of the space and its inhabitants' lived experiences:

> On a formal level Zhenya wanted to avoid objectification at all costs, to avoid dehumanizing and distancing subjects from the spectator in cold expressions, or to show a state of being which is normal, but is displayed as exotic. You know, where at one time you had the display [in public life] of Soviet-style apartments, where nothing was at all like an apartment, really, but displayed to be an apartment that reflected all of Soviet idealism. For Zhenya it was important not to place objects or object-people in the apartments in her project.[111]

Where Plungian conditions the post-Soviet environment of the photos as the decay of cultural memory in the failure to create something "new," Tchermalykh portrays their Soviet kitsch as an ironic reprieve from official discourse. In an important sense, then, both critics deliberate on how the patronizing stereotypes that infantilize the life of the Soviet citizen as totally dependent on the state have actually carried over into the post-Soviet era in Ukraine.

It is apparent that Plungian writes from Moscow and not Kyiv. The Russian capital of the former USSR occupies a very different contemporary relationship to the past than does Kyiv, the once thriving, but now struggling former capital of the Ukrainian Soviet Socialist Republic. The ironies of Soviet ideology that Tchermalykh points to are less strident in the Russian context, where Moscow's once Soviet hegemony makes the past possibly appear more earnest in its desirable qualities.

For the Russian critic, the photos appear to fall into "the sad impasse of obedience and fear" in a failure to leave the "familial home" of the now disintegrated Soviet Union. For Plungian, the project also carries with it an optimism not afforded to Russia, perhaps, as she suggests later in the essay, simply because Ukraine's national identity can be more readily disassociated from the Soviet experiment.

The framing of everyday life in these photos, then, at least in their reception, is marked by their national context, despite the nonspecificity of the Soviet aesthetic of domesticity that serves as their main background. The tensions between normalization and exoticization that Tchermalykh, writing from the former "periphery," points to are less about the discourses of the past than about evading idealism at all costs. These tensions culminate in statements that resist the objectification of individuals into "object-people" with prescribed social roles. In showing the dynamics by which the ideologists of the USSR once projected *homo sovieticus* into the landscapes of daily life, the images make the normative environments once designed to produce and constitute this ideal Soviet citizen appear all the more surreal and unnatural. The result encourages audiences to question the mechanisms of citizenship, and the seeming naturalness and ease by which some norms come to arbitrarily exclude others.

Normative versus Non-Normative Time

In the images of Roman discussed earlier he has adopted the symbols of the institution of Orthodoxy in order to address a gay Christian community within the privatized space of a modern apartment. These photos of Roman in a black robe and rainbow vestment illustrate a radical break with the very limited terms upon which gender is recognized and regulated in Ukrainian civic life. Roman's needing to conduct his religious services from within the private sphere also reflects the overall absence of any institution in Ukraine willing to support a gay Christian church. Audiences viewing the photograph of Roman standing ceremoniously before his altar are invited to temporarily take up the position of the absent church members.

These photos apprehend a public that does not yet exist in institutionalized or mainstream post-Soviet Ukraine and Russia. The fact that Roman is disconnected from any larger state or social structure that would sanction his queering of the church places him outside the frame of "productivity" that is automatically granted to normative appropriations of time and space. Thus, the photo inverts the boundaries around the systems – financial, parliamentary, familial – that privilege heteronormative ideals grounded in the nuclear family above all others. Judith Halberstam, in discussing the figure of the transgender individual in postmodernism, has coined the term "Queer time" to denote models of temporality that emerge once one leaves the temporal frames of bourgeois reproduction and family, longevity, risk/safety, and inheritance. In turn, "Queer space" refers to "the place-making practices within postmodernism in which queer people engage and it also describes the new understandings of space enabled by the production of queer counterpublics."[112] Where the sovereignty of normative time regulates the family unit at the foundation of public life as the primary social vehicle for monetary accumulation, it also creates barriers that exclude non-normative membership from that public. Roman's repurposing of a post-Soviet home into a queer church allows for alternative performances of gender that do not fit prescribed cultural manifestations of time and space elsewhere in Ukraine.[113]

Time in the photos also reflects the broader political conditions in Ukraine. Belorusets describes the isolating effects of social conformism under an oppressive regime:

> This project helped me to understand what it means to toss aside a "norm" through an artistic medium, to feel how gender identities can dissolve and binaries between couples disintegrate, and to question down which roads the progressive and inevitable transformation of the institution of the family will go and what larger role each of these micro-changes might play in the lives of each man and woman and in the future design of society in general.[114]

It is no coincidence that Belorusets, like many artists in Ukraine working during the same period, views her primary role as a photographer in civic terms. The censoring of her photos in Ukraine led to some of her protagonists facing extreme threats and constant harassment from the far right.[115] The psychological pressure eventually compelled Roman to emigrate. He was able to receive amnesty in Amsterdam. Nonetheless, the material and political effects of the "micro-changes" Belorusets mentions continue to surface in Ukrainian public life. Attempts to unravel gender binaries in "the future design of society" resist the streamlining of everyday life within the logic of neoliberalism; in this case, the social inequalities of that logic are made all the more apparent by the photos' multiple political backdrops and their emergence at the height of Yanukovych's corrupt regime.

Thus, *A Room of One's Own* could also be viewed as an evasion of what Tamara Martsenyuk has noted in passing as the "institutionalized society" of official NGOs.[116] Writing on Ukrainian women's activism in the 1990s, anthropologist Sarah D. Phillips identified a gap between women's grassroots articulations of need and the terms defining welfare provisions. Her research reveals how the ideology behind the new economy being piloted at the time caused NGOs to import labels for certain groups. These labels then gravitated towards functioning along the lines of local stereotypes, for example, by excluding large families who had been associated with either extreme wealth or poverty in popular cultural associations in the USSR.[117] In Phillips's words, her informants had to learn "needs talk" or "claims making" to assert their deservedness for state and NGO grants. The stakes of the terms they used were balanced precariously between asserting what they contributed to society and defining what they lacked. The ability to do this well depended on a multitude of factors, but most keenly rested on calculations of sociocultural ideals and identity roles.

Positioning oneself so as to avoid being excluded from the new regime, in effect, became highly dependent upon language. The ideal citizen was weighed against the ability to conform to an external ideal, thereby greatly reducing in public life the tolerance for deviation from that ideal. These photos problematize characterizations of the private sphere as a feminine space of domesticity and reproduction. The Soviet-turned-modern apartment frames the intersection of church, state, and family. The resulting image is a bold statement on the exclusion of sexual and gender minorities from public discourse during a specific moment in time, the 2000s, and in the context of the eternal juggling between stereotypes and need.

The photos themselves soon became public sites. Protests erupted around their display in 2012, in the broader context of the shutdown of the Visual Culture Research Center for the exhibit *Ukrainian Body* and feminist workshop, discussed in more detail later. Many protagonists featured in the series were subjected to ongoing harassment. As visual documents of the everyday lives of the marginalized LGBTQ community in Kyiv, the photographs became controversial in their remapping of the divisions of public and private spheres that are assumed by the norms and assumptions that guide everyday experience. Both 32 Gogol St. and A Room of One's Own destabilize normative timeframes in ways that pose challenges not only for Ukrainians, but for experiences of post-Soviet life more universally. In the Russian context, Valerie Sperling points to homophobia and misogyny as largely stemming from the gender regimes promoted by the authoritarian Russian state under Putin in the mid-late 2000s. Her political science approach includes sharp analyses of how official projections of the leader's masculinity through campaign technologies and other media shaped gender norms, assumptions, and behaviours that have led to increasingly regressive policies in the Russian Federation.[118]

While all of the photographs discussed in this chapter directly concern the gender binaries that sequester minorities in the private sphere, the broader social assumptions and behaviours stemming from this binary split have emerged from a unique combination of phenomena in the post-Soviet context: ideologies inherited from the Soviet past, the state-church political nexus, and neoliberal idealizations of heteronormative productivity. By contrast, artistic productions such as Belorusets's photography and associated events and exhibits can be considered extremely valuable sites for viewing multiple angles in the production of post-Soviet political subjectivity and its translation into speech and agency more broadly. Similarly, as will be explored in more detail soon, Ofenzywa's symbolic march through the Ukrainian capital of Kyiv worked on several levels to resignify where authoritarianism replicates itself through gender regimes that are written into the fabric of the city.

VII. Resignifying Gender in Kyiv's Urban Environment

Opinion polls show that sensitivity towards gender and sexual minorities declined in the periods leading up to and following the Orange Revolution, even as LGBTQ and feminist activists' visibility increased in urban street demonstrations. Discriminatory statements targeting sexual and gender minorities by officials continue at even the highest levels.[119] Despite backlash from conservative groups, the overall increase in public discussion about gender-related issues is promising. Olga Plakhotnik attributes the "critical revolutionary potential" of feminism in Ukraine to street demonstrations having helped usher gender into public discourse in a more radical way. The routes, slogans, and events of Ofenzywa's 2012 march mapped a path of symbolic meaning through Kyiv's city streets. A closer look at these alternative appropriations of public space can further illuminate where gender ideologies are impressed into landscapes, and how such impressions shape civic life.

Marchers first gathered at Mykhailivska Square near the memorial to Prince Volodymyr, who has historically embodied the fusion of ecclesiastical rule with state legislature. They had chosen the separation of church and state as the theme for their protest in response to recent surges in intolerance by religious groups across Ukraine, including one entitled Love Against Homosexualism. Marchers aimed to draw attention to impending laws supported by Yanukovych's Party of Regions that would levy a tax on childless women over thirty, and another that would limit artificial insemination for single women above a certain age. Opponents from the other end of the political spectrum also showed up at the rallying point for the march, the far right in Ukraine being marked, as elsewhere, by protectionist stances towards a unified church and state, homophobia, and xenophobia. Roughly a hundred men and women, self-proclaimed "antifeminists," touted family values in opposition to "feminism and homosexualism." Many carried brooms with them to signify a desire to "sweep out the feminists" and chanted this phrase along with "Keep Ukraine pure!" and "Stop homosexualism, gender ideology, and degradation of the justice system!"

These slogans, besides being illogical, conveyed a policing of the nation through exclusion. Their choice in words, for example, "homosexualism" instead of "homosexuality," fit the religious nationalism and expulsion of difference that they argued for on national news. In one such interview, a man stated, "Homosexualism is killing the nation"; in another, a couple agreed, "It is just natural for a man to be a man and a woman to be a woman." These statements reveal that, for a segment of the population in Ukraine, sexual difference is perceived as an ideological pathology harmful to the nation. The elevation of the conflict to the level of national survival by this segment of the population revealed that more than reproductive laws were at stake in the protest. The clash unfolded as a large-scale re-evaluation of the justice system, debates on the ties between church and state, and fierce opinion on everything from immigration, welfare, and social autonomy: all sides, on issues going well beyond feminism alone, were being aired on the open city square.

Despite the opponents' aggressive stance towards the marchers, neither side of the conflict experienced physical violence or arrest. Police in riot gear barricaded any contact between the two sides, and Ofenzywa's marchers were able to continue along their planned route. They continued past the Cabinet of Ministers and through Maidan Nezalezhnosti where nearly 300,000 demonstrators had gathered to protest unfair elections during the Orange Revolution. They also marched past the Ministry of Bioethics where, in September 2010, state officials and clerical leaders jointly signed a proposed amendment to the constitution to ban abortion and revise sex education in schools to "promote marital fidelity and premarital abstinence."[120] This is only one example of a deeper preoccupation with sexuality and the body inherited from Soviet projections of political anxieties onto corporeal metaphors.

Eric Naiman roots these metaphors in the NEP era, when sexuality was largely bound up with ideas of individuality.[121] Past "incarnations" of the citizen's inner life have carried over into postcommunism: many prior ideological compulsions still govern public assumptions around proper conduct. Whereas in the West, Judith Halberstam has observed that "the transgender body has emerged as futurity itself, a kind of heroic fulfilment of postmodern promises of gender flexibility," in post-Soviet Ukraine, gender flexibility is perceived by many as a threat to the nation and its citizens.[122] Where the concept of "queer time" is bound up with late capitalist economies of flexibility, in the postcommunist context, the relations between sexuality, time, and space take on a different structure linked to the region's unique historical context. Writing in 2019, Ukrainian feminist scholars and former Ofenzywa members Olga Plakhotnik and Mariya Mayerchyk looked back on two decades of feminist protest to identify how different forms of colonialism combine with the regressive impact(s) of nationalism on homophobia, antifeminism, and the rise of the far-right in Ukraine.[123] Plakhotnik's and Mayerchyk's analyses support many of my own early observations on how Ofenzywa's rally around a socialist holiday politicized gender in Ukrainian public speech, pointing to a particular dynamic in which past Soviet discourses continue to inform the ways in which citizenship is equated with masculinity and with certain forms of labour that are seen as masculine.

The Russian leftist newspaper *Worker's Gazette* reported on the march in an article entitled "The Stern Face of Feminism," in which the author declared that Ofenzywa had finally overcome the "provincialism" of Femen's topless protests. Filtering the story of Ukrainian feminism through a Russian imperialist gaze, the article's nationalist undertone animates the conservatism of the Soviet past for its audiences in the present, asking, "Is it not a form of radical feminism to run half-naked through the streets, thinking that if you yell for something, showing your torso, someone will believe you? Surely, our feminists have now decided that if you want to fight for your rights, then do it seriously, sternly, like a man." The emphasis on "acting like a man" to achieve gender equality, coupled with the author's nationalist sentiment, grants men superior status as the architects of public life. As in the right-wing papers that diametrically opposed feminism to masculinity, the idea that women must fight for their rights in the "masculine" realm of the symbolic nation rests on the notion that the female body can simultaneously be both a lyrical defence of the nation and a threat to its borders.

Ukrainian presses and television stations covering the march all emphasized the controversy between "feminists" and "antifeminists" on Mykhailivska Square. Depending on the political leanings of the journalist, the point of the march ranged from "reclaiming women's rights" to "marching against men." Nonetheless, for the left and the right sparring over gender in Kyiv during the march, the form of the debate over women's rights staged in the streets conveyed a wider belief (shared by both sides) in street protest as a way to exercise democracy.

The march concluded in Mariinskiy Park. Members of Ofenzywa gathered to place a purple scarf around the neck of the monument to Ukraine's canonized poet and playwright, Lesia Ukrainka. Ukrainka lived at the turn of the twentieth century. Perhaps the most prominent woman author in Ukrainian history, she is considered a national poet in contemporary Ukraine and enjoyed wide cultural influence during her lifetime. Monuments are dedicated in her memory throughout most cities and towns. Lesser known among her achievements is the fact that she communicated frequently with her contemporaries Ivan Franko and Ol'ha Kobylians'ka on issues such as poverty, rural education, and legal reform.[124] Her ambition was reflected in her political thinking and its focus on radical change. As with many figures posthumously claimed by the state as civic symbols, her reconstruction for the mainstream leaves out her more radical sides. She translated Marx, expounded socialist views, and in her private life was rumoured to have had a romantic relationship with the writer Ol'ha Kobylians'ka. Given the cultural and political significance that canonized authors receive in Ukrainian public and official life, Ofenzywa's decision to associate Ukrainka's memorial with their march was a rhetorically powerful move.

The Italian feminist Rosi Braidotti's writings on dissonance and her more recent trope of "nomadic subjectivity" can help to illuminate Ofenzywa's symbolic intervention into the politics of citizenship. The group's symbolic output counters the patriarchal characterization of the state inherited from the Soviet era by "find[ing] a more accurate, complex location for a transformation of the very terms ... [which specify alienation] and of political interaction."[125] It is notable in this context that Lesia Ukrainka has also become a very visible state symbol of national identity: her face is on the 200 hryvnia banknote, she appears in standardized humanities textbooks, and she is featured in ceremonies on the Soviet holiday dedicated to students and knowledge still celebrated on the first of September. Placing a feminist symbol on her monument in Kyiv inscribed over stone an alternative idea of gender in civic life that had not yet entered the official terms of the state.

Essentially, the fervour over "feminism" that erupted between the left and right during the course of the march was also a staging of *how* to protest by challenging the identity categories available for expressing oneself in a publicly meaningful way.

It is also significant that the overall design of Ofenzywa's protest adopted an iconicity adapted to the virtual age. In Certeau's terms, they appropriated the "immense texturology" of the city's representations as "optical artifacts" in a topology of physical places that were also re-represented as virtual sites for public speech.[126] One poster featured commentary about pending internet censorship laws with the words "Google Is With Us" scrawled above the company's logo for March 8 that year (a rainbow montage of the male and female symbols). Participants wore purple scarves and carried flags of the same shade marked with the fist symbol – international signs for a broad umbrella encompassing many feminism(s). One woman wore a t-shirt with the ironic statement, "This Is What a Feminist Looks Like."[127] Three protestors wore fake beards in solidarity with French participants from the group LaBarbe, while a few others carried signs resembling the elaborately embroidered flags of Orthodox religious ceremonies. One sign featured politicians with church cupolas instead of heads, indicating that the church remains the primary legislative body in Ukraine. Slogans included the phrases "Church and State: Live Apart, Perish Together!," "My Body, My Business," and "Zetkin, Davis, Kollontai – To All the Oppressed We Cry!" Images and texts from the physical space of the street protest interpolated the online media surrounding the event. This dynamic aided activists in further suspending the divisions between the public and private spheres in order to stage their conversation on the cultural processes denoting gender roles in Ukrainian civic life.

VIII. Conclusion: Ethics and Competing Rhetorics

Ofenzywa's collective politics and Belorusets's photographs juxtapose the rhetoric of feminist marches of the early twentieth century with their own contemporary statements. In both instances, feminism is a valuable frame for a critique of Ukrainian civic life in terms that pre-exist both the Soviet period and the Ukrainian constitution. This way of "reclaiming" March 8 airs anxieties around shifting gender roles that are tied to broader social upheavals and nation-building efforts that have been reflected in the day's official commemorations over time. Ofenzywa's manifesto advances a philosophy of language formulated by the early Soviet avant-garde in a visual paradigm that assumed art is always bound up with action. Unlike the early avant-garde, however, Belorusets's photography conveys a concept of political subjectivity as not being founded upon the state, but rooted in everyday life, which is also the primary site for constructing gender roles.

Throughout the course of events on Kyiv's Maidan during the winter of 2013–14, leaders in Ofenzywa put their activism skills to use in practical ways, even though they were initially sceptical of the meanings of the broader demonstrations taking place. In late January 2014, Nadia Parfan and others organized a "Night of Women's Solidarity" to draw attention to the barring of women from certain activities on the square. The rally expanded into a grassroots group entitled "Half the Maidan: Women's Voices of Protest" that operated through Facebook to document women's protest activities. Ofenzywa members also joined up with activists from other groups in order to stage free workshops to teach nonviolent protest strategies. Yet, despite widespread efforts by many to keep the peace, events progressed and the situation turned critical. After Berkut riot police fired into the crowd in late January 2014, protestors fortified the square with burning tires, defending the barricades with Molotov cocktails and cobblestones pulled up from the streets. Hundreds were either wounded or killed. Ofenzywa members among the crowd applied the social organizing skills that they had learned and maintained throughout the Yanukovych years. They quickly organized to create independent media sites, acquire medical supplies from abroad, and guard the wounded from being kidnapped by the opposition in hospitals spontaneously set up inside local churches.

Nothing would remain the same. Ofenzywa split on 7 February 2014. In my ongoing interviews with members over the years that have passed since then, their reasons for ending the group vary, but nearly all consistently state that the end came about because of disagreement over the form of their involvement in the more mainstream protests. Some spoke of a lack of consensus on the question of whether or not to adopt militaristic means within their activist practice by taking up arms against the state alongside the other protestors. Their disbanding shook the entire network of feminists in the region.

Ofenzywa's end on 7 February 2014 also coincided with the date of Pussy Riot's first US visit, when Pussy Riot's members-at-large issued a public letter disassociating themselves from the two formerly imprisoned members of Pussy Riot, Nadya Tolokonnikova and Masha Alyokhina, on the grounds of "not wanting to be part of the commercial institutions of art and activism."[128] This was all taking place in the background of the Sochi Olympics in Russia, which spanned 7–23 February 2014 and saw protests by athletes who stood down from participating as the violence continued to mount on the Maidan – reaching its height in the mass shootings on 18 February 2014.

In the weeks intervening between the anonymous letter and the mass shootings, two much broader women's squads had formed on the Maidan: Ol'ha Kobylians'ka Sotnia and Zhinocha Sotnia.[129] The former adopted a more militaristic image, but preserved the leading symbol from Ofenzywa's Kyiv march on March 8 in the writer Ol'ha Kobylians'ka. On 8 March 2014, the first International Women's Day to take place after the Revolution of Dignity, Ofenzywa co-founder and scholar Mariya Mayerchyk published a journal article in *Krytyka* contextualizing the group in the context of the Maidan.[130] Tamara Martsenyuk followed up with a response article. Both of these texts evidence a firm commitment to the continuation of feminist social organizing and education in the context of the Maidan and beyond.

In 2018 I attended the march with Olha Martynyuk, one of the original organizers of the march, a feminist, a former Ofenzywa activist, and a historian at Kyiv Polytechnic University. She said that the mood of the earlier marches had been more playful, and mentioned as an example the "more radical, more separatist" Samba drummers' group that she has performed with at many protests over several years, including at the Maidan in 2013–14.[131] We marched together with a sign we made the night before that read Більше Ректорок, Деканок, Професорок, Вихователів, і Секретарів. This statement in Ukrainian works to the effect of reversing the gender bias in the occupation of academic positions of the highest rank by more men than women; the message is achieved by replacing the masculine endings of nouns that denote professional titles with feminine ones (except for the role of secretary, which is gendered male here): "More (female) Rectors, Deans, and Professors! More (male) Instructors and Secretaries!" Taken as a whole, the diversity and the size of the crowd made clear that public opinion and awareness around the meaning of this particular day had grown exponentially since Kis' letter in 2009 and Ofenzywa's first march in 2010.

Thus, although Ofenzywa had fractured apart on the Maidan in 2014, their efforts have been extremely important for preserving feminist actions and ethics in Ukraine, along with the two broader women's movements that have been described elsewhere; as a result of all of these women's efforts, a collective ideal remains that is not completely subjugated to the national ideal. And while many of these women's stories have made their way to international audiences, many have yet to be written. Now recent history, Ofenzywa's aesthetics and protest experiments were part of an early staging of a still ongoing search for a more continuous, alternative history of local feminist activism. A particularly important page in Ukraine's history belongs to them, and I only hope that as more and more researchers work on this period, they will take up the mantle of exploring the full range of members' ideas.

Like so many others participating in the revolution, Belorusets also captured the events unfolding there through a camera lens. As artistic artefacts citing prior avant-garde forms that once stood for "revolution," the images that she and others created are texts that go beyond conventional notions of social change that more traditional understandings of protest typify.

Arguably, all of the images from the events that took place on the Maidan in 2013–14 depict how politics are synthesized in people's relationship to their environments. Yet this dynamic resonates most clearly in the hands of artists.

In figures 3.20 and 3.21, a woman stands in place of the stone Lenin statue that demonstrators had just dismantled. While in *32 Gogol St.* Rodchenko's aesthetic underscores Belorusets's project, here the parallel between them can be viewed once again as a depiction of memory

Figures 3.20–3.21. *Maidan: Occupied Spaces*, by Yevgenia Belorusets, 2014.
Shared with permission of the artist.

disintegrating against the backdrop of Soviet documentary. The narratives of social emancipation and economic equality once signified by the statue, in turn, motivate the temporal disjuncture within both images. The overall picture thus contains within it an epochal achievement of the 2013–14 demonstrations against the backdrop of the failure of a bygone revolution. The Maidan takes on shape as the ultimate site for unravelling grand narratives. In the series *Maidan: Occupied Spaces,* Belorusets's depictions of gender echo the tenement home from 32 Gogol Street as a post-Soviet symbol of the "losers" of the transition period. Both series make visible the feminization and stigmatization of poverty that had infused even the social gatherings on the Maidan.

The ways in which power is leveraged through spaces emerges here as a narrative of the everyday, affording a view of the mythic qualities that guide how events unfold in the restoration of equilibrium and predictable conduct, to which all revolutions aim. The utopian spaces and suspended timeframes of revolution are revealed to be just as subject to discrimination as the practices of spaces/times marginalized by society in more stable periods. The occupied Parliamentary building in another of Belorusets's photos from the Maidan Revolution, like the house at 32 Gogol Street, appears as an allegorical production of space, showing how public discourses can both suppress and amplify social differences.

Social transformation is always first and foremost a question of individual perception. Where Belorusets carried over her semantics into the Maidan Revolution, her work became a valuable part of broader visual language experiments, discussed in the following chapters, around how power is leveraged through communal spaces, in this case represented by the occupied Parliament building. The inclusion of everyday material items into another image, such as cabbage and coat racks, reveals the transient nature of regime change by highlighting its micro effects. As in the concept of feminist politics that I document in this chapter, Belorusets along with former members of Ofenzywa, especially Nadia Parfan in her initiative Film86, and associated artists from connected collectives, would continue to utilize visual language as a medium. On 19 November 2014 Belorusets would give the keynote address at Vienna Art Week, which featured her series alongside work by over twenty Ukrainian artists in an exhibit dedicated to the Maidan.[132] The event included the visual art collectives REP and HudRada, which are the focus of the next chapter. As the artifacts of a generation positioned between two revolutions, these texts contain unique affective registers for viewing how societies contest public life by re-inscribing symbolically loaded public spaces.

Chapter Four

Museum of Congresses: Biopolitics and the Self in Kyiv's HudRada and REP Visual Art Collectives

We alone are the *face* of *our* time.
Through us the horn of time blows in the art of the word.
— D. Burliuk, Alexander Kruchenykh, V. Mayakovsky,
Victor Khlebnikov, *A Slap in the Face of Public Taste*, 15 December 1912

The open way leads to the public square.
— Marshall Berman, *All That Is Solid Melts into Air*, 1982

I. Introduction

The interactive exhibit discussed in this chapter, HudRada's *Draftsmen's Congress* (Конгрес рисувальників), now appears in hindsight as a premonition of things to come. The exhibit took place at the National Art Museum of Ukraine (NaMU) in the summer of 2013, not far from where clashes between police and protestors would soon engulf Hrushevsky Street in some of the most violent events of the Maidan Revolution. HudRada is a curatorial team formed in 2008 by then-emerging Ukrainian artists, authors, and critics affiliated with the Kyiv-based journal *Prostory*, rooted in the word *prostir* (простір), the term for space, or locus, in Ukrainian.[1] HudRada has sixteen members, some of whom are also in a related collective named REP or Revolutionary Experimental Space (Р.Е.П. Революційний Експериментальний Простір). REP's unofficial founders, Nikita Kadan and Lesia Khomenko, are now each highly regarded visual artists independently, although they do still work together on projects.[2] Both of these groups organize themselves by nonhierarchical means in which open collaboration takes precedence over more structured modes of cultural production. Common aims across these organizations overlap in the sharing of grants-based

NGO, state, private, and educational resources in order to create inter-active public art events in Ukraine aiming at political dialogue.

The compound noun HudRada is itself an eponym for the Soviet Arts Council. Given the council's original focus on making Kyiv's art scene more publicly accessible, this appellation is also a tongue-in-cheek unrav-elling of Soviet styles of censorship still active in Ukraine. From 18 May – 8 June 2013, the group essentially converted the official functions of Ukraine's National Art Museum into a roundtable workshop for new di-rections in art and politics. There were two parallel programs: an inter-active public mural in which participants were invited to "communicate through art" on a white surface installed throughout an entire room on the ground floor; and an installation on the second floor featuring a series of paintings, photography, and sculpture, entitled *Disputed Territory*. Partly due to the conflicted history of the Soviet avant-garde, none of Ukraine's public museums since 1991 have made contemporary art a priority in any substantial way. Thus, HudRada's roundtable and exhibit stood in stark contrast to the rest of the National Museum's permanent collection of Or-thodox icons and late-baroque paintings. A note from the curators reads:

> We move along a volatile border, from which we can see the constant shift-ing of battle lines, the focal point of the violent outburst manifesting itself again and again. But where exactly is this disputed territory? It lies in social interactions, in exclusions, in marginalization, gender and sexuality, in war over private and common interests, in public space and its acquisi-tion, in choices people make as civilians, politicians, and activists, and it is above all in the field of power.[3]

Over the three weeks of the exhibit, volunteers hosted discussions in the adjoining foyer on topics ranging from censorship to antiabortion initiatives to the criminalization of homelessness.

I observed the event as armed police patrolled the museum steps and hallways. My conversations with organizers from VCRC and Kyiv-Mohyla University, Oksana Briukhovetska, Vasyl Cherepanyn, and Katia Mishchenko, each of them writers like myself, involved facing the fact that there were hardly any people in the audience. Looking back now, those days seem a century ago. All of this marked the be-ginning of a series of unexpected events that would soon reveal the state's deception in previously unimaginable ways. Ukraine's contem-porary art collectives, as a community of friends and intellectuals, have proven remarkably resilient. Despite challenges in funding, political instability, and social change, the institutions that this generation has crafted continue to introduce important debates into public discourse.

Meanwhile, they have done so while inventing a visual language that synthesizes the aesthetics of Kyiv's early avant-garde and local 1990s trans-avant-garde with a new emphasis on the body, urbanism, and materiality. Framing critical ideological junctures between state, museum, and public, the common aesthetic across each of these art collectives pivots on the empty rhetoric of utopianism in allegories of the Ukrainian state to point out its anachronisms – and its failures – in protecting basic rights, including freedom of expression.

Retrospectively, the timing and location of HudRada's exhibit and activists' gatherings at the National Art Museum of Ukraine reveal the multiple planes of power that intersected and shaped the event itself. The main gallery in Kyiv is on the same street as the parliament building. The museum building was located at the centre of the seven major clashes between Berkut riot police and Maidan demonstrators that took place in January 2014. A program of political discussion, referred to as the *Congress*, took place in an atrium located next to an interactive, oval-shaped white space installed on the ground floor of the museum. The gatherings of civic activists and artists that ensued stood out from the rest of the museum and its hierarchical display of state authority. The circles of activists who staged the event, and the roundtable of debates that took place within it, destabilized the museum as an ideological space. This was most visibly apparent in the teams of armed police that patrolled the gallery and museum grounds during the exhibit. The content of the debates that took place and the mural itself – both symbolically and in the theme of disputed territory – prefaced the standoffs and fatal clashes that would occur between Maidan protestors and police just a few months later. Hrushevsky Street would later be renamed for the protestors who perished in holding back the police lines.

REP and HudRada were unified in this particular exhibit conceptually, but also materially and socially. Individual members had staged critiques of centralized power before by targeting other issues, not all of them related to artistic expression. LGBTQ and feminist struggles for parity in pay, HIV/AIDS awareness, labour unions, interfaith dialogue, better standards in orphanages, homelessness, and substance abuse rehabilitation are but a few of such issues. They have continued their work in the face of state repressions, ongoing social discrimination, and in some cases, even violent physical attacks by far-right groups and police. Individual artists have worked across these two collectives, sometimes collaborating with outside groups, usually on the left, in organizing public assemblies, petitions, and volunteer opportunities through NGOs. However, their primary concern has always centred on inventing new venues for public engagements with art.

Both collectives are working to reinvigorate public access to museums and their operations, including by putting on display the dynamics of various censorship regimes in contemporary Ukraine. Many of these artists take as a point of departure the traditional concerns of the avant-garde such as public performance, interface, and the symbolic agency afforded by public display in order to investigate economic and social injustices in contemporary Kyiv. Alexei Yurchak has made reference to REP using the term "Generation 2004" in categorizing them as part of a Third Avant-Garde. While this term may work in the Russian context, it is insufficient in the Ukrainian, and in REP's selective disengagement from all Russian state-funded sources. The idea of bringing art to the masses that Yurchak underlines in his characterization is much less, if at all, considered in Ukraine's emerging generation and its conceptualizations of socially engaged art, which is very much tailored to specialized audiences and not readily accessible to the masses. I do agree with his observation that one of the distinguishing features of artists of this generation is that they put themselves into actual confrontation with political authorities, sometimes endangering their bodies and/or art objects in the process. Yet the critical fact that Yurchak overlooks in his overall assessments is that this technique derives not from a readaptation of prior avant-gardes' theories of agitation, but from precisely the opposite: an attempt to cut against mass culture in Ukraine, and the monopoly of traditional folk aesthetics from the protest pop culture introduced by the Orange Revolution.[4]

Scholars of the region have coined a dilemma in the literature on democracy and transition as a search for a "third way" between communism and capitalism. Yet much of this literature, as has been argued elsewhere, has failed to consider postcommunism as a global condition.

Artists in Ukraine sometimes play with the surfaces of different projections of folk culture over time in its various manifestations as a vehicle for state ideology. The body, especially when gendered female, appears as a particularly profound site for revealing breaks and continuities between the Soviet and contemporary contexts. For example, in figure 4.1 the Soviet socialist realist heroine as a conveyor of production/reproduction in concepts of "fertile soil" and the emancipated "modern woman" who joins the factory workforce are refracted through an image of women's contemporary experience of rural life in Ukraine as one of hard work and sacrifice, but also resilience and the backbone of social autonomy from corrupted state and private enterprises.

Reading these artists' conceptualizations of local politics entails going beyond mere rejections of "transition" narratives from the 1990s. Ultimately, these artworks contain nuanced stories about intellectuals' and minorities' experiences. They are also stories about being in-between two revolutions: the advent of the second only sketched

Figure 4.1. *Dachna Madonna* series, by Lesia Khomenko, co-founder of REP Group, 2013. Shared with permission by the artist.

out here by these artists' works as a revolution of self-knowledge; and by their actions, as a collective attempt to evade the oppressive systematization of cultural production in Kyiv.[5] The exhibit's title, *Disputed Territory*, now appears Cassandrian after the literal annexation of Crimea in early 2014, and the disputes that followed with regard to the future of Ukraine's sovereignty. All of this further illustrates the suppressions that these artists had long been facing, and also *the value of artistic autonomy to public discourse in a revolutionary state.*

To understand "the political" in relation to the two intellectual collectives in this chapter, we must question why they are concerned with making and displaying art in the first place. It would be far too easy to simply label the HudRada collective a group of activists. Such a critique would miss the point of artistic autonomy and risk falling prey to the powerful figure of the Soviet dissident, all too recognizable in his more reductive costume of a defector or other populist hero, who only just happens to make art or write poetry. The more complicated and rewarding path, I think, is to abandon the search for heroes in order to better see the archetypes that societies hold onto and produce into heroes.

The stories that these artists tell about themselves in their artwork are ambivalent and open-ended: they are often about the museum itself, more than they are about revolutionary change per se, or realpolitik. The irony to this situation may be that, in turning to the site of the museum as their outlet, these artists' attempts to interpolate their audiences both as institutional and informal public sphere(s) are wrapped up in one of the core creative legacies of communism. The museum itself, after all, was the moral arm of the state with its ideological didacticism of socialist realism and visions of the enlightened social role of the artist. This being the case, much of the work produced by these artists who position themselves in conflict with the museum directly concerns the most inalienable site of ideology – the human body – in exposing what has since manifested itself externally, but at the time of the exhibit discussed in this chapter, had remained wholly internal to the Ukrainian populace: an alien state.

Using copies, collages, maps, acronyms, signs, and symbols from a range of modern political parties and movements, the images in *Draftsmen's Congress* and *Disputed Territory* pose challenges to the conditioning of post-Soviet reality as collapse and nostalgia. Combining cartographical notation in maps of Eastern Europe and Russia with formal aesthetic elements from Kyiv's architectural and Soviet pasts, the exhibit also employs physical landscape as a metaphor for the body in confrontation with shrinking spaces for self-expression.

This generalized focus on oppositional thinking and marginalization in the HudRada collective's work, as curators, pivots on montage and participatory painting, bringing into relief the central role of biopolitics in the state's attempts to legitimize itself. Furthermore, to read these artworks as an expression of civic dissent is to see in them not a tale of heroism, but an inventory, or even an etymology, in an evolving search for a more viable vocabulary with which to critique not only the institution of the museum (a site that is, arguably, always contested by artists) but the power systems beyond its walls that aim to muffle that critique.

In the second half of the chapter, I return again to Svetlana Boym's writing on concepts of "freedom" in late Soviet and post-Soviet modernism to explore some of the key events, ideas, and venues around which these collectives cohere. Piotr Piotrowski's notion of "agoraphilia" in Polish, Ukrainian, and Russian contemporary visual art also helps to clarify where these geographical sites share attributes that are absent from Western theories of democracy, which tend not to include negative critique or dissensus. Eric Naiman's work on corporeality in early Soviet ideology again becomes relevant to our discussion, as these pieces play upon the verisimilitude of past socialist-realist murals, architectural drawings, and mosaics from the twentieth century. Post-Soviet art emerges as less than social change, but certainly more than art: evidence of a problematic paradigm. The images here, created in participatory public-artistic events, I argue, populate with multisensorial displays the limbo and unpredictability – the gaps – left by East/ West clashes and ruptures between state, nation, citizen, and territory in Ukrainian spaces: private homes, streets, harbours, and others, including virtual spaces.

The notion of an inner citadel, a strengthened sense of inner freedom, as opposed to the threat of the censor (in the history of authorship under the tsar and then, later, socialism) remains in these artists' creative uses of what I call "negative space" in a sociocultural sense explored shortly. Ultimately, I propose that these artists ascribe to an ethos of collective compassion set against the fictions of a corrupt and parsimonious state. The content of their exhibit essentially manifests the imaginary and unfulfilled possibilities that were opened up by two revolutions in 2004 and 2013 that were, in both cases, co-opted by elites at different times throughout this period.

II. Art and the State

In the West, the rise of the museum in the nineteenth century was tied to the systemization of power by colonial states. Benedict Anderson writes that with the emergence of the printing press, and the shift of empires into modern nation states, there arose a sense of conquest through new mechanisms by which to measure space and plot time. Anderson includes the museum, along with the census and the map, as one of many technologies that supplied a vision of power that manifested in the state's infinite ability to reproduce itself.[6] In the territories that comprise modern Ukraine, museums also developed through the regulation of cultural artefacts by a dominant central authority. One might even argue that the cultural erasure suffered under the transfer of Bolshevik power from Russian imperial rule was equally, if not more severe than in more classical cases of colonial transfer. The speed of the transition contributed to the violence. After the Bolsheviks seized power, hundreds of churches, former palaces, industrial properties, and private collections of cultural artefacts formerly held by the deposed aristocracy were handed over to the state. Many of these acquired properties and their rich stores of paintings, ancient books, sculptures, and so forth were then turned into museums in a series of decrees by the new cultural apparatus.[7]

In 1917 the People's Commissariat of Enlightenment (Narkompros) was founded to carry out the enormous task of reorganizing cultural production, consumption, and exchange by decree of the Second All-Russian Congress of Soviets. Art became a category under which the economic requisitioning of public space occurred on a massive scale. In February 1919, the First Museum Congress convened in Petrograd to discuss further consolidation. It was decided that all museums would be financed by a single reserve fund (Gozmuzeifond): "in a single unified state, museums cannot pursue a separate economy."[8] The art system became an all-pervasive hierarchy in which directives were carried out from on high. Thousands of private mansions became repositories for the surplus of objects labelled "art" that had been abandoned or confiscated. The methods by which planners under Lenin brought art to the workers thus implicated museums in a grand utopian project that was reminiscent of Russia's imperial nineteenth century. The force of rule by the tsar replicated itself in the museum complex of the Soviet authoritarian state, a fact that would be brutally illustrated to anyone who dared to challenge its dictates in the regular interrogation, purging, and execution of artists, writers, and all brave souls associated with them. These terrors would persist across all territories under Soviet rule in the twentieth century.

But utopias are never permanent, nor are collections. The amplification of state power through illusions of permanence is a highly recurring theme in Slavic literature, and also includes its opposite: the unravelling of authority through brilliantly wrought irony, parody, and sarcasm.

Beginning with Gogol's petty clerks, countless authors have criticized the state in all of its forms by pointing to its surplus of bureaucracy. Fanfare is both a ridiculous decoration and a sign of weakness linked to a more generalized failure to gain the trust of the people over which the state claims to preside.

The stifiling atmosphere of hierarchy appears in the figuration of the museum in early twentieth century Russian letters as a trope for the old imperial system withering away. Few scholars have turned their attention to the predominance of the museum in this sense, or in the gendered qualities of the patriarchial order underlying museums; perhaps future research could illuminate how these qualities have carried over into the Soviet and post-Soviet eras.

At the turn of the twentieth century, the young poet Marina Tsvetaeva describes her father fulfilling his dream of creating a Russian museum of sculpture. Yet she casts her observations in language that reveals the strict borders around female access to such endeavours and institutions. Cixous's *écriture féminine* manifests in the language of "My Father and His Museum" as marginality and abjection, and yet, it is precisely this marginality that produces, ironically, a thoroughly modernist aesthetic well ahead of any concept of a museum cast by the old imperialist order. Tsvetaeva transcribes details that also convey arbitrariness, unthinking ritual, and even ridicule in the project of colonial expansion:

> I – am the one writing, the illiterate Asya is drawing museums and Ural mountains, on each Ural peak – one museum. "And here's another Ural, and here's another Ural, and here's another Ural" and, in her diligence drawing out her tongue almost to the edge of her cheek, "And here's another museum, and here's another museum, and here's another museum ..." While I, also with my tongue sticking out, dutifully and painstakingly produce: "Have you found the marble for the museum and is it strong? In Tarusa we have marble too, only not strong marble ..." But I'm thinking: "Have you found a cat for us – and is it a mountain cat? In Tarusa we also have cats, only not mountain cats." But by the laws of our house, I can't bring myself to write it down.[9]

In her prose piece "The Opening of the Museum," Tsvetaeva utilizes repetition as a device to draw out the futility of imperial ceremony in order to undermine the solemn authority of the tsar and his power. She accomplishes this by depicting an inaugural visit from Tsar Nicholas II to mark the opening of the Emperor Alexander III Museum of Fine Arts in 1912, the construction of which had been overseen by Tsvetaeva's father:

> Today the whole old-age of Russia seems to have flowed into this place in homage to the eternal youth of Greece. A living lesson of history and philosophy: this is what time does with people, this is what it does – with gods. This is what *time* does with a man, this is what (a glance at the statues) *art* does. And, the last lesson: this is what time does with a man; this is what a man does with time. But because of my youth I don't think about that, I only feel a cold shudder.[10]

Time, like reason and art, is an abstraction in the essay – the province of the statesman is far removed from the narrator's own experience. Penning her account as an eyewitness from the perspective of a child, Tsvetaeva frames the museum in light of a creeping sense of artificiality, which the author equates with the unpopular emperor.

Tsvetaeva leaves us with a final image of her father lauding another portrait, of Princess Zinaida Volkonskaya, the commissioner of the museum. Her father compares the latter's beauty, talent, and generosity to Mycenas: "Did she ever think that her dream of a Russian museum of sculpture would be destined to become the heritage of the son of a poor village priest, who until the age of twelve had never even seen a pair of boots ..."[11] These final images of longing and benevolence, encompassed by these two portraits of the museum's late female benefactresses, stand in contrast to the superficial show of power embodied by the tsar. Metaphorically, the museum is transformed at the end of the story from an environment of social rank and obsessive deference – the illusion of mastery over time – to a space characterized by familial care, learning, and generosity; in both instances the space is depicted through personal qualities that transcend time. Tsvetaeva's and her father's memories of these deceased women come to enliven and distort the synthetic order expressed in the museum's arranged sculptures. The "eternal youth of Greece" projected into "the whole age of Russia," embodied by the tsar, is limited. Tsvetaeva the child, in viewing this "youth" from a cold distance, senses a barrier between herself and the "childlike" quality she sees in the tsar. Whereas in her father's living memories, evoked by the portraits, Tsvetaeva sees completion "by going back into the past to the arc of spiritual continuity."[12] The museum comes alive as soon as time is released from the overpowering grip of the tsar and everything that is supposed to emanate from him within the museum.

At the time of the Orange Revolution elites attempted to justify national autonomy by breaking completely from the Soviet past in overtures to nineteenth-century Romanticism. The cultural establishment followed suit by blotting from the record Kyiv's important twenti-eth-century legacies in film, graphic art, and literature produced by the wave of artists who inhabited and travelled to the city at the peak of high modernism in the 1920s. In March 2005, the chair of the National Association of Artists of Ukraine, Volodymyr Chepelyk, stated his aims in an official speech:

> to defend our traditional artistic culture from various influxes and from pollution ... to strengthen the progress of the nation [natsio postup] in art and to defend the traditional flow of our ancient culture, so that Ukrainian art does not lose its specificity and originality in the world art space.[13]

Ironically, the new allergy towards modernist aesthetics that was supposed to signify national autonomy instead mimicked the very attitude towards culture that it had claimed to reject by creating a set of strident parameters for art. In doing so, this failure to adequately appraise a cultural past apart from ideological manoeuvring in the present effectively dismissed one of the most prolific periods in Kyiv for the purposes of installing yet another censorship regime. The relationship between the state and the cultural establishment in Ukraine remained stable in the shift from communism to independence – only the enemy changed.

In Eastern Europe and Russia, the question of artistic autonomy has continually plagued artists, driving them to rethink the inherited conceptual horizons of the museum at the core of state-managed culture. With the fall of communism, new opportunities and barriers in the practice, display, and market exchange of artworks emerged as museums played a central role in projects aimed at legitimizing national independence.[14] In Ukraine, the state has mostly maintained the regulatory functions of the Ministry of Culture from the Soviet period. Public museum officials have addressed practical problems such as the lack of funding and poor staffing, but have failed to account for more ideological issues, such as the selective omission of controversial themes from exhibits. Private museums in the country are equally selective, although they operate according to the interests of outside NGOs and oligarchs and are oriented towards trends in the global marketplace and the personal tastes of the investor; thus they remain more or less severed from local contexts.[15] The situation is such that grassroots collectives formed by well-established local artists (who have presented individual works in PinchukArtCentre and Kyiv's Mystetskyi Arsenal, and abroad in Biennales) have had to struggle to install new exhibits in their own city. As a result, local artists, critics, and curators have gone outside of both state and private art institutions to conduct more radical experiments that call into question Ukraine's entire art establishment.

III. Censorship and Negative Space

Members of Kyiv's contemporary visual art collectives cultivate a politics of detachment and scepticism of mainstream political initiatives in order to mount critiques of state power. It might be said that members of the radical intelligentsia of the 1860s were equally misunderstood by mainstream society, yet also desired by it. A century and a half later, Ukraine's contemporary generation of artists springs from a similar negative logic of detachment. Yet this time, the impulse to detach from mainstream politics seemingly derives not from the anomie of an aristocratic upbringing, but from what is perhaps the greatest of all of the oxymorons of post-Soviet life: that the most educated in society often tend to come under attack for their ideas. Upon closer reading, many of these artists' statements, not only on canvas, but also in the modes by which they organize their cultural production, echo Rousseau's social contract. Many of their activities directly involve the allocation and sharing of intellectual and material resources in order to ensure work for a wider number of people in a socially and economically marginalized community.[16] These emphases on self-education, sustainable income, fair labour practices, and artists' rights to legal representation raise several important questions about the role of the artist in society.

How is the voice of the citizen conceived of in these groups' creative processes and their relation to the state? How do the sites of their art exhibits and installations, which take place both in the Soviet-style interiors of state museums and across Kyiv's wider built environment, create sensorial cartographies – negative spaces – with shared meanings? How are these cartographies politicized?

In the post-Soviet case, museums are a battleground for shaping the future of independence and nationhood because they supply audiences with a critical immediacy, an immediacy that differs from the shock tactics of art often deemed political or subversive in the West. In my conversations with artist Nikita Kadan, he has emphasized the retrograde tendencies of the museum in the Ukrainian art system as a place where artists face particular challenges in the climate of the decommunization laws and the Russia-Ukraine conflict. Artists of his generation have already reached a level of notoriety abroad, and yet many choose to stay in Ukraine.[17] It is an open question as to whether the experience of two revolutions, and now a war, have driven artists of this generation to become more committed to local contexts than their predecessors. To be fair, many young people that I have spoken with tell me that the opening up of Ukraine's borders, combined with increased sources of income domestically, have provided them with the ability to travel abroad more often for work or vacation, making them more likely to choose to remain in Ukraine on a permanent basis.

These dynamics are also rooted in memories of the Orange Revolution. Thematically, much of the work by REP artists concerns language, communication, and the autonomy of art/politics. In the 2005 performance *We Will REP You*, members dressed in absurd costumes and held mock "protest" signs featuring Andy Warhol and slogans such as "every person is an artist."[18] Set on Kyiv's Maidan, this surreal political theatre conflicted with the "real" politics that had taken place on the same spot just a year earlier, pointing to the latent, and even violent, potentials of a space highly saturated with symbolic meaning. In *Patriotism Project* (2006), REP created an "artificial visual language" based on graphic symbols whose "universal" meaning could be interpreted by an accompanying "dictionary."[19] Both acts were consistent in the tendency to "expose a spectrum of negative emotions." Taken together, these acts could be understood as a kind of reclaiming of the Rosetta Stone from the centripetal force of the state, wherever its policies drive cultural conformism.[20] This absurd mock-protest on the square, hearkening back to the 1980s, poked fun at the sanctity of civic etymology itself; both of REP's stagings could be said to have temporarily collapsed the autonomy of art – once so vital to survival under totalitarianism – to reveal the political mechanisms underlying its systematization in the present.

There is considerable overlap between artists, critics, and curators in REP and other groups in Kyiv, including HudRada, whose members have worked closely with Kyiv's Visual Culture Research Center (VCRC) since its founding in 2008. As briefly noted earlier, VCRC was based at Kyiv-Mohyla Academy, but was forced out after their exhibit *Ukrainian Body* was shut down due its controversial uses of corporeality to dismantle ideology. By framing Ukraine's poverty and fractured government with literal and figurative nakedness, the exhibit tapped a central nerve in the national imagination and epitomized the artists' radical critique of democracy. The exhibit featured, among other media, drawings and photographs of nude men and women by Sasha Kurmaz and Anatoly Belov, Oksana Briukhovetska's pictures of destitute elderly women in Kyiv, and a piece by Mykola Ridnyi layering the image of a vagina over a photo of parliament.[21] Pointing at deep wells of ideological fissures seething just below the surface of Ukraine's statehood, the exhibit framed poverty, corruption, and gender inequality in allegories of coercion featuring exposed bodies of aging, nude, gay, disabled, and other marginalized populations. Three days after its opening on 7 February 2012, university president Serhiy Kvit shut down the exhibit space and indefinitely postponed all VCRC activities on the premises of Kyiv-Mohyla Academy.[22] VCRC, nevertheless, would continue by maintaining affiliates in the NGO and publishing sectors.[23]

Materialist Aesthetics and the Notion of Freedom

Recalling Homi K. Bhabha's idea of the postcolonial postmodern, discussed in the context of Vitaly Chernetsky's scholarship on Ukraine in chapter 2, I argue that the exhibit's materialist aesthetics negotiate nationness by questioning how the body, as an ideological site, can be framed in provocative ways that initiate a "shift of attention from the political as a pedagogical, ideological practice to politics as the stressed necessity of everyday life – politics as performativity."[24] HudRada's drive to organically create a broad local audience for their work interrogates the geohistoric frames of art-systems and the values, tastes, and judgments that these systems generate. Nikita Kadan, who has often spoken publicly on behalf of HudRada, has commented on the group's exhibits as a sort of disruption in the public scripts that a museum is supposed to follow: "It's a ritual, because every surviving post-Soviet museum is ritualized, and they all continually repeat the same message."[25] The source of social confrontation in this exhibit, as is the case elsewhere in these groups' work, lies in its challenge to the very idea of a museum and what it is supposed to do – it goes against the overwhelming institutional message that a strict code of behaviour must be observed at all times. The exhibit attempted to reinvent the rigid and closed functions of the national museum system in a counternarrative of the homogeneity and objectification of the materials on view.

In *Fixing*, a series by Kadan, featured in the exhibit *Ukrainian Body*, sexuality and gender are positioned within the frame of regulatory and ideological systems of control over the body (figure 4.2). The series combines Soviet-era calisthenics excercises and the suprematist typeface experiments of El Lissitzky and Kazimir Malevich. In *The Corrupted*, bloc apartments anthropomorphically link female reproductive capacities to urban planning in surreal black-and-white sketches (figure 4.3). The work was displayed on five light boxes bearing images of drawings from a Soviet medical encyclopaedia of the 1950s. Art historian Katerina Gregos writes,

> The work refers to the instrumentalization of the human body and the violence exercised upon it by the Soviet state: whether in competitive athletics where athletes were pushed to the limits and used in national showcases abroad; or the actual hardships that workers and farmers endured, often with tragic results, such as the famine during the period of forced collectivization of farm land and labour, which caused the deaths of millions of peasants in 1932–22.[26]

I would add to this interpretation that the sexualization of the social body – through blueprints – foregrounds the utilitarian, biological

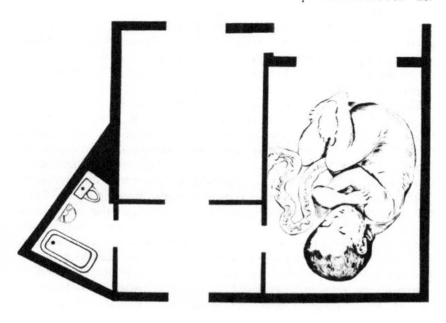

Figure 4.2 and Figure 4.3. From the series *Fixing*, 2010, and *The Corrupted*, 2012, by Nikita Kadan. Early exhibitions included *Ukrainian Body* (Kyiv-Mohyla Academy, VCRC Collective) and *Disputed Territory* (NaMU, HudRada Collective), Kyiv. Shared with permission by the artist.

aspects, over the pleasurable benefits of the sexual act, throwing into sharp relief the political manipulation of natural processes. The images also convey the feminization of the domestic sphere as an inherent factor in the regulation of the social body in how official state regimes distribute populations across urban space.

Censorship is a relative term that also contains its opposite by implying varying degrees of freedom wherever it is applied. A day before the exhibit *Great and Grand* in the summer of 2013, the director of Kyiv's Mystetskyi Arsenal Museum, Nataliya Zablotna, ordered that black paint be thrown on REP member Volodymyr Kuznetsov's mural *Koliyvshchyna: Judgement Day* and that a painting entitled *Molotov Cocktail*, by Vasyl Tsagolov, be removed from the building (figure 4.4).[27] Though Zablotna herself had overseen preparations for the show as one of its curators, she deemed these two works too controversial for the occasion for which they were curated, which was the 1,025th anniversary of the baptism of Kyivan Rus', which was to be marked by a visit from President Yanukovych and the Ukrainian Orthodox Patriarch. In response, the independent artists' organization, Self-Defense Initiative (ICTM), issued an open letter describing the act, which soon garnered international support. Two foreign curators invited to oversee Kyiv's Biennale in 2014 withdrew their acceptance, and the editor of the prominent industry journal *Art Ukraine* stepped down from her position.

In addition to the destruction of artwork, it is critical to document the fact that the exhibit itself was designed from the outset as somewhat of a baptismal ritual within Ukraine's leading art institution. The cultivation of public preferences for art within the bounds of religious doctrine placed artistic production in the service of shoring up state power under Yanukovych.[28] Artists Nikita Kadan, Yevgenia Belorusets, and others who sat for weeks in the courtroom and spoke as witnesses at Kutnetzov's trial tend to publicly position themselves as socially engaged artists unaffiliated with any established institution. In this case, the artist Kuznetzov had initiated the civil suit over copyright and moral damages. The trial has dragged on (still unresolved as of 2019). A group called Method Fund, led by REP artist Lada Nakonechna, continues to fundraise in order to help pay the court fees, along with raising awareness around this and other issues related to artists' relations with cultural institutions in Ukraine.[29]

Although a singular incident on the margin of the mainstream, the ongoing case highlights a much wider phenomenon in Ukraine's cultural establishment that draws equivalency between "religion" and "progress," a line that persists in part due to the history of the atrocities committed by the atheist Soviet state and its repressive regime.[30] At times

Figure 4.4. *Koliyivshchyna: Judgement Day*, work in progress, 2013, painting on the wall, text, photos, video, archives, screenshots, official letters, media publications, official documents, the lawsuit. By Volodymyr Kuznetsov. volodymyrkuznetsov.com. Shared by permission of the artist.

Soviet artists chose the strategy of complete detachment from the public sphere. It is significant that Zablotna acted in a Soviet manner, without consulting anyone, but then destroyed the painting in the same way that Orthodox monks in Kyivan Rus' would have destroyed religious icons that did not conform to the strict rules that govern the formal properties of icon painting. To condemn Zablotna's act, protestors gathered inside Kyiv's museum Mystetskyi Arsenal and returned her gesture in-kind by holding up large black paper squares over their faces.

The black square is a reference to the early Soviet artist Kazimir Malevich's famous painting from 1917, reindexed in the demonstration as the mark of the censor. Artists responded to similar trials against Yevgenia Belorusets, Andriy Movchan, Serhiy Movchan, and Aleksandr Volodarsky in the mid-2000s by organizing a program of discussions, publications, and artworks under the name Court Experiment Project.[31] They effectively transformed the conditions and environment of limited agency into the material for an alternative grammar on creative legality. It appeared as though history were turning back on itself in the coding of speech versus silence.

The history of Malevich's life and work is intertwined with the development of the Soviet art establishment and the self-contradictory pressure placed on artists to create nonconformist art in the interest of the state. Malevich himself, like many painters of his time, was inducted into the Artists Union as an official member and therefore became tasked with the dangerous, and somewhat oxymoronic, position of a "professional" revolutionary. Foundational to the modernist canon, his black square came to define the anti-aesthetic concepts rooted in the deconstructive graphics and industrialist aesthetics that the Soviets would then counterbalance with socialist realism throughout most of the twentieth century. Malevich's sign for revolution in this context subverts the eclipsing effect of the black paint that Zablotna had used to destroy Kuznetsov's painting as a language with which to frame the framer.

The protest worked against the instrumentalization of art by recalling the earlier suppression of abstract art. The point was not to locate what was permitted inside or outside the museum (or to attribute moral judgment to Malevich in a reactionary gesture), but to destabilize the practices encrypted into the frame. It is worth mentioning that Zablotna responded to the protest by labelling her destruction of the artwork her own "performance."[32] The artists, students, and scholars involved in the protest were drawn into a fight with the state over the definition of censorship. Necessarily, this fight occurred on the negative terrain of demanding the right to self-expression by being able to express what it is *not*; in other words, the stakes of the conflict hinged on the rhetorical conditions providing the right to publicly name censorship.

The notion of an individual revolution, internal to the self, has a particular past in the history of repressive regimes. In literature and art across cultures, varying notions of censorship have fostered the development of specific formal artistic devices for illustrating conceptions of the self in an oppressive environment. By showing what is *not* permitted in print or in public, authors and artists have long dealt the cards of their own poker game, so to speak, revealing the irony of the need for a game face at all. There are many anecdotes about writing "for the drawer" in Slavic cultures, and so self-censorship makes its way into the arts as a thematic device in and of itself. Dostoevsky is well known for his characters' disembodied voices, whose conversational threads become finely wrought and entangled in the narrative, destabilizing the linear plot structure of the nineteenth-century Russian novel and the concept of authority in ethics and polemics, as Bakhtin argued in his theory of dialogism.

Fantastic beings and hauntings also appear throughout both Russian and Ukrainian texts in the nineteenth century as allegories for the self, which is often multiple or doubled. In the twentieth century, authors diffused the weight of the censor while writing under socialism by employing, in some cases, elements from folk tales and legends in political metaphors and allegories for the state. In perhaps the most well known depiction of censorship in the literary establishment, *Master and Margarita*, Mikhail Bulgakov's protagonist, Master, wrestles to write his manuscript about Pontius Pilate while a pesky devil – a playful Slavic folk devil (quite different from Milton's or other Western devils) – keeps returning to him in the form of a shape-shifting feline foreign gentleman named Woland. At the end of the novel, the devil leads both the Master and his Margarita out of Soviet Moscow into a realm resembling purgatory, after which the Master frees Pontius Pilate from punishment. Common to these examples and countless others is a vision of creativity as negative freedom: an outpouring of the inner self that at once counters, and is shaped by, the terms upon which it is silenced externally.

The independent artists' union Self-Defense Initiative (ICTM), formed by artists in Kyiv, is based on a set of objectives connected to democracy and "the formation of new cultural policy principles and how they are put into practice" in Ukraine.[33] Larissa Babij explains the union's mission as creating spaces for reflection as a "thinking community," without any aspiration to govern. Individuality and revolution are emphasized:

> We make no claims on the empty space designated for a leader. On the contrary, our work is aimed at creating open spaces for reflection on the very conditions that fill that space with restrictions on ideology, or events. Such a "thinking community" cannot be dictated from above. It can only expand horizontally on an individual basis, as a series of individual revolutions.[34]

Articulating the creative self against a backdrop of public repression, the "thinking community," and the "individual revolution," Babij refers to prior conditionings of the self within the contexts of the twentieth century. Here, the self becomes most vibrant when in retreat from society – it is a vision of the self constantly articulated in language that is flexible enough to circumlocute the authority of the state.

Arendt observed how the Stoics' conception of the self as an "inner polis" estranged from public life emerged with the fall of Athens during the rise of the Roman Empire, a time of great disappointment in democratic ideals. In the Soviet era, an author's ability to inhabit the space of the book morphs into a supple game of masks to avoid the censor; the game itself moves to the centre of art. Upon returning to Soviet Russia from exile, Viktor Shklovsky, along with the other Formalists, came under attack by Marxist traditionalists who denounced him as a practitioner of comparative literature, considered bourgeois (by 1930 "aesthetic estrangement" had become an intellectual crime). Svetlana Boym has pointed to a parallelism in the Soviet modernist period between the surveillance of the polis and the confinement of the writerly imagination: "The two deaths of the author – one a playful self-constraint and the other the acceptance of the state *telos* – are not the same."[35] Boym derives her concept of freedom from among artists and writers whom she terms the "off-moderns" of the Soviet period, in which freedom is "an existential imperative" to be found in "co-creation." She refers to Shklovsky's diagram of the knight's chess move (khod konia), which he named the "tortured road of the brave," as an allegory of the intelligentsia under Soviet rule and the sideways manoeuvres between pawns and kings that its members were forced to invent just in order to survive beyond the dictates of the regime. In 1926 Shklovsky penned *Third Factory*, a text about censorship as an artistic problem. An example of the concept of freedom from above, his text contained literary devices that would serve as blueprints for the parables and codes by which the Soviet intelligentsia would learn to speak in order to circumvent the censors.[36]

In the twentieth-century Soviet city, the metropolis became the embodiment of these exchanges as the epitome of unfreedom, but also a vital source of inspiration. Despite the bureaucratic restrictions, and sometimes fatal, consequences of becoming an author at the time, a veritable renaissance ensued in early Soviet Kyiv. Kyiv became an important centre for film and graphic art, even in spite of the fact that the Ministry of Culture and the Writers' Union in Moscow centralized all production, closely managing the visual graphics and composition in advertising, cinema, public announcements, textbooks, and other genres to ensure they conformed to a unified ideology. In the 1920s fast cuts and montage, for example, were developed extensively as cinema became the government's preferred mode of communicating its policies to citizens. Propaganda trains with mini cinemas set up inside their cars travelled throughout the countryside to "educate" the peasants. Beginning in 1929 Stalin pursued his policy of collectivization and its transferral of Ukraine's large peasant population into communal farms and factories. But the city provided only a temporary refuge for artists. The tangible effects of man-made famine under Stalin in 1931–33, officially recognized as Holodomor, were soon felt everywhere. This contradicted the happy-go-lucky imagery of the films aimed at exporting the revolution beyond the city.[37] Artists themselves felt the pressures acutely, as they came to occupy an especially dangerous role in having to learn to navigate the tightrope of artistic innovation versus conformism in their work. The ideology demanded of them was based on a coming future utopia, but was, in reality, the fetishization of revolution itself – the impossibility of utopia rendered in art and text.

Recodings

The visual experiments of the twentieth century have left deep traces, as both scars and achievements, in post-Soviet Kyiv artists' investigations into the politics of the self, censorship, and the question of what freedom and progress could look like. Svetlana Boym has explored the history of the idea of freedom in Soviet modernism, using the image of Tatlin's tower and Shklovsky's diagonal chess move to point out differences from the West.[38] She traces the development of a sense of being in-between, circumlocution, and evasion as sources of both creative expression and democratic thinking.

REP's and HudRada's work is rooted in a similar antipolitical ethics in which their artistic expression becomes subversive in its total detachment from being neither in service to the state nor directly counter to its logic in any way. Artists often pose questions about freedom in space within formal experiments that employ scale and prior formal conventions from Monumentalism and Futurism. Artists in Kyiv have founded artist-run spaces as well as an alt gallery (LabGarage) in which organizers invite contributors to create pieces that are visible twenty-four hours a day through apertures on the side of the garage.[39] Many of the works focus on sites that were, at one time or another, places of everyday social interaction under socialism and have since been overlooked or ignored in the new economy. Such sites also function as important places in these communities for gathering to share ideas, celebrate achievements, and mark other significant events. Public gatherings and manifestations recode spaces such as garages, large avenues, or crumbling seas of grey apartment blocs, or *Khrushchovka*, as they are now commonly called, in reference to their construction in the 1960s under then president of the Soviet Union, Nikita Khrushchev – all spaces that were once central to Soviet planners' utilitarian zoning of urban space into places for personal reflection, socializing, and intellectual exchanges. This site specificity also provides participants with a modicum of artistic autonomy. The resulting forms and conflicts between urban space, media, and design can be read as conceptualizing and challenging the limits of where more mainstream galleries, museums, and normative spaces fail to represent lived experience.

In a series for the exhibit *Ukrainian Body*, artist Anatoly Belov created condensed sketches of sexualized women's bodies rendered from hundreds of image searches. The result resembles Femen's projections of the imagined sexual female ideal. The body and its position within space is in and of itself a function of ideology and politics: the internet here appears less liberating than amplifying of private consumerist desires and their shaping of sex and gender. The "shock" of Belov's work, this drawing being part of a larger project entitled *The Most Pornographic Book in the World* (figure 4.5), lies in the fact that the sexuality it expresses is quite banal. The female body appears in complete submission to the desires expressed within the social body, which is repeated here as we would expect it to appear in its marketed form. As in Kadan's surrealist apartment landscape, the feminization of virtual space also stems from the manipulation of the natural sex drive in an ideal that also serves a regulatory function. Here, however, the function is the consumption of the whore taboo, rather than the reproductive function of the domestic feminine ideal. The hand-drawn format transfers these idealizations from the sphere of mass production to the personalized image. In shifting the interlocuters across these two genres, the image challenges viewers to question its authenticity as advertisement or portrait. The outcome calls to mind Ralph Steadman's aesthetic or Femen's hyperbolic "sextremist" headlines in the scrawled black wording and the citation of commercial pornography.

The HudRada collective could be said to put into social action what it tries to imagine in art: a total aversion to the trappings of ideological "–isms" through attempts at voluntary disassociation and detachment. The value of this experiment is linked to its public nature. By drawing contrasts between the individual and the state, I argue that across all these artworks the concept of the self emerges more truthfully, highlighting the fictitious terms upon which the social contract always rests.

In *Civil Disobedience* Arendt reasons through the flaw inherent in the social contract as a "fictitious origin of consent" by premising inalienable individual will upon its capacity to enter into voluntary association with others. Dissent, then, as opposed to the Kantian conscience that entrusts itself to tacit "consensus universalis" (Tocqueville), in Arendt's view, admits the fiction of democracy in order to approximate it: "Dissent implies consent, and is the hallmark of free government; one who knows that he may dissent knows also that he somehow consents when he does not dissent."[40] By reappropriating and recoding urban space, HudRada, as a voluntary association of artists, mounts a critique of the state against the backdrop of vanishing public freedoms.[41] Through the opposing motifs of liberation and constraint, the thematic content of the *Draftsmen's Congress* characterized these spaces as sites for communicating the role of art in the National Gallery to local and global audiences in the summer of 2013, just before the Maidan Revolution would scatter and rearrange these negative spaces even further.

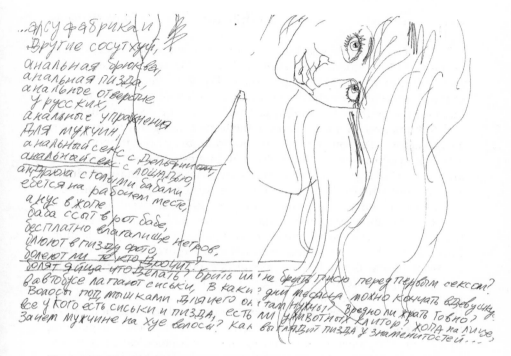

Figure 4.5. *The Most Pornographic Book in the World,* by Anatoly Belov, Kyiv, 2011–2012. Exhibited by VCRC. Printed in *Prostory: Documenting Maidan.* Shared with permission of the artist.

IV. Inside the Assembly: Marginality in *Draftsmen's Congress*

The notion of "the political" deployed by participants in *Draftsmen's Congress* has antecedents in the supra-national orientation of the early avant-garde. The mural at the centre of the exhibit takes its technical cues from action painting, but mimics the format of the 1990s European trans-avant-garde where *tusovkas* (get-togethers) in Kyiv often featured gigantic collaborative paintings and murals. A member of this prior avant-garde, the Polish artist Paweł Althamer, founder of Grupa Nowolipie,[42] first created the concept for *Draftsmen's Congress* and was joined in Kyiv by VCRC and HudRada.[43] The format of the *Congress* followed that of a *tusovka*: it involved a room totally covered in a white surface containing paints, charcoals, pens, markers, and other materials with which the public was invited "to draw one's inner emotions, convictions, and demands."[44] At the end of the installation, its surfaces were dismantled into pieces and distributed at no cost to participants and passersby.

The first in Althamer's series premiered in an abandoned cathedral in Berlin, with subsequent installations in Venice, Warsaw's Praga District, and Eisenhüttenstadt, a small town on the Polish-German border where, in the absence of an established museum, participants donated the dismantled pieces from the exhibit to small shops for display. HudRada and Althamer retain mutual roots in the trans-avant-garde in two ways: a negotiation with power hierarchies to promote artistic autonomy, and a critical eye towards authority. Both are interested in pointing out the anachronisms of post-Soviet contexts by juxtaposing mass-produced art-for-profit with the legacies of the Soviet systematization of culture.

Each of the individual images works on different semantic levels to convey ideas about dramatic social, economic, and national change; on the whole, they cohere around diverse experiences of marginalization. For example, the most visible slogan in the Kyiv mural directly confronts the trope of loss through which people's experiences were previously translated into collective meaning during the transition from Soviet to post-Soviet life: "There are no victims. There are no criminals."[45] One of the exhibit's organizers, Mykola Skyba, described the exhibit as an attempt to shift the focus of museum activity towards society, explaining that "after Ukraine's independence, once the ideological current was switched off," the local, post-Soviet museum "essentially became a no-man's land."[46] The metaphor aptly fits Ukraine's ongoing position as a borderland between Poland and Russia, with the museum as a microcosm of public life orchestrated almost entirely from above:

> It is clear that this area, left outside the influence of state agencies, has not become an entirely public zone. The institutionalization of civil society, practically speaking, is still going on today. So in fact we're talking about the creation of, again, a no-man's land, which sooner or later will fall under the expanding control of those with influence in socio-economic processes.[47]

Skyba casts the conflict between the old and new guard of professionals in the museum as a clash of generations. My idea of the superfluous woman, which is, essentially, rooted in a similar generational gap, fits within this clash. Skyba turns to the language of the *raznochintsy*, railing at the failures of Tsar Alexander II's emancipation of the serfs:

> Within the museum community a tense encounter played out between the generation of museum functionaries and the new generation of museum professionals, who actually are not allowed to make strategic decisions, though they have sufficient capabilities. As an illustration, the former

could be compared to vassals who have received fiefs from their over-lords. The latter could be called "self-made" men and women: this gen-eration values self-realization and development based on free initiative.[48]

Appearing in the exhibit catalogue and circulated in several online jour-nals with an international readership, the essay frames the social role of an artist in locally polyvalent terms. The author adopts the archetype of the organic intellectual in a stance that challenges official state mu-seum institutions on the whole not for being foreign, as the Slavophiles who subscribed to the archetype would have done, but because the mu-seum, in failing to encompass its own public of intellectuals, patrons, and nonexperts, has become rigid and alien.

Towards "Agoraphilia"

HudRada's drive to organically create a broad local audience for their work interrogates the national frames of art systems and the values, tastes, and judgments that these systems generate. Critic Piotr Piotrowski has called this impulse more broadly "agoraphilia" – "the drive to enter the public space, the desire to participate in that space, to shape public life, to perform critical and design functions for the sake of and within the social space."[49] This is key in the artistic culture of the countries of the former Eastern Bloc, where states have at one time or another possessed methods for subordinating the public sphere to political doctrine.

Aesthetically associated with a radicalism that fetishizes the pub-lic square in and of itself, the manifestation of "negative space" in the open centre of the mural in *Draftsmen's Congress* is thus a metaphor for oppositional thinking more generally that is present throughout all of the projects associated with HudRada and REP. It comes as little surprise that members of both of these groups and the grassroots art union ICTM were also among the demonstrators on the Maidan who organized media outlets and hotlines, and worked with student unions advocating nonviolence. As participants in various protest activities on the left – not all directly related to art – throughout Kyiv's interrevolu-tionary decade, these artists had long depicted the ideologies govern-ing civic life in Ukraine as emanating from a rotten throne.

In 1989 the Kyiv artist Dmitry Kavsan created a triptych, *Trees in the Garden of de Sade*, that – in both form and content – could be said to convey similar messages about the corrupted centre at a time of radical political and social upheaval. First displayed as part of the exhibit *The Smell of Fish*, all three panels, shown in figure 4.6, were installed in Kyiv so that they spatially formed the shape of a well (as in a village), at the centre of which contained a cardboard box with an actual rotten fish.[50]

Figure 4.6. *Trees from the Garden of de Sade*, by Dmitry Kavsan, 1989, Kyiv. From the personal collection of Dmitry Kavsan. Courtesy of PinchukArtCentre.

As part of the so-named South Russian Wave (Pivdennorosiis'ka kh-vylia) of avant-garde tusovka artists, Kavsan in this work discursively linked Kyiv to the massive changes taking place in nearby Poland, which gained independence that year. The paintings are also interesting in their address to the legend of the Marqi de Sade by contrasting beauty with decay, and their situatedness within the lands of the former Pale of Settlement, heightening the Chagall quality of this aesthetic rendering to that of a shtetl myth. The display of large canvases on the floor, arranged around an object, doubly frames the space. This rendering of revolutionary time and space evokes Bruno Schulz's *Street of Crocodiles* – stories that unfold as intersecting planes propped up along the byways and red-light district in the city of Drohobych, which is described in text in a way that makes it impossible to map out: the narrative moves in spirals. Here Kavsan's garden of de Sade, as in the *Disputed Territory* mural, is a microcosm of imaginary Kyiv – and by extension Ukraine – inside another/other Europe. Moreover, this is a Europe that contains multitudes: the layered past(s) of Ukrainian, Polish, Jewish, and

Western fantasies, doublings, and a shared well that can be at once corrupted by memory and spontaneously life-giving.

The aesthetics of the Kyiv *Draftsmen's Congress* mural revolved around a collage of impressionistic realism, pop culture, graphic art, graffiti, and expressionism. Standing at the centre of the installation's concave walls, the spectator becomes part of the exhibit and can create, block, or intercept messages between images inscribed on the walls. The placement of new slogans, shapes, and colours alongside, below, across from, directly over, or in any other relation to the other traces left by previous participants comprises an open text (figure 4.7). This radically unfinished form contrasts with the halls of polished gilt frames and nineteenth-century portraiture under heavy glass in the museum's more permanent collections. The prioritizing of anonymity over recognized authorship in the mural's unsigned graffiti – itself a contradiction in terms – worked against the selective profiling of the canon in Ukraine's National Art Museum, where few works were shown from the twentieth-century collection that dated later than 1917.[51]

The total and freeform use of surface in the mural lent the panels an interlocking, nonsequential expansiveness. In modernism the theme of expansion, as well as the idea of building and dismantling things, was equated with invention. Marshall Berman describes Jackson Pollock's drip paintings as a symptom of symbolism's withering away at the turn of the century: a time when "man loses himself in a forest of symbols, only to find himself again."[52] Around the same period in Soviet art, it is not the poet or the painter, but the modern scientific industrial engineer who comes to represent the epitome of human creativity. By contrast, Berman roots constructivism in Dostoevsky's fascination with London's Crystal Palace. It is not the actual structure that amazes him, but its impracticality as a kind of spectacle of its own that is valued more for the process of drafting and designing than for the quality of the final structure.[53] The process is the form. Negativity becomes the horizon of critique.

In the Kyiv mural, the images can be read as a chronicle of messages that parody the state's language for apprehending its own citizenry – the outcome appears as a system in disrepair, or a display of construction-in-progress: "LGBT heals everyone! LGBT is good for people!" and "After death, nothing matters." Religious iconography associated with the Orthodox Church appears in several places, but in a mestizo graffiti style that includes references to local pagan rites: the bright colours, ancestral skulls, and the motif of female sainthood mirror the goddess portraits in the urban murals of Mexico City and Los Angeles, as much as they echo Ukrainian village funeral rites.

Figure 4.7. *There Are No Victims. There Are No Criminals.* Fragment. Photo by the author, Kyiv, 2013.

Attempting to excise from the mural different images to read them as individual statements with subversive political content would miss its intertextual dimensions. The work of participants in constructing the mural, and their assembly into a collective, however provisional and guided by the curatorial collective preceding the artwork itself, I would argue, is also a kind of polemic on the mural as public art, a "test of its specificity" as an "art with a politic" that "seeks to produce a concept of the political relevant to our present. A purchase on this concept is no doubt difficult, provisional – but that may well be the test of its specificity and the measure of its value."[54]

Participants who contributed to the mural identified themselves within it as gay, left, feminist, HIV positive, eco-punk, pro-choice, anti-war, and more, in a wide range of graffiti and other markings indicating ontological stance. Signs and symbols are blended across several representational schemes and genres signifying dissidence within the mural. Taken together, they communicate a detachment from mainstream politics that also resonates within the same paradigmatic cultural economy of "dissidence" as Pussy Riot's and Femen's body rhetoric. The difference here, however, is that the HudRada curators who worked with Althamer on an installation in Ukraine's National Art Gallery are more committed to site specificity, employing virtual audiences in their work almost exclusively with reference to local issues. One effect of this is a reclaiming of the physical spaces in which art "takes place" in site-specific installations that provoke questions about the role of the body in political processes, and what it might mean for creativity to have political relevance.

It is significant that the mural evolved in conjunction with similar events held elsewhere in Europe, connected by video and internet. Bruno Latour's "assemblage" in his Actor-Network Theory offers a good starting point for interpreting this visual collage as an *art-efact* caught in the gap between the European Union and Ukraine, the flow between the Orange Revolution and the Maidan Revolution of Dignity, and the shift of generations. He asks, "Once the task of exploring the multiplicity of agencies is completed, another question can be raised: What are the *assemblies* of those *assemblages*?"[55] A few months after the exhibit, then-incumbent president Viktor Yanukovych's refusal to sign the EU Association Agreement would spark the Maidan Revolution. Ukrainian artists' positioning of themselves within a complex set of international political relationships would evolve, but not change shape.

To understand the images in the mural as somehow signifying a one-to-one description of participants' identities risks reducing its layered meanings into static units of expression. Instead, the potential meanings in the conflicts between images are like Lyotard's diffèrends: for example, the statement "Everything is alright with us" (У нас все нормально) over a rainbow flag, or the word "fight" below the triangle prism from Pink Floyd's *Dark Side of the Moon*. The signs have no clear referents. Some images suggest solidarity with global movements around gender, health, ecology, civil rights, and antiglobalization.

In the tensions between local and global the mural goes one step further to open up the possibility that the "assemblies" of people, supposedly represented by these civic symbols, are themselves collectively empowered by calling their local contexts into question. The social "assemblage" in the mural, in this sense, does not really refer to identity politics at all, but to what gender critics often point to as a politics of difference in which identities are always in flux through performance. The dialectical recombinations of sign/signified within the mural bring together powerful tropes of "the dissident" from disparate cultural sites, albeit in a localized post-Soviet form. The fall of the Berlin Wall is pervasive in the design of the event, lending the entire exhibit, its images, and its material objects a sense of collective monumentality. A camera placed in the centre of the mural recorded everything as people wrote and painted on the walls – and then disassembled them – distributing their fragments among themselves and interested passersby for free.

The pieces of the mural structurally resemble artefacts of a conversation that might be considered as a breakdown in communication. Nation, the body, notions of civic freedom, and a broader range of discourses attached to these ideas were reaching a boiling point in Ukraine in late 2013. At the time this mural was created, crackdowns on protest were at an all-time high: Femen activists had permanently emigrated to Paris, Pussy Riot members had gone to jail and been attacked at Sochi, several activists in Ofenzywa and other LGBTQ-friendly groups had been attacked by the far right, and at least three censorship cases against artists were pending in the Kyiv municipal courts. Perhaps due to the shrinking availability of physical spaces for dissent under an oppressive regime (street protest being the only form of peaceful civic disobedience left in a corrupt court system), the body remained central to the Kyiv mural, not only in its imagery, but also in its position within the public sphere.

In one mural fragment the word "Фуко" (Foucault) appears beneath the red rays of a panoptical camera tower. A factory with a death's head on it spews toxic fumes, under which appears the Spanish anarchic slogan *"No Pasarán!,"* a slogan adopted by Nadezhda Tolokonnikova of Pussy Riot in court while on trial in mid-2012. A female prisoner in blue stripes carries a sign with a message in solidarity with Turkish women and stands behind a black podium on which is written: "Freedom Is

Never Free." Another fragment features a cartoon of a nude woman with a speech bubble, stating "Мої ліки – без мети збуту" (My medicine – without intent to sell), behind which is written "Cures Not War"; this exchange is likely a response to stigmas attached to different drug therapies in prevention and treatment programs introduced at the time to address Ukraine's ongoing, soaring HIV/AIDS epidemic. The black text in both panels and the references to news headlines transfer media aesthetics to a paint medium. Yet unlike the so-called information wars that drive media regimes, the overall message here stands at a far remove from party politics. The common denominator is detachement itself – pacifism according to an internet generation that grew up during the Orange Revolution and the Iraq war.

The political valences in the mural's rainbow motifs might be thought of in terms of "sexual dissent." Coined at the height of the debates over pornography legislation in the United States in the eighties, the term itself originates in the history of censorship. Lisa Duggan, founder of the Feminist Anti-Censorship Task Force (FACT), defined it as "a concept that involves a unity of speech, politics, and practices, and forges a connection among sexual expressions, oppositional politics, and claims to public space."[56] The representation of the individual in sexual dissent depends less on the nature of expression than on the publicity of the representative vis-à-vis the collective. Returning to Arendt's concept of "voluntary association," in which the civil disobedient is defined by their individual membership in a group that is bound by opinion (rather than actual or achievable interests, as in the case of the conscientious objector), the individual conscience thus stands in tenuous relation to other consciences, but is also bound to them as an opinion adhering to a group. Affiliation in the group is reinforced by the number of its members and the group's shared opinions, as opposed to incentives that are bound to concrete outcomes.

Many scholars of democracy have tested the paradox that the social contract at the very core of democracy depends on civil disobedience. Later in life, Hannah Arendt mounted a defence of the public value of dissent, observing the explosion of protest in the United States in the fifties and sixties. She based her position on the fact that law, by definition, cannot legislate its own transgression, even though democracy is strengthened by civil interpretations of the law.[57] Artists' individualized expressions of a marginalized subjectivity might be viewed similarly: as a critique and therefore, ultimately, also a defence of their own bodies as the vehicles of such transgression. Contributors to the Kyiv mural contested the social codes that govern the marginalization of the body in Ukraine's public spaces. The images evidence multiple discursive strategies by which individual participants became interlocutors in a network, each speaking about their own locality.

Thus, negative space differs from pure negativity in the concept of the political deployed by participants working on the mural. Altogether separate from true anarchy or nihilism, although aesthetically associated with both in a radicalism that fetishizes the public square, the manifestation of "negative space" in the mural emerges as a sign for oppositional thinking more generally.

The notion of an *aesthetic of anarchism* and the idea that it can encompass a radical critique of democracy appears as a sceptical counterweight to utopianism writ large. In the context of post-Soviet art, anarchism is the epistemological rejection of both the permanence of the Red Revolution and the neoliberal promises of "shock capitalism" introduced in the 1990s. Given anarchism's Slavic roots, often traced to Bakunin and Makhno, it is also a radical signifier that gains traction in artists' evasions of the proscribed models of rebellion from the Cold War: those associated with being a dissident, versus an artist-citizen in service of the state (models that both the Soviets and the West each adopted in their own ways). I agree with Piotr Piotrowski that the symbols, customs, and habits that guide public life in postcommunism tend to be more continuous with the socialist past, despite official state attempts to force a break with those symbols. A highly synthetic and specious type of cultural governance entrenches itself on all scales through leaders who shore up their power by presenting themselves as "adversaries of the fallen system," and who, by association, lean totalitarian.[58]

Piotrowski argues that in emerging East European art, anarchism has come to stand not for a program of any kind, but for a critical appeal rooted in the impulse to investigate and remain sceptical of utopian rhetoric. He describes this opposition as "democratizing democracy," which I interpret to be anarchism as a critical mediator for making visible political methods of coercion, without having to directly critique individuals.[59] In this view of anarchism-as-aesthetics, ambivalence is figured as a radical performative technique, supplying an exit strategy from the traps of blame, victimization, and binary polemics that have plagued the region's politics (Piotrowski traces the particularities of his claim to Zbigniew Libera's renderings of the Polish experience, but similar appropriations of anarchism as a sign for general suspicions towards the status quo also exist in the history of punk music beginning with London in the 1970s).[60]

In Ukraine, where access to art is managed by the Ministry of Culture, heavy centralization still contributes to the overall bureaucratization of creative production. Artists complain that their work so often does not fit preconceptions of what art "should do," and so they find themselves relegated to the periphery. The state and the market work arbitrarily and in tandem in the cultural sphere. Art, even as praxis, is itself maintained as a marginal category, sequestered from public access and left out of the curriculae of major universities. This inaccessibility manifests in public disinterest, and policies that block artists in contemporary Kyiv from attempting to question the logic of marginality reproduced by state institutions of art that still cling to a Soviet format. The alienation of the individual in Western art thus differs from the post-Soviet artist's renderings of the self, the latter being more inflected by inert bureaucracy.

State and Nation in (Anti)Representational Art

Postmodernist literary scholars have also linked the prevalence of direct address, fragmentation, and sarcastic readaptations of Western countercultural symbols in Russian and Ukrainian letters of the youngest generation to the radical individualism brought on by market reform in an "aesthetics of anarchy."[61] The anarchist symbol itself appeared more than a few times in the several layers of paint that participants applied over the Kyiv mural's changing surfaces. Indexing anarchy as a global signifier for dissent, the mural now appears as a window into visionary gestures towards a city, and a nation, about to undergo mass revolution.

The artist David Chichkan, in the same circles and generation as the participants in the Kyiv mural, created a painting in 2018 featuring three women carrying a sign with the anarchist slogan "No God, No King, No Lord, No Nation" (figure 4.8) The title of the image links the brief window of Ukrainian independence in 1919–21, after the civil war, when Nestor Makhno led the Ukrainian anarchist army, to the only other of its kind on the territories of modern Europe, the Spanish anarchists fighting Franco's repressions in the 1930s.

On a formal level, the collapse of artistic display into practice in post-communism shifted art from representation to language, in which the spectator is no longer objectively removed from the production of art, but intervenes as an interlocutor. The artist becomes a manipulator of signs, more than a producer of an object, through the mural's situational address to participants standing at its centre. A probing of the material basis of art revealed itself in intertextual references that equated the museum with the Ukrainian state. In one segment, cutout leaflets from the museum's marketing materials were recombined in a collage involving national symbols: the trident, colours of the Ukrainian flag, and quotes from recent official speeches. Here and elsewhere, artists contrasted state symbols with images of completely opposite emotional charges.

Figure 4.8. *This Could Happen in Ukraine Earlier than in Spain / No God, No King, No Lord, No Nation, No Borders*, by David Chichkan, 2018. Shared with permission of the artist.

Focusing first on the institutional frame, and second on the economics of the modern art commodity, signifiers in the mural shifted within the contemporaneity of a constitutive public, tracing gaps between itself and Ukraine's ideological museum complex. The outcome is an illustration of the limits to the state museum's original referents in the latter's claiming to encompass or represent *the* nation before a public.

The mural is further grounded in the politics of location in both its content and form. In one figure, the rendering of a ballerina points to contrasting aesthetic forms, ballet having remained a major export of a heavily censored, centralized, and nationalized state art system since the nineteenth century and well into the twenty-first. The figure's alternative rendering challenges the homogenization of culture by underwriting the tradition of ballet with graffiti. Given that modern dance, like modern art, has more or less remained absent from Kyiv's cultural scene, the image undercuts the ongoing monopolization of the arts into state commodities. This phenomenon is inherited from the Soviets' attempts to level aristocratic sociality with peasant folkways through the heavy regulation and subsidization of theatre (dance being central to both high and low art forms). The quote in yellow chalk added to the layers of messages covering the dancer conveys a sense of exhaustion and release from an unjust state of affairs: "How much can you complain? Finally just say something good!" The ball of thread in the dancer's left hand combines the revered "high" form of ballet with the "low" knitting work of a peasant woman, further juxtaposing the physically demanding, but gracefully hidden labour of dance with the dutiful performance of more mundane tasks.

The interpretation of the overall image is left open to the viewer, although the playful tone of the colourful cartoons and phrases around the dancer bring out a hopeful element from the darker, impressionistic tones of the portrait. As elsewhere in the mural, a general sentiment of detachment prevails in its phraseology. There is no direct mention of individuals or groups; rather, the mural contains a more generalized critique of local power hierarchies on a surface insulated from attack or suppression (even if only momentarily so, and not elsewhere in the city). Louis Althusser's definition of ideology as how one legitimizes oneself vis-à-vis politics is relevant here.[62] Anonymous graffiti arguably demonstrates a notion of freedom specific to a generation's singular experience of postcommunism: the total lack of any consistent vocabulary with which to localize the dominant practices that have created marginal social categories in the first place. The mural's position as a grassroots project – staged from within the National Art Gallery – is an antipolitical stance towards the extraction of profit from the art object as commodity, and labour from the artist as cultural worker. It is a disarticulation of state hegemony under Yanukovych in a radical comment on dissent itself. Artists' actual struggles to form unions that would give them a living wage by reforming Ukraine's privatized art scene are thus bound up with the abstract question of freedom in their art. Both impulses involve a search for the freedom to define which forms of dissent are permitted by the state and legitimized by the public, and which are not.

The site-specific, concave format of the Kyiv mural also shapes the interpretive possibilities and limits to its design. After the exhibit, the mural was dismantled and placed upon the steps of the museum for participants and passersby to take at no cost (figure 4.9).[63] Instead of a signature, each piece was stamped with the words Конгрес рисувалників 2012 (*Draftsmen's Congress* 2012) in black ink with a standard rubber stamp. Each bore neither the legislative mark of a copyright seal nor the aura of an original signature; the anonymous authorship and unregulated circulation of the artwork signalled a critique of commodity value as arbitrary and unrelated to taste. The material act of dismantling a wall of graffiti, and the comment on dissent in the content of the mural itself, recall the dismantling of the Berlin Wall.

In both instances the notion of resisting, overcoming, and then memorializing not the wall, but the very absence of the wall – the power to create and then break down the wall – is tantamount to the object's significance. In the end, as with the Berlin Wall, it is not owning a piece of the larger mural that is important, but the moment of collective will that it signifies. The uniqueness of the piece *as art* resides in its original production. The value of the remaining art object lies in its ability to reproduce an individual connection to a specific moment in time through its material claim to authenticity.

Thus, the geographic location of the Kyiv mural is also central to its interpretive scope, the Berlin Wall being one of the most immediate discursive backdrops in an exhibit as much about "disputed territory" as redrawing notions of static identity. HudRada's particular artworks reference the frame of their own display to expose the absurdities of local cultural policies. Much of the work in the collective is site specific to the post-Soviet context. In a contrasting example, the artist Mark Wallinger's exhibit *State Britain*, installed in the Tate Britain in 2007, featured a detailed replication of Brian Haw's anti-Iraq-war protest camp that he had set up and maintained in Parliament Square from 2001 until the Arab Spring of 2011, when the British High Court tightened restrictions on public gatherings precisely where the protest had been taking place (figure 4.10). I was visiting London in 2003 and remember observing people serving food and camping in tents. It so happens that the main atrium in the centre of the Tate Britain splits the same perimeter line of one kilometre that was demarcated by the parliament's new law as part of the laudably named Serious Organized Crime and Police Act.[64] Both the original site-specific installation, and its reinstallation, protested against the state's suppression of pacifist anti-Iraq-war activism by contesting the physical boundary of the state's jurisdiction over the museum.

Averring that the Occupy Wall Street movement of 2011 foregrounded an "iconography of non sovereignty and anonymity," W.J.T. Mitchell

Figure 4.9. Dismantled pieces of the Kyiv Mural distributed to the public, on the steps of the National Art Museum of Ukraine (NaMU). Photo by the author, 2013.

discusses Jeffersonian democracy within the exhibit as the image of "perpetual revolution ... in the form of election cycles, requir[ing] that the place of sovereignty and power remains empty in principle (but certainly not in practice). The important thing is the office, not the flesh-and-blood occupant."[65] Thus, he contends that memorials will incline even more towards "not those of *face* but of *space*; not figures, but the negative space or ground against which a figure appears." The exhibit at Tate could never achieve this sort of resonance in Kyiv's museum. While in the West the museum is generally a backdrop – a highly polyvalent space in which culture is rearranged, constructed, and dismantled – Ukraine's National Museum clings to an outmoded authority in everything it fails to do (by turning art into objectification and ritual). Contemporary artists thus engage with these spaces as they are: an open battleground for the future of Ukraine, embedded in the institutional logic of the state and its instrumentalization of the creative mind.

Figure 4.10. *State Britain,* by Mark Wallinger. Mixed media installation, 5.7 × 43 × 1.9 m detail, installation at Tate Britain, 2007. Courtesy of the artist and Hauser & Wirth. Photo © Mark Wallinger.

V. Biopolitics in *Disputed Territory*

Many of the works in HudRada's exhibits challenge regional conditionings of post-Soviet life against collapse and nostalgia. By juxtaposing the formal devices and graphic notation used in cartography with emotionally charged images of the body, the works defamiliarize moral narratives proffered both by and about socialism. Prior visions of the enlightened social role of the artist unravel as the didacticism of socialist realism begins to look as absurd as protocols on the museum as a moral arm of the state. These jabs are also attacks on Ukraine's contemporary state-museum complex and the utopian thinking, ideological purity, and oppressive outcomes involved in the attempt to codify a national art. Together, as elsewhere in HudRada's works, like the mural of *Draftsmen's Congress* and the metaphor of "disputed territory," their ideas portray a common landscape – playful and terrifying – that transcends any static notion of politics or the nation.

Writing oneself into the mural and the museum, one engages notions of the self in communication with others about what a shared public space *should* or *could* become. Picking up where Foucault left off, Giorgio Agamben contemplates the rise of state sovereignty in ancient Roman law in the figure of the *Homo sacer*, the body that could be killed but not sacrificed. The regulation of flesh and blood in space and time, Agamben argues, constitutes the origin of the modern nation state: "The production of a biopolitical body is the original activity of sovereign power."[66]

Artists in Ukraine extended the Orange Revolution in the decade intervening between then and the events of 2013–14 by confronting the post-Soviet state in its failure to mediate spaces for dissent and self-expression. In the 2012 action *Territorial Pissings*, three activists created a video of themselves tracing a red trail of paint along a path from Kharkiv's Secret Security Services to the Kyiv Zoo, City Hall, and finally, to the Circus (visually aligned with Security Services). Named after the song by Nirvana, the video was part of a broader set of footage spanning the years 2009–12 involving several artists connected to the Kharkiv-based SOSka Group.[67] As in other artworks produced by SOSka, the central activity in this piece could be viewed as an experiment in the spatial limitations on art in Ukraine's heavily patrolled and regulated cityscape. By "vandalizing" a pathway between old Soviet landmarks, the action's legal ambiguity posed a challenge to the public valuation of art and its supposed function. Positioned somewhere between private spectacle and protest (two opposite impulses that polarize private and state galleries), the experiment's ridiculousness, coupled with its relative harmlessness, challenges audiences to reconsider market and state-driven mandates as equally impairing to the idea of freedom of speech in Ukraine.

The conceptual design of *Territorial Pissings* could be compared to the 1997 propaganda pastiche *Painting by Numbers* by Moscow artists Komar and Melamid. Experimenting with statistics and data as creative material, the two artists polled thousands of random citizens in Russia and the United States on various aesthetic principles, and then mapped their responses into "ideal" paintings. In Komar's and Melamid's works, the manipulation of individual consciousness through statistical notation is revealed by the transferral of mathematical and cartographical language from the contexts of its deployment, back into arbitrary shapes and patterns. This is arguably the same dynamic at work in the action by SOSka's Mykola Ridnyi, Alina Kleytman, and Ulyana Bychenkova.[68] In both instances the physical world is depicted as neither preceding nor following any ideal, but as experienced through processes of writing and painting. Mapping and plotting data are revealed as creative functions of an imaginative template with multiple interpretations.

Ridnyi, Kleytman, and Bychenkova show us that a walk through the city puts the body at risk of arrest, conveying that the regulation of space and its imprints on actual people's everyday lives have tangible effects on what one is able to say, think, and do. This characteristic is palpable among artists identifying themselves as body and performance artists throughout the region's avant-garde and experimental communities.

But there are deeper roots to these flash-mob-style guerrilla tactics that stem from resistance to a resurgence of the surveillance-style societies of the past, but in new, digital forms. The repetition of eyes elsewhere in Ridnyi's work, in my reading of his aesthetic, stems not only from the experience of walking through panopticons everywhere in the post-Soviet built environment, but from the body itself at the centre of new media.

Eric Naiman writes that in Soviet ideology the body remained disturbingly present and central to the tales and pictures that expressed and sought to defuse ideological anxiety. He points to a 1919 work, entitled "Muscles," by Sergei Malashkin:

O muscles of stern labor,
O muscles of arms, O muscles of rumbling legs
you make the wires buzz like bees; you make the bends of the roads
hiss like snakes.
Villages, stations, and cities, having forgotten the bloody years
The apotheosis of bones, the deep groan,
turn the sky red with the joy of banners –
All because of you.
It is because of you that the bodies of factories and plants
The abscesses of purulent mines and pits
Goggle their eyes
and gaze with the electricity of their pupils.
O muscles, O muscles, life comes from you
And scraping with iron against stone, concrete, and granite
It thunderously boils and glorifies you and the ecstasy of creation.

This example captures just how powerfully incarnate, corporeal images suffused ideology in the NEP era, revealing a broad obsession with the body fostered by the Proletkul't. Naiman writes, "All of Russia [was] a body, and its eyes – body parts that observe rather than do – watch with fury as proletarian muscles empower arms and legs across the land."[69]

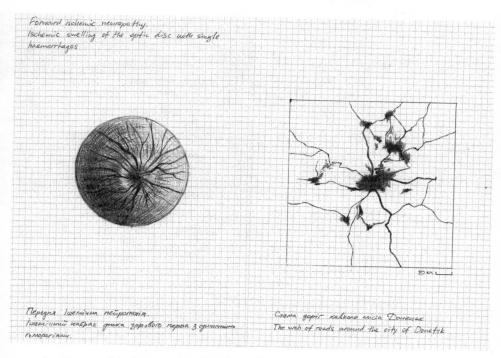

Forward ischemic neuropathy.
Ischemic swelling of the optic disc with single
haemorrhages

Передня Ішемічна нейропатія.
Ішемічний набряк диска зорового нерва з одиничним
геморагіями.

Схема доріг навколо міста Донецьк
The web of roads around the city of Donetsk

Figure 4.11. "Forward Ischemic Neuropathy" and "The Ring of Roads around the City of Donetsk," *Gradual Loss of Vision* series, by Mykola Ridnyi, 2017.

In Western and Central Europe, the surrealists' obsession with eyes, the earliest example of which, in Max Ernst's and Paul Eluard's exchanges, appears in the odd figure of J.J. Grandville's rare etching *The Cynosure of Every Eye* (1844), printed in the broadsheets of Paris in the eighteenth century, re-emerges in Ridnyi's and others' works (especially Vlada Ralko, discussed in the next chapter) around the media production of the Ukraine-Russia conflict. The "Gradual Loss of Vision" expressed through the ring of roads around the city of Donetsk is, in many respects, also about the invisibility of the experiences of people living there in global mass media (figure 4.11).

In *Territorial Pissings*, the language of the map, census, and museum is portrayed at the site of its production: colours and graphics come to stand in for whole populations in the culturally determined processes through which ideas about citizenship are expressed in spatial notation. Ridnyi, Kleytman, and Bychenkova's videorecording of themselves involved painting a red path leading from the Offices of the Secret Service (SBU) to the zoo (figure 4.12). The outcome could be read as being *against the*

Figure 4.12. *Territorial Pissings (Security Service Department – Zoo / Town Council – Circus)* video, 4' 26, by Ulyana Bychenkova, Alina Kleytman, and Mykola Ridnyi, Kyiv, 2012. Shared with permission of the artists.

panopticon: a repositioniong of Komar and Melamid's aesthetic in a metaphor for population control. At once an illegal act, the video is also an affront to Kyiv's commercial galleries, which are owned by local oligarchs who maintain public tastes by privatizing and monopolizing access to contemporary art. The animalistic quality of marking territory through urination underlying the stunt also functions as a statement about reclaiming ownership over individual freedom of expression, however vulgar, against predetermined canons of taste and valuation.[70] Alina Kleytman was the only one of the three artists detained by the police. Meanwhile, Mykola Ridnyi managed to evade the officers' attempts to erase all footage by creating a backup recording of the video.[71]

Yuri Solomko's photography in the series *Human Planet* projects topographical maps onto human bodies with disabilities, conveying overlap and disjuncture between actual borders (national, municipal, economic) and the cultural and social myths that uphold them. In figure 4.13, the female nude stands in for Ukraine and its tenuous relationship with Russia. Crimea is foregrounded as an amputated limb. The pose, matte ivory composition, and the truncation of the body into just a torso, convey not a portrait, but an artefact of sculpture from the height of Athenian Greece. Equating modern photography with an ancient "living" statue, as though in veneration of a goddess or matriarch, the stripe of folk cross-stitch also cues the viewer to draw connections within the ordering of social hierarchies.

As in *Territorial Markings*, the projection of maps directly onto flesh in the construction of the photo can also be read as commentary on

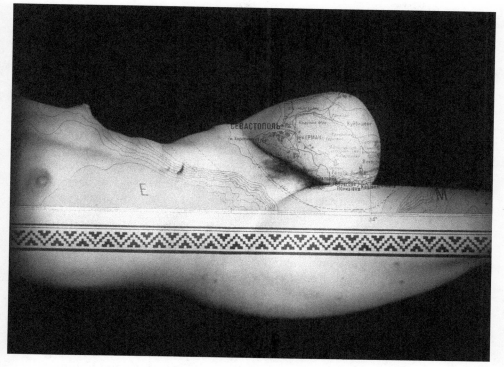

Figure 4.13. *Sevastopol*, from the series *Human Planet*, by Yuri Solomko, 2000. Shared with permission of the artist.

the totalitarian ordering of populations across time and space. In the context of the Russian conquest of Crimea, the map itself now appears highly synthetic, a comment on the discourse of mapping as the manipulation of human perception.

In this interpretation, the photo reveals the arbitrary relationship between culture and the state, employing a female body to draw upon the assumed causality between borders and language in the political rhetoric of the nation state as "motherland," with Russian versus Ukrainian parrying for the status of "mother tongue." The inclusion of both the Ukrainian peasant folk stripe and the Russian language in the map also suggests misalignment between the civilizational identities imposed by borders, as opposed to the coexistence and blending of multiple identities and norms within the actual cultures that transverse them.

Gaps begin to emerge between the illusory "objective" sciences of landscape, and how they are challenged/reinforced by culture.

Discourses of conquest implicit in cartography further underpin the fact that the subject in this photo is a woman, her body the sea, and Sevastopol the seat of the Russian Navy. The absence of any notation from the segment of her body below the folk stripe suggests, through the principle of asymmetry, the contingency and ambivalence with which history becomes grafted upon nature. Had this photo been created after the annexation of Crimea by Putin in early 2014, its resonance with the idea of amputation might be slightly different, appearing more as a comment on overcoming and accepting challenges in national history, rather than averting them.

However, in either instance, time in the photo appears roughly the same: completely unhinged from the map. While in Benedict Anderson's well-known description of the nation-state, the alignment of map and power preceeded borders by mapping space "triangulation by triangulation, war by war, treaty by treaty," here, the territory that is being disputed in this photo is abstracted from actual experience.[72] The projected image of the map is artificial and decorative. The nude female torso is manipulated into a single frame. The black background into which the flesh fades, unlike a sculpture or an actual body, cues the realm of memory while drawing the viewer's attention to the edges of the map. The meaning of the signs for ocean, land, city, nation, etc. and their inherent political and geographical systems are morphologically extended outward towards a "phantom limb," suggesting the impermanence of the living, human qualities that shape our perceptions of time, space, and history.

The photo reflects the central theme of the exhibit in portraying the region as a blank slate, or an empty space – a no-man's-land, like the museum – drawing attention to potentials, more than definitions of what Ukraine should or could become. In this sense, the concept of "negative space" can also take on terrifying tones: an unprotected agora open to seizure by totalitarian ideologies.

It is worth noting that *Disputed Territory* (without *Draftsmen's Congress*) first premiered in Kroshitsky Art Museum in Sevastopol, Crimea, from 26 September to 7 October 2012.[73] The metaphor of "disputed territory" that artists depicted through corporeal metaphors and cartography was later manifested in the political disputes that took place over Ukraine's territory throughout the literal invasion and annexation of Crimea by Putin's command in early 2014. As an image of the nude female body curated by HudRada, which had been censored earlier that year in the *Ukrainian Body* exhibit, the photo already contained traces of meaning linked to public outcries around issues such as "homosexual propaganda" and reproductive rights. The ongoing targeting and attack on LGBTQ and feminist activists that had been occurring for years would manifest in Yanukovych's wider attempt to stifle all civic dissent by ordering Berkut riot police forces to shoot and kill peaceful demonstrators on Kyiv's Maidan.

Thus, the metaphor of "disputed territory" can be read not only as a microcosm of society, but also (and perhaps even more directly connected to the concept of micro/macro) as an externalization of the self unmoored from society in the search for what is forbidden, lost, or uncharted in the production of a uniform citizenry.

Transparency versus Invisibility

The Soviets often used metaphors of anatomy to talk about the nation as a productive unit in order to elevate the worker and idealize the proletariat. One of the curators of *Disputed Territory*, Larisa Venediktova, adopts the language of medicine in her essay about the project, entitled "Homeopathic Aggravation. Simila similibus curantor." She sanctions controversy as a necessary crisis point in a larger process of healing society, referring to Jacques Rancière on aesthetics as a "radical combination of various things" that suffers a viewer "the ability to think in contradiction."[74] Paradox, in her description, is both a source of hypocrisy and the prerequisite for its relinquishment. In this view of art, the curator doles out paradox in an attempt to simulate what subjugates individuals within society, thereby also "curing" its ills through perception. Venediktova leaves open the source of these ills, although the Ukrainian state's repressive measures and the constant fear faced by civil rights demonstrators hover just below the surface of her writing.

Metaphorically, the essay compares such fears to a kind of disease, emerging wherever Venediktova parallels internal medicine with the struggle of the self to express itself. Her corporeal rhetoric departs from earlier Soviet formulations that exhibited an obsessive compulsion towards purification. Thus, freedom in the essay is equated with a blank expression, however inadequate, that still remains preferential to the limits of a totally empty terminology. The body becomes not the repository of the state's anxieties, but an enclosure of individual knowledge. The curator points to this gap between the self and the public as a matter of form. Venediktova writes,

> Homeopathic aggravation "from the similar," from a small dose of a remedy, can be considered an operation of creating empty spaces, transforming the human body (just like the public) from a crowd into society. Here the body (and the social body) becomes a disputed territory for the theory of similarity and the theory of counteraction.[75]

In this theory, the curator seeks to frame the differences between actual bodies in the crowd versus how they are represented – illustrating contrasts within a collective social ideal. The dispute over similarity and counteraction includes the idea that incorporating what is dissimilar in society is not a ready human impulse and that society, like a body, cannot always naturally heal itself. Comparing Ukraine's geography to disability, the photo suggests a gap in the larger process of inclusion/exclusion in the mythmaking of national history, here represented in the insider/outsider relations between Russia and Ukraine on the Crimean peninsula.

Solomko's depiction of the female nude affords a broad range of interpretations in the rhetorical links between nation/anatomy/gender. Nevertheless, and perhaps in its lacking a clear position on actual politics, the photo expounds on the centrality of sex to ideology by offering its own erotic aspects in lieu of the supposed "objectivity" of territorial acquisition. This semantics of the social-as-erotic mirrors the Russian intelligentsia of the early twentieth century. Their similar shift to corporeal metaphor included an overall abandonment of symbolism and its according the individual author or artist a level of spiritual significance aligned with "the norms of the universe"; that was around the same time when, Naiman writes,

> public statements about the importance of sex began to be perceived as an essential component of an intelligent's worldview, and the interplay between sexual and political desires had become a crucial topic with which the writer depicting a better world (or the path thereto) had consciously to grapple.[76]

Here, while the sex of the body is obviously female, the gendered aspects of the photo remain largely neutral. There is no straight line connecting maternal reproduction or masculine virility to the nation and its productivity.[77] By contrast, the attitude towards the biopolitics of post-Soviet statehood is rather ambiguous: here is a body, in visibly good health and most likely of a member of a privileged class, although there is insufficient information to determine much about this person's identity. We only know that the body itself is subject to sets of categorical divisions in its production into the citizen-subject of the state, regardless of whether or not that body is designated to have any rights. The arbitrariness and subjugation involved in this process are represented here as random notations on a map projected onto flesh. The Russian language on the map further adds to the postcolonial undertones between Russia and Ukraine in both nations' relationship to Soviet Crimea.[78]

With the end of communism, the binary between East/West was renegotiated at the same time as the male/female binary in gender theory.[79] Ambiguity also feeds the irony in Venediktova's pharmacological allegory. Her emphasis on negative space, like the turn inward in prior dissidents' notions of freedom under socialism, supports the idea of the curator as occupying a democratic ethos within a receding public sphere. Yet there is also a zero at the heart of the radical premise that withdrawing from public discourse on rights can renew its own critique.

The curator, in writing about her own public role as framer, ultimately curates herself as well:

> What then, if not hypocrisy, constitutes an "exhibited" person, who finds oneself before the gaze of other people? What if there is no person if one hasn't succeeded in becoming "transparent"? Here it is important to avoid the illusion that the "open" already exists, has arisen, that the squares are waiting for us to also arise there, as people, as a society, as "public," "exhibited," "unconcealed"; that a practically empty space exists, where one can arrive, where cooperation is possible, where each of us is part of the common, where conflict or "publicizing experience" is possible (what the Greeks called the "agora").[80]

Here, the "exhibited person" is also the person misrecognized by society and barred from the category of citizen. In the instance of exhibition, of standing in for an ideal, the illusion of possibility can also mean erasure of the self into a vacuum. Where Arendt had written that the strength of democracy rests with the "the voluntary association of divergent minds," on the ideal square, where no one can fully "arrive," there is no pretext for making rights public. One must think for oneself, Venediktova seems to be saying, and that this alone is the gift of the curator.

The regimentation of critical art, or art that attempts to mount a critique of its own limits to describe, can be easily observed in the Soviet-style police surveillance of state museums and the destruction of artworks in contemporary Ukraine. Thus, the fetishization of transparency also produces a blank slate: *What if there is no person if one hasn't succeeded in becoming "transparent"?*

In the years between Kyiv's two revolutions, the citizen became superfluous to the obsessive language in policies equating freedom with "transparency" in democratization efforts, mirrored by an obsession with "corruption" that was equally limiting, however extremely well placed that accusation may have been in the case of the Yanukovych regime. Milan Kundera included the term "transparency" among his sixty-five keywords in *Art of the Novel*. He comments on its popularity in journalism, defining it as "the exposure of individual lives to public view," containing residues of the nineteenth-century obsession with the glass house: "an old utopian idea and at the same time one of the most horrifying aspects of modern life."[81] In post-Soviet Ukraine, the glass house projects easily onto the walls of all of the museums it contains.

The terror of the glass house also resides in the possibility of actually having to dwell within it; like the city square, it is most beautiful only in theory, seen in passing for its many parts, each imparting a story about the fallible human processes by which its illusory perfection remains, in the end, just a made thing: "This means that architecture aimed at creating public space must simultaneously become 'anti-architecture.' Art, in turn, should convey the impossibility of art."[82] The challenge to invention has always been the province of art and, possibly, is the only territory within which dispute leads to the creation of new territory. Venediktova affects an affinity for construction: "Public space must be built, it requires the entirely artificial creation of the emptiness in which society could arise." The belief that one can create something new from the combination of unlike elements is, I think, the alchemy in Kyiv's visual culture collectives' concern with public spaces going stale: an awareness of past appropriations of art, and a practiced vigilance against the state turning citizenship into its own kind of specimen for display under glass – a Kafkaesque insect, or a prisoner's dilemma.

VI. Conclusion: The Politics of Display

Adopting many of the formal conventions of Kyiv's early avant-garde, the art collectives discussed in this chapter attempt to push what one is permitted to say in order to extend what one is capable of imagining and speaking. The collectives Revolutionary Experimental Space (REP) and HudRada, in name only, reflect the Soviet ideal of bringing art to the masses. By contrast, the intellectuals affiliated with these groups are more concerned with deregulating the systems that have narrowed public interest in contemporary art in Ukraine. The HudRada collective has stated their aim is to address a "crucial vacancy" brought on by the instrumentalization of art by the state and the privatization of nearly all markets and legal processes by local oligarchs. Emphasizing the body as an ideological site, aesthetically, much of these collectives' work coheres around diverse experiences of marginalization. In members' dissenting from repressive policies targeting minorities (many of these policies crystallized into entrenched social norms during Yanukovych's regime), these artists have attempted to dismantle the established art system not only in aesthetic terms, but also as activists risking their bodies in protest actions alongside others outside these collectives.

Near the end of her life, as an émigré in Paris in the 1930s, Marina Tsvetaeva attempted to make sense of the revolution that she had lived through. Penning several theses on poetry, in *Art in the Light of Conscience* she defends the impulse towards artistic creation as an act of conscience and of individual will, going against the charge of superfluity sometimes attributed to art amid times of political chaos. She severs art's value from any claim to legislative status: "The moral law can be introduced into art, but can a mercenary corrupted by so many changes of master ever make a soldier of the regular army?"[83] Tsvetaeva's tone and her personal reserve in this passage reflect the experience of many in her circle at the time, such as Aleksandr Blok, whom she mentions in the essay "Fleeing from Death into the Street." Art became a way to preserve an inner sanctum of sanity, an exemption from the laws of the revolution. Art was perceived to be a renunciation of absolutes: "Artistic creation is in some cases a sort of atrophy of conscience – more than that a necessary atrophy of conscience, the moral flaw without which art cannot exist."[84] This vision of art is nonpolitical insofar as the artist is neither arbitrator nor litigator; it is "art without artifice," which Tsvetaeva expounds is "not yet art, but already more than art."[85] This description cut against the centralization and repression of art under Stalin at the time. The negative space is therefore a space riddled with gaps in perspective, conflicts, and rupture. It is a trace on the geographical ordering of space – like the square, the museum, or Plato's cave wall – always just out of reach, and thus, constantly rewritten.

Throughout this chapter I have outlined in two of Kyiv's collectives a notion of the political within their experiments in cultural form. In the ongoing history of Ukrainian and East European art, the creative process is highly tangled up with the struggle for working concepts of inner freedom and viable depictions of negative space – set apart from oppressive external surroundings marked by authoritarian leaders and social decline.

The question of creative autonomy is a long-standing theme in Slavic intellectual history writ large, given that so many writers from the region stretching from Russia to Poland have faced persecution and even death for their work. One could argue that the immediacy of politics in art in this region has produced an anxiety that has, through various conventions that writers and others have had to employ in wrestling with manifest forms of censorship, evoked new patterns of display that have, over time, become devices of expression. Disembodied voices hover in a dialogue above these texts: there are many instances of the creation taking over the creator as characters attempt to describe a context, or frame a situation in which the expressive subject becomes the object of the description. The creative processes in making an artwork – writing, drawing, painting – can sometimes become more real than the self. The artist depicts the creative process as though from an empty space where one might see, in full consciousness, a reflection.

The central paradox in the exhibit that I focus on in detail in this chapter now emerges in conflict with the real. This gathering takes on shades of an instance of strange historiography in which, upon Putin's invasion of Ukraine, *the literal suddenly caught up with the metaphorical*. Both the "congress" and the works in HudRada's increasingly prolific experiments now mark the decade following the Orange Revolution as a circle: the internalization of speech against self-censorship, and the rights to a nuanced history – an ouroboros to inoculate the future against silence. As long as Ukraine's curators, artists, and writers will continue to strive for event rather than artefact, at transforming the museums that dominate the core of cultural life, and at making of "the open square" not the object, but the very material of their art, their efforts will not go overlooked. Politics, as artifice, always depend upon the means of their display.

Chapter Five

Bad Myth: Picturing Intergenerational Experiences of Revolution and War

Now, a hundred years later, the future is, once again,
not where it ought to be.
Our time comes to us secondhand.

– Svetlana Alexievich,
Secondhand Time: The Last of the Soviets, 2013.

For if Ariadne has fled from the labryrinth of old,
the only guiding thread for all of us now,
women and men and others
is a tightrope stretched above the void.

– Rosi Braidotti, *Patterns of Dissonance,* 1991

I. Introduction

Five years after the Revolution of Dignity, the annexation of Crimea, and occupation of eastern Ukraine by Russia, I find myself in Kyiv again. At the time of writing this chapter, the war is still ongoing and has claimed thousands of lives. Millions of people are displaced from their homes and have been forced to resettle throughout the continent. Economic sanctions between the United States and Russia continue to reshuffle Ukraine's economic landscape, complicating all diplomatic efforts. President Poroshenko's signing of the EU Association Agreement, a direct and positive outcome of the Maidan Revolution, has resulted in increased trade with European companies, in addition to a visa-free travel regime for Ukrainian citizens introduced in late 2017. Yet the overall situation remains unstable due to the president's low popularity ratings and the far-right groups that have largely occupied the public domain. Media channels remain in the hands of the oligarchs, as ongoing war with Russia spurs on an "information war" fuelled on by international propaganda schemes and intrusions into governmental and financial systems and databases by hackers in global cyber conflicts. Support from the International Monetary Fund in Ukraine, as well as military training assistance from the United States, Canada, and the European Union remains tenuous due to continually backsliding efforts at anticorruption and court reform, and changing perceptions on the role of NATO and intelligence agencies in the post-Soviet context.

Despite expectations to the contrary, in the years following the Orange Revolution, Ukraine's parliament (Verkhovna Rada) slid further towards authoritarianism and sidelined many rights. The failure to sign an Anti-Discrimination Law was overlooked in the talks leading up to the EU Association Agreement extended to ousted president Viktor Yanukovych. One success of the Maidan Revolution is the fact that the bill was signed and put into effect in November 2015. In 2010, the pro-Western opposition leader of the Orange Revolution, former president Viktor Yushchenko, established a censorship bureau charged with monitoring media and public information (the National Expert Commission of Ukraine on the Protection for Public Morality). Protests went largely unnoticed against the Commission's Anti-Abortion Bill in 2011, which was spearheaded in partnership with the Ukrainian Orthodox Church (Moscow Patriarchate) at a conference on bioethics. Ukraine then followed suit behind Putin's similar initiatives by instituting a "gay propaganda law" criminalizing any behaviour, display, or distribution of information conveying same-sex desire. Kyiv's Commission functioned in an authoritarian, Soviet manner; it has since been disbanded, but its effects remain in pervasive censorship practices and negative public attitudes towards minorities.[1]

As revolution shifted into war in 2015, feminism as both a term and a debate disappeared from global news streams about the region, even as socially engaged and nonconformist artists in Ukraine experienced a surge of opportunity to express themselves in public exhibits and conferences in many major cities throughout Europe. Local artists contesting the commodification and institutionalization of the art system in Ukraine against the backdrop of how to memorialize the Maidan Revolution became known and collected abroad, yet their ideas were less appreciated in their own country. They continue to publicly complain and lament the fact that their ideas are not appreciated in their home country. This dynamic intersects with debates around the decommunization laws, discussed throughout this chapter, and the rise of populist groups within the capital in the lead-up to the next election cycle.

Perhaps, most critically, the social, creative, and emancipatory capacities of the revolution are at risk. This is clearly evident in the content and themes of the activities and artworks produced by the artists featured here, who anticipate their audiences from within the dissident fabric from which they draw their content: the closely knit social networks in which topics conveniently deemed unimportant or too controversial elsewhere are debated openly.

War is not a distant memory in Ukraine. The Russia-Ukraine conflict poses distinct challenges for the nation's memory politics about how to inherit the Soviet past. These challenges are most obvious in the passage of a set of laws by President Poroshenko in 2015 mandating the *decommunization* of public space and discourse, to be carried out under the jurisdiction of the Ukrainian Institute of National Remembrance, which was established on 31 May 2006. One of the most troubling aspects of these policies is the combination of the authoritarian dictate to remove all symbolic references to the Soviet Union and the arbitrariness by which the laws are directed against not only public monuments but also texts, objects, and individuals.[2] Given the presence of so many self-described art-activists and dissidents in Ukraine, as well as comparative protests for free speech taking place in other parts of the world, I argue that these laws are, ultimately, a death knell for civil society – and by extension the state.

Arbitrary rule can also be observed in other areas of governance concerning human rights and civil liberties. In post-Maidan Ukraine there remains an absence of public statements by government officials condemning acts of civilian violence, despite ongoing petitions from Amnesty International and Human Rights Watch.[3] A 2018 report published by the Atlantic Council identified this government inaction as a sign of state weakness and institutional breakdown in the classical definition of Western democracy.[4] The monopoly over violence in all forms usually rests with the state via its legislative power guaranteed by the social contract, but in this case, the enforcement apparatus is failing to uphold its normal functions in protecting citizens from civilian violence both preventatively and when it appears in the populace. Absence of corrective action by the state is evidence of weak or absent rule tending towards a paramilitary structure. My assessments above second the Atlantic Council's 2018 report in including art exhibits in a wider set of activities and demographics targeted by far-right extremists.

The revolutionary who dies on the square is not the same as the figure who is memorialized. The symbolic economy underwrites the foundations of the state. This economy can be traced in the artworks created in Ukraine since the Orange Revolution by the generation featured in this book – these symbolic codes' highest cultural stakes are now taking shape in the destruction of those same and other artworks in the occupied territories of the Russia-Ukraine conflict, and in the authoritarian impulse to control and censor public space. In 2018 members of HudRada and Revolutionary Experimental Space (REP) worked with locals to restore the museum in Stanytsia Luhanska that had been shelled, and in which locals had sought refuge during the battles that took place there. The project, which was partially funded by USAid, prompted dialogue about extending UNESCO protection to other Soviet modernist architectural structures and artefacts. The art collective Izolyatsia was also forced to relocate from Donetsk to Kyiv in 2014 and lost several art pieces in the process. Mikhail Minakov uses the term *demodernization* to describe the retrenchment of oligarchic clans and stalled court reforms in the years following the Maidan Revolution; decommunization functions as only one of many impulses strangling the democratic energy and "political creativity" of that moment.[5]

In the words of artists, poets, authors, filmmakers, and others I have worked with side-by-side as a researcher, writer, teacher, translator, and friend, I understood the immediacy of the overall situation. Soviet authoritarian behaviours and logics are repeating themselves over and over again in Ukrainian statecraft post-Maidan through various applied mechanisms that have led to new forms of censorship, which are felt acutely in the museum, educational, and cultural spheres.[6] While much of the modernist aesthetics in Kyiv in the 1920s were co-opted or subjugated by the ideological mandates of the state, many artists and writers from this period were then targeted and executed for those same works. Theirs is a story of dissent from tyranny. Figures such as Mykhaylo Semenko and others, discussed later, had once designed specific aesthetic forms in order to circumvent the censor, to challenge Moscow's imperialism within the Soviet project, and to resist programmatic dictates that compelled conformity to authoritarian, absolutist ways of thinking. Nonetheless, many of the texts and images produced by artists and authors, at times labelled "dangerous" by past regimes in the territories that comprise modern Ukraine, led to sophisticated literary and artistic devices that have since entered the canons of film, poetry, and painting globally.

Locally, the aesthetic forms of the Soviet past are deployed as a reference point to illustrate the limits, rather than the sources, of today's ongoing social and political conflict. The emerging generation of artists in Kyiv is mining Ukraine's local artistic vaults, in order to reflect upon the violence of the twentieth century by innovating their own visual language for facing new challenges in the twenty-first. In my conversation with street artist Vova Vorotniov, he explained his motivation behind making (and selling) a pop series of miniature replicas of the Artem worker statue: "It is better to explore the full constellation of experiences of the twentieth century, instead of erasing its unappealing and even terrifying aspects completely – which is an unquestionably authoritarian reflex in and of itself."[7] By modifying or editing the aesthetics that once served propagandistic purposes, Vorotniov and others like him apply limitations to the signs and icons that were once stamped with grand narratives that delegitimized individual experience. The true shock here is that the work of these artists is destroyed or censored by officials. The state chooses to enact the same monopoly as the Soviets by ensuring that all symbolic power (along with symbolic capital) is held by the centre, not democratized.

The eternal flame is still burning brightly in the crucible – only the colours of the wreaths adorning the pedestal have changed! How do images, having a particular semantic relationship to the history of the censor, pose questions about the creative freedom of the individual in the present? What does art mean in a time of war? And what does art mean in a time of war against symbols? Against (dis)information?

The grand narratives about revolution and war, as we will encounter them in this chapter, are rooted not only in official ideological myths that were invented and monopolized by the Soviet regime, but also – and possibly even more powerfully – in the myth of the dissident who, from the outside, deliberately plays with the law of opposites dictating the internal logics of authoritarian states. Persecution borne by intellectuals, artists, and others throughout the twentieth century can never be incorporated, either in form or content, into the grand narratives of tragedy and suffering that once drove the glorification and cathartic functions of the Red Army victory narrative in the Soviet monopoly over memory. Contrasting pressures to remember versus erase are still operative within these older myths today. This dissensus can also lead to their reinvention: a new discourse of resistance by dissidents as the claiming of public spaces and the creation of new institutions.

These debates are occurring among Ukraine's generation to have emerged between the two revolutions as the first to take shape in social networks of commentary on local politics occurring, to a large degree, almost completely online. And yet elsewhere the Soviet vernacular persists as a parallel genre, one that is now just emerging in published texts and images as a documentation of society in secondary sources. Older generations of authors writing anthropological, thick description about their experience – Svetlana Boym, Svetlana Alexievich, Serguei Oushakine, Alexei Yurchak, and others – are, from a linguistic standpoint, inscribing the features of this shared language. An important aspect of these texts is the way each positions the features of this language below the level of official state discourse, or lyrical national narratives. When we consider this vernacular, it is also attached to the Maidan Revolution and the Russia-Ukraine conflict – functioning sometimes counter to the ideologies of narratives in Soviet-era documents and literary texts, which unfold as myth. Time is marked as being before/after the Great Patriotic War (the official Soviet designation for the Second World War). The shift to decommunization legislation works similarly in making pretence to the (violent) idea that a myth could ever be totally erased from the personal memories and experiences of the USSR shared by the majority of the post-Soviet population.[8]

The Soviet vernacular genre for these "personal histories," as they are described by one artist in her graphic narrative about the Maidan featured in this chapter, almost always unfolds as myth. Svetlana Alexievich's Nobel Lecture "On the Battle Lost" – a pacifist speech act – unravels these masculinist victory narratives by foregrounding defeat, yet the genre remains the same. Contrast this with "everyday life," *byt*, also discussed in chapter 3, so often depicted as a "grind unfolding," in the narratives of social and cultural decline dominating public life after 1991.[9] In both generations, everyday experience is about retelling several versions of the same story: The war. The fall. The revolution.

II. Urban Space as Medium for Aesthetic Experiment

The School of Kyiv – Monuments, Museums, Soviet Architecture

This chapter zeros in on the Visual Culture Research Center in Kyiv, demonstrating how authors, artists, and others connected with their projects have put on display the enduring cultural mythologies that shape public discourse. As with Vova Vorotniov's statuette, which was produced in the context of the 2017 Kyiv International Biennial, modification, framing, juxtaposition, fragmentation, and collage borrowed from earlier visual forms unify the technical approaches of artists and authors associated with the group. A contemporary art collective, VCRC was founded in 2008 as a "platform for collaboration between academic, artistic, and activist communities"; it has since become an important venue for creative work that has struggled to survive in light of repressive actions from the authorities and far-right groups.[10] VCRC has been housed in three different venues in the city due to controversial relations with state representatives over the content of the artworks; for instance, as discussed in chapter 3, the collective was expelled from Kyiv-Mohyla Academy in an act of censorship by university president

Serhiy Kvit for the exhibit *Ukrainian Body* (2011), which depicted same-sex couples. The group politically positions itself as an alternative educational centre critical of the centralized institutionalization of the art system in Ukraine. Widespread efforts locally and among partners abroad to keep the initiative afloat in Ukraine's politically regressive environment attest to the fact that VCRC has broken new ground for art and its impact on local civic struggles.[11]

A powerful message resides in the parallel between the artistic process and public dialogue. VCRC describes its central aim as fostering "a new discourse of Ukraine," in which "representation means gaining political subjectivity – being present, visible, and voiced as a separate entity."[12] This emphasis on representation is a valuable point for addressing local demands for more autonomy from which to gain critical vantage in evading propaganda clashes between the nation's EU and Russian neighbours. Creating public space for free discussion also responds to misrepresentations of Ukraine in the propaganda daily synthesized by the "information war," only one outgrowth of Putin's ongoing disregard for Ukrainian sovereignty and international treaties.

The repetition of false binaries across media coverage on Ukraine as a site of crisis and conflict (national, fiscal, linguistic) reveals the manipulative surfaces that can limit and stymie conversations about democracy. Contrary to these limiting devices, in the years between the Orange Revolution and the events of winter 2013–14, artists in Kyiv continued to carve out pivotal public sites for making visible the symbolic, often hidden, violence that the state had asserted against its own people. The public activity involved in the design, creation, and display of art has fostered a creative and intellectual community independent of the state and its institutions. This type of free association is extremely precious and becoming all too rare in post-Maidan Ukraine. While I would argue against the idea that any one art collective should or could have a monopoly over this thinking community, at present this type of model is the single pathway through which the democratic ethos of the revolution will survive.

Intergenerational conflicts over the Soviet past appear in both visual artworks and activities by participants in VCRC. The iconoclastic policies in Ukraine today that target Soviet history drive local social conflicts that survive beyond, and are even strengthened by, the processs of removing statues or demolishing buildings.

The distribution/perpetuation/resolution of civilian debates across and within urban spaces, and about architecture, are both profoundly counterbalanced by the "antiarchitecture" of reinscribing these sites with social meaning that outlasts their stone façade. Much of the participatory actions by artists and activists in Kyiv offer new platforms for understanding global concerns around the repressive effects of state-run media and government access to and control over information. These platforms pose broader questions not only for Ukraine, but for how we think about the effects of power systems (including data) on the body.

The works featured in this chapter, especially the monument to Lenin, expose where local sites can be especially powerful for international scholars working on the question of surveillance regimes. The Soviet experiment was unprecedented in its fixation on the body, projections of nation and ideology onto the body, the forms/functions of internal organs, and rituals marking mortality in wider social manifestations of sexuality, reproduction, and the state regulation of borders, populations, the built environment, and time.

The excerpt below is from *The Book of Kyiv,* a compilation of essays by approximately twenty artists containing local accounts of the many changes that have resulted from the nation's recent experience of revolution and the ongoing war.[13] The narrative often stretches back to the city's origins in the tenth century, visually framing the present in layers of dialogue, parable, and metaphor that lead readers to confront their surroundings critically, irreverent of taboos in prescriptive uses of space; instead, revealing how memory inscribes and alters environments.

> The address of the booth selling scrap metal is on Mirnaya Street, a term which denotes both world and peace, though the street was formerly known as Chorny Yar, or Black Ravine. Nearly a century ago local residents petitioned the city to change the name of their street. The notion of a Black Ravine called to mind a necropolis. No one wanted to rent a room there. "Sign, seal, and deliver what you will, but give us Peace!" went the slogan.[14]

The text trespasses into alleyways between churches and a mosque where the homeless rest, into secret gardens growing near forgotten graves dating to "sometime after Oleg the Prophet was interned," in which all were "buried in rows: first the locals, then soldiers, then Roma, Muslims, Jews, then victims of the plague." The narrative scales all walls – showing, in images, how the city populates and moves counter to divisive strategies in the mainstream media stories of national conflict. Pathways emerge:

> Today the outskirts of the market are filled with Tatars, who, having fled Crimea after its annexation by Russia now bake and sell cheburek, a dough pastry filled with seasonings. In 1980 a covered building was added to the marketplace. The structure resembles a seagull, and the air there smells of seagulls as well, due to the stray cats that compete with the birds in retrieving any discarded fish. But these newly displaced Tatars from Crimea

have actually been here before; there is even a hill nicknamed after them, returning it to its original inhabitants – "Tatarka," now mostly abandoned, lies on a weedy slope hidden from view.[15]

The texts in the book function as a guide to an event named The School of Kyiv.[16] Spread out across eighteen venues in the city, what began as an art event soon became a multinational phenomenon and a springboard for dialogue about the Maidan Revolution. The performances, public lectures, and art installations that manifested from September to November 2015 were originally supposed to be the Second Kyiv Biennial, which had been postponed from 2014 because of the revolution.[17] Only six months before the 2015 opening, the Ukrainian Ministry of Culture cancelled the state funds earmarked for the biennial, stating that art is not a priority in a time of war. This sudden turn of events galvanized the local art community further in their efforts to sustain the project.

In October 2017 VCRC organizers followed their 2015 School of Kyiv Biennial with the concept of Kyiv International – an open experiment on the centennial of 1917. The Academy of Arts, Academy of Fine Arts and Architecture, National Museum of the History of Ukraine, and the National Library for Architecture all lent out their spaces to VCRC organizers for relatively small fees. This was a thorn in the side of the privatized monopoly over contemporary art. The main site of the 2017 Biennial was located in an historic Soviet structure (nicknamed "Plate," or "Tarilka"/"UFO" for its shape) slated for conversion into an extension of the Ocean Plaza shopping mall. The event also led to a broader movement, #SaveKyivModernism, dedicated to the historical preservation of the city's Soviet architecture.[18] Although extreme political flux involving many international organizations has saturated Kyiv's public spaces with many layers of loaded meanings, the Kyiv International remained quite local in the links it drew between the conflicts over the proposed demolition of the structure "Tarilka" as the hosting site, and the legacies of free speech spanning post-Soviet space.

The question of how to inherit the history of the USSR threaded throughout every discussion I observed in the form of questions on how to document history in a vacuum of memory politics:

In Ukraine, together with Soviet memorials, the visuality of the modernist avant-garde tradition has been wiped out from the public space as a disturbing symbol for counter-memories and alternative historical narratives. "Patriotic" populism externalizes the Soviet period and retroactively nationalizes historical memory, using the communist past for redistribution of political and symbolic capital today. This repression of memory results in the revenge of memory in all new forms of social destruction that we observe today. The regressive politics of memory lays the grounds for conflicts that will tear the social fabric to pieces in the future, widening the funnel of violence and pulling the whole society into it, a society for which it is becoming harder and harder to come to its senses and to its own memory.[19]

These statements by Vasyl Cherepanyn, co-founder of VCRC, issue a warning about the consistency of censorship across regimes. The Soviet past is deployed as a reference point to illustrate the limits, rather than the sources, of today's ongoing social and political conflicts. By modifying or editing the aesthetics that once served propagandistic purposes, the many artists and thinkers that cluster around VCRC are protesting decommunization in their work, and as activists: "Creation of the international cooperative of politically engaged institutions acting together on the basis of common ideas, conducting transnational politics in spite of existing borders and new walls at the age of globalization – that is the art piece we really need most."[20] The task set forward is more than art. The critique is aimed at the spectre of the communist past in its worst form: the grand narratives entrenched in Ukraine today that delegitimize individual experience, fail respond to anger at promised reforms, and serve to justify a war in which it is not clear to civilians who is fighting whom.

In the 1970s the architect Edward Bilsky developed a project for the Museum of Contemporary Art to be constructed on Instytutska Street (formerly October Revolution Street), the present site of the memorial to the Heavenly Hundred (Небесна сотня) who lost their lives defending the city from government attacks during the Maidan Revolution in 2013–14. These plans were made during the stagnation period and served a pragmatic end: the development of cultural institutions near the corridors of power was intended to co-opt and pacify artists, thereby preventing them from getting too involved in dissident activities. Repressions against the intelligentsia in the 1970s resulted in limiting the museum to a single gallery. With the end of the USSR, the unfinished museum was demolished and the territory was slated for a "shopping center and hotel," but court battles continued and nothing was accomplished. A later architectural pair, Miletsky & Shevchenko, proposed a project that included not only a new museum, but also an annexe that would unite the old and new museum buildings into a single complex. Hrushevskoho and Instytutska Streets – separated by a steep hill and several buildings – were to be joined.

The two main corridors that provide access to the government quarter would have formed a broad pathway up from the Maidan. Had this alternative state-art complex been realized, it might have led to a different outcome to the revolution. It is significant that the memorial to the Heavenly Hundred, and former site of the Soviet Museum of Contemporary Art, is demarcated as the location for the future Maidan Museum. On 18 February 2018, the fourth anniversary of the clashes and coincidentally also the date of my birth, I observed over forty prototypes for the future design of the museum in a temporary exhibit installed on the square itself in a showcase of public involvement into its memory.

Living not far from the site of the future museum for over the course of several months that same year, I also witnessed firsthand several marches, gatherings, and speeches by others in disagreement with the memory of revolution, including those who would seek to erase or distort its civic narratives beyond recognition, such as the former mayor of Odesa, Mikheil Saakashvili, and his supporters. The most astonishing of these public manifestations around the events of 2013–14 was the revealing of a plot by Ukrainian member of parliament and former military helicopter pilot, Nadiya Savchenko, to violently take over the government quarter with support from Russian-backed rebels in Donetsk.[21]

Data and Knowledge

In format, VCRC challenges the traditional idea of a biennial and an exhibit because it functions not as an annual art event or a market, but as a social experiment that includes resuscitating Ukraine's past cultural institutions. This again is another thorn in the side of the privatized monopoly over contemporary art in Ukraine. By contrast, the VCRC concept relies on global knowledge and volunteer labour flows through networks, many which have been strengthened in Ukraine over the past decade through NGOs. The self-organized crisis centres that emerged out of the Maidan Revolution have also catalyzed the motivation to reverse outflows, or "brain drain," by increasing aptitude around media and financial sustainability in order to combat critical issues facing Ukraine such as the digital divide, social intolerance, and rising income inequality.[22]

With the boom in big data, access to information and communication have become a basic human need around the globe equal to the right to shelter, water, and life-sustaining resources. In 2013 the United Nations adopted an Open Charter, "The Principled Use of Humanitarian Information in the Network Age," for "the implementation of open-data policies by 2015" to streamline data sharing between governments and humanitarian responders.[23] The charter includes a system of checks-and-balances for signatories. But information at this scale can easily be misused. The impacts of data collection and sharing by governments and corporate entities ("big data") on human rights are evident in the

rise of populism due to lack of public access to information and the repression of civil liberties. Inequalities across the digital divide in globalized Ukraine are driven not by access issues or cost (Ukraine remains
among the top nations for internet affordability), but by insufficient and
corrupt management of communications and data infrastructure.[24]

Adorno proclaimed there could be no poetry after the atrocities of the
Second World War. We might ask a similar question about Ukraine during the ongoing conflict with Russia: Why art now? Historically, artists
and activists have adopted similar roles in applying pressure against
public silence. Art does not signify protest in the traditional sense of a
state versus society, or group versus society approach to social change.
Art is the practice of displaying and interpreting information: it leverages self, audience, and public in critique.

In the regions of the world stretching from Eastern Europe to Russia,
declaring the social role of an artist has often led to more than co-optation,
reduction, or mechanization of the content of any medium – a simple
turn of phrase could mean the difference between life or death. The expressive languages that structure art in the post-Soviet context are inherently bound up with the perpetuation of competing regimes, and thus
nearly always contain some element of social controversy. The Soviets
formally recognized art as subversive at every level – the roots of its very
definition were deeply intertwined with the communist bureaucratization of material culture. In 1917, the Bolsheviks seized and installed all
possessions from land-owning peasantry (kulaks) into collective repositories at village, oblast, and municipal centres. The official state museum
complex thus functioned to prevent the individual accumulation of items
of material value through a centrally managed display of revolutionary
propaganda, versus the dangers of capitalist spectacle.

When Viktor Yanukovych fled Ukraine in early 2014, the self-defence
brigades from the Maidan seized his palatial private estate, Mezhyhirya.
They discovered embezzled property valued into the high millions,
including rare ecclesiastical texts and objects from the tenth century.
Items of interest were shipped to the National Art Museum of Ukraine,
where I observed how curators from several state museums organized
them into an ad hoc exhibit entitled *Codex Mezhyhirya*.[25] The artefacts
were displayed on the very crates they were shipped in, surrounded
by their wrappings and marked off from the crowds with nothing more
than a thin yellow string. Each room formed an inventory of the deposed
dictator's strange tastes, framed in sections such as "The Book of Idols"
and "The Book of Vanity," a room filled with gaudy self-portraits (figures
5.1, 5.2). The exhibit proved that the former criminal's plundering of resources in private resembled the same kitsch veneer as the campaigns

Figure 5.1. Two men stand near a statuette of Yanukovych from his palatial Mezhyhirya Estate, seized by Maidan demonstrators. Along with photos showing the opulence of the estate and its hoarded, stolen items of wealth, the statuette appeared in a room filled with hundreds of fanciful cartoonish self-portraits, including renditions of Yanukovych and his cronies as soccer champions, Napoleonic soldiers, and so forth. The items mirror totalitarian-style portraits in other political contexts in an obsession with self-image bordering on extreme narcissism. Displayed in the National Art Museum of Ukraine (NaMU), Kyiv, 2014. Photo by the author.

invented by the oligarchic clans that ruled the 2000s. Their rule had created an information vacuum in the fallout of the Orange Revolution.

A new museum structure might thus envision ways to depart from older practices of state-sponsored centralized culture, in order to facilitate public access to the provenance and meriting of artefacts and artworks. By adopting the same format of the codex, and organizing themselves into "books," The School of Kyiv symbolically returned Yanukovych's stolen texts to the public, but did so by coordinating events across the city to propose a new kind of "museum." The initiative was promising in its ambivalence towards East/West regionalism and other polarizing narratives (the event and its outcomes have no official language, no central bureau of review, and no firm attachment to any one sponsor). Given the relatively young age of the organizers (mostly in

Figure 5.2. Ecclesiastical artefacts that had been appropriated illegally by Yanukovych and stored in his Mezhyhirya Estate, seized by Maidan demonstrators and put on display in the National Art Museum of Ukraine (NaMU). Kyiv, 2014. Photo by the author.

their thirties), the projects foregrounded in this chapter have political corollaries in both the twentieth-century avant-garde and the street gatherings of the early 2000s. Many of the texts reflect ideas espoused by youth groups, such as PORA, that were instrumental in the Orange Revolution and whose members have survived into the present through student unions.[26] Many works co-opt the language of the state to poke fun at it (a technique utilized by the second wave avant-garde groups in the region, such as BuBABu in Lviv). The concept dates to Poland's "flying universities," which were maintained by the underground resistance during German occupation. Later, activists from the Solidarity movement would continue to broker many NGO networks between the West and Ukraine in local projects.[27] It is significant that Vasyl Cherepanyn is editor-in-chief of the Ukraine branch of the Polish journal *Krytyka Polityczna* (founded by Sławomir Sierakowski). The author

Jerzy Onuch has also been instrumental in supporting the group Revolutionary Experimental Space (REP), discussed in the previous chapter. By no small measure, the emerging generation of artists in Kyiv has been at the forefront of sheltering public debate with support from Poland in the years between Ukraine's two recent revolutions. The focus of their civic efforts has evolved into mitigating the negative impacts of regressive laws on independent venues that extend citizens' agency around more than just art, to include: freedom of expression, corruption reform, elections, and even LGBTQ rights.

Prioritizing cultural development and education foregrounds pedagogy over ideology. The ideas espoused by VCRC are based on aims stated in terms that are equally ambitious to those of a manifesto. Again VCRC's mission to create "a new discourse of Ukraine," is significant in how it signals a shift to the language of experiment in which "representation means gaining political subjectivity – being present, visible, and voiced as a separate entity."[28] Adopting the familiar rhetoric of dissidence, these statements gesture towards more institutional autonomy, a noble, if not inadequately realized aim that could also introduce more critical vantage points in the propaganda clashes between Russia and the West. Along this line, I agree with Cherepanyn, who writes:

> The Biennial is a continuation of the idea of the Maidan, operating as a political *agora* in the cultural field ... Learning is the finest antidote to counter-revolution, especially in the form of war. We are in the right time and in the right place – Kyiv, a key city for today's Europe – to implement that.

What art offers, as a platform in Ukraine deeply rooted in the rise and fall of regimes, is a vector of movement out of crisis and war by challenging audiences and participants to absorb a turbulent history without the blame involved in the naming of perpetrators and victims.

In "Declaration of the School of Kyiv," Cherepanyn issued a comprehensive mission for the role of art in public life.[29] The document unifies the six divisions of the school by establishing several key aims for its participants in a sociopolitical experiment focused on "understanding what we have lived through." Each division engages a different cluster of concerns about transformation, neocolonialism, and dispossession in Ukraine's post-revolutionary moment. The School of Abducted Europe lists the following among its objectives of study: "exclusion of the European 'Other' and the new 'Schengen wall'; 'the end of ideology' and the rise of the far right in Europe and beyond; the conflict of historical memories and the remaking of war; cultural wars between pornography and religion; 'the hatred of art,' iconoclasm and image wars."[30]

The varied foci across the schools within the larger project convey concerns about the site of civic agency in the global discourse on democratic reform in Ukraine. For example, The School of the Displaced involved refugees and displaced peoples to ask how participatory and performative actions might ameliorate states of crises. The School of Realism and The School of Landscape investigate the contentious past lives of these aesthetic forms, while The School of the Lonesome teaches the theory and practice of documenting contemporary history in open workshops, such as "How to Remember? How to Archive?" led by Zeyno Pekünlü. Perhaps most immediate for international observers is The School of Image and Evidence, which synthesizes a curriculum based in user-generated online video to facilitate documentary reports by participants that contest mass-media propaganda about the war.[31]

With the more recent spread of fake news to stoke fear and confuse citizens, increased impetus towards control over big data by the state seems to be outpacing local efforts to decentralize cultural institutions to support a diversity of perspectives.[32] The private cultural sector has either remained solidly in the hands of a few oligarchs, or grown in new market directions through global IT outsourcing. Meanwhile, state educational, museum, and scientific institutes remain in ruin. Interstate and market debates on the free flow of information leave open the ongoing question of how to address these gaps. Social inequalities continue to lead to physical and cyber targeting in discrimination towards minorities on the ground. In January 2015 Cherepanyn survived an attack by an unknown far-right group.

Incidents like this are still common among those who speak out in Ukraine on behalf of civil liberties. On 16 October 2015 a screening of *This Is Gay Propaganda! LGBT Rights and the War in Ukraine* was attacked by far-right groups in Chernivtsi.[33] Social media played a role on both sides. During an earlier Toronto screening, the film's director, Marusya Bociurkiw, discussed her work with another director from Uganda; they agreed that the church-state bond in both countries had restricted the free flow of information and compounded discrimination against minorities. A separate screening was held under police guard as a direct outcome of a public petition to the mayor of the city of Ternopil, Ukraine. In 2013 Nataliya Zabolotna, director of Ukraine's prominent museum, Mystetskyi Arsenal, destroyed a controversial painting on display the night before a visit from Yanukovych to mark the anniversary of the Christianization of Kyivan Rus'.[34]

Threats to information access and increasing censorship in Ukraine can still be observed at the highest levels. Reform efforts have continuously unravelled alongside Western leaders' fatigue with both President Petro Poroshenko's and then President Volodymyr Zelensky's backsliding anticorruption efforts and the ongoing hybrid war with Putin. One could argue that a media "information war" has catalyzed and sustained the conflict on all sides, but that is a separate debate. A pressing, interrelated concern may be how to simply sustain participation in these debates. The events on the Maidan in 2013–14 were a watershed for protest, but the conflict in the east has left many ambivalent about democracy in the country. Freedom House reports in 2017 and 2018 list Ukraine as "partly free," with aggregate scores of 61/100 and 62/100. However, as in other countries in Europe, there has been a drop in tolerance and free speech. Amnesty International and Human Rights Watch released statements in early 2018 in response to attacks on Roma and journalists in Ukraine.[35] Zabolotna and other incumbents appointed by Yanukovych in the cultural world only recently left, or still occupy their posts, many clinging to the oppressive daily practices of the old regime.

There can be no regeneration without pluralism in the cultural sphere: a decentralization of the private monopoly over art coupled with financial restructuring and greater protection for free speech in public educational institutions, including both museums and universities. Leaders and institutions, including universities, have a responsibility in sheltering public access points for the critical exchange of information and knowledge. The prison complex located across the street from the planning centre of The School of Kyiv is a stark reminder: the former has heating, a full staff, and is always filled with residents, while the second is a nearly empty textiles warehouse.

Thus artists, writers, and activists associated with VCRC and other collectives featured throughout this book highlight the responsibility that leaders and cultural institutions have in fostering civic freedoms. Their themes point less to Ukraine's national identity than to criticism of local notions of civil rights in a global comparative of nations (the overlap between "European," "humane," and "dignity" here sometimes leading to problematic forms, including those stemming from older "second / third world" discourse in compulsion towards total erasure of the Soviet experience). These theatre performances, debates, and participatory actions in Kyiv's urban space are providing new platforms for sharing information that challenge the blanketing effects of big data and mainstream media on democracy. For example, panel titles at The School of Kyiv included "Art as Something Else: Artists Making Institutions"; "Who Is Supposed to Build Bridges?"; "Learning Europe: Making Space for Self-Education Practices"; and "Writing Across Borders: Prospects for a European Public Sphere." The performance group DIS/ORDER held a "Queer Chapel," featuring a performative, interactive LGBTQ marriage ceremony. Nikita Kadan's sculpture installation

Figures 5.3. *The Possessed Can Testify in Court*, Nikita Kadan, Kyiv, 2015.
Photo credit: Kostiantyn Strilets. Courtesy of the artist.

piece, "The Possessed Can Testify in Court," employed Soviet-era everyday items in order to deconstruct how ideological meanings are assigned to random objects (figure 5.3).

As mentioned earlier, the political corollaries between the collectives of the early twentieth century and the protest street gatherings of the early 2000s have survived into the present. However, the marginalization of artists and activists associated, or perceived to be associated, with a left-leaning political position has become ubiquitous in the post-Maidan era. Tacit agreement between the state and cultural institutions has allowed for ongoing attacks by far-right groups on a wide range of individuals. The situation is compounded by a package of "decommunization laws" aimed at removing past Soviet references and symbols from public spaces; these laws have been arbitrarily interpreted and applied in acts of censorship.[36]

Nevertheless, the autonomous artistic alliances that have emerged out of past contexts have grown between authors, curators, artists, and others in Kyiv associated with VCRC, HudRada, REP, and others. Individual members have continued to work together to shelter public access points for turning information into knowledge. I would argue that their events have evolved into mitigating the negative impacts of regressive laws on independent venues for citizens to discuss not only art, but also freedom of expression, censorship, memory politics, civil rights, and a number of other issues. Part of their ability to withstand the extreme political and financial volatility of two revolutions resides in their detachment from any one sponsor or governmental ministry. This is a first priority for mitigating ongoing sanctions and preventing oligarchic clans from overtaking independent venues. A new museum and university structure might thus look to these experiments and discussions for models in facilitating alternative spaces to support more public access to interpretive practices.

III. Nonconformist Women – an Unofficial Archive

As in the idea of an artistic "avant-garde" that came before them, the art collectives active in Ukraine vacillate between art and anti-art; and yet, their material has changed: they mine the chipped ideological fragments of the past in search of an alternate future in the face of a largely borderless war. There are no Red Heroes left to celebrate. What, if not war, is there left to inherit?

The official artists' unions and writers' houses – like countless other Soviet ruins – can perhaps only be repurposed for the sake of study and careful contemplation of a civilization preserved in the living memories of Ukraine's older generations. Careful dialogue and nuanced discussion are more innovative than the cycle of perpetrating perpetrators now driving the idea of decommunization, a cycle of inheriting those very same Soviet practices that the idea seeks to overcome in its politics of memory. Late Soviet documentary claimed to represent the "truth" about "what really happened" under Stalin (by directors such as Juris Podnieks, Marina Golovskaia, and Stanislav Govrukhin). By contrast, contemporary directors, such as Serguei Loznitsa, have taken a more indirect approach to documentary filmmaking that seeks to expose the reflexes in society that replicate entrenched Soviet myths.

Maidan: Rough Cut is a collective work by several young independent filmmakers, some of them film school students who chose to create a film as their primary mode of involvement in the protests, forming themselves into a collective called BABYLON'13.[37] The film raises the important issue of artists' and filmmakers' engagement and responsibilities in the context of political unrest. The need to film developments as they happened, which was also the case during the revolutionary events of 1968 in France, led to the organization of several filmmakers' collectives. In the context of Ukraine's Maidan in winter 2013, BABYLON'13 worked with the surfaces of focused segments and locations, later shaping their footage into short narratives. Films about the Maidan Revolution now number into the hundreds globally, each of them arguably showing a different revolution with its own unique timeline and outcomes for national and international audiences.

Maidan: Rough Cut follows a chronological timeline over three months of the events and is structured as a visual chronicle, each episode taking place in a different location in and around the Maidan. The film begins in front of the Monument of Independence, where peaceful protesters were first attacked by police. The scenes that follow travel through the occupied Kyiv city administration building to Besarabska Square. The pendulum of history in this particular space in Kyiv is extremely loaded. Besarabska Square is the site of the first Lenin monument erected in 1917 in the territories of the Ukrainian Soviet Socialist Republic; the monument was rededicated in 1919 after Ukraine's short period of independence. In a profound cycle of national breaking and remaking, it was exactly this same Lenin that was the first to fall in the Maidan Revolution of Dignity; others would follow suit in "Lenin-falls" throughout the country, discussed in more detail later.

The film consists of a sequence of several shorter clips stitched together. The segment by Kateryna Gornostai, entitled "Lenin's Teeth" (6:20–12:00), presents a powerful interaction between the young and the elderly amid the crowd. Three young people bend down and hug an older man who begins to weep as he sits nearby and watches a larger group of people of all ages crack apart the stone Lenin with pickaxes and cobblestones. A few of the other protesters argue among themselves about their motivations. One middle-aged woman carrying a lap dog shouts, in Russian laced with a combination of anger and nostalgia in that special tone reserved for moments like this familiar to all in these regions of the world: "I used to walk by this statue every single day on the way to school. We should keep it!" A slightly younger man provokes her by bringing up past wounds and throwing salt in them: "Maybe we'll replace it with Stepan Bandera! Ha! Take that!" Zooming in on a different man, the filmmaker's lens starts to go in and out of focus as she asks this new suspect his opinion. He stumbles, straightens his black winter hat, and then belts out a hoarse laugh that could have been cut straight from the debaucherous scenes in the opening sequence of Andrei Tarkovsky's *Andrei Rublev*. It becomes apparent that he is completely drunk. His watery bloodshot eyes peer deep into the lens – searching for the filmmaker behind it – and, not finding her gaze, he looks askance, moving to steady his balance. It is precisely at this point, and on this man's face, that everything that came before in the sequence suddenly crystallizes. The old man crying. The woman with the dog. The taunting young man. *The painful history.* These themes come crashing together in the expression on the drunk man's face – sorrow so profound that it breaks the whole dialogue. He stands in silence. Reverence. Fear. We see the gaze he was searching for inside the camera lens vividly reflected back at us in the brilliant light glinting off of his tears. He is the statue that the crowd cannot dismantle *because he contains all of their emotion.* A rough cut.

"Divchata!" he yells sharply, overcompensating with authority his inability to address the filmmaker by name as he looks back into the camera, this time more self-composed. He is using the general term of address applied to young women reserved for those moments ranging from the kind to the demeaning, his tone balanced somewhere between the range of how one would address a sister or a close friend: "divchata (girl) – listen to me ... you know ..." He starts to weep, saying, "those people, those people could give a shit about me." The filmmaker replies with empathy "Why? Why do you think that is so?" She persists in holding the camera steady. Frusterated, he pushes his emotion away a second time. Then – in a sudden flash – he pulls out an automatic pistol from his coat, brandishing it towards the crowd. It is a scene straight from a nineteenth-century duel, but this time there is nobody on the other end of the gun. He sees no fight worth fighting. *He is a superfluous man.*

Staggering, he twirls, looks towards the camera, then away in the opposite direction – into the darkness not far from the lights of the metro station. The swarm behind him is still caught in a net of arguing, cheering, and crying below a constellation of photo flashes sparking all around the broken Lenin, as if in some kind of absurd fireworks display. Mustering the last of his strength, he roars at the top of his lungs in the direction of the crowd: "YOUR TRUTH IS ONLY YOUR TRUTH!" (ВАША ПРАВА, ТО ВАША ПРАВА!). The scene ends without any resolution.

The Soviet "Great Myths" of the twentieth century are coming into conflict with what could also be thought of in broader terms as the post-communist *interrevolution* marked by nostalgia, the preservation and resignification of cultural commodities, concern with class inequalities (labour rights, zoning), and a de-emphasis on the official use of language (Ukrainian and Russian are integrated). *Maidan: Rough Cut* premiered in March 2014 at the opening ceremony of Docudays, a film festival in Ukraine dedicated to the theme of human rights, and was screened again three months later at the Odesa Film Festival, and in Budapest, Vilnius, Tblisi, the Czech Republic, Amsterdam, Moscow, and many other cities. Although the film travelled widely, its small, unscripted interactions between different generations can only be fully understood as symptomatic of several traits shared by students, cultural workers, artists, scholars, and others that are unique to the generation of Ukrainians now in their twenties and thirties. There is an imperative towards the exploration of alternative histories of their parents' and grandparents' living memories of Soviet life in oral histories, autobiography, material artefacts, industrial design, and maps. Marginality and alienation drive the younger generations' narratives of isolation, loneliness, and anxiety.

How could they not? Inheriting "the fall" of the USSR or "the transition" implies an end. The emotional fallout of revolution and war makes explicit the younger generations' more immediate experience of these paradigms. This experience undercuts the twentieth-century myths of "progress" and the propagandistic qualities of Lenin and other artefacts from that era. The totalitarian "uses" of the past are set into sharp relief as a kind of feedback loop that replays as static and confusion in the multiple, conflicting ways in which symbols that were once designed to convey absolutist, unquestionable messages now appear ambivalent: Lenin means something different to each person – there is no longer a monopoly on "truth."

The film's premiere itself manifested this new paradigm. The critic, curator, and anthropologist Nataliya Tchermalykh, of the same generation as the filmmakers, in writing about "a collective purifying feeling," situates herself and her students within a powerful emotional exchange that is both genuine and, at the same time, ambivalent and emptied of sense:

In March 2014 I was teaching in an Art School in Kyiv and had a chance to discuss the festival screening of *Euromaidan. Rough Cut* and what happened after with my students, who had also been in the audience during the screening. They shared with me their emotional responses towards what they were seeing: some of them confessed that they almost felt shivers running up and down their spine while watching the movie. However, not all of them defined this communal experience as positive. One girl, Maria M., acknowledged to me that she was disturbed by the "regulating power" of the experience that she had undergone in the cinema hall: she realized that she was not able to escape, and automatically repeated the gestures – and even emotions – of those who stood around her: standing up, singing the anthem and crying. Afterwards, as she told me, she felt a mixture of sorrow and shame.

Today, several years after the deaths on the Maidan, and despite an internationally supervised investigation, none of the cases of sniper shooting have yet been resolved judicially. It seems that, notwithstanding the collected evidence, in Ukrainian society there has not been a real, articulated and coherent demand for a public trial – a judicial way to restore societal harmony. Ukrainian society has already asked for forgiveness for a hundred of innocent deaths through a collective cathartic expression of mourning, which happened on Maidan and was then replicated repeatedly through symbolic performances, including the ones that I witnessed in the cinema hall.

My student's description is quite close to what I felt myself. Despite my sympathy towards the filmmakers, my activist path, my sincere tears and the feeling of a lump in my throat, which I feel each time I hear *Plyve Kacha*, the irrationality of the nationalist pathos that emerged immediately from the emotional communion provoked by the end of the film left me with mixed feelings. If I had experienced a collective catharsis, this catharsis didn't purify me.

Today, from a distance, I can confess that the emotional "mixture" I experienced contained also the feeling of shame. Retroactively, I felt ashamed of my strong, almost uncontrollable physiological reactions towards a discourse that I do not necessarily approve of intellectually, and yet I am driven by it, as one can be driven by the movement of a crowd. The essence of catharsis and its profound ambiguity may lie here: a break in a chain of human reasoning, when emotional, bodily reactions are almost blurred with intellectual ones. Under this effect, a collective aesthetic experience can be easily translated into a collectively shared, yet semi-conscious political affect, driven by a necessity to momentously resolve the effects of violence, inexplicable by means of reason.[38]

Perhaps this neutralizing dynamic is also due to the immediacy of events and immersive local context. The site specificity of the screening, in Kyiv, among participants of the revolution as it was just ending, and then the author's reflection on the power of emotional catharsis of her experience, raises the iconography of the spaces of the city into an allegory for the new paradigm. The alienation brought on by her students' feeling of automatic gestures, descriptively linked to catharsis, points to the impossible in being unable to resolve or to assimilate the extreme range of emotional experience as either/or: a logical narrative, or an arcane "purification" ritual, both of which serve to transfer "collective aesthetic experience" into "political affect." The unfathomable of revolutionary violence here is transformed into a shared sense of authenticity and empathy. Whose revolution are we witnessing? The dismantling of the Soviet project? The failure of the Orange Revolution? Or the promise of a new era in the Maidan protests? The film in its reception among the youngest generation becomes an unofficial archive that reveals the *bad myths* – the ritualized narratives, taboos, nostalgia, and search for redemption in the passing of generations, and the painful shifting of regimes.

The Drawings of Alevtyna Kakhidze

The shift in generations has also led to whimsical and humorous expressions. The protagonist of the graphic novel *Strawberry Andreevna*, by Alevtyna Kakhidze, is based on her mother, who chose to remain in the occupied Donetsk region where Kakhidze was born (figure 5.4).

She died tragically in late 2018 from exhaustion due to waiting outside in line for her pension.[39] In an interview about the project, the artist states, "I didn't come up with this pseudonym on my own; it was given to ... [my mother] by the kids who looked up to her in the kindergarten where she used to teach. But that's all the distant past now, long before the war."[40] Kakhidze recalls when her town was taken over by Russian forces in September 2014: "My mother called me everyday from the local cemetery because that was the only place with any cell phone reception. It all seemed symbolic to me – that the cemetery was the only place in Zhdanovka with a connection to the outside world." The story unfolds in maps and telephone conversations.

Kakhidze's drawings present memory by activating the Soviet past within a certain legibility of place: encounters particular to women's experiences of the peculiar peripheral spaces of war.[41] The events on the Maidan and the war with Russia both appear as alien to everyday life as the ideological narratives about them that pervade common language. Ambiguous characters and the lack of any stable plotline in the sequencing of images suggests, rather than prescribes, the arbitrary stories that people tell themselves in order to make sense of their individual experience of place and time. The Soviet vernacular genre for these "personal histories" almost always unfolds as myth. Here the mother-daughter relationship is depicted among "worlds" that problematize time and gender. She writes,

I think that still present within me to this day there exists what I call "*mother-father complexity*." My mother is a very austere man. She keeps a simple home with a minimal number of personal belongings. Everything is the opposite with my dad. He has an enormous number of things and a huge house. My childhood unfolded between two worlds: the world of asceticism, versus the world of affluence and materialism.

I could feel a great sense of misunderstanding growing in the Donbas during the Maidan protests in Kyiv. When Russian flags started appearing in Donetsk in March 2014 I went there and delivered two presentations with the title "A Study on History in Drawings." I showed many of the sketches I'd made over the course of events on Maidan, beginning with November. I talked on the phone with my mom about what was happening for six hours. It wasn't easy – we cried, fought, and then reconciled. Her very first question was: "Do you really think it's alright to throw stones at the police?"

I knew that my mother more or less only watched state-funded television channels. Before Yanukovych fled the country, the news reports on both Russian and Ukrainian stations were nearly identical, and I'd said

Figure 5.4. *Strawberry Andreevna* graphic novel, by Alevtyna Kakhidze, 2014–15. Shared with permission of the artist.

"enough with this!" From that moment onward, we began to open up more and I described to her everything I'd observed and felt.[42]

The spatial text of Kakhidze's drawings depicts an alternate world of women's experience in contrast to a "material" male world, the world in which war is waged, where to survive as a single mother requires becoming an "austere man" (Kakhidze's mother's wording) and war itself risks becoming ordinary, in fact, so common to everyday experience as to be nearly invisible. Audiences are invited to question the cognitive and affective means by which spatial environments come to shape politics.

Are the inhabitants of the occupied zone different from the rest of post-Soviet society or any society? Planting strawberries, rolling out dough for varenyky or pierogies, and losing the family pet all fold easily into experiences that are sometimes culturally specific, and sometimes just a part of life – quotidian. The impacts of war on the daily conversations between a mother and daughter transgress the chaotic din of the media dramaturgy playing out elsewhere, supplying narrative detail to dispel myth: "I haven't heard from you in a hundred years: get dressed, eat well, don't slouch, don't raise your voice, don't get upset ... no matter what's wrong."[43]

This environment in her drawings is also part of undoing the processes that drive ossified art institutions. She writes, "In Ukraine, the figure of the curator grew out of Komsomol [the All-Union Leninist Young Communist League]. I understand why, in Ukraine artists then become curators. Not every artist needs a counselor." She continues, "I like it when a curator offers you the work of a curator of your own project, within the scope of the wider curatorial project he or she is undertaking. But under such difficult conditions there were with Manifesta in Russia, such an approach would be impossible."[44] Lada Nakonechna, closely associated with artists and curators through both her artworks and active organizing within the groups REP, HudRada, and Method Fund, and who is also an artist/curator and a curator/artist, writes, "We do not just organize the exchange of knowledge, but, first of all, we create discursive spaces: contexts for the existence of contemporary artistic practice."[45]

Since 2008 Kakhidze has organized a creative environment where she hosts artists on short residencies in the village of Muzychi in the Kyiv region where she lives.[46] Her artworks have expanded to include these surroundings through the visual and descriptive languages of botany woven throughout her ironic portraits of everyday encounters between people and places. When I met her in 2018, we talked as though we had been friends for a long time. It was the height of strawberry season. She shared with me a story about a past lover to whom she had dedicated a painting, emphasizing the ambivalent qualities in the drawing as though it were a plant that nobody could identify – apart from its spellbinding properties.

The Paintings of Vlada Ralko

Another artist contemporary to Alevtyna Kakhidze, Vlada Ralko, also created a chronicle of the events on the Maidan as they slid into war. As graphic narrative, the text of Kyiv Diary (Київський щоденник) consists of 358 drawings that the artist created from 2013 to 2015.[47] She writes,

The "diary" contains many allusions to Shevchenko's protagonists, who, along with the characters from national mythology or folklore (Cossack Mamay, a cloth doll, etc.), seemed to have become active participants of recent events, or, rather, were made newly relevant by them. Extraordinary

Ukrainian reality seemed to offer, again and again, proof of its identity, or even proof of its existence, through resistance, pain, trauma and death.[48]

Ralko exhibited the first set of drawings in February 2014 in an exhibit named after the Taras Shevchenko poem "These Pages White."[49] The influence of Shevchenko's sketches can also be seen in the lines of her drawings, evoking his early drafts in which he sketched several figures on one page in order to save on paper. This gave the appearance of floating bodies in space. Images of women's billowing peasant dresses, or finery among revelers in his drawings *Bahanka, Harem, Oksanas*, and others appeared to sail above or alongside the Dnipro River, blend into willows on the Kyiv shoreline, or rest in clouds piled tall over the surrounding steppe. In my conversation with Ralko in Kyiv in the summer of 2019, she confirmed the deep inspiration and solace she draws from the region of Kaniv, where Shevchenko was from, and where she has spent a good amount of time working on her projects.

In Kyiv Diary, the abstract images – pencil, ink, watercolour, and marker layers over many sheets of paper torn from sketchbooks – appear as surreal dreams and nightmares, hauntings, comic book frames, or edited film stills; they are woven throughout with Soviet symbolism and vivid depictions of Slavic lore mixed with modern violence: bleeding bears, domes on fire, "babusiyas" in brightly coloured headscarves waving red carnations that burn black smoke across the sky (figures 5.5, 5.6). Foreboding shadows, barricades, weapons, and all-seeing eyes are pervasive.

The metaphor of the all-seeing eye strikes to the core of the text as an experience of history that is particular to Ukraine – protection from danger signified by the eye is a magical theme in local folklore. Fetishization of protection abounds in Ukrainian culture, and while the all-seeing eye carries with it elements of Turkish tradition, its popularity in the post-Soviet context functions in direct opposition to the traumatic memories wrought by the brutal panopticon of the Soviet surveillance apparatus. Vladko writes, "I first envisioned a series of drawings structurally similar to a diary after I saw a giant eye in the evening crowd [on Maidan] in turbulent Kyiv, that is, a man dressed as an Eye, it must have been an advertisement ..."[50] A surreal image from the earliest graphic works in Parisian newspapers featured just such an eye in the crowd. The image entered mass consciousness in the late nineteenth century, at a time of fear of violence on the public square with the rise of the first crowds, mobs, and reports of terrorism; after it was printed in Paris it found its way across the Atlantic. In my reading of Ralko's depictions of the Maidan, the eye is a metonym of the psyches of those carrying over the traumas and myths from the Soviet experience that the artist's generation seeks to understand, but cannot fully know.

Medieval Kyivan Rus' was filled with chroniclers. This chronicle radically reimagines the revolution in emotional qualities that draw attention to "bad myth" as a return of the repressed. Taboos and nightmares of all kinds take hold of the psyche. Although they do not disappear completely, there is paranoia around the total breakdown of the reference points – spatial, verbal, temporal – that structure identity and nation. The images do not supply or apply ready definitions or templates from prior aesthetic forms. They can thus also be read as creative blueprints towards a civic vocabulary for post-Maidan Ukraine that is, as in Svetlana Boym's citation of Taitln's Tower in *Another Freedom: The History of an Idea* – open, diagonal, and unfinished. Deconstructed socialist-realist icons, folkloric creatures, garlands, graffiti, floating heads, crying babies, grotesque streams of blood, dismembered torsos, and guerilla warfare undercut transcriptions of upheaval on the territories of modern Ukraine past and present that tend toward any official ordering or grouping of populations. Nonsequential symbols dating as far back as the pre-revolutionary Cossack Sich forgo documentary claims to "truth" by overwriting linear chronology.

As a "diary" that is also a chronicle with many depictions of women at the centre of the narrative, the language of the text further undermines the authority of the Soviet canon wherever state officialdom in the present seeks to extend communist ideology of perpetual emancipation in illusions of time and space. The past appears as an angry ghost, rather than a trace, nostalgia, or absence.

For those who have no direct memory of the events of the twentieth century, only second-hand encounters in fragments and material artefacts, these myths appear in sharp relief – emptied of their lived experience. Ralko's watercolour forms, for example, resonate with artists working from different points on the globe, such as Nalini Malani in India, who engages the profound resilience of the human body in the face of war and today's shifting forms of colonial power.

Painting, as an artificial aesthetic language, is an effective means by which to contrast representations of "reality" in public life with its myths. Unlike a photograph, speech, or state document, a drawing or painting can make no documentary claim as evidence of a specific moment. It can thus allow for gaps in time in which an individual's memory comes into conflict with the historical paradigms that come to constrain imagination. Ralko stakes an axe into the empty plinth in Kyiv's Besarabka Square (figure 5.7), where, as in the BABYLON'13 film,

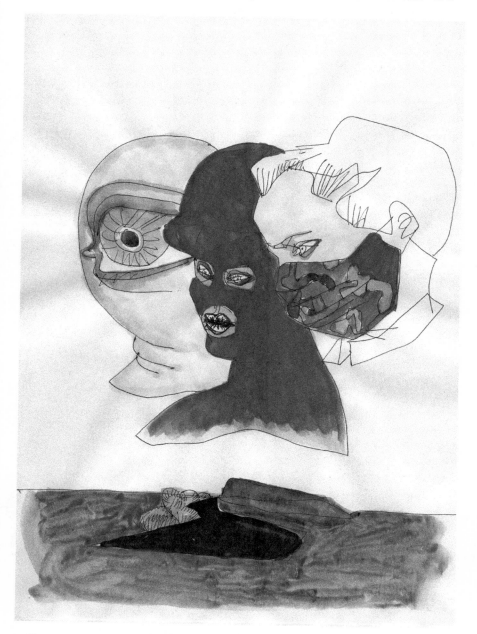

Figure 5.5. *Kyiv Diary*, by Vlada Ralko, 2014. Shared with permission of the artist.

Figure 5.6. *Kyiv Diary*, by Vlada Ralko, 2014. Shared with permission of the artist.

Figure 5.7. *Kyiv Diary*, by Vlada Ralko, 2014. Shared with permission of the artist.

the monument to Lenin that was the first to stand and the first to fall in the territories of Ukraine is the stage for laying claim to the future. And where the future no longer takes shape in a red hammer and sickle, but a pink axe tipped with blood left by the hand of a giant, time belongs to another myth, one that moves counter to the linear vectors this plinth once supported. Time now appears out-of-joint and more readily lends itself to the axes in Hutsul forest lore that is both menacing and liberating, buried deep in the Carpathians, as though called forth from a scene in Sergei Parajanov's *Shadows of Forgotten Ancestors*.

IV. Decolonizing Political Creativity

In the years immediately following Maidan, the impulse towards silence and total discipline manifested in the removal of Lenin statues throughout the nation as part of broader legislation on the decommunization of public spaces.[51] Many of the critiques and scandals around the invoking of these laws in acts of censorship and corrupt power grabs have actually mirrored the attacks that the Soviets once leveraged at the early Modernists and their descendants in the 1990s. In 1994, Yurii Mushketyk, first secretary of the Writers' Union, wrote an article denouncing the "modern Ukrainian post-avant-garde" for trying to

> create [art] on a wholly different basis – fanciful, abstract, self-willed, beyond ideals, beyond nationality ... the "pure," "complete" avant-garde is supranational, anational. For them national problems (as with social problems) do not exist ... It is possible to allow a Frenchman or an Englishman to play around with literature, they have a strong state, a nation, prosperity in the country ...[52]

This idea has survived, in a slightly different form, with the false logic running that because Ukraine is a "small" nation (despite a population of 46 million), it should tread carefully in presenting any views that might destabilize alliances, sources of trade, and aid packages linked to more powerful countries. While some of the radical feminists and artists featured in this book largely disappeared from the post-Soviet cultural landscape, others have become very central to its increasingly digitized and networked spaces.

The first structure to rise over the pedestal of the toppled Lenin monument on Besarabka Square was an art installation constructed on 7 July 2016 that ran for two weeks. The piece was entitled *Inhabiting Shadows*, by Cynthia Guiterrez, a Mexican artist invited to create the work as a result of an international competition that garnered interest from applicants from over twenty countries (figure 5.8).[53] The competition was

Figure 5.8. *Inhabiting Shadows*, by Cynthia Gutierrez, 7 July 2016. Social Contract Project, curated by Kateryna Filyuk for IZOLYATSIA. Photograph by Dima Sergeev. Photograph shared with permission by IZOLYATSIA.

created by Izolyatsia Art Group and named the Suspilny Dohovir Project (Community Trust), directed by Kateryna Filyuk of Izolyatsia Art Foundation, an art group that was forced to relocate from Donetsk to Kyiv after their offices and art pieces there came under attack by Russian so-called separatist forces during Putin's invasion and occupation of the Donbas region.[54]

The installation draws up a polyvalent image of revolutionary change not dissimilar from Kakhidze's and Ralko's deconstructed chronicles. The piece simulates both liberation and subjugation by placing participants in the position of the former dictator. The 360-degree open space on which participants were invited to stand splits apart the gaze of the missing stone Lenin, once aligned with the long avenue of poplar trees that still runs the length of this hill in Kyiv. The aesthetic of an unfinished construction evoked by the metal structure over the plinth also shifts the narrative of "progress" into something different. Ubiquitous mobile phones replicate and circulate images captured from atop the platform, forming a panopticon for networks on social media, news reports, and other digital surfaces. The gaze that once marked totalitarian power is thus rearticulated in the social and digital networks that combine not only in new forms of social freedom, but also, along with these forms, in new challenges brought on by the impacts of reduced privacy, the sale of demographic information, and the ethical questions around state surveillance of IP addresses, people, and territories.[55]

As of 2018 the plinth on Besarabka Square, like many others throughout Ukraine, remains empty. The material afterlives of the deposed stone Lenins vary widely: some have been tossed aside, while others have been put into museum repositories. There has been discussion about creating an open-air museum with many Lenins on display in one location, as in Budapest, despite widespread criticism abroad of Hungary's museum efforts in the 2000s as catering to markets over careful research, in order to attract profit from foreign tourists. In *Secondhand Time*, Svetlana Alexievich comments on the ideological contradictions in similar pop clichés that she observed in the perestroika generation in Russia: "I met young guys on the street in t-shirts with the sickle and hammer on them, holding portraits of Lenin. Do they know what communism is?"[56]

In light of the above examples, I believe that the more critical engagements with Soviet monuments and symbols by artists of the emerging generation in Ukraine are yet to be fully appreciated or understood. For example, Yevgenia Belorusets also addressed Lenin in her curatorial and photographic practice. She utilized fragments from the faces of broken Lenin statues to comment on contemporary social issues in *Let's Put Lenin's Head Back Together Again!*, a collection of photographs and sculptural installations that were exhibited in 2017. Nikita Kadan, Mykola Ridnyi, Oleksiy Radynski, Vasyl Lozynsky, and others associated with the journal *Prostory* continue to experiment with similar integrative concepts in filmic language, poetry, sculpture, and other media as a unifying forum for independent artists and collectives. *Monument to a Monument* by Zhanna Kadyrova, an artist from REP (chapter 4), featured computer-generated images and actual installations of statues in a park covered with white fabric, as though yet to be unveiled in a dedication ceremony (figure 5.9).

The outpourings of creativity around the figure of Lenin in Ukraine may be read as an extension of the first installation over Lenin's plinth in Kyiv taken to its full historical value – the internationalization and replication of the space of postcommunism: Who owns what? Who views who? Who is fighting for whom in the Russia-Ukraine conflict?

Lenin statues, like other Soviet ruins, have taken shape locally as a medium of expression and a trope for exploring the "bad myths" – the paradoxes of the Soviet system and the full extent of its advantages and disadvantages. Svitlana Alexievich's receiving the Nobel Prize for Literature in 2015 is also significant for the fact that her texts were nearly banned by the state and were only published in Belarus by private publishing

Figure 5.9. *Monument to a Monument*, by Zhanna Kadyrova, 2009. Former Lenin Square, Shargorod, Ukraine. Courtesy of the artist.

houses after 1993. Her ideas in *Secondhand Time* are as relevant today not only for the experience of Ukraine's youngest generations, my global peers, but also for so many authors like myself and others throughout the world who are at present situating our own voices in the discursive shift at the turn of the century: "On the eve of the 1917 Revolution, Alexander Grin wrote, 'And the future seems to have stopped standing in its proper place.' Now, a 100 years later, the future is, once again, not where it ought to be. Our time comes to us second-hand."[57]

In 2014, the film *The Tribe* (Плем'я), by Myroslav Slaboshpytsky, reached international audiences in an Oscar nomination for Best Foreign Film along with wide recognition at Cannes. Set in a boarding school for the deaf, the film depicts the struggles of a teenage boy forced to hustle sex and drugs in order to survive in the school's gang. Yet the protagonist comes to question the ethics of the entire system of criminal exchanges in which all residents of the school are forced to survive. He falls in love with a female student who has been assigned to him by the other gang members as his first target in becoming a pimp.

Instead of erasing the symbolic codes of Soviet society, Slaboshpytsky appropriates them for a canvas. The same blue wall as in the graffiti artist Vova Vorotniov's contribution to Belorusets's series *Ya i Ona*

(Me and her), discussed in chapter 3, appears here once again as a meto-nym for the state. This ubiquitous Soviet holdover, which still officially marks nearly all public space in Ukraine ranging from state institutions to apartment hallways, is a highly potent signifier for total bureaucratic indifference. For some, this is arguably the single most stable factor in the transition between the Soviet and contemporary Ukrainian state. In the film, this sign is motivated and repeated in visual language as the primary backdrop that throws into relief, by contrast, all forms of alternate, illicit, and illegal symbolic capital as it is leveraged among the boarding school students across liminal transactions.

Nudity in the film, as in the focus on the gendered body in Beloru-sets's photo series, heightens audiences' attention to the state's mech-anisms of population control. By literally "laying bare" the people in front of the wall in the most fundamental of exchanges, their con-structed and regulated roles as citizens are shed like clothing. The biopolitics of officially sanctioned behaviours breaks down into fights, manipulations, and provocations in a Darwinian struggle to secure ba-sic needs. Exploitation, greed, and pride characterize the microcosm of this self-interested Hobbesian world that Slaboshpytsky formu-lates within the walls of the school. The biopolitics of the unregulated exchanges among the schoolboys are formed through their gang hierar-chies, which mirror the brutality of the Soviet regime, both portrayed as equally Orwellian. Although the formal mark for public/private con-duct is still written on the wall, so to speak, in dark blue paint, in the film, there is no escape from its clutches over the minds of the youth – this is made all the more apparent in the dehumanizing transactions that devolve into mutual exploitation in brute competitions for power in front of it: sex, fighting, sale of drugs, and so on.

As a microcosm not only for Ukraine, but for all of post-Soviet soci-ety, the blue wall is also significant as a spatial language among other languages. The film contains no subtitles or musical soundtrack. All characters speak in Ukrainian sign language, which, alongside other visual elements, is underscored by noises and sounds from the settings of the school, the streets of Kyiv, and a large truckstop where the male gang members pimp the girls in the school. Sign language mixes with many other languages developed between individuals, most promi-nently body language.

The images are alienating in their brutality, yet every scene is uni-versally intelligible, even if you do not know Ukrainian sign language. In the context of the Maidan Revolution of Dignity and the Russia-Ukraine conflict, which were both occurring at the time the film was made, the overall neutrality of the language factor in the film is extremely important. Sign language, unlike spoken Ukrainian or Russian, still shares roots in both of these languages and has not been codified strictly into either/or.[58] The body language in the film is highly gestural and occupies an even more central role than the sign language does. Mimeographic gestures between characters create repetitions that drive the plot and dialogue in a technical ballet of languages. Spontaneous movements, as in modern dance choreography, are only an affect of the more lyrical repetition of stanzas in bridges between statements. Lastly, the total absence of subtitles gives viewers the opportunity to enter the microcosm without applying geopolitical qualifiers. The borderless and allegorical qualities are tantamount here: the deaf school in Kyiv could be anywhere.

This is a society of the superfluous. All are insignificant and thrown away by the mainstream. Marginal leftovers. This is a story familiar in all cultures. Here, the broken mess of the mainstream seems to lay waste to a forgotten younger generation. Where are the parents, the caretakers, the police? We know nothing about how the students in the school got there. In fact, where are any members of the older generation – other than the truckers who pay for sex? There is not a single person in the film capable of providing guidance, as the few teachers and one doctor we encounter look past their young charges indifferently. There is no ethical figure to stand in for the rule of law.

The younger characters in the film prove to be incredibly creative and compassionate in their resilience. Their struggles to understand themselves are also about learning to see each other; they fight, but do so without aiming to kill or harm, moving in a visual choreography that runs counter to the stagnation of the Soviet past which remains still and silent around them. The overall cinematographic effect marks Soviet time and space as cyclical, but not impossible to overcome. This is perhaps the single most powerful element of the film because cyclical time and unregulated space are highly malleable materials for the reinvention of history. Younger generations are co-opting, rather than submitting, to the authoritarian legacies inscribed into the environments surrounding them.

The blue wall, the Soviet code for public space – like Lenin – is a central trope for the emerging generation. These tropes are invaluable because they are ideologically loaded material structures. They serve to visually mark where the selective distortion of history meets contemporary manipulations of power by way of ongoing bureaucracy and willed "obsolescence." While these tropes are primary, they are just two among many in the spatial codes utilizing the body to contest the most significant space – the public square – alongside the values and ideas of the Orange Revolution and Revolution of Dignity, both watersheds for this generation. These values continue to come into conflict with real and imagined propaganda wars, the militarization of society in the context of the Russia-Ukraine conflict, and policies on how to memorialize and "modernize" what were once considered "highly modern" Soviet public facilities. As in Ralko's paintings and Kakhidze's drawings, the projection of nation and ideology onto the body throughout all of the chapters in this book also functions as an allegory. The public/ private divide is being challenged, as in the liminal spaces of the boarding school's boiler room, hallways, and Kyiv's urban parks and public zones of transit. Return to the microcosm of the school: ultimately, gender difference drives the transactions in front of the wall. The central female protagonist is depicted outside of any traditional familial private life: she is both liberated and trapped by her sexuality, forced to sell herself in order to negotiate her survival. The only thing that the boys have to offer her in exchange, in the informal economy run by their gangs, is their protection from the outside world, the world of the hearing that all too often walls off the deaf. In these exchanges, the forms/functions of the body and its internal organs are also rituals marking mortality in wider social manifestations of sexuality and reproduction.

These bodily forms stand in for the state regulation of borders, architectural forms, and time. The younger generation's renegotiation of that regulation shows that erasure is not an option, and escape is futile. So they invent themselves through language. The film reaches its apex with the protagonist falling in love with his assigned worker-protégé. Each risks excommunication from the gang, but also gains the potential to change its mode of survival from competitive to collaborative. The survival mechanisms of body language used solely for commodity exchange are forfeited for others that run counter to its objectification and dehumanization: the survival mechanisms of empathy and compassion (figure 5.10).

But love in the film is not romantic or ideal. The brutal abortion scene in the nearly defunct hospital – also in front of a blue wall – is perhaps the starkest reminder that, in the post-Soviet context, for the most vulnerable, the state exacts its price on the body by constantly reminding all that everything but life and death can be regulated. Deafness lands in silence in trying to "hear" the languages of the older generation. As in the dystopian British novel Lord of the Flies by William Golding, the survival of a civilization depends on both material and existential reference points. There is no indication in the deaf school that the younger

Figure 5.10. Film Still. *The Tribe (Плем'я)*, directed by Myroslav Slaboshpytsky, 2014. Shared with permission of @AlphaViolet.

will attain the means or will to reproduce, indicating that the future is either open, or absent – as in revolutionary time. All are alienated from the past: individual will, in a constant fight for visibility and mutual intelligibility, is in a zero-sum relation to the world outside the deaf school, and yet, it is this paradox that the youth alone face, and as much as it entraps them, the brief moments of their perception of being trapped that arise are also the backbone for survival within the school, as much as for negotiating and interpreting a better future beyond its officially marked blue-and-white Soviet era walls.

V. Conclusion: The Interrevolutionary Generation

War is not a distant memory in Ukraine. The nation's youngest artists are seeking continuities with their grandparents' lived experiences by inhabiting Soviet spaces as public gathering places. This goes against the "noise" of the information war, in which the past is often drawn in stark East versus West terms. These grand narratives delegitimize individual experience, and cannot account for popular ambivalence towards the many regime changes that have amounted to shuffling elites unable to deliver on reforms. There is little open public discussion in contemporary Ukraine about its troubled long twentieth century, as can be seen in a recent motion to outlaw all symbols connected with the Soviet regime. This silence only contributes to Putin's propaganda machine wherever it co-opts the Soviet past as pro-Russian. More critical dialogue can be an antidote to the information war that provokes actual combat.

What emerges across all of the specific works in this chapter is the cultural turn of what I am naming Kyiv's *interrevolutionary generation*, defined by what they do not remember – the Soviet Union – as they live out its effects under the rule of those who do. Arguably best poised to critique the resulting impacts of the ideological shifts occurring from within the post-Soviet space are its internal "outsiders." This outsider status extends especially to gender and sexual minorities, whose identities were never fully formed according to the Soviets, and whose local interests oftentimes appear most clearly when understood as part of a global phenomenon in human rights protest occurring almost completely online (despite The Woman Question and Ukraine being the first republic to decriminalize homosexuality in 1991). Amid state elites' attempts to rebuild society in Ukraine after the Orange Revolution, and again after the Revolution of Dignity, any semblance of "stability" remains elusive.

Gains have been made. Increased trade with the European Union and a visa-free travel regime were introduced in 2016 and 2017. But for those fighting on the front lines of the war with Putin's Russia, or living on the low end of rising inequality – the revolution can also feel like a metaphor for a stalled life. The noble aspirations of Ukrainians from diverse political, ethnic, religious, and class backgrounds who stood and fought on the Maidan are to be admired as the revolution is still very much a work in progress.

Artists are readaptating broader Soviet aesthetic conventions that, in Ukraine's climate of "decommunization laws," could also be viewed as provocative in their disassociating the past from the hegemonic role that Moscow played in the Soviet project, a theme touched upon in chapter 4 in the context of Ukraine's museum system. The material spaces of post-Soviet society are serving as metonyms and microcosms in film, painting, and texts that utilize the oppressive spaces of the Soviet past in order make its continued lawlessness in the present all the more apparent.

Ideologically saturated material artefacts of the Soviet era, ranging from the most concentrated symbolic unit in the figure of Lenin, to the banality of the ubiquitous blue wall, to the small details of everyday life in communal spaces, serve as reminders not to fall prey to accepting any ideology wholesale. There is no alternative, no escape from these symbols according to the texts and ideas of the younger generations. Attempting to do so, like attempting to erase the past, only further subjugates one to the risks of a blank slate – a vacuum for new forms of hegemony and exploitation. By contrast, artists create their own economy to survive, initiating their own future by negotiating signs and codes in a vocabulary unique to our generation, which shares many experiences with others, including myself and my peer researchers, whose self-reflexivity and positioning with regard to Ukraine involves ongoing negotiation of multiple meanings, contexts, and identifications in shifting frames, discursive fields, and definitions of human rights.

The durability of the Cold War is still visible in its material traces on both sides of the iron curtain, but its limits are evidenced in human interaction between the generations. For those who have no direct memory of the events of the twentieth century, only second-hand encounters in fragments and material artefacts, its grand myths appear in sharp relief – emptied of their lived experience. The works throughout this book show the durability of these tales, but also their limits. For all generations, the Soviet myths have already taken on religious dimensions, yet perhaps for the younger ones, and especially those who have witnessed two revolutions, perhaps only we are positioned to view the full range of archetypes, deities, and fetishes operative within the epic (and from a perspective beyond its stable time frame).

The ideological myths that order our lives can be universal, or they can wall off our worlds – as they did in the Cold War. Art, as an artificial aesthetic language, is an effective means by which to contrast the representations of "reality" that drive human communication in all forms and languages. Unlike official historical documents, creative production can make no documentary claim as evidence of a specific moment: it can thus allow for gaps in time that open up the possibility for a more global view, a lens by which to explore where memory comes into conflict with the historical paradigms that can constrain us in our thinking, speaking, and living. This is the gift of imagination as the language of experiment, of revolution, a language that has no value, mode of expression, or meaning other than through invention.

As Ukraine struggles to reinvent itself against the stream of violence, life loss, and displaced populations unleashed by Putin's invasion, occupation, and war, new forms of civic participation will cede to new histories. Global engagements with the past will produce new images that will push against the binaries of the Cold War. Not only Ukrainians, but also my own generation in the West will, inevitably, disassemble the timepieces to examine the clockwork in *the mirror image* of the Soviet myth – Western liberalism – where it silences nuanced ways of seeing the occupied territories of Ukraine, the DNR (Donetsk National Republic), LNR (Luhansk National Republic), and Crimea as more than just territories in a geopolitical contest, or provokes views on the people living there as obsolete Soviet "Others" – simple unfortunates at best, and fossils of the past, at worst. Ironically, elements of both sides of the Cold War myth can be observed in Russian media, which selectively plays Western discourses against a rehash of denationalization policies. Exploring the past is always linked to securing survival in the future. For artists such as Kakhidze, this search is tied to individual will, and resilience. Her story of the Russia-Ukraine conflict rummages among the old myths, looking for fragments and chards to carry into the new epic that will, inevitably, be forged in the years ahead. She forages for the unsung heroes among those who were once so callously described as the "losers of the transition" – teachers and others like her mother:

> It seemed like I finally came to understand what was being implied by the word "escalation." It isn't cruelty, violence, or aggression, but the expansion of a conflict situation to the point where all social norms no longer apply. This theme underlies the darkness in my work. But what is perhaps more interesting is that after experiencing violence amnesia sets in ... a desire to forget everything ... And yet it is at that point that the restoration of memory becomes especially critical. Without memorialization you cannot build a future. It is for the same reason that I always carry with me small shards from the mines in Slavyansk – so I don't forget the experience.[59]

Access to information, increasingly linked to class conflict in the widening of the digital divide, also conditions the material experiences of everyday life from which all politics proceed in the twenty-first century, shaped by memories of multiple revolutions that cohere around different ideas of progress. These ideas often outpace territory and language, although both are exploited by elites in positions of authority by different means and ends. After the Maidan Revolution of 2013–14, Ukraine slid into conflict with Russia. Kyiv became a site of international concern. Ukrainians, in their efforts to tell their own stories in the onslaught of "fake news" and an "information war," were first responders who now share much with others around the globe in standing against rising authoritarianism and extremism. Some are seeking ethical solutions to problems without clear answers. And yet, in Kyiv at the centre of this search is a particularly keen aptitude for survival, cultivated over many generations, that is manifesting in a cultural renaissance.

Art continues to have urgency in Ukraine where minorities, artists, and journalists who speak out can easily become targets, forcing retreat from a hostile political environment. This situation is not unique to Ukraine; it is no fault of its citizens, who have fought tirelessly for democracy, nor is it the product of an "ethnic" conflict. The outcome of regressive legislation and elite shoring up of resources is a population starved of information, the very basic fabric from which knowledge can be cultivated through education.

New engagements with urban space and art can be sites for innovation as they allow interactive experiences that disperse educational processes not only across traditional sites, such as the university and the museum, but by recasting the public value of learning in local terms. The School of Kyiv, VCRC, and others are innovative because they are significant attempts to extend these processes during an era of reinvention – which will require deft navigation through the twin siren songs of decommunization and propaganda. Further, this means peeling back the layers of the histories of the Orange Revolution and the Maidan Revolution as a project of autonomous values and membership in the international community, rather than an imitation of Europe:

> Ukrainian Eurorenovation of the 2000s consists of replaceable surfaces, drywall and plastic; a cheap dream, the temptation of advertising, physically displacing an unworthy reality. Eurorenovation is a self-identification through consumption, an expensive spectacle of representative democracy rapidly deteriorating in meaning, the euphoria of an "eternal today," a plastic sheet of printed advertisement glued onto the granite of the Soviet metro ..."[60]

Class aspirations and specious displays of democracy in "Eurorenovation," as Anastasiya Riabchuk points out in her essay on a REP artwork by the same name, disappear, but only on the surface: "Eurorenovation simultaneously contributes to social marginalization and encourages the labelling and stigmatization of any deviation from the norm."[61] Among what is often rendered defunct or obsolete, Soviet-era spaces have become important sites for experiments in social dialogue among all who grew up during the Cold War as microcosms of post-Soviet society that have global significance.

In this context, artefacts from Ukraine's history are also valuable for dismantling the modes and behaviours by which totalitarianism replicates itself. Global audiences traversing this part of the world will encounter here more than a painting, a lecture, or a textbook, but the public square itself – lived, remembered, defended, and invented by those who have long inhabited its geometric coordinates at the crossroads between East and West in the former Soviet territories. Reading the signs and icons in these codes in the twenty-first century will require deft skill by scholars engaging with multiple revolutionary processes as they unfold on all social, cultural, and political layers: "The humanitarian thinker is an intellectual smuggler; it is only through overcoming borders that new ones may be drawn. The modern world requires two types of talent: the ability to apply, and the ability to learn."[62] In the School of Maidan, the most profound discoveries are made along those unmarked trails and footpaths that veer far off from the main trade routes that have zigzagged through this kaleidoscopic terrain over several centuries.

Conclusion

Do revolutions ever end? Some have written that after any revolution fatigue sets in, but how do we recognize fatigue in this sense? In the years following the Orange Revolution, a range of emotions clustered around "the ideals of the Maidan" in Ukrainian public discourse. Scholars, journalists, and international commentators in the West tended to note that the ideals of the Maidan had faded. The image evokes a dream. The leitmotif of those years was that the harder people had fought for their civil rights, the deeper the nation's sleep became. In the decade intervening between the Orange Revolution and Putin's war, the civil liberties that Ukrainians had once striven for slowly slid into obscurity. The reforms promised by the Orange leaders Yushchenko and Tymoshenko had undergone a steady dissolution under Yanukovych. However, throughout even the darkest periods of that oppressive regime, among young civil rights activists, there grew an intense belief that some kind of awakening was imminent.

Active in the decade between Ukraine's two revolutions on Kyiv's Maidan, the dissenting activists, artists – and feminists – whose stories are documented here were an important, if underestimated, catalyst for airing repressed individual fantasies and anxieties about collective identities latent to the public square. These anxieties took shape internationally as well: an ideological mirroring of elites that protesters throughout the post-Soviet region had fought against in their actions against corruption in the 2000s would fully come to bear in the ongoing investigations of Russian meddling in the US 2016 presidential election, in addition to the charges against Yanukovych's former campaign consultant, Paul Manafort, for conspiracy against the United States brought by US Justice Department special counsel investigator Robert Mueller III.

In the years between Kyiv's two revolutions, many intellectuals, artists, and others became activists against their own will – forced, at times, to risk their own bodies in the face of physical violence in order to express themselves freely. State violence driven largely by infighting among corrupt elites played out over an entire decade of regime change. This resulted in a heavy burden of injustices that has been disproportionately shouldered by women and other minorities. Artists in Kyiv have continued to carve out pivotal public sites for making visible the symbolic, often hidden, violence that the state had wreaked against its own people. It is my hope that this study not only offers up critical material for viewing the relationship between gender and protest in the context of revolution, but also provides blueprints for interpreting the intersection of art and politics in a civic vocabulary about power, self-expression, and the body.

There is another revolution still ongoing in Kyiv. It can only be described as one that is non-national in the sense it is about totalitarian rule over the nation coming into conflict with multiple, simultaneous, and varied enactments of civic identity; as a result, it is even harder to mark as having an end or an outcome.[1] The Soviet past of the twentieth century, for those living in its immediate shadow in Ukraine, never faded completely. Many on both the left and the right are sceptical of postcommunism as a viable paradigm, or a condition of being, as it is sometimes described in neoliberal policies focused on undoing the communist "mentality." Questioning local constructions of race, class, and gender in lived experience, however, has provided local feminist thinkers and artists on the left with strategies for negotiating between the grand narratives of capitalism and socialism. These narratives, and their twentieth-century utopian origins, seem to be losing their foothold in the region. Women activists in particular are bridging conversations within emerging feminist scholarship that overturns older East/West divides.

Agata Pyzik has compared growing up between London and postsocialist Poland to living in a "dream factory."[2] Ongoing exchanges across the former Bloc and Western Europe have profoundly changed people's relationship to each other and, perhaps even more significantly, their memories of the past. Pyzik's own descriptions of her life comprise a unique perspective that works to unravel previous assumptions around the isolation of socialist societies. Her metaphor of a "dream factory" turns upon the fabrication of time: in particular, the industrial past and its teleologies that tether "progress" to the myths, stereotypes, and grand narratives of the Cold War. Many of these ideas still haunt East-West cultural relations. The utopian dreams of the early twentieth century and their imagined modernities, in hindsight, appear astonishingly similar on either side of the Iron Curtain. The expression "former East" now sounds ironic, even parodic.

The organization of spatial and temporal experience by activists in Kyiv's most recent Maidan demonstrations differed significantly from descriptions of protest elsewhere, for example, in Poland 1989. In May 2014 I observed first-hand the space of the Maidan, noting how the people still living within the lingering tents and scorched barricades had altered the physical landscape in order to attract the attention of satellite cameras. One sign made from upturned cobblestones spelled out a message in large letters: "Patriotism is the idea of the Maidan. Stop Propaganda! There is no Fascism Here!" The image, shown in figure 6.1, makes apparent just how extensively digital culture has shaped sensorial narratives of immediacy on the Maidan, shifting the *optics* of protest, including local attempts to both come to terms with the past and prevent misperceptions about Ukraine in foreign media, especially those circulated by Kremlin propaganda. In attempting to translate these discourses, perhaps no one can completely escape the "dream factory" and its idealism. How does one stave off fatigue – by sleeping, or waking?

Scholars of social movements often base their critiques in alternative, nonlinear timeframes unmoored from mainstream discourses. The juxtaposition of real/virtual spaces on the square had long been familiar to feminist activists in Ukraine's capital. These activists, already positioned outside the mainstream, had carried the mantle of this marginal viewpoint. They were, arguably, better suited than anyone else to understand just how weakened the centre of government had become long before the Maidan demonstrations had even begun.[3]

In a sense then, there were many "Maidans" in the events over the winter of 2013–14. The different encampments, parties, social groups, observers, and others on the physical space of the square plotted themselves in cartographies of politics tethered differently for each, depending on their views. Some writers and intellectuals stated their independence from all established political parties (Serhii Zhadan, Oksana Zabuzhko, and Yurii Andrukhovych). Despite these early attempts, the large gathering on the Maidan grew and turned violent in January 2014 after demonstrators on the far right responded to the initial attacks on student protestors by Berkut riot police.[4] After approximately three weeks of demonstrations, a moment arrived when many realized that the wide range of demands on the Maidan could never be met. Two authors whose works have been aligned with the youngest generation of feminists in Ukraine, Irena Karpa and Viktoria Narizhna, drafted a document entitled Agenda 5/12 petitioning opposition leaders on the right who had gained a substantial following to follow through with three points they believed would keep the peace and move all involved demonstrators towards reform.[5] The document

Figure 6.1. "Stop Propaganda! There Is No Fascism Here!" Maidan, Kyiv,
1 May 2014. Photo by the author.

included protection of protestors from police, a demand for members of
parliament aligned with Yanukovych to resign, and for the opposition
to present and follow through on several reforms. The petition received
thousands of signatures, and opposition leaders agreed to its demands.
This took place early on during the demonstrations, on the cusp of the
mass mobilizations that took place on the second Sunday of December
known as the March of Millions. Despite the coming together of diverse
agendas to keep the movement peaceful, the deployment of state riot
defence units would result in more deaths in February, after which the
police themselves would defect from the regime.[6]

Many of the artists and writers discussed in this book, including
feminists in Ofenzywa and activists united by Kyiv's Visual Culture
Research Center have maintained ambivalence towards the conflicting
ideologies represented on the Maidan.[7] What they did share with demonstrators, however, was deep scepticism towards the regime and a desire to form a public consensus. Many individuals in these communities
had prior organizing experience and shared their time and knowledge
by contributing to the communications centres, hotlines, fundraising

for medicine, "flying universities," and manual labour needed to keep the movement going.[8] Individuals in Ofenzywa, HudRada, and Revolutionary Experimental Space (REP) took part in the initial efforts to reinforce nonviolence among protestors. They worked tirelessly in every capacity to prevent deaths among the wounded by delivering medicine during the police attacks. They worked with independent media to translate information and counter the streams of propaganda that circulated throughout the demonstrations. Many also took on banal tasks such as making sandwiches, hauling trash, and organizing transportation. Throughout these events, Femen activists remained in Paris. They incorporated messages of support for the Maidan demonstrators into their photo-ops, but largely remained bodies in front of the camera, in spite of the fact that their origins on a post-Orange Maidan were very much part of the story of its transformation into *the* Maidan.

Perhaps the only tangible political idea that everyone involved in the Maidan had in common was the square itself: less what it was officially venerated as being about, or was popularly imagined to be, *or never became* in the Orange Revolution, but its symbolism, which had finally been called into question. The idea of the square emerged as a totally transparent space – a negative space – drawing everyone into its centre for what it might become, for better or worse: opportunity or tragedy. The square was sought, shared, and contested because of its polysemy. The defining measure of the moment was the square itself (figure 6.2).

After ousted president Viktor Yanukovych fled to Moscow, the material wealth that he had stored up in his private estate was seized by protestors and put on display in the National Art Museum of Ukraine in Kyiv, not far from the Verkhovna Rada (parliament). This calls to mind a prior revolutionary moment in the Bolsheviks' confiscation and transferral of private wealth in the process of solidifying the institutionalization of museums. Thus, the exhibit discussed in chapter 4, *Disputed Territory*, organized by HudRada at the same site two months prior, reaches its culmination at this point in the complete reversal of the Soviet cultural artefact. It is an example of the public taking back what the state had stolen.

This reversal illustrates a reclaiming of both the state figurehead's privatization of art and the museum's defunct exclusionary policies. One portrait in the exhibit featured Yanukovych in a cartoonish rendition of Napoleon. The deposed dictator's face had been scratched out of the picture (figure 6.3). The display called to mind Tsar Nicholas II's portrait, which was covered in bayonet scratches by the revolutionaries who had stormed the Winter Palace in 1917. This is not to equate the Bolsheviks' confiscation of private wealth with the appropriation of Yanukovych's stolen material wealth by the new post-Maidan ruler and his state.

Figure 6.2. 1 May 2014, *Kyiv's Maidan*. Photo by the author.

Rather, I want to emphasize how these acts split apart by pointing out the reversal of consolidated power in the interregnum: the return of public property to the Ukrainian public meant overturning its own definitions – and how, ultimately, it is this process that is at the root of democracy.

Among the kitsch self-portraits and other artefacts in Yanukovych's hoarded collection were state and ecclesiastical treasures: icons and rare books dating to 900. The exhibit was named *Codex Mezhyhirya* and featured several rooms divided into "books" chronicling different aspects of "the story of a dictatorship." Objects were grouped and placed on the crates that they had been shipped in. Yellow and black tape separated viewers from the objects, evoking an investigative scene, but also serving a practical purpose in that the exhibit had gone up within merely a few weeks. One room featured a roundtable with experts and a sign that read "Ask me about this exhibit." Large banners running the exterior length of the building announced the event with a single word: *Revolution*. Displaying the embezzled wealth of the ousted president in this particular way thus also signalled a radical shift in the public's engagement with state museums in the postcommunist era, pointing to imminent change in the future accessibility and involvement of the public in institutions.

Figure 6.3. Portrait of Yanukovych from the palatial Mezhyhirya Estate, seized by Maidan demonstrators, on display in the National Art Museum of Ukraine (NaMU). Kyiv, 2014. Photo by the author.

Perhaps there can be no true story of a revolution, only transformation. The artists and activists discussed in chapters 3 and 4 are continuing to create visual artworks, performances, and other texts that respond to their experiences on the Maidan. During the course of the revolution, Ofenzywa became two groups: Zhinocha Sotnia (Women's Hundred) and Kobylians'ka Sotnia (Ol'ha Kobylians'ka's Hundred).[9] Yevgenia Belorusets undertook a project featuring her photographs of the barricades surrounding the square. Her portraits include commentary on the gendered divisions that occurred within the encampment.

As a virtual exposition, the project re-maps the boundaries of "#euro-maidan" as a protest symbol. VCRC curator and author Kateryna Mishchenko and Berlin photographer Miron Zownir created photographs and essays in creative ethnographies featuring everyday life in Ukraine over the course of a year.[10] Many of their works open possibilities for alternative perspectives that complicate depictions of Ukraine in the media, particularly those which condition viewers to accept grand narratives that demand either a pro-Russian or a pro-Western bias and to see only heroes/villains in the ongoing conflict in the region. An empty press booth with graffiti commentary that I passed by on 20 April 2014, which happened to be Orthodox Easter, located at the foot of the street along which the heaviest clashes took place and where the barricades were still smoking captures the situation better than words (figure 6.4). This particular street has since been renamed Nebesna Sotnya, or Heavenly Hundred, after the defenders who perished there (figure 6.4).

Artists in Ukraine have continued to carve out new public spaces for their artworks, despite attacks from the far right on the sites of these collectives' activities and on individuals across all segments of society involved in minority rights movements. In only one of the many other examples, the anonymous burning of the location of the Visual Culture Research Center (VCRC) at the historic Kino Zhovten (October Cinema) in late summer 2014 further united artists with outside activists. Individuals gathered in regular meetings to call for investigations into the burning. These meetings expanded to include demands for reforms in the Ministry of Culture linked to the art world. Shortly thereafter, VCRC was reinstated in a new space and continues to serve as a venue for discussion among activists on the left concerned with a wide range of social issues.

Three distinct court cases were brought to the Kyiv municipal courts in 2009, each concerning an artist in HudRada, raising questions of censorship due to the destruction of works and closure of exhibits by local museums. The collective responded by creating an auto-referential exhibit called *Court Experiment*, held 12 October–12 November 2010 at VCRC, before the center lost its location at Kyiv-Mohyla University due to a reactionary decision by then director Serhiy Kvit. As of early 2018 Volodymyr Kuznetsov is fighting for recognition in the municipal courts for the destruction of his painting *Judgement Day*, discussed in chapter 4.

Despite a sharp rise in organizing among nationalist far-right groups, along with increasingly narrow legislation on decommunization restricting freedom of expression throughout Ukraine, projects and dialogue continue to grow across collectives and between individual artists, many of whom are receiving more and more critical attention abroad. Yevgenia Belorusets is working on a new project dedicated

Figure 6.4. An empty press booth with graffiti commentary, 20 April 2014, Kyiv. Photo by the author.

to the conflict in the occupied territories; she has continued to exhibit throughout Europe since she headlined Vienna Art Week in November 2014 in an exhibit entitled *Maidan* that brought together fifty artists from Ukraine, including many from the collectives in this book.[11] Despite the war, new art initiatives have continued to thrive, such as the independent film festival group FILM 86, in which former Ofenzywa member Nadia Parfan plays a central role. Pathways for public conferences, exhibits, and publications continue to be built not only by feminists, but also by many others allied with them, whose early activism skills and critical actions have paved the way for future creative experiments. Looking back, Femen's story is very much a part of the city square in the interrevolutionary dynamics, and the energy that has carried over into the new era in Kyiv is revivified in the installations and gatherings by the local art-activists described in chapters 3, 4, and 5.

Exploring these intergenerational and international experiences can open two critical pathways in Ukraine. Securing freer spaces for education and open debate must be facilitated in a grassroots capacity in order to reduce propaganda about identity (ethnicity, nationality, religion, and sexuality) proliferated by the unprecedented falsification of the present state-to-state combat between Russia and Ukraine as a conflict driven by civilians. Second, the extensive lessons for strengthening global solidarities around information access, knowledge networks, and delivery channels for material support should be considered a defence strategy in the de-escalation of conflict and human rights infringements. Many scholars, artists, and activists throughout the region have worked to break barriers to global access to scientific journals and other information markets in order to counter local misinformation; it is crucial that Ukrainians' unique cultural and civic viewpoints as being "between" the West and Russia are not reduced to economic and military tactics.

Investment in private arts institutions rose dramatically in the years after the Maidan Revolution, especially through the platforms of PinchukArtCentre and Mystetsky Arsenal. By contrast, the landscape for public Soviet-era museums and independent projects has been far slower to adapt to rising interest. In 2016 the state issued a charter for a museum dedicated to the events on the Maidan 2013–14; the museum was slated for the formerly named Instytytska Street, where the defence brigades perished in the bloody clashes that took place on 18 February 2014, yet as of 2020 the site still stands empty.[12] Scholars and curators continue to work with international partners in the European Union in planning and hosting new programs, exhibits, and other events. The critical need for more public educational outreach only continues to rise.

April 2014. I am standing on Kyiv's Maidan at Eastertime. Everything around me is scorched and covered in flowers. Handmade memorials

Figure 6.5. *Barricades and Drone*, Kyiv Pride March, 2019. Photo by the author.

and carefully arranged miniature displays of bullets and other debris labelled as "proof" of what happened stand outside the tents of this mostly Carpathian and Zaporizhian people's encampment. A city within a city surrounds me: from the middle of the square I can see a graveyard, a church, a military training zone, a psych ward, a hospital, a canteen, a press centre, and even a piano. Vibrantly coloured drawings and paintings posted to the stone façades of Khreschatyk's Stalinist-era buildings and the gilt marble entrances of the metro flutter in the midday sun. A banner near the stadium reads "A Polish Sign of Solidarity with Ukraine." Several people are bowed in prayer in front of Dynamo Stadium, the site of the barricades between riot police and demonstrators where many lives were lost. Two Orthodox priests dressed in black vestments wave censers in a circular motion, and the pungent scent of myrrh covers the smell of hickory burning beneath the cauldrons of gruel boiling on the back of a recuperated Soviet-era Red Army military vehicle nearby.

Later that day, I join a small crowd in front of Taras Shevchenko University to observe a demonstration by student union activists calling for educational reform. Someone in the crowd, I will learn months later, would be physically attacked and hospitalized. I follow others as they travel in a group to the subway, protecting themselves in numbers. Individuals here are targeted regularly for speaking out against the corrupt practices that continue to eat away at people's life opportunities. The students I speak with that day tell me that there is no trust for the older generation and their leadership. While participating in the women's marches and Kyiv Pride marches nearly five years later, I observed how the size of the crowd had grown exponentially since I had first come to Ukraine to research feminism. I also observed how the threat of the opposition not only to those marching for gender justice, but also to minorities of all kinds outside of the context of the marches, had grown and shifted into online groups organizing with the far right, the authorities in Ukraine too often turning a blind eye to the activities that foster hate crimes, as has increasingly become the case elsewhere in the world (figure 6.5).[13] I find myself wondering how there can be any trust in the future without building international solidarity with the help of my local peers in addressing the conditions of speech affecting us all in the present.

If the past two decades in Ukraine can provide scholars with any lessons, we can be sure that they will unfold in dialogue with the bold thinkers, scholars, artists, and mavericks of all stripes who have become visible and found their voices in Ukraine in the 2000s. It is this generation that spans the former Cold War divide – our ideas, and our deviations from the legacies of the twentieth century around the globe – that will determine the rest of this story.

Notes

Introduction

1 Szymborska, "A Tale Begun," in *View with a Grain of Sand: Selected Poems,* 161–3.

2 Judith Butler argued "that even as the war is framed in certain ways to control and heighten affect in relation to the differential grievability of lives, so war has come to frame ways of thinking multiculturalism and debates on sexual freedom, issues largely considered separate from 'foreign affairs.'" *Frames of War,* 12.

3 Szymborska, "A Tale Begun."

4 Anna Hutsol, interview with Kateryna Mishchenko, Nadia Parfan, and Oleksiy Radynski, "Mriiemo vyvesty na vulytsiu tysiachi holykh zhinok: rozmova redaktsiia PK z hrupoiu Femen," *Krytyka Polityczna,* February 2012, accessed 25 March 2012, http://vcrc.ukma.kiev.ua/uk/pk3/femen.

5 The groups Zhinocha Sotnia (Women's Hundred) and Zhinocha Sotnia Kobylians'ka (Women's Hundred Kobylians'ka) emerged from the feminist group Ofenzywa, featured in chapter 3. While individual members worked together throughout the events that transpired on Maidan, the question of violence, specifically whether or not to adopt a militaristic approach to rights, and whether to join demonstrators taking up arms in defence against the state, eventually split the group into two camps. Sarah D. Phillips analyses the impact of the debate on feminism within the context of Euromaidan in "The Women's Squad in Ukraine's Protests."

6 McFaul, "The Orange Revolution in a Comparative Perspective," 193.

7 Phillips examines this dynamic in detail among several groups of women in the early 2000s in *Women's Social Activism in the New Ukraine.* In particular, she observes that the definitions of social need articulated by elderly women activitists do not readily dovetail with the language that dominates in Western NGOs and granting agencies.

8 They outlined their demands for equal representation in a letter addressed to officials in Yanukovych's parliament in 2009. The document's circulation catalysed ongoing demonstrations around March 8. Kis, "Lyst posadovtsevi" (Letter to an official).

9 Verdery writes, "The several ways in which gender equality was legislated [under socialism] served to reinforce the significance of gender difference even while ostensibly undermining it. This makes gender, like nationalism, a strengthened vehicle of post-socialist politics." *What Was Socialism?*, 14.

10 Naiman quotes the philosopher and publicist Mikhail Gershenzon on his taking stock of the intelligentsia in the academic journal *Landmarks* in 1909. *Sex in Public*, 45.

11 Naiman, *Sex in Public*, 48.

12 Ibid.

13 Ibid., 47.

14 Benjamin, "Theses on the Philosophy of History."

15 Verdery, *What Was Socialism?*, 14.

16 Chernetsky, "Introduction," in *Mapping Postcommunist Cultures.*

17 Femen's public satire has involved them in several lawsuits. In January 2012 they were arrested and tortured in Belarus for their nude demonstration outside of the state's secret police headquarters. A few months later, three activists were arrested again in Russia for attempting to steal a ballot box during Putin's 2012 re-election campaign. April 2012 group members faced charges in the Ukrainian court system that included a four-year jail sentence at the request of the Indian Embassy in retaliation for Femen's protest on the balcony of the Indian ambassador in downtown Kyiv.

18 Mayerchyk and Plakhotnik, "Radykal'nyi Femen i novyi zhinochyi aktyvizmu," 8.

19 "Femen: «Конечно, а Как Же Ж» Colta.ru," accessed 5 February 2013, http://www.colta.ru/docs/12363.

20 Verdery, *What Was Socialialism?*, 82.

21 Avant-garde groups like Bu-Ba-Bu from the 1990s are finding critical corollaries in more recent initiatives by groups throughout both Ukraine and Russia similar to HudRada discussed in chapter 4, which is a self-described "curatorial union" that uses subversive aesthetics founded in early modern montage. Depictions of war, collectivization, interrogation, exile, and other events from Ukraine's long twentieth century are provocatively juxtaposed with the modernist utopias of both capitalist and communist "progress."

22 These political references are comparable to Yekelchyk's position on Verka Serduchka, as a "carnivalesque, liberating take on the very real cultural

and political tensions caused by the imposition of political correctness."
Yekelchyk, "What Is Ukrainian about Ukraine's Pop Culture?," 219.

23 Ilnytzkyj, *Ukrainian Futurism*, 184.

24 Quoted from the 1921 manifesto of the Ukrainian futurist avant-garde
group Nova Generatsiia, by Mikhail Semenko, in "Platform and
Environment of Leftists," in Lawton and Eagle, eds., *Words in Revolution*, 25.

25 Lawton and Eagle, *Words in Revolution*, 184.

26 The poet Oleh Olisevych wrote, "'[The Lviv pacifists] are a radical group,
and we are for proactive methods.' There were several more demonstrations in 1987, culminating in one planned for December 26 to commemorate the eighth anniversary of the Soviet invasion of Afghanistan.
This one was preempted by arrests. There were also protest letters, fasts,
and ever more contacts with Poland, the Ukrainian émigré community
in London, and the Independent Peace Association in Czechoslovakia."
Qtd. in Risch, *The Ukrainian West*, 220; Padraic Kenney explores the same
collectives in Lviv and Kyiv within his book *Carnival of Revolution*.

27 Risch, *The Ukrainian West*, 250. The term "Banderites" is a reference to
the followers of Stepan Bandera, the controversial leader of the former
Ukrainian national movement in the years during the Second World War
until his assassination by the KGB in 1959. The term is often used as a
derogatory metonym for absolute thinking and far-right nationalism.
These uses of the term stem from critiques of the actions and ideals of
Bandera's branch of the Organization of Ukrainian Nationalists (OUN-B),
and their collaboration with the Nazi regime under his leadership.
Bandera and his unit were later sent to German concentration camps.

28 "According to one of the band's early leaders, it was originally a
Russian-language group. It turned to making Ukrainian-language hits
out of inspiration from jokes band members made about local Ukrainians
with the aid of Galician Ukrainian slang. The rise of Ukrainian-language
groups like Vopli Vidoplasova (V.V.) in Kyiv also inspired them to
perform in Ukrainian. By the time of the first Red Rue festival in 1989,
as noted by scholar Romana Bahriy, the group's songwriter Serhiy
Kuzminskyi ('Kuzia') had written a number of Ukrainian rock songs with
deliberate themes of political protest, including a song that described
recent police beatings of a peaceful demonstration in Lviv." Ibid.

29 See my articles on Femen: "Two Bad Words"; "Femen, A Photograph";
"Global Protest Movements in American-Ukrainian Dialogue: From
Femen to Occupy"; and "Performing Protest: Femen, Nation, and
the Marketing of Resistance"; see also Zychowicz and Tchermalykh,
"Asymptotes."

30 Serhy Yekelchyk aptly described the main conflict driving the situation
in terms of rising economic inequality, rather than cultural difference.

Despite the country's pronounced regional differences, and the 2004 campaign platforms of Yushchenko as pro-Ukrainian and Yanukovych as pro-Russian, most Ukrainian voters wanted a nation unified by civic egalitarianism and an end to oligarchy, rather than a protracted battle in the Rada. In *Ukraine: Birth of a Modern Nation*, Yekelchyk points to the simultaneous vernacular usage of Ukrainian and Russian languages in everyday modern life as one example of cultural fluidity, as opposed to the projection, manipulation, and marketing of identities through linguistic categories in political campaigns. This view supports the position that the divisive ethnic tensions embedded in Ukraine's political landscape were reinforced by a handful of elites who co-opted nationalists' rhetoric in order to maintain their power, even after the country gained independence in 1991. Also see Way, *Pluralism by Default*; and Minakov, *Development and Dystopia*.

31 Her work has been exhibited in Berlin, Moscow, and Warsaw; she has been featured as a writer-in-residence in Vienna and has led translation workshops for the Goethe Institute.

32 Alexei Yurchak discusses the visual art collective REP in the context of a broader span of civic activism on the left in "Revolutions and Their Translators."

33 Phillips, *Women's Social Activism in the New Ukraine* (2008); Hrycak, "Orange Harvest?" (2006).

1. Performing Protest: Sexual Dissent Reinvented

1 Anna Hutsol, interviewed by the author, 22 August 2011, Kyiv.

2 "Mission Statement," Femen website, accessed 10 November 2013, http://femen.org.

3 To be sure, Hutsol's statement is overly dismissive of the many important gains that numerous scholars who identify themselves as Ukrainian and feminist have and continue to make in all sectors of society, including on the levels of intellectual, policy, and social development. Solomiia Pavlychko in Kyiv, Irina Zherebkina, and Tatiana Zhurzhenko in Kharkiv, and Oksana Kis in Lviv, and others have been frontrunners in this regard since the 1990s. A seminal text that documents the debates on feminism in a transnational context in the early postcommunist context is Gal and Kligman, *Reproducing Gender: Politics, Publics, and Everyday Life after Socialism*. Also see Pavlychko, *Dyskurs modernizmu v ukrains'kii literaturi*; Pavlychko, "Feminism in Post-Communist Ukrainian Society"; and Pavlychko, *Feminizm*.

4 Hutsol stated, "As for feminism itself and whether [Femen] is feminist or not, I think this question belongs to researchers and historians.

Generally, I think I agree with those dear people who say that women have rights, for example, that I have a right to protest. Whether these rights are radical or not radical, justified or unjustified, is a different question altogether. People like myself who say women have the right to do what they want are in a way feminist, slightly so, but feminist." Hutsol, interviewed by the author, 22 August 2011, Kyiv.

5 "Femen is a product of the post-Soviet system, they are out in the streets as the generation of 20-25 year olds who have group up during the independence period ... Femen is also a post-revolutionary phenomenon in terms of the powerful opportunities for street protest that were brought on by the Orange Revolution." Mayerchyk and Plakhotnik, "Radykal'nyi Femen i novyi zhinochyi aktyvizmu," 8.

6 Ibid.

7 "[Femen is] looking for their own interpretation of feminism; experimenting with the term as a neologism, they manoeuvre around the Sword of Damocles, which is maintained by antifeminist stereotypes. While attempting to sift their ideas out from an older, 'bad' feminism, they are simultaneously trying to construct their own, 'egalitarian,' new feminism." Ibid.

8 While based in Ukraine, Hutsol and other members often referred to their mission this way in the media and in interviews; their position would later shift after their move abroad.

9 Vitaly Chernetsky's theory of the "postmodern postcolonial" nation in his study on 1990s Ukrainian and Russian literature encompasses many of the complex historical processes that manifest as contradictions in postcommunist art. See *Mapping Postcommunist Cultures*.

10 Irigaray, "Women on the Market," in *This Sex Which Is Not One*, 170–91.

11 Historian Roman Adrian Cybriwsky includes chronological timelines of these protests alongside other key political changes in Kyiv in his book *Kyiv, Ukraine: The City of Domes and Demons from the Collapse of Socialism to the Mass Uprising of 2013–2014*.

12 Femen, *Livejournal* (blog), 8 August 2011, accessed 10 September 2011, http://femen.livejournal.com.

13 When I queried Hutsol whether Femen would ever perform in a theatre, versus outside on the street where the group usually makes its appearances, she quickly replied: "Nothing would change if we did that, it would distract from our aims. Women cannot remain timid and quiet in Ukraine. In principle Femen's ideas, our protests, are highly visible, but full of ideological motivation: a philosophy of life in action. Men seeking something like a show or a cabaret can go view those in a theatre – we're doing something else, we're involved in protest." Hutsol, interviewed by author, 22 August 2011, Kyiv.

14 The group almost never circulated or published any photos of themselves cuffed by women officers.

15 At the time of Femen's founding in Kyiv in 2008, according to Article 14 Ch. 173 of the Code of Ukraine on Administrative Offense, public nudity was listed as minor hooliganism and was punished accordingly, with a modest fine, or arrest and only a few days of custody. In 2009, the code was amended to allow for more frequent arrests.

16 Several movements across Central and Eastern Europe in the twentieth century have used similar strategies involving humorous street theatre; see Kenney, *Carnival of Revolution.*

17 Femen activist Inna Shevchenko described her thoughts while being covered in gasoline and threatened by Belarusian state secret security agents: "I suddenly saw the huge potential of this. Maybe it's strange to say this – I know some people already think we're kamikaze – but that's why I now say I'm more of an activist than a person, because I know that tomorrow I could be killed." Cochrane, "Rise of the Naked Female Warriors."

18 Femen has attributed their funding to private donors including a musician named D.J. Hell and the owner of KP Media Holding Company, Jed Sunden. Several artists, filmmakers, and journalists have created artworks and short documentaries about the group's activities; in early 2013 two popular books were published on Femen; see Ackerman, *Femen*; and Tayler, *Topless Jihadis.* The journalist Jeffery Tayler initially published his first-hand accounts of Femen's headquarters in Paris in *The Atlantic*; see "Femen: Ukraine's Topless Warriors" and "Topless Jihad." He portrays Femen's core members as media labourers and underwriters. Inna Shevchenko reports in Ackerman's book that participants are paid living wages out of a fund of which she is the primary public relations and accounts manager, and that Femen is fully invested in maintaining a public image based on highly reproducible media protest imagery.

19 "Mission Statement," Femen website, accessed 19 November 2012, http://femen.org/en.

20 Qtd. in Cochrane, "Rise of the Naked Female Warriors."

21 "We [Femen members] are smart people who live in the modern world; we're not barbarian or crazy. The war we are in is more ideological and in the sphere of communication. As for actual conflict, I hope that will never come to pass. We are completely for peaceful protest without casualties or other losses." See Cochrane, "Rise of the Naked Female Warriors."

22 Mouffe, "Artistic Activism and Agonistic Spaces," 5.

23 Rubchak, "Seeing Pink."

24 Rubchak, "Ukraine's Ancient Matriarch as a Topos in Constructing a Feminine Identity," 133.

25 "Ukrainians sought to authenticate their ethnic uniqueness by rejecting the collective masculinized Soviet model of quintessential womanhood in favour of their own legendary 'hearth mother' Berehynia. They created important links with their past by reaching into pre-history for a lasting symbol of Ukrainian cultural identity as a historically matriarchal society. It was projected onto a contemporary culturally determined female stereotype to produce a new paradigm of the ideal woman, exemplifying the 'mother of the nation.'" Rubchak, "Seeing Pink," 57.

26 Rubchak noted, "Femen meets some of the formal criteria for a women's movement, for example, as described by Carol Mueller: 'specific individuals must be identified who have formed emotional bonds from their interaction, negotiated a sense of group membership, and made a plan for change ... [creating] a collective identity' (1994: 246), but this has yet to translate into a national phenomenon although, as noted above, branches are springing up in other cities." Rubchak, "Seeing Pink," 69.

27 Ibid., 55.

28 Mayerchyk and Plakhotnik, "Radykal'nyi Femen i novyi zhinochyi aktyvizmu," 8.

29 Early Femen actions in Ukraine resulted in domino effects among protestors from other groups. Rubchak wrote of the impact of Femen's initial street actions: "On 25 February 2010, Victor Yanukovych, a twice-convicted felon, was inaugurated as Ukraine's fourth president. Exhibiting an almost pathological fear of public criticism, he and his cronies moved swiftly to restrict public assemblies and muzzle the press, often resorting to brutal police tactics to achieve their ends. Consequently, a peaceful assembly of young people opposing the proposed legislation barring public assemblies without prior government approval brought hundreds of youthful activists to Kyiv's central square on 17 June 2010. They did score a temporary victory, but the struggle is far from over. This rally for freedom of assembly followed on the heels of a FEMEN demonstration on 3 June 2010 against limitations on democratic liberties and freedom of the press. Its protest was timed to coincide with, and comment upon, Yanukovych's first 100 days in office." "Seeing Pink," 69.

30 Gal and Kligman, *Reproducing Gender*, 3.

31 Ibid.

32 Schechner, "Speculations on Radicalism, Sexuality, & Performance," 98.

33 Kenney, *Carnival of Revolution*, 163.

34 Ibid.

35 Hrycak, "The Coming of Chrysler Imperial."

36 See Andryczyk, "Four Bearings of West for the Lviv Bohema."

37 These playful demonstrations have more recently been described as the progenitors of a movement given the term "monsration," yet such

claims that these phenomena originated in Russia overly reduce a much more complex amalgam of aesthetic styles in Central and Eastern Europe, as well as the influence of pop culture, among art-activists working throughout the 2000s in post-Soviet regions outside of the Russian Federation. It is easy to see why ascribing a Russian origin to this term is an overstatement when one considers closely the very notion of the art collective in the mid-twentieth century, which differed greatly from its later counterparts under glasnost in which small intellectual circles blended with the proliferation of mass-culture and pop-culture – both of which entered at a more rapid pace those territories that were the first to withdraw from the Soviet Union, or already existed beyond its borders. Critiques of Russian imperialism and Western capitalism were always equally subject to parody, as in the rock opera *Chrysler Imperial* in Lviv. Rock, pop, and the early modern avant-garde collective became fused with political scepticism of both Russian and Western imperialism. In both Lviv and Kyiv, "global countercultures, including those of hippies, bikers, and punks" appeared by the early 1990s and were more closely connected to the West through proximity to Poland. Pop culture's influence on collectives was almost always deeply political, even in the later years of the dissolution of the regime, as in the case of Bu-Ba-Bu in Lviv: "In the sphere of rock music, the forces of pop, rock, and nationalism made their greatest fusion at the end of the 1980s, thanks to a nascent political upheaval in Kyiv. A new republic-wide rock festival, the Red Rue, organized in memory of Ivasiuk in 1989, did much to articulate young people's demands for the Communist Party to step down and for Ukraine to become independent." Risch, *The Ukrainian West*, 220, 259–60.

38 For a thorough discussion of these performances throughout East-Central Europe in the twentieth century, and their implications in the broader historical changes leading up to 1989, see Kenney, *Carnival of Revolution*.

39 Quoted from Michael Kirby's seminal description of the diverse elements of happenings, which he derived from observing his contemporaries in New York, also referring to the art form as "theatre of effect" published in the Introduction to several performative statements and texts by Allan Kaprow, Red Grooms, Robert Whitman, Jim Dine, and Claes Oldenburg in *Happenings: An Illustrated Anthology*, 19.

40 In both cases, ambivalence is as much about creativity, as it is a form of strategic inoculation against the radical economic fluctuations of late- and post-Soviet political regimes in Ukraine. For example, Mark Andryczyk describes the Lviv Bohema as follows: "Welcoming to, but wary of, today's presence of 'the West' in Lviv, these men and women recognize the dangers in swapping once mass culture (Soviet) for another (Western pop culture). They are inspired by their position between 'the East' and

'the West'; through the art they produce and the lifestyles they choose to lead, they navigate the course of post-Soviet Ukraine as it oscillates between these two poles." Andryczyk, "Four Bearings of West for the Lviv Bohema," 248–9.

41 For a more extensive discussion of counterculture in the USSR in the second half of the twentieth century, see Yurchak, *Everything Was Forever*.

42 The challenges of a postmodern feminist theoretical model can most notably be seen in the case of Nancy Fraser's critique of Habermas's public sphere in *Fortunes of Feminism*. Some Ukrainian feminist scholars have held to a similar line of critique in their evaluations of Femen, for example Maria Dmytriyeva in "Femen na tli hrudei," 20–3.

43 Benhabib, *Situating the Self*, 204. Benhabib's scepticism is driven by a more extant feminist critique of postmodernism, inclusive of the idea that the constant deferral of signs negates the subject-position that is needed to articulate rights. She asks, "Are the meta-philosophical premises of the positions referred to as 'postmodernism' compatible with the normative content of feminism, not just as a theoretical position but as a theory of women's struggle for emancipation?"

44 Chernetsky, *Mapping Postcommunist Cultures*, 237.

45 "Zabuzhko is a writer in whose work one can find a combination of powerful explorations of Ukraine's colonial legacy with a challenge to the familiar paradigms of patriarchy that often reemerge in the openings created by the breakdown of the empire." Chernetsky, *Mapping Postcommunist Cultures*, 252.

46 Spivak, *An Aesthetic Education*.

47 Anna Hutsol, interviewed by author, 22 August 2011, Kyiv. Inna Shevchenko has also waxed nostalgic in news interviews while looking back on the Orange protests of her childhood: "I was just a girl then, but for the first time in my life I understood that we could have democracy in our country." Qtd. in Tayler, "Femen, Ukraine's Topless Warriors."

48 CANVAS has since come under scrutiny as having provided consulting and branding in the Arab Spring, and for receiving financial support from private multinational corporations invested in by Western governments. For a comprehensive overview of the group, see Rosenberg, "Revolution U."

49 Manning, "Rose-Colored Glasses?," 175.

50 Ibid., 171.

51 Ruslana, Grynholy, Okean Elzy, Mandry, and many other pop musicians contributed to a common aesthetic of Ukrainian independence characterized by a diverse blend of nineteenth-century folkways, European jazz, myths and legends from Kyivan Rus', Orthodox liturgical music, and other genres disassociated from the Soviet period.

52 Qtd. in Neufeld, "Femen Activists Get Naked."
53 Yekelchyk, "What Is Ukrainian about Ukraine's Pop Culture?," 18–19.
   Yekelchyk has discussed elsewhere how political elites' campaigns in the
   lead-up to the Orange Revolution adopted ethnic models when beneficial
   to solidifying their power bases. By contrast, he argued, nation-builders
   in parliament and voters on the left and right wanted democratic reforms
   that embraced civic models over ethnic ones. In late 2000 a set of private
   tapes brought to light Kuchma's fraudulent and criminal behaviour. In
   February 2001, protestors formed a small movement called "Ukraine
   without Kuchma!" After Tymoshenko joined the anti-Kuchma movement
   other oligarchs in parliament soon engineered her dismissal; however,
   she later emerged as a charismatic populist leader and went on to establish her party, BYuT. Yushchenko remained prime minister until April
   2001 due to a coalition of oligarchs and communists in parliament working in his favour. Both of these leaders would go on to unite the Orange
   opposition. For a more detailed discussion, see Yekelchyk, *Ukraine: Birth
   of a Modern Nation*, 208–25.
54 Michael McFaul has pointed out that the peaceful gatherings on the
   Maidan in 2004 triggered by a falsified election "mirrored 1991 in form
   by affirming Ukraine's autonomy through putting into practice the
   democratic laws already on paper." The citizens who demonstrated
   on Euromaidan in 2013–14 ultimately attempted to testify further to
   this democratic autonomy. Their demand for a referendum regarding Ukraine's EU Association Agreement, and then general elections,
   deserves recognition as a powerful instance of the Ukrainian citizenry's
   lasting faith in the democratic process. See McFaul, *Revolution in Orange*,
   55, ed. Aslund.
55 Wilson, *The Ukrainians: Unexpected Nation*, 209.
56 McFaul draws this parallel in *Revolution in Orange*, 55.
57 This is mostly the case in the historiography of the Orange Revolution
   in the comprehensive studies produced in the years just after it took
   place: Yekelchyk, *Ukraine: Birth of a Modern Nation* (2007); Wilson, *The
   Ukrainians: Unexpected Nation* (2009); McFaul, *Revolution in Orange* (2006).
58 Tymoshenko remained in prison under Ukrainian jurisdiction despite
   Western governments' and human rights groups' ongoing grievances
   over her sentence. Ongoing domestic protests by Ukrainian citizens also
   did little to change the course of her internment. In autumn of 2013,
   Tymoshenko issued a public statement that she would be willing to relin-
   quish her Ukrainian citizenship if this would lift the obstacle that her jail
   term posed for Ukraine-EU integration.
59 Youth groups such as PORA and Rukh in western Ukraine played a key
   role in the early stages of the revolution. For example, PORA barricaded

Yanukovych's motorcade from being able to access the Parliament building while Yushchenko held an inauguration ceremony.

60 The group's parodies often make reference to the elusive language
around target issues, such as pension reform, that Ukrainian politicians
had promised the Orange Revolution would resolve.

61 Lisyutkina, "Soviet Women at the Crossroads of Perestroika," 283.

62 Ibid., 293.

63 Ibid., 284.

64 Helena Goscilo gives a detailed overview of the cultural politics of the
"sexual revolution" in the late-Soviet period and 1990s in her introduction to *Dehexing Sex: Russian Womanhood During and After Glasnost.*

65 Nikolai Gnatyuk, "Vyberi menya, vyberi menya, ptisya schastya
zavtrashnego dnya," accessed 10 May 2015, http://www.youtube.com
/watch?v=ZQrZ00JGjWk.

66 At the World Economic Forum in Davos in 2011, President Viktor
Yanukovych told international media: "Come to Ukraine to see our
beautiful girls!" On 8 March 2012, Prime Minister Mykola Azarov wished
women well and mentioned that he hoped spring would make them "blossom" with "bright colors" to put on display to the world. Martsenyuk,
"Ukraine's Other Half."

67 Irigaray, *This Sex Which Is Not One,* 186.

68 Herbaut, "Dans L'intimité des Amazones."

69 Others have argued that Ruslana's Amazon image contains a
"combination of individualism and hedonism that many would see as
paradigmatic for the life practices of contemporary Western societies."
See Pavlyshyn, "Envisioning Europe," 474.

70 Mikhail Bakhtin probes a similar concept of the inversion of power relations between centre and margin in his theory of carnival in *The Dialogic
Imagination.*

71 Kyiv's tallest structure is a monument entitled Мати-Батьківщина,
or "Mother of the Fatherland." Built by Yevgeny Vuchetich in 1981, the
statue stands over the memorial museum to the Great Patriotic War
on the Dniepro in Kyiv. It features a steel woman sixty-two-metres tall
bearing a sword and a Soviet shield in her raised arms.

72 Wolff, *Inventing Eastern Europe,* 62.

73 The Latin term used on maps in the seventeenth and eighteenth centuries
demarcated all lands to the east of the cartographer's territorial depictions
of Western Europe. The term loosely translates to "Where there are lions."

74 Sacher-Masoch, *Venus in Furs,* 43.

75 Wolff, *Inventing Eastern Europe,* 62.

76 Mucha wrote that in his paintings women should be "elevated and
turned into impersonal bearers of all beauty." When sketching, if the

face of a model excited him too much, he covered it with a veil. He did not do this when taking photographs; Josef Moucha and Jiří Řapek have noted that the main purpose of Mucha's figures "is not to allure with provocative expressions" but to convey "the source of the profane level of Mucha's nudes as collections of erotic diversions and curiosities." Underlining the ubiquity of his nudes in Czech modern photography only one generation later, one critic remarked in 1934: "The nude in photography, not to mention the original Czech nude, is a kind of Cinderella." R. Viktor, "O Fotografickém aktu u nás," *Fotografický obzor* 42, no. 7 (1934): 101–3, qtd. in Moucha and Řapek, *Alfons Mucha*, 15–16. Also see Husslein-Arco, Louis Gallemin, Hilaire, and Lange, *Alphonse Mucha*.

77   Kyiv's tallest structure is a monument entitled Мати-Батьківщьина, or "Mother of the Fatherland," built by Yevgeny Vuchetich in 1981. The statue, which stands over the memorial museum to the Great Patriotic War, features a steel woman sixty-two metres tall bearing a sword and a Soviet shield in her raised arms.

78   "To create a new language Khvylovy fused various linguistic levels: the traditional concerns of the Ukrainian intelligentsia were interspersed with references to Western literature, Marxist political theory, the macaronic language of the Russian civil service, and the racy idiom of the town proletariat. The twenties were witnessing a democratization of culture of unprecedented proportions: the introduction of mass education, mass publications, radio and cinema meant a rapid expansion of culture beyond lyrical poetry and the theatre of ethnographic realism." Shkandrij, *Modernists, Marxists, and the Nation*, 55.

79   Zabuzhko, *Pol'ovi doslidzhennia z Ukrains'koho seksu*.

80   The work was published as a book entitled *Ukrainian Folk Tales / Ukrainskie narodnye rasskazy*.

81   Humesky, "Marko Vovchok vs Turgenev," 595. Vilinska later sent copies of her stories to the poet and Ukrainian revolutionary Panteleimon Kulish (1819–1897), who called them a "living ethnography" and soon published Turgenev's translation of them in the Russian journal *Narodni opovidannia*. According to Humesky, the stories immediately caused a sensation for their depiction of serfdom; many critics attacked them as a brutal depiction of the Empire, while other critics saw in them a just evaluation of ethics. The poet Taras Shevchenko, a name often invoked as a euphemism for the nation of Ukraine itself, called the young Vilinska "his daughter" and even went so far as to dedicate a poem to her.

82   The photo is also another example of how Femen's protests stimulate the commercial media and art industries. Rayss, "Award of Excellence for Photo 'Sascha from Femen.'"

83 Featured in the exhibition *Iconoclaste* at Galerie Mansart (Paris), curated by Azad Asifovich, 12–19 June 2016, accessed 3 November 2018, http://www.galerie-mansart.fr/iconoclaste--oksana-shachko.html.

84 Nancy Condee describes prison tattoos as permanently engaged in subversive dialogue with the administration: "This dialogue, so to speak, between the prisoner's sloganed body and the prison administration's sloganed space was intensified by the reality that the body could not be confiscated. It could be mutilated, coerced, controlled, and neglected; but as long as the prisoner lived, his body was a potential interlocutor with the prison administration." Condee, "Body Graphics," 350.

85 Condee notes, "Women's tattoos were more frequently hidden from view and not as associated with the performance of criminal power. They were often autobiographical, recalling a first experience of heterosexual or lesbian sex, marriage, birth or narcotics; or a death, often of a mother or a child." Ibid., 347–8.

86 Taras Shevchenko, "Iakby vy znaly panychi," *Kobzar*, 238, my translation.

87 Translation by the author as part of Dr. Omry Ronen's Seminar in Ukrainian Poetry, University of Michigan, Winter 2012.

88 Humesky, "Zhinocha symbolika u Shevchenka," 108, my translation.

89 Ibid., 110, my translation.

90 Vitaly Chernetsky applies Rosi Bradiotti's postmodern nomadic feminism from *Nomadic Subjects* to Ukrainian postcolonial literature: "'Time is not frozen for the postcolonial subject, as the memory of the past is not a stumbling block that hinders access to a changing present. Quite the contrary, the ethical impulse that sustains the postcolonial mode makes the original culture into a living experience, one that functions as a standard of reference.'" *Mapping Postcommunist Cultures*, 229.

91 "The possibility of collectivity is persistently foreclosed through the manipulation of female agency"; Spivak, *In Other Worlds*, 150.

92 Femen's manipulation of online images that, in turn, mediate socialization and consumption around their imagining of "protest" as popular politics capitalizes on an earlier notion of spectacle as alien commodity. In *Society of the Spectacle*, originally published in French in 1967 with the first translation into English published by Black & Red Press in Detroit, poststructuralist philosopher Guy Debord defines "spectacle" in his foundational postmaterialist critique of Western societies, which he traces in the advent of film: "The spectacle is the other side of money: it is the general abstract equivalent of all commodities. Money dominated society as the representation of general equivalence, namely, of the exchangeability of different goods whose uses could not be compared. The spectacle is the developed modern complement of money where the totality of the commodity world appears as a whole, as a general equivalence for what

the entire society can be and can do. The spectacle is the money which one only *looks at*, because in the spectacle the totality of use is already exchanged for the totality of abstract representation. The spectacle is not only the servant of *pseudo-use*, it is already in itself the pseudo-use of life." Debord, *Society of the Spectacle*, 25.

93 "By making him no longer self-identical, it allows him the negativity, not simply reason or criticism, but an identification with a disembodied public subject that he can imagine as parallel to his private person." Warner, *Publics and Counterpublics*, 164.

94 "As the bourgeois public sphere paraded the spectacle of its disincorporation, it brought into being this minoritizing logic of domination." Warner, *Publics and Counterpublics*, 167.

95 Ibid., 169.

96 Rancière, *Dissensus*, 145.

97 Warner writes, "Where consumer capitalism makes available an endlessly differentiable subject, the subject of the public sphere proper cannot be differentiated. It can represent difference as other, but as an available form of subjectivity it remains unmarked." *Publics and Counterpublics*, 168.

98 Ibid., 179.

99 Ibid., 177, 179.

100 Ibid, 176.

101 Ibid., 183.

102 Mayerchyk and Plakhotnik have noted that, for Anna Hutsol, "the measure of a successful Femen action is a popular action. Popularity, for Femen, is publicity that draws attention to social issues, for them, this is the way out of obscurity." During the years Femen was based in Kyiv, the core group of original Femen members' amorphous media spectacles remained bound up in Mayerchyk and Plakhotnik's early assessments of their design: "In our opinion, Femen is a local, postsocialist, and postcolonial project. Femen's position and actions, if you try to correlate them with the western principles of feminism, simply will not coincide with the parameters of any of them." "Radykal'nyi Femen i novyi zhinochyi aktyvizmu," 7.

103 Balmforth, "FEMEN Topless Activists Plan Euro 2012 Soccer Tournament Protests."

104 Warner, *Publics and Counterpublics*, 184.

105 Ibid.

106 "Other than a brief three-year period following the Civil War, after which the beginning of a Ukrainian state was absorbed by the Bolsheviks, there was no period of independent Ukrainian statehood to point to in the modern era." Wanner, *Burden of Dreams*, 131. Scholars also reference this period as the "Ukrainian Revolution" instead of "Civil War." While this

particular point is beyond the scope of this study, it is important to note that the Ukrainian People's Republic (1917–1921), however brief, is significant to any understanding of independent Ukraine and its civic identities in the contemporary political landscape.

107 "In the age of the nation-state, 'uncovering' a sense of Ukrainian identity was part of the strategy to challenge the legitimacy of Soviet rule." Wanner, *Burden of Dreams*, 121.

108 "Performers throughout the evening tried to steer the anti-Soviet feelings of anger, deception, and disillusion, which they had purposefully evoked, into a strategy of empowerment by advocating Ukrainian independence as a cure-all strategy for the ills currently plaguing their society." Wanner, *Burden of Dreams*, 126–7.

109 Wanner discusses the negative, exclusionary impact some of these performative strategies had on Russian festivalgoers in underscoring Moscow as imperial capital of the USSR, although she weighs more heavily the alternative cultural memories that festival organizers attempted to achieve: "Cognizant of the fact that as a site for the transmission of a post-Soviet national culture, the Chervona Ruta music festival, through its celebratory crowd setting and ensuing solidarity offer[ed] the potential of facilitating reorientation of individuals to a nationalized collective. To ensure that this reorientation [was] lasting and not fleeting, Chervona Ruta [was] institutionalized with state funding that has been steadily forthcoming." *Burden of Dreams*, 140.

110 Pavlyshyn, "Envisioning Europe," 474.

111 Ruslana's song "proposes to its domestic audience that the assertive and forceful emancipation celebrated by the song as a whole has a predecessor in, and is not so very different from, a Romantic emancipation that is more familiar and therefore acceptable." Ibid., 475.

112 Pavlyshyn underscores Ruslana's ahistorical fantasy as agentive: "[She avoids reference to actual history] because this would almost inevitably mean grounding identity in experiences of suffering and victimhood and run[ning] the risk of contaminating collective identity with *ressentiment* toward the historical perpetrators and their contemporary heirs." Ibid., 479.

113 Yekelchyk, "What Is Ukrainian about Ukraine's Pop Culture?," 219.

114 Ibid.

115 Warner, *Publics and Counterpublics*, 171.

116 Rancière, "Ten Theses on Politics," in *Dissensus*, 37.

117 The photo was taken in Ukraine by South African photographer Brent Stirton, upon an invitation from the HIV/AIDS NGO organized by Olena Pinchuk. Local Ukrainian circulations of the image included discussion on the larger structural and legal disparities that replicate

cyclical patterns of addiction and incarceration in the lives of individuals and communities in Ukraine. Women, in particular, face these disparities in even greater numbers. The Ukrainian newspaper День (*The Day*) reported that according to the Leonid Vlasenko Foundaton, which works to rehabilitate substance uses in Kryvyi Rih, the woman in the photograph, Maria, was a typical case: "The Ukrainian drug policy hardly provides any social and medical protection for addicts, and usually resorts to repressions against them. The Ukrainian legislation provides for three years of imprisonment for keeping drugs. As a result, over 70 per cent of drug addicted people spend some time in prison. After being released, most of them do not manage to integrate into society. Women are yet even more vulnerable in this world of criminalization than men. That is why when they lack money to maintain themselves and their addiction many of them engage in prostitution ... All of these people are ill, left without their relatives' support and need the minimum social attention and support from the state ... Maria is 32 now. She has a little daughter who lives with Maria's mother-in-law. Her husband died because of using drugs. Maria prostitutes to maintain herself and her daughter. This is typical." Skuba, "Madonna."

118 In 2012 Green spent fourteen months travelling, living, and participating in protests with Femen's core members gathering footage for her documentary film *Ukraine Is Not a Brothel: The Femen Story*.

119 Qtd. in Neufeld, "Femen Activists Get Naked to Raise Political Awareness."

120 Hutsol often employed the term "sexpats" in posts on Femen's blog and in interviews; the term was adopted by journalists in international media coverage on Femen.

121 Members of the group publicly grabbed the tournament trophy while it was on display in the cities of Kyiv and Dnipro (formerly Dnipropetrovsk) during the summer of 2012. *The Huffington Post*, 21 May 2012, accessed 20 February 2015, http://www.huffingtonpost.com/2012/05/21/femens-euro-2012-protest-_n_1532989.html.

122 Martsenyuk, "Ukraine's Other Half."

123 Anna Hutsol, looking back on Femen's half-decade-long history, observed, "I consider what we've done for women's protest in Ukraine very important. People now relate to one another differently, for us, the fact that women's issues are now up for discussion and debate is highly important. Women are now able go out in the streets and protest without punishment, though, of course, if [Femen] were to do the same thing, naked, we'd be punished. I think we've contributed to similar positive changes in Russia. Overall, these are the first steps towards democracy and a new, free nation, our main objective is to save women – to help

them realize that they can achieve freedom, but that they have to fight for their rights." Qtd. in Azar, "Femen: Konechno, a Kak Zhe Zh."

2. An Anatomy of Activism: Virtual Body Rhetoric in Digital Protest Texts

1 W.J.T. Mitchell, Judith Butler, Chantal Mouffe, Brett Lunceford, and other scholars working at the intersection of politics and aesthetics have renewed interest in the role of the body in protest.

2 Suzanne Lacy and Leslie Labowicz, founders of the feminist media performance collective Ariadne: Social Art Network, formed in Los Angeles in 1978, claimed that "it was violence – in the media and in society – that gave birth to feminist media art." Lacy and Labowicz, "Feminist Media Strategies for Political Performance," 133.

3 Formed in April 2011 in Toronto, Canada, Slutwalks is an international street protest phenomenon that also adopts a performative strategy in which participants dress in revealing clothing to protest against explanations of rape based upon a woman's appearance. Anna Hutsol and other Femen members collaborated with Slutwalks in 2012 in producing a calendar to protest the trial of Aliaa Elmadhy in Tunis for posting nude photos of herself on Twitter.

4 Jason Miks, "Naked Protest."

5 Ellis-Kahana, "Transformative New Amazons."

6 See, for example, Fraser, *Fortunes of Feminism*. In her 2013 re-evaluation of Judith Butler, Fraser claims that the roles that culture and economics have played in envisioning "the political" in second-wave feminism differ from contemporary feminist conditionings of global solidarities. She argues that economic struggles leverage cultural difference by transcending national borders. This view has since been taken up by critics, especially feminists of colour, as too universalizing to account for local resistances to global hegemonies.

7 Susan Gal and Gail Kligman have assessed the public transformations brought on by mass media in the shift to postcommunism in the early nineties: "The development of more open public spheres since 1989, and the arrival of capitalist mass media, have swept away censorship and 'official' discourse in this classic sense ... Yet the apparent plurality and openness of mass media veil the fact that certain issues remain undiscussed, some perspectives suppressed." *Reproducing Gender*, 3.

8 Between the years 2012 and 2014 approximately 1,000 articles on Femen were published in major periodicals in Germany alone. For a detailed study of Femen in German media and its impacts on the wider EU media landscape, see Thomas and Stehling, "The Communicative Construction of Femen."

9   Mayerchyk and Plakhotnik, "Radykal'nyi Femen i novyi zhinochyi aktyvizmu," 7.
10 Pussy Riot, *Pussy Riot! A Punk Prayer for Freedom*.
11 For detailed list of protests in Kyiv during this period, see Cybriwsky, *Kyiv: The City of Domes and Demons*.
12 Masyuk, "Posle prygovora."
13 Bateson, "On Femen, Pussy Riot and Crosses." Also see *Der Spiegel Online*, "International Support for Pussy Riot."
14 *Der Spiegel Online*, "International Support for Pussy Riot."
15 "Pussy Riot on Prison, Putin, the Ukraine Crisis & Activism," Channel 4 News, 14 November 2014, accessed 18 December 2017, https://www.youtube.com/watch?v=ruMclx5Gy7M&t=197s.
16 Leturcq, "A Meeting with Oksana Shachko."
17 Bernstein, "An Inadvertent Sacrifice," 1.
18 Masyuk, "Posle prygovora."
19 Elena Gapova and Nataliya Tchermalykh have each made observations along this line about Pussy Riot's "Punk Prayer" performance in Russian popular discourse.
20 Alek D. Epstein traced this debate early in its formation within the Russian literary and cultural spheres: "Arest uchastnic gruppy 'Pussy Riot' kak katalizator hudozhestvenno grazhdanskogo aktivizma izdatel'stvo."
21 Safea Lebdi is a founding member of the French women's rights organization Ni putes, ni soumises (Neither whores nor submissives) and is a politician in the Green Party.
22 Interfax-Ukraine, "FEMEN Says Their Male Activist Brutally Beaten Up."
23 Lunceford, *Naked Politics*, 138, 141.
24 BBC, "Femen's Inna Shevchenko Inspired France's Marianne Stamp"; BBC, "Topless Protestor Inspired Marianne."
25 Lunceford, *Naked Politics*, 138.
26 Ibid., 141.
27 Naiman, *Sex in Public*, 15.
28 Valerie Sperling provides extensive analysis of Putin's impact on gender dynamics in the Russian context. See *Sex, Politics, and Putin*.
29 See Naiman, *Sex in Public*, 15.
30 Femen website, 10 March 2012.
31 This particular photo appears in an article by Joscelyn Jurich, who also interprets it as an example of the objectification of non-Western cultures in contemporary journalism. The article is named after her critique of W.J.T. Mitchell, and borrows his famous title, "What Do Subjects Want?"
32 Sarah D. Phillips outlines Ofenzywa's emergency strategizing, contact with journalists, and eventual transformation into two separate factions during and after the clashes on Maidan in 2013–14 in "The Women's Squad in Ukraine's Protests."

33 Joshua A. Sanborn and Annette F. Timm provide a valuable overview of this particular event in a history of gender and sexuality across the entire European continent in the twentieth century. They position Femen at the forefront of generating unforeseen manifestations of feminism in the twenty-first century. See "Femen's Challenge to European Feminism."

34 Announcement of the World Press Photo Contest, accessed 20 May 2012, http://www.worldpressphoto.org/people/samuel-aranda; MacDonald and Furst, "A Painterly World Press Photo Winner." Shachko's photo was featured in the exhibition *Iconoclaste*, curated by Azad Asifovich at Galerie Mansart (Paris), 12–19 June 2016, accessed 3 November 2018, http://www.galerie-mansart.fr/iconoclaste--oksana-shachko.html.

35 Hutsol described her group's strategy this way in an interview with the author, 22 August 2011, Kyiv. Later, in 2012, Inna Shevchenko repeated this sentiment on Ukrainian and French national news. Mie Birk Jensen has documented her experiences as a trainee in Femen's Paris "feminist camp," in which she describes in detail the media apparatuses in the group's performative strategies. See Jensen, "The Body Theatre."

36 Elena Gapova and Maria Dmytriyeva critiqued Femen early on from a Marxist perspective by arguing that members enjoyed a certain level of class privilege. See Gapova and Soroka, "Hola svoboda i tila na drabyni" (2010); Maria Dmitreyevna, "Femen na tli hrudei" (2010).

37 Lacy and Labowicz, "Feminist Media Strategies."

38 Munster, *Materializing New Media*, 20–3. Digital embodiment is "an arena across which material and incorporeal forces will continue to engender further connection and differentiation," and "information culture can lead us from aesthetic to ethical considerations of new media. The issue is no longer one involving just body-computer relations, but one involving bodies networked in information culture as its flows disconnect and connect the heterogeneity of embodied lives.".

39 Haraway, *Simians, Cyborgs, and Women*, 149–82, 243–8.

40 Piotrowski, *Art and Democracy in Post-Communist Europe*, 50.

41 While scholars contest whether to describe post-Soviet Ukraine as post-colonial, I generally agree with the critics, such as Vitaly Chernetsky, whose diagnosis of postcommunism reflects an instance of nonclassical postcoloniality.

42 Bhabha, *The Location of Culture*, 772, 766.

43 Ibid., 766.

44 "By making visible the forgetting of the 'unhomely' moment in civil society, feminism specifies the patriarchal, gendered nature of civil society and disturbs the symmetry of private and public which is now shadowed, or uncannily doubled, by the differences of genders which does not map onto the private and public, but becomes disturbingly supplemental to them." Ibid., 773–4.

45 This is one thesis that emerged from Nancy Fraser's critique of Habermas and subsequent feminist engagements with critical theory in the 1990s.

46 Lisyutkina, "Fenomen Femen: malyi vybukhovyi prystrii made in Ukraine," 161.

47 Her novel, *Fieldwork in Ukrainian Sex*, was once included in a photo on Femen's blog of one of their members being released from jail. In *Fieldwork*, the protagonist O. remarks to her American colleague and friend Donna that Ukrainian women are doubly subjugated in their support for men who struggle for the national idea. "The conceptual approach: women's struggle for their rights. What can I tell you, Donna-dearest? That we were raised by men fucked from all ends every which way? That later we ourselves screwed the same kind of guys, and that in both cases they were doing to us what others, the others, had done to them? And that we accepted them and loved them as they were, because not to accept them was to go over to the others, the other side? And that our only choice, therefore, was and still remains between victim and executioner: between nonexistence and an existence that slowly kills you?" Zabuzhko, *Pol'ovi doslidzhennia z Ukrains'koho seksu / Fieldwork in Ukrainian Sex*, 158.

48 Zabuzhko articulates systems of patriarchy within Ukraine in terms of male expressions of eternal youth, a notion closely connected with utopia: "For you see, prior to the appearance of *Fieldwork* the voices heard in our literature were predominantly male, and misogyny, either overt or latent, became part of a fashionable writer's make up – all those guys playing the role of 'eternally young' macho boys, to the cheers of the same 'eternally young' macho critics ... The male protagonist of the novel, 'the genius painter' (a fact, by the way, that the heroine honestly believes – her own poetic 'genius' doesn't matter that much!), belongs, undoubtedly and recognizably, to the same type. That the book uncovered behind this 'invincible' make up a deeply hidden insecurity and social helplessness was, of course, taken as a feminist 'cultural answer.' But that was not my principal message. What I attacked was, basically, a system of social lies extending to the point of mental rape, and affecting both men and women. That is why I don't divide my readers along male/female lines. I don't believe that intelligence is gender-specific – women, too, know quite well how to protect patriarchal standards with the utmost bile against their 'dissident' sisters." Hryn, "A Conversation with Oksana Zabuzhko."

49 Popova, "Feminine Femen Targets 'Sexpats.'"

50 Ibid. The interview also included Femen's citing of unconfirmed statistics indicating that Turkish men are the primary consumers of sex tourism in Kyiv: "Together with the Institute of Political, Sociological and Marketing Research, Femen polled 1,200 female students in Kyiv. Their findings

suggest that nearly 70 percent of those polled were proposed sex for money and most offers came from Turkish men."

51 Sify News, "Topless Ukrainian Feminists Protest Iranian Woman's Death Sentence."

52 In writing about Femen for the Ukrainian scholarly journal *Krytyka*, gender scholars Mariya Mayerchyk and Olga Plakhotnik point to these Saudi and Iranian protests as the turning point when Femen first gained serious international attention: "For two years they had tried to overcome their own sex appeal in order to force us to hear their voices and take their words as a challenge." Radykal'nyi Femen i novyi zhinochyi aktyvizmu, 9, my translation.

53 Femen website, accessed 10 June 2011.

54 See Glenn, *Female Spectacle*.

55 Lorde, *Sister Outsider*.

56 For comprehensive comparisons, see Kibler, "The Corking Girls: White Women's Racial Masquerades in Vaudeville," in *Rank Ladies*.

57 Krasner, "Black Salome," 175.

58 Bean, "Black Minstrelsy," 176.

59 Ibid.

60 Discussions about race linked to the idea of postcolonialism in the context of post-Soviet Ukraine are contentious due to the imperial legacies of the nineteenth century and the Soviet denationalization policies that followed. For a comprehensive overview of these debates and their terms, see Bilaniuk, "Race, Media, and Postcoloniality."

61 In a footnote to this excerpt Alaina Lemon includes the following: "see also Hirsch 1997 on the debates among experts responsible for devising and compiling the Soviet census over whether to include 'physical type' as a criteria for constructing the category 'nationality.' The recurrence of these debates at high levels suggests that race was indeed a salient 'commonsense' category." *Between Two Fires*, 63–4.

62 Krasner, "Black Salome," 176.

63 Dmytriyeva, "Femen na tli hrudei," 20–3.

64 Mitchell, *What Do Pictures Want*, 25.

65 Defending her radicalism as the right to peaceful protest, Hutsol distanced herself from extremism: "Unfortunately it is not our fault that seventy percent of sex tourists are from Turkey. This is official data and has nothing to do with racism or xenophobia. However, at one point the [Ukrainian] nationalists suggested we go and burn the club where Turkish men meet, but we refused because that is not our method." Qtd. in Mishchenko, Parfan, and Radynski, "Mriiemo vyvesty na vulytsiu tysiachi holykh zhinok."

66 Anna Hutsol, interviewed by author, 22 August 2011, Kyiv.

67 Bhabha, *The Location of Culture*, 775.
68 Ibid., 765.
69 Imre, *Identity Games*, 133.
70 Anna Hutsol, interviewed by author, 2011, Kyiv.
71 The digital divide also plays a role. Elena Gapova's assessment of class conflict in the links between technology and activism illuminates this point in the post-Soviet context through the Pussy Riot affair in Russia. Yet I would also argue that this assessment does not fully account for precarity in class formation among younger generations, and thus is overly critical of younger feminists, not all of whom enjoy privileged social positions. See Gapova, "Becoming Visible in the Digital Age."
72 Adorno, "Aesthetic Theory," 103.
73 Ibid.
74 Irigaray, *This Sex Which Is Not One*, 55.
75 Transnational feminism has recently renewed interest in interrogating the critical relationship between politics and the artistic image debated by the Frankfurt School during the cultural turn of the 1970s. Nancy Fraser claims in her reevaluation of Judith Butler that culture and economics play twin roles in the idea of "the political," which she says transcends national borders in contemporary feminist global solidarities, versus in the second wave. She has been heavily critiqued by women-of-colour feminists, in particular, as overstating her case by ignoring the real material needs of intersectional groups. Fraser, *Fortunes of Feminism* (2013).
76 Imre, *Identity Games*, 13.
77 Claire Bishop gives a detailed overview of the art commodity in European visual culture post-1989. She examines individual searches for artistic equivalents to political positions in Western societies, the collective creative process, and citizenship-making in *Artificial Hells: Participatory Art and the Politics of Spectatorship*. Russian critic Alek D. Epstein places Pussy Riot in a similar critique of action, agency, and audience in *Iskusstvo na barrikadakh: "Pussy Riot."*
78 Aspects of early 1970s feminist body art were appropriated by various protest campaigns. Femen has been compared to PETA's 1990s marketing campaigns protesting the use of fur in the textiles industry. These campaigns also featured radical nude actions (see, for example, Pamela Anderson's banned ad depicting her body as a diagram for butchering meat, with the slogan, "All Animals Have the Same Parts"). While this comparison is valuable for thinking through the central conflict in Femen's advertising of themselves in order to protest the hypersexualized female body in commercial advertisements, the link is conceptually weak considering the metanarrative in PETA. Activists baring their skin in order to protest the fur industry is critically limiting for parsing Femen's

role-playing of prostitutes from Ukraine, a subject position with multiple archetypal associations.

79 See Biesenback, *Marina Abramović: The Artist Is Present*; Denegri and Miscetti, *Marina Abramović: Performing Body*.

80 The incident was widely covered in international media. See "Polish Protest after Gallery Removes Suggestive Banana Art," *BBC World News Online*, 29 April 2019, accessed 4 July 2019, https://www.bbc.com/news/world-europe-48096188.

81 Mayerchyk and Plakhotnik, "Radykal'nyi Femen i novyi zhinochyi aktyvizmu," 8.

82 Femen website, "Bodymessagers against Putin! Part 1," accessed 12 March 2014, http://femen.org/gallery/id/309#post-content.

83 Mikhail Minakov's analyses of oligarchy and patronage in Ukraine during the years just before and after 2014 reveal little change in the public sphere wherever it is controlled by clan-like pyramidal labour practices and limits on civic expression; Minakov, *Development and Dystopia*.

84 The Krasnals! "EURO 2012."

85 Ibid.

86 This line of thinking follows from Judith Butler's seminal work *Gender Trouble*.

87 Although not initially designed for museum spaces, both activist groups' works have since been commodified into art objects. In this sense they share a similar fate with past conceptual feminist and Soviet dissident artists, whose work has also entered the institutions of profit and enterprise in galleries around the world (e.g., The Krasnals! paintings have been displayed at Tate Modern). See "The Krasnals w Tate Modern."

88 Anna Hutsol has since modified her stance on sex work by claiming her support for the Dutch model in which the criminalization of sex work reverts to the client-consumer, not the sex worker. "Le féminisme à l'épreuve du sextrémisme," *Le Monde.fr*, accessed 12 March 2013, http://www.lemonde.fr/societe/article/2013/03/08/le-feminisme-a-l-epreuve-du-sextremisme_1844822_3224.html.

89 For a comparative "sex positive" approach documenting the legal and social impacts of over five decades of sex worker activism in Canada, the United States, and Europe, see Chateauvert, *Sex Workers Unite*. New and promising directions in research on sex work in Ukraine are exploring this approach. For one leading example from the field of anthropology, see Rachok, "Seks-rabota: ot abolytsionyzma k dekrymynalyzatsii."

90 The range and style of Femen's media platform recall the activist duo the Yes Men (Jacques Servin and Igor Vamos), whose tactical media in the wake of the WTO protests involved parodic public appearances designed to critique government and corporate interests. The term "culture

jamming," coined by Kalle Lasn, editor of *Adbusters* magazine, founded in 1989, and initial supporter of the Occupy Wall Street Movement of 2011, has since been employed to describe a range of media art and activism that seeks to expose the social mechanisms embedded into the language of mass advertising.

91 Briukhovetska, "What in Me Is Feminist?" 22.

92 Oksana Briukhovetska curated two feminist art exhibits in the years following: *Motherhood* (2014) and *TEXTUS* (2017). Both exhibits were dedicated to women, work, and migration. Also see *Feminist Strategies* (2017) and *Right to Truth* (2019), collections of interviews with feminists in Kyiv and Lviv, as well as in Paris and Russia, conducted by Briukhovetska and Lesia Kulchinska. For an excellent overview of constructive dialogue between Ukraine and Russia through feminist cultural practices, see Dmytryk, "I'm a Feminist, therefore ... The Art of Gender and Sexual Dissent in 2010's Ukraine and Russia" (2017). Key contemporary academic works dedicated to feminism also include Mariya Maerchyk and Olga Plakhotnik's online forum on feminism in Ukraine hosted at *Krytyka: Journal for Ukrainian Studies* (2016), and Martsenyuk's book *Gender for All: Against Stereotypes* (Гендер для всіх: проти стереотипам) 2017.

93 Briukhovetska, "I Am Ukrainka."

94 For extensive interviews with the newest feminists in Ukraine, leaders of FemSolution, founded in 2016, along with Feminist Workshop (Lviv), and several other feminist groups in Europe started around this time, see Briukhovetska and Kulchinska, *The Right to Truth*.

95 See Gapova and Soroka, "Hola svoboda i tila na drabyni" (2010); Dmitreyevna, "Femen na tli hrudei" (2010); and Lisyutkina, "Fenomen Femen: malyi vybukhovyi prystrii made in Ukraine" (2011).

96 Rubchak, "Seeing Pink."

97 Considering the notion of "the political" in Femen's subversive protest media, Mariya Mayerchyk and Olga Plakhotnik critiqued Femen early on, arguing that the group's performances conflate the idea of feminism in the realm of realpolitik, where the very idea of "good" and "bad" feminism gets folded into other economic and social development agendas: "They are looking for their own interpretation of feminism; experimenting with the term as a neologism, they manoeuvre around the Sword of Damocles, which is maintained by antifeminist stereotypes. While attempting to sift their ideas out from an older, 'bad' feminism they are simultaneously trying to construct their own, 'egalitarian,' new feminism." Mayerchyk and Plakhotnik, "Radykal'nyi Femen i novyi zhinochyi aktyvizmu," 8.

98 Nataliya Tchermalykh makes the point that Femen's visual rhetoric in their move abroad was "aligned with a conservative, protectionist stance

toward the Ukrainian national idea" in her essay "Feministychnyi analiz politychnyi amal'hamy mizh radykal'nymy i pomirkovanymy natsionalistamy ta relihiinymy pravamy" ("Feminist Analysis on the Political Amalgam between Radical and Moderate Nationalists and Religious Rights") 2012. Hommen's anti-gay marriage rallies in Paris further evidence Tchermalykh's claim that Femen's visual rhetoric is not readily emancipatory and is distinct from actual gender politics.

99 Jan van Dijk and Kenneth L. Hacker map the functions by which the export of politics through information campaigns may also function to reduce democratic participation in some contexts in *Internet and Democracy in the Network Society*.

100 Tchermalykh, *Art Ukraine*, 92, my translation.

101 Ibid.

102 Pyzik, *Poor but Sexy*, 141.

103 Building on Heidegger's idea of the social and political as *existential*, Chantal Mouffe argues that the two cannot be separated, and that identities are "never pre-given, but are always the result of processes of identification." Mouffe's definition of critical art aligns with a broader school of thinking on the topic including Jacques Rancière in his claiming symbolic dissensus can provide a challenge to hegemony. Mouffe, *Agonistics: Thinking the World Politically*, 46.

104 Martsenyuk, "Ukrainian Feminism in Action."

105 Kis, "Lyst posadovtsevi (Letter to an official)."

106 Museum of Women's History and Gender Movements website, accessed 11 December 2011, http://gendermuseum.com/.

107 Angelina Diash, interviewed by the author, July 2013, Kyiv.

108 Tchermalykh's quote continues: "Something has to happen – positive or negative – and yet, nothing happens. Everyone continues to wait for something to occur, always just around the corner: the valuation of the hryvnia, the Kyiv Biennale, Euro 2012, and then it turns out that nothing changes – or at least, almost nothing. Is no news really good news? To the contrary, there is little reason for optimism considering last year's closure of the Visual Culture Research Center by [Serhiy Kvit, president of] Kyiv-Mohyla Academy, accompanied by his Khrushchev style evaluation: 'This is not art – it's shit!' in a direct attack on the exhibit *A Room of One's Own*, by Yevgenia Belorusets, not to mention the failure of the first Ukrainian gay pride parade upon the eve of an unanimous homophobic vote in parliament." Tchermalykh, "Temni Chasy," 32.

109 Hutsol has called for both the criminalization of the client in prostitution and the illegalization of pornography in an effort to eradicate sex tourism in Ukraine. Other Ukrainian feminist activists and scholars have expressed scepticism at these strategies. See Mishchenko, Parfan,

and Radynski, "Mriiemo vyvesty na vulytsiu tysiachi holykh zhinok: rozmova redaktsiia PK z hrupoiu Femen."

110 Mayerchyk and Plakhotnik, "Radykal'nyi Femen i novyi zhinochyi aktyvizmu," 10.

111 *The Guardian, The Atlantic, The New York Times, Kyiv Post,* as well as *The Moscow Times* and *Pravda* along with many other Western and Russian media outlets reported on Femen in 2009–11 as the piedmont of a new grassroots feminism in Ukraine. Subsequent reports on the group have included the question of whether or not Femen is able to transmit a feminist message through the display of the female body. These reports have instantiated an ongoing metarhetorical discussion about the depiction of the female body in mainstream media.

3. The Image Is the Frame: Photography and the Feminist Collective Ofenzywa

1 Announced at the International Conference of Socialist Women, which Zetkin attended as editor of the German newspaper *Die Gleichheit* and as an already well-known theorist of the working women's movement.

2 Ofenzywa, "Mission Statement," my translation.

3 Boym, *Common Places.*

4 Halberstam, *In a Queer Time and Place,* 1, 13. Halberstam borrows the term "geographies of resistance" from S. Pile's introduction to an anthology of the same title.

5 Belorusets, email message to author, August 2018.

6 Official discourse on women and labour in the first half of the twentieth century privileged ideologues such as Alexandra Kollontai and her experiments in communal child-rearing and were based on Engels's theory of the bourgeois family unit as the primary obstacle to the proletarian revolution, a theory he first articulated in *The Origin of the Family, Private Property, and the State* in 1884. The official rhetoric on women's rights proffered by the Soviet state helped to encourage popular views of feminism as collaboration with the regime, views that continue to obfuscate discussions about grassroots feminism(s) within the former USSR.

7 Untitled article, *Rabotnitsa* (Moscow), no. 1 (1914), 2. Photographs about the history of March 8 were exhibited online by Tatiana Isaeiva in *The Truth about March 8th.* The photographs are in the Museum for Gender History in Kharkiv.

8 While originally Krupskaya's distinction between bourgeois and working women positioned the former "against men," and the latter alongside their male comrades, a general fear of "lawlessness" and an overall desire for greater economic equality prevails in her assessments of her own paradigm.

9 Mouffe, *Agonistics: Thinking the World Politically*, 125–6.
10 Ibid.
11 Kis, "Ukrainian Women Reclaiming the Feminist Meaning of International Women's Day," 225.
12 Kis's description of Yushchenko's speech. The speech itself begins with the following: "Dear Ukrainian women! Greetings on the occasion of the holiday of spring, the holiday of women's beauty, which blossoms in Ukraine today. My heart is filled with most tender feelings for you..." Ibid., 221.
13 Chantal Mouffe has argued for a need to rethink communism, stating the word "connotes an anti-political vision of society" in which power antagonisms and the politics of the self, in what she and others have termed "the political," are evacuated from society. Mouffe, *Agonistics: Thinking the World Politically*, 83.
14 Ibid., 222.
15 Kis, "Lyst posadovtsevi" [Letter to an official], 12 February 2009.
16 "What Gramsci called 'hegemony through neutralization' or 'passive revolution,' a situation in which specific demands [feminism] that challenge the hegemonic order are appropriated by the existing system so as to satisfy them in a way that neutralizes their subversive potential." Mouffe, *Agonistics: Thinking the World Politically*, 73.
17 Kis, "Ukrainian Women Reclaiming the Feminist Meaning of International Women's Day," 230.
18 "In recent decades March 8 has turned into a holiday of spring, women's beauty, and love, celebrated both in public settings and in Soviet families. By the late 1980s, Soviet citizens had interiorized new ways to celebrate this day at which men and boys were expected (or even required) to solemnize the 'eternal femininity' of their counterparts by expressing their love, respect, and attention to women and girls of all ages, to greet them with flowers and gifts and to fulfill all their (rather modest) wishes one day a year." Ibid., 219.
19 Ibid.
20 Beauvoir, *Second Sex*, 23.
21 For an in-depth history of women's organizing in Ukraine in the interwar period, including communication with transnational movements in North America, see Bohachevsky-Chomiak, *Feminists Despite Themselves*.
22 "The problem of ideologies is as follows: how can consciousness at all levels (individuals, groups, classes, peoples) be mistaken about itself and its content – its being – when it is that very content and that very being which determine it? Only by taking the formal structure of consciousness and its content as inseparables and submitting them to a complex analysis will we be able to understand any particular form of consciousness, or any particular ideology." Lefebvre, *Critique of Everyday Life*, 96.
23 Ibid., 97.

24 Ofenzyva, "Акція «За Рівність! Проти НЕКвізиції!"

25 The term "biopolitics" refers to Michel Foucault's idea on the extension of state power over populations through the regulation of bodies in time and space. He sees an inadequacy in Marxism's failure to fully account for an embodied politics: "It's as though 'revolutionary' discourses were still steeped in the ritualistic themes derived from Marxist analyses. And while there are some very interesting things about the body in Marx's writings, Marxism considered as an historical reality has had a terrible tendency to occlude the question of the body, in favour of consciousness and ideology." Foucault, *Power/Knowledge*, 58–9.

26 The blue wall has since emerged as a trope in works by Ukraine's emerging generation. In the feature-length film *The Tribe* (2014), directed by Myroslav Slaboshpytskiy, the wall appears in a boarding school for the deaf and serves as the main backdrop for a series of scenes depicting the violence, sex, and desperate crimes committed by its young protagonists. Kyiv-based graffiti artist Vova Vorotniov also created a blue wall painting for the exhibit *Ukrainian Body* (2012).

27 "Early pronouncements by socialist regimes in favor of gender equality, together with policies to increase women's participation in the workforce, led optimists to expect important gains for women; the internationalist bias of Soviet socialism promised to resolve the 'national question,' making national conflicts obsolete; and the Party's broadly homogenizing goals bade fair to erase difference of almost every kind from the social landscape." Verdery, *What Was Socialism and What Comes Next?*, 61.

28 As part of the exhbit's program I delivered a lecture on transnational women's organizing in the early twentieth-century labour movement, and published the following article: "*My, Autsaiderky*: Virginia Woolf i feminizm u hlobal'nii perspektyvi." An extended version of the article will be published in 2021.

29 The exhibit was curated by Tatiana Kochubinska and Tatiana Zhmurko, supported by PinchukArtCentre Research Platform. See *Space of One's Own* (Свій простір), Kyiv, 30 October 2018 – 6 January 2019, accessed 12 December 2018, https://pinchukartcentre.org/ua/exhibitions/sviy-prostir.

30 Approximately thirty copies of the text, *Ya I Ona*, were printed by PinchukArtCentre, Kyiv, in 2008. The text was edited by Darina Bazhynska and designed by Uliana Bychenkova at IST Publishing Kharkiv.

31 Bieńczyk, *Transparency*, 76.

32 See Plakhotnik and Meyerchyk, "Zahoplyenna logik, abo Svit bez Zhinok [Seizing the Logic, or A World Without Women]," announcing the official end of the group on 25 January 2014.

33 See Phillips, "The Women's Squad in Ukraine's Protests."

34 My ongoing interviews in 2011, 2013, 2016, 2017, 2018, 2019, 2020 with Ofenzywa members Olha Martynyuk, Nadia Parfan, Nataliya Tchermalykh, and others closely connected to the group show wide variation on the exact reasons they chose to end the group, but all referred to violence on the Maidan as the turning point in its dissolution.

35 Ofenzywa, "Manifesto." Also see the discussion of feminist art in Kyiv and Moscow by former Ofenzyva member, Olenka Dmytryk, "'I'm a Feminist, Therefore ... The Art of Gender and Sexual Dissent in 2010s Ukraine and Russia."

36 Excerpted from "Ofenzywa Manifesto" distributed at marches and posted online. My translation.

37 "Among the employed, 56% of women have higher educations, though there remains an overall 30% pay gap between men and women, and for women 20-30 years of age, their pensions will differ from men's by 50%. Women are hardly represented in the higher echelons of power and leadership. Out of 179 academics at the National Science Academy of Ukraine only 3 are women. Women also constitute the absolute majority of migrant workers in Ukraine." Martsenyuk, "Ukraine's Other Half."

38 Bourdieu, "The Perception of the Social World and Political Struggle," in *Language and Symbolic Power*, 236.

39 Lefebvre linked labour to this transformation: "if we consider the overall life of the worker, we will see that his work and his attitude towards work are linked to social practice as a whole, to his experience as a whole ... What is more, this 'whole' must be taken in the context of a specific country and nation, at a specific moment of civilization and social development, and as involving a certain set of needs. And this brings us back to the critique of everyday life." *Critique of Everyday Life*, 88.

40 Concluding that they needed to tighten their ranks in order to pursue "true" communism, they set forth a plan: "*Lef must bring together the leftist forces. Lef must survey its ranks*, after having discarded the past that stuck to them. *Lef must create a united front* to blow up old junk, to fight for the integration of a new culture. We will solve the problems of art not by majority of vote of a mythical left front which so far exists only as an idea, but by action, by the energy of our steering group which year after year leads the work of the left and of those who have always guided it ideologically." Lawton and Eagle, eds., *Russian Futurism through Its Manifestos*, 195.

41 "We act: in street actions, marches, protests; in our words, in articles and discussions; by organizing conferences, discussions, seminars; by organizing exhibits, film screenings, and other cultural events; by initiating women's groups for raising awareness." Ofenzywa, "Mission Statement"; also see Ofenzywa, "Акція «За Рівність! Проти НЕКвізиції!»"

42 "If history is made up of modes of production, the subject is a *contradiction* that brings about practice because practice is always both signifying and semiotic, a crest where meaning emerges only to disappear. It is incumbent upon 'art' to demonstrate that the subject is the absent element of and in his practice, just as it was incumbent upon political economy to prove that history is a matter of class struggle." Kristeva, *Revolution in Poetic Language*, 215.

43 Lawton and Eagle, eds., *Russian Futurism through Its Manifestos*, 25.

44 Ibid.

45 Ofenzywa occasionally worked with leftist youth groups, although individual members have most consistently identified themselves to me in interviews as distinct from any of those groups and from the wider LGBTQ movement. The terms "separatism" and "radical feminism," according to one of the original March 8 march organizers, Olha Martynyuk, were from the outset quite important in the sense of distinguishing a platform that priviledged the demands of women-identifying genders, lesbian, and bisexual individuals. The activist groups Left Opposition, Avtonomiia Union, and Priama Diia Student Union helped to organize Ofenzywa's 2012 march. The LGBT NGO, Insight, organized later marches, including as recent as 2018.

46 Chernetsky, *Mapping Postcommunist Cultures*. Chernetsky bases his term on his survey of 1990s Ukrainian and Russian literary representations of the nation through alterity to the West. He claims "globalization of resistance" is especially the case within the postcolonial underpinnings that he argues are pervasive throughout modern Ukrainian literature, including its more recent feminist developments in the late-twentieth-century regional tendencies he defines as "postcommunist-postmodernism."

47 Contemporary artists in Ukraine are pushing for more radical forms of expression by demanding greater creative licence and professional autonomy. Some have founded initiatives in Ukraine sponsored by international and local organizations to protect artists' freedom of speech. As a well-known photographer, translator, poet, and critic, Belorusets is at the centre of these events. She is the founder of the prominent Ukrainian literary magazine, *Prostory*, and is a member of both Ofenzywa and the curatorial artists' union HudRada. In 2012, Belorusets joined other artists in founding a professional union (ICTM) to protect their professional and creative rights. One of their aims is to coordinate with the state to regulate artists' employment by levying taxes on the sale of their works and offering financial and social assistance when necessary.

48 The series *32 Gogol St.* received international acclaim. The project was awarded by the Royal Photographic Society of Britain in 2010 and received *The Guardian*'s Joan Wakelin Award. See "Unfit for Living."

49 Belorusets, "Комментарии к Фотопроекту Гоголевская 32/Gogol 32," Все ж Продолжает Нерей в Аонийских Свиреπствовать Водах: Повседневность Как Событие, 2011 [Commentary on the photo project Gogol St. 32 / Everything follows Nereus on the raging Aonian waters: everyday life as an event], my translation. Subsequent citatons referred to as Belorusets, blog.

50 Belorusets, blog.

51 Shklovksy proposed his theory of estrangement in his 1917 essay "Art as Device," cited here. Shklovsky experimented with the idea that "truth" could best be approximated through distorting human perspective. He wrote of images that "an image is not a permanent referent for those mutable complexities of life which are revealed through it; its purpose is not to make us perceive meaning, but to create a special perception of the object – it creates a 'vision' of the object instead of serving as a means for knowing it." For Jakobson, like Shklovsky, images in poetic language could also reveal truth by defamiliarizing objects "through the slowness of perception." Shklovsky and Sher, *Theory of Prose / O teorii prozy*, 219.

52 Belorusets, blog.

53 Ibid.

54 Julia Kristeva developed a theory of the abject to convey marginalization in the breakdown of the linguistic subject as Self/Other into negativity (Not I), in *Powers of Horror*.

55 "Kino-eye as the possibility of making the invisible visible, the unclear clear, the hidden manifest, the disguised overt, the acted nonacted; making falsehood into truth." Vertov, *Kino Eye*, 210.

56 Benjamin, *The Work of Art in the Age of Its Technological Reproducibility*, 32.

57 "As soon as the criterion of authenticity ceases to be applied to artistic production, the whole social function of art is revolutionized. Instead of being founded on ritual, it is based on a different practice: politics." Ibid., 25.

58 Ibid., 35.

59 Benjamin drew this idea out to an extreme in his famous expression written in 1936 on the eve of the Second World War: "Such is the aestheticizing of politics, as practiced by fascism. Communism replies by politicizing art." Ibid., 42.

60 Ibid., 43.

61 Ibid., 37.

62 Belorusets writes on her blog associated with the project: "These images and interview extracts may also be used as an illustration of inadequate living conditions of millions of other post-Soviet citizens."

63 Todorova, "Balkanism and Postcolonialism," 45.

64 Boym, *Common Places*, 130. Boym apprehends her own visit to her former communal apartment as a return home, in which she reconstitutes a sense

of self through traces in the landscape that are embedded with particular memories of former ways of inhabiting space. She writes, "What an architectural utopia does not take into account is history and its narratives about inhabiting places. Thus the utopian Common Places turn into 'places of communal use' in the apartment, a shabby stage for many scandals between the neighbors and a ruin of utopian communality."

65 Boym, *Common Places*, 19.
66 Ibid.
67 Jakobson, *Language in Literature*, 20.
68 Ibid., 27.
69 Boym, *Common Places*, 151.
70 "This narrow, nearly one-dimensional space behind the glass of the bookcase reflects the image of the resident; it is his or her carefully arranged interface with the world." Boym, *Common Places*, 155.
71 Boym writes that "in Soviet Russia there was no interface between public and private, no space of conventional socialization, the space that is governed neither by the official decorum, like the Soviet subway, nor by the unwritten rules of intimacy that reign in the overcrowded domestic nooks. The space between is the space of alienation – the Soviet zone – the space on the outskirts of the Soviet topography." *Common Places*, 142.
72 Boym, *Common Places*, 159.
73 Boym comments on the feminization of domestic work in communal dwellings in the Soviet era: "The burden of the communal interactions and negotiations rested entirely on women; the world of the communal kitchen has often been called matriarchal, but I would add that it has been matriarchal by necessity and not by choice." *Common Places*, 147.
74 Boym, *Common Places*, 148.
75 Belorusets, blog.
76 Certeau, "Spatial Practices," in *The Practice of Everyday Life*, 108.
77 Certeau, *The Practice of Everyday Life*, xxiv.
78 Benjamin, "The Ruin," 180.
79 Belorusets, blog.
80 "... which prevented its apartments from being privatized. As a result the inhabitants of this building live in public units and do not have the right to sell or exchange them. According to official statistics, there are more than a hundred such houses in Kyiv; many of these houses are absent from maps of the city; for all intents and purposes, it is as though they do not even exist; at any moment they may be torn down or permanently locked without notice or consultation with their residents." Belorusets, "Комментарии к Фотопроекту Гоголевская 32/Gogol 32."
81 Yevgenia Belorusets, email message to author, trans. by author, 28 December 2018.

82 While living and working in Kyiv on a Fulbright in 2017–18 I often passed by the building at 32 Gogol Street. I observed with regret how its walls had become even more dilapidated to the point of being uninhabitable. The structure is likely beyond restoration, and the site remains abandoned as this book goes to press in 2020.

83 For Certeau this process is descriptive rather than representative: "not in substituting a representation for the ordinary or covering it up with mere words, but in showing how it introduces itself into our techniques ...and how it can reorganize the place from which discourse is produced." *The Practice of Everyday Life*, 6.

84 Ibid., 6.

85 Ibid., 10.

86 "Escaping the imaginary totalizations produced by the eye, the everyday has a certain strangeness that does not surface, or whose surface is only its upper limit, outlining itself against the visible." Ibid., 93.

87 Ibid., 94.

88 Lacan has been criticized extensively for theorizing from a particularly hegemonic view of language that ignores the body and its role in the processes of signification and identification through which subjectivities form. Many postcolonial thinkers and feminists of colour (e.g., Akhil Gupta, Chandra Mohanty, Seyla Benhabib, and Rosi Bradiotti) challenge this approach.

89 Azoulay derives her theory of photography in opposition to Walter Benjamin's appraisal of art and politics. She locates her position within this classical dichotomy as a transferral of the politicization of art onto its practice, beyond categorical judgment: "What appeared to me to be problematic in the first place was the unsubstantiated transition from the differentiation between 'the aesthetic' and 'the political' to a distinction between 'aestheticization' and 'politicization' in a manner that renders them equivalent ...this makes of aestheticization or politicization a form of action reserved chiefly for those works of art that either strengthen or weaken these attributes of the image." Azoulay, *Civil Imagination*, 35.

90 Ibid., 3.

91 Ibid.

92 "The ontological properties of photography enable one to rebel against the paradigm of sovereign spectatorship, and to undermine that which constituent violence renders self-evident." Ibid., 225.

93 Yevgenia Belorusets, interview by author, 10 May 2018, Kyiv.

94 Belorusets, "Все ж Продолжает Нерей в Аонийских Свирепствовать Водах."

95 Lefebvre observes that consciousness "not only reflects the outside world, and things, but also human activity, practical power over nature ...

the equally objective conflict between man and the 'environment,' between the human world and nature, [and] between individuals in the human world." *Critique of Everyday Life*, 95.

96 Certeau, *The Practice of Everyday Life*, 106.

97 Belorusets, "Стихійний ринок. Фоторепортаж"; Anastasiya Riabchuk, "Криміналізація споживачів ін'єкційних наркотиків в Україні."

98 Riabchuk, "Homeless Men and the Crisis of Masculinity in Contemporary Ukraine," 218.

99 See Phillips, *Women's Social Activism in the New Ukraine*; Kuehnast and Nechemias, *Post-Soviet Women Encountering Transition*.

100 I am referring to Sarah D. Phillips's use of the term differentiation to describe the prescription and fulfilment of social needs by the Ukrainian state and Western-leaning NGOs in the 1990s. She argues that many grassroots definitions of need were overlooked in favour of top-down descriptions that fit a capitalist-production model. Phillips, *Women's Social Activism in the New Ukraine*.

101 Mouffe characterizes the artist as an organic intellectual: "Today, artists can no longer pretend to constitute an avant-garde offering a radical critique. But this is not a reason to proclaim that their political role has ended; they have an important role to play in the hegemonic struggle. By constructing new practices and new subjectivities, they can help subvert the existing configuration of power." *Agonistics: Thinking the World Politically*, 105.

102 The Visual Culture Research Center (VCRC) was suspended from Kyiv-Mohyla Academy in the spring of 2012. Belorusets's works were among others in the feminist workshop that resulted in the permanent expulsion of VCRC. Much of the art involved depicted the state's role in the lives of minorities who face ongoing discrimination and backlash from heightened censorship laws and an overall absence of social protections in Ukraine. The center's shutdown incited a wider student protest, and many prominent intellectual figures, including Slavoj Zizek, Judith Butler, and former Polish president Aleksander Kwasniewski, signed an ongoing petition to reinstate the center in the university. The center continued its activities for some time at the nearby October Cinema (Kino Zhovten). "Ukrainian Body Petition for Support," accessed 15 October 2012, http://vcrc.org.ua/ukrbody/.

103 Nataliya Tchermalykh, interview and translation by author, 18 July 2013, Kyiv.

104 The quote continues, "Yes, there is, and I've seen it with my own eyes growing all around me in well-organized street activism, in talks about the need to rethink the structure of the nuclear family, in annual feminist conferences, and in groups raising their self-consciousness." Plungian, "Как Выжить в Проходной Комнате" [How to survive in the hallway].

105 Tchermalykh, interview and translation by author, 18 July 2013, Kyiv.
106 Lefebvre, *Critique of Everyday Life*, 92.
107 Ibid., 125.
108 Ibid., 42.
109 Ibid., 90.
110 Plungian, "Как Выжить в Проходной Комнате" [How to survive in the hallway], my translation.
111 Tchermalykh, interview and translation by author, 18 July 2013, Kyiv.
112 Halberstam, *In a Queer Time and Place*, 6.
113 All kinds of cultural alterity, not only queer identity, are excluded from normative time. Halberstam argues that a certain discourse of "gender flexibility" has arisen with the advent of appropriative notions of queer identity in neoliberalism. She emphasizes a new kind of capitalist worker linked to idealizations of adaptability suited to a global increase in short-term contract labour. Social scientists are reinvestigating all prior assumptions about mating and marriage for best social outcomes in terms of economic sustainabilities, health, and reproduction in the patterns that are emerging in twenty-first-century practices. For example, see Geoffrey Miller, *The Mating Mind: How Sexual Choice Shaped the Evolution of Human Nature* (New York: Doubleday, 2000).
114 Belorusets, "Международный Фестиваль Квир-культуры в Санкт-Петербурге."
115 The display of this series of photos in Kyiv in 2012 resulted in fierce backlash from conservative audiences that eventually caused the LGBTQ couples featured in the photos to become targets of harm; in response, some chose the solution of emigration.
116 Martsenyuk, "Ukrainian Feminism in Action."
117 The influx of Western aid was spurred on by discourse that incentivized such investments by linking the future of the free market to the promotion of "civil society" in the newly independent countries of the former USSR. This dynamic led to a situation in Ukraine, along with the rest of the post-Soviet nations, in which the factors determining the recipients of social welfare predominantly rested with the ability to win successful grants from Western donors. In evaluating how this dynamic impacted various demographic groups, Phillips looked at processes of "differentiation" in which social needs, or "who gets what," so to speak, were sifted and determined across a set of shifting priorities. These priorities were largely contingent upon shrinking state provisions that were buffered by donations from Western NGOs. See Phillips, *Women's Social Activism in the New Ukraine*.
118 See Sperling, *Sex, Politics, and Putin*.
119 Zhurzhenko, "Gender, Nation, and Reproduction."

120 Hankivsky and Salnykova, *Gender, Politics, and Society in Ukraine*, 15.
121 New Economic Policy (NEP) was first proposed by Lenin and pursued from 1921 to 1928 as a retreat from hardline communism and enforced centralization.
122 Halberstam, *In a Queer Time and Place*, 13. Yet this observation is limited because it is drawn from the Western context. In post-Soviet Ukraine gender flexibility is perceived by many as a threat to the nation and its citiens.
123 Mayerchyk and Plakhotnik, "Between the Time of Nation and Feminist Time."
124 Holdings at the State Archives of Lviv Oblast (Tsidial) include correspondence between Ukrainka and Kobylians'ka discussing the reorganization of schools to increase Ukrainians' access to urban institutions.
125 Braidotti, *Nomadic Subjects*, 7.
126 Certeau, *The Practice of Everyday Life*, 92.
127 The only NGO in Ukraine to support both gay and transsexual individuals, Insight, helped Ofenzywa to organize the event along with the Autonomous Workers Union, Priama Diia student union, the Left Opposition Party. Interviews by author, August 2018, Kyiv.
128 See Katz, "An Open Letter from Pussy Riot"; and Ofenzywa, "Feminist Ofenzywa Ceases to Exist" (Феміністична Офензива припиняє існування).
129 Phillips describes this formation process in "The Women's Squad in Ukraine's Protests"; however, the question of representation, aesthetics, and violence in the article does not fully reflect the nuance of the debates between feminists, as the artists discussed were not associated with members' ongoing art-activism before, during, and after Maidan.
130 See Mayerchyk, "On the Occasion of March 8th / Recasting of Meanings"; Martsenyuk, "До 8 березня / Жіноча сотня або право на смисли."
131 Olha Martynyuk, interviews by author, 2018, Kyiv.
132 Lesya Prokopenko and Kateryna Taylor (curators), *Through Maidan and Beyond*, 17–30 November 2014, accessed 10 January 2015, http://www/throughmaidan.org/artists.

4. Museum of Congresses: Biopolitics and the Self in Kyiv's HudRada and REP Visual Art Collectives

1 Founders include the authors Yevgenia Belorusets, Nataliya Tchermalykh, and Katia Mishchenko. As of 2019 the editorial board consists of approximately seven members. See https://prostory.net.ua/ua/, accessed 10 August 2018.
2 HudRada's website states, "HudRada acts as a curatorial and activist interdisciplinary group. HudRada's members are architects, political activists,

translators, writers, designers, and artists. Projects organized by HudRada are based on discussion combining the experience of participants. These projects take the form of exhibitions, which become a platform for theoretical work and public campaigns using posters and screenings in city space." Accessed 10 July 2015, http://hudrada.tumblr.com/About%20Hudrada.

3 HudRada, *Disputed Territory* exhibit website, accessed 10 March 2014, http://disputedterritory.org.ua/en/node/1.

4 See Yurchak, "Revolutionaries and Their Translators." It is potentially important for me to also mention, given the title of the article, that these individuals are members of my same peer age group, including those I have collaborated with as an author, curator, and translator working across Ukrainian, Polish, Russian, and English.

5 Vitaly Chernetsky also makes this case in his discussion of the prevalence of what he terms the idea of a "postmodern postcolonial" in Russian and Ukrainian literature after 1991; see *Mapping Postcommunist Cultures.*

6 "A characteristic feature of the instrumentalities of this profane state was infinite reproducibility, a reproducibility made technically possible by print and photography, but politico-culturally by the disbelief of the rulers themselves in the real sacredness of local sites ... It had all become normal and everyday. It was precisely the infinite quotidian reproducibility of its regalia that revealed the real power of the state." Anderson, *Imagined Communities*, 182–3.

7 The "Decree on the Freedom of Conscience, Church, and Religious Society" guaranteed that all property owned by the Orthodox Church would become "the property of the people." Another decree dated 22 September 1918 reads, "On the announcement that all those who have not returned from their dacha are considered to have disappeared and their property is liable for confiscation." Several more decrees governed the removal of art for sale abroad, requisitions, and nationalization. Nationalization certificates were issued for all cultural property that had come under Narkompros's jurisdiction, under which buildings and land were headed under the Section for Property of the Republic, while the protection of works of art and antiquities was transferred to the Section on Museum Affairs. See Semenova, "A Soviet Museum Experiment," 87.

8 Semenova, "A Soviet Museum Experiment," 87.

9 Tsvetaeva, "My Father and His Museum," 179.

10 Tsvetaeva, "The Opening of the Museum," 201.

11 Ibid., 206.

12 Ibid., 207.

13 Volodymyr Chepelyk, "Shliakhom mystets'kym i odniieiu hromadioiu!" Obrazotvorche mystetstvo 2, 2005, cited in Shkandrij, "Contemporary Ukrainian Art and the Twentieth Century Avant-Garde," 424.

14 Robin Ostow, in *(Re)visualizing National History*, provides an overview of museum exhibit styles in Eastern Europe throughout the 2000s. She pays particular attention to the political struggles that emerged between different contemporary interest groups in depicting war and tragedy of the twentieth century.

15 In Kyiv, PinchukArtCentre, independently supported by the oligarch billionaire Viktor Pinchuk, has until only recently dominated local public perceptions of contemporary art, even though much of the art in the museum has historically been selected for display based upon trends in the global marketplace. The CCA (Center for Contemporary Art), funded by George Soros between 1993 and 1999, started as a gallery space, but switched to an educational and grant foundation in 2008 and often partners with Polish organizations. EIDOS Arts Development Foundation, established by Dr. Ludmila Bereznitsky, Lubov Mihailova, and Petro Bagriy, also offers grants and recently opened a new gallery. EIDOS prioritizes critical art and aims to "become a communication platform to develop the arts situation in Ukraine," but faces some limitations (www.eidos-fund.org/eng/news/read/688/, accessed 10 March 2014). The author Serhii Zhadan has also spoken out in public with regard to the situation that artists face in finding venues for their works, which is a case in point closely linked to the thematic content of his literary production – *Big Mac* (2003), *Anarchy in the UKR* (2005), *Anthem of Democratic Youth* (2006), and *Voroshilovgrad* (2010) – in which nonspaces, violence, chaos, and anarchy define the life of the young in the era of new capitalism. It remains to be seen whether independent artistic venues will be able to develop and survive with regard to the twin poles housing art in Ukraine: privatization/commodity markets, versus the state-funded museums, which, as in the case of the majority of cultural institutions across the country, are in dire need of funding and management reform.

16 One example of this is the Art Workers Self-Defense Initiative (ICTM: Ініціатива самозахисту трудящих мистецтва), founded in 2012, with the main objective being "to defend the artist and his/her labor practice in relation to the institutions and agencies that solicit, organize and present their work." Members are Lesia Khomenko, Nikita Kadan, Larissa Babij, Kateryna Badyanova, Anatoly Belov, Yevgenia Belorusets, Oleksandr Burlaka, Ksenia Hnylytska, Anna Zvyagintseva, Yuriy Kruchak, Yulia Kostereva, Vasyl Lozynsky, Mariana Matveychuk, Andriy Movchan, Ivan Melnychuk, Kateryna Mishchenko, Lada Nakonechna, Alexey Salmanov, and TanzLaboratorium. ICTM website, accessed 10 November 2017, https://istmkyiv.wordpress.com/manifest/.

17 Some Ukrainian artists of the 1990s such as Oleg Kulik and Sergey Bratkov emigrated to countries with stronger contemporary art markets. Babij and Kadan, "Blacked Out in Ukraine."

18 Piotr Piotrowski also describes REP's artists' works as a parody of politics in the Orange Revolution: "The reactions of the public and of the 'real' political groups gave the R.E.P. demonstration a social meaning. The action achieved its critical objective: it revealed conflict ... It exposed a spectrum of negative emotions and the absurdity of politics, in particular public political demonstrations. The autonomy of art, which was so important under a totalitarian system where it functioned as a defensive shield against political manipulation, was in this instance completely eliminated." *Art and Democracy in Post-Communist Europe*, 108.

19 REP on HudRada website, accessed 20 March 2015, http://hudrada .tumblr.com/.

20 Piotrowski, *Art and Democracy in Post-Communist Europe*, 108.

21 Briukhovetska, Cherepanyn, Radynski, Kulchinska, and Klymko, *Ukrains 'ke tilo* [*Ukrainian Body* exhibit catalogue].

22 Kvit responded to media coverage condemning his act, including an article in the *New York Times*, on his personal blog hosted by the university. He posted a letter from fellow rectors with comments supporting the shutdown: "In preserving human dignity modern culture does not offer ready solutions ... Kyiv-Mohyla is more precious to us than any victory won at the cost of a threat to our unique community." Kvit, "Personal'nyi zhurnal Serhiia Kvita."

23 An international response ensued as cultural figures Slavoj Žižek, John Paul-Himka, Eric Fassin, Artur Zmijewski, Sara Goodman, and many others signed a petition in March 2012 calling for the "restoration of academic and artistic freedom" in the country. After the university closed the exhibit, VCRC managed to find offices for their operations at the historic, but then deteriorating, Soviet Kino Zhovten (October Cinema). The cinema was restored in 2014 after protests ensued in response to a fire in the building; the site was then converted once again into a cinema. VCRC relocated operations to another site in a nondescript office buiding nearby where they remain as of January 2018, despite a break-in and an attack on an exhibit there by members of a far-right group in 2015. See Visual Cultural Research Center, "Ukrainian Body Petition for Support."

24 Bhabha, *The Location of Culture*, 43.

25 HudRada, *Disputed Territory Exhibit Catalogue*, 16.

26 Gregos, "On the Politics of Transformation," 35.

27 This incident was reported on widely in Ukrainian art periodicals, and also abroad, by Radio Free Europe / Radio Liberty's Ukrainian Service, "Ukrainian Museum Director Destroys Critical Painting Ahead of President's Visit."

28 A few critical distinctions are in order. Unlike in Russia (where the Russian Orthodox Church reigns supreme), in Ukraine there are many different churches. The Yanukovych government aligned itself with the

Ukrainian Orthodox Church of the Moscow Patriarchate and attempted to model the relation between church and state after Putin. The Poroshenko government after the Maidan Revolution of 2014–15 worked to facilitate the unification of all three orthodox churches in Ukraine, the other two being the Ukrainian Orthodox Church of the Kyivan Patriarchate and the Ukrainian Autocephalous Orthodox Church. The Ukrainian Greek Catholic Church, Roman Catholic Church, Protestant churches, Jewish, Islamic, and other faiths also exist among Ukraine's diverse populations. For excellent new research on the politics and public relations campaigns of the Russian Orthodox Church and its practices vis-à-vis Ukraine, see Diana Dukhanova, Religion Dispatches (website), accessed 1 November 2018, http://religiondispatches.org/author/diana_dukhanova/. Also see Andrew Sorokowski, "The Status of Religion in Ukraine in Relation to European Standards," in *Contemporary Ukraine on the Cultural Map of Ukraine.*

29 Method Fund website, https://sites.google.com/site/methodfund/news.

30 The artist Nikita Kadan links this to censorship: "Through this careful balance between Western values and Orthodox spirituality, the reigning government has effected an untenable way of life. Neither democratic representation nor international conventions have overt influence on the laws that govern existence here ... Censorship exists, and is even admitted to, but only as long as the word 'censorship' isn't uttered." Babij and Kadan, "Blacked Out in Ukraine."

31 VCRC, HudRada Curatorial Union, and Center for Society Research, *Art Ukraine.*

32 Radio Free Europe / Radio Liberty's Ukrainian Service, "Ukrainian Museum Director Destroys Critical Painting Ahead of President's Visit."

33 "In a country that declares democracy the preferred mode of interaction, we, as art workers, must impact the formation of new cultural policy principles and how they are put into practice," in "Open Letter from the Art Workers' Self-Defense Initiative to the Ukrainian and International Art Community," 31 July 2014. ICTM, Ініціативу Самозахисту Трудящих Мистецтва / Art Workers' Self-Defense Initiative.

34 Babij and Kadan, "Blacked Out in Ukraine."

35 Boym, *Another Freedom: The Alternative History of an Idea,* 8.

36 "Inner freedom and the space of the writer's creative exploration are shrinking in the context of public unfreedom." Boym, *Another Freedom,* 222.

37 Kharkiv and Odesa were also Soviet cultural capitals of film production, though Kyiv was among those territories most deeply affected by the Holodomor.

38 Boym, *Another Freedom,* 8.

39   Although Ukraine's contemporary art scene has grown exponentially
     since the Maidan Revolution, the local demand for nonconformist art re-
     mains relatively small. Oftentimes an artist associated with a collective or
     a journal will double as a curator, critic, or translator for another journal,
     membership across forums being highly variable and sometimes tied to
     funding streams from key Western supporters (e.g., Soros Foundation,
     Henrich Böll Foundation, Krytyka Polityczna). A benefit of this dynamic
     is adaptiblity, experimentation, free debate, and flexible local cultural
     contexts sometimes supported by artists themselves (even at great per-
     sonal expense). Commonly held aims involve educating the public and
     debating outmoded state museum practices as sites for contesting history.
     These efforts have evolved within the contexts of communities facilitated
     by social media networks, as well as new publications developed from
     the legacies of nonconformist samizdat strategies of the twentieth century.
40   Arendt, "Civil Disobedience" in *Crises of the Republic*, 88.
41   Some of the key virtual journals that have hosted Kyiv's grassroots ex-
     periments in public art are *Zombie* (www.zombie.ccc-k.net), *KrAM, Durch-
     schlag* (http://durchschlag.ho.ua), and *Prostory* (www.prostory.net.ua).
42   Grupa Nowolipie involves the mentally and physically challenged in
     major art projects. See Syba, "Paweł Althamer."
43   Althamer's description: "The idea behind the Congress grows and trans-
     forms through artistic strategy, the idea that the path of least resistance
     may be transformed through strategies that are both artistic and political,
     that speak about democracy and power." *Art Ukraine*, 6–2, 31–33 (2013):
     118–21.
44   The full invitation read: "Draftsmen's Congress is a meeting of people who
     communicate with the help of images rather than words. Draw your inner
     emotions, convictions, and demands. Speak the truth, express yourself!" /
     "Конгрес рисувальників – це зустріч різних людей, які спілкуються за
     допомогою образів, а не слів. Намалюйте свої емоції, переконання та
     вимоги. Скажіть правду, висловіться!" VCRC, *Exhibit Catalogue.*
45   Hearkening back to postwar Soviet ideologists' attempts to document
     the remnants of war, post-Soviet rhetoric conveyed the disorientation of
     the transition to a market economy in grand narratives of suffering that
     produced socially meaningful subject positions: "Questions of political
     responsibility were eventually displaced by collective practices of grief
     and discourses of bereavement, as if no positive content could functions
     a basis for a sense of belonging and a community must envision a shared
     experience of loss in order to establish its own borders." Oushakine, *The
     Patriotism of Despair*, 5.
46   Ibid., 5.
47   Skyba, "Who Do Museums Belong to?"

48 Ibid.

49 Piotrowski, *Art and Democracy in Post-Communist Europe*, 7.

50 From the personal collection of Dmitry Kavsan. Image shared with permission from the PinchukArtCentre Research Platform, https://archive .pinchukartcentre.org/. This image also appears in V.D. Skdorenko, "Postmodernists'ki tendentsii u suchasnomu vizual'nomu mystetstvi Ukrainy kinstsia 1980-pochatuk 1990," 117.

51 The situation improved after the Maidan Revolution of Dignity in 2014, yet the display of Soviet works is still rare in many smaller and regional museums. From 15 December 2017 to 18 February 2018 the National Museum in Kyiv held an exhibit featuring 100 years of history of the Kharkiv avant-garde entitled *Misto Ha City Karkiv Avant-Garde: Research Project*, curated by Tatyana Tumasyan and Sergiy Bratkov. There was also a separate exhibit in 2018, also in the National Museum of Ukraine, featuring Mykhailo Boychuk and the generation of artists in the 1920s surrounding him.

52 Berman, *All That Is Solid Melts into Air*, 241.

53 Berman cites Dostoevsky: "Man loves to create and build roads, that is beyond dispute. But ... may it not be that ... he is instinctively afraid of attaining his goal and completing the edifice he is constructing? How do you know, perhaps he only likes that edifice from a distance and not at close range, perhaps he only likes to build it, and does not want to live in it." Ibid., 242.

54 Hal Foster makes this distinction as a key feature of postmodernism: "One might distinguish between a 'political art' which, locked in a rhetorical code, reproduces ideological representations, and an 'art with a politic' which, concerned with the structural positioning of thought and the material effectivity of practice within the social totality, seeks to produce a concept of the political relevant to our present. A purchase on this concept is no doubt difficult, provisional – but that may well be the test of its specificity and the measure of its value." Foster, *Recodings: Art, Spectacle, Cultural Politics*, 155.

55 Latour, *Reassembling the Social*, 260.

56 Duggan and Hunter, *Sex Wars*, 5.

57 Arendt began to work this thesis out in the context of the civil rights movement in the southern United States, where racially marginalized subjects confronted the tyranny of the majority. The resulting text was one of the last things she ever wrote, and was never completed before her death. Perhaps the questions it poses can offer comparative starting points for understanding human rights, violence, and the suppression of dissent through revisiting the US civil rights movement, and the Maidan Revolution of Dignity in Ukraine. Arendt, "On Violence," in *Crises of the Republic*.

58 "Contrary to what one would expect, the post-communist condition does not require a rejection of communism and a return to the 'former' state. In fact, it can signal a certain type of continuity, if not of symbols, then certainly of the modes of thought, customs and habits, as well as the ways of wielding power by the former adversaries of the fallen system, now mainly identified with the political right." Piotrowski, *Art and Democracy in Post-Communist Europe*, 44.

59 Ibid., 151.

60 "Art can not only function as a catalyst, but also as a provocateur with a significant range of influence, something that fathers of anarchism have missed. Moreover, the artist-provocateur does not have to be solely a rebel; he or she could also take on the role of a critic." Ibid., 128.

61 The trend also includes postsocialist authors and artists. Serhii Zhadan, Andrii Bondar, and Oksana Lutsyshyna epitomize the postmodern generation in Ukraine. Some have attributed their image of the nation to "part of a non-hierarchical and open project of cultural globalization." Chernetsky, "From Anarchy to Connectivity to Cognitive Mapping," 114.

62 Even in cases where attempts were made to totally appropriate art in the service of social discourse, as Walter Benjamin pointed out in the aestheticization of politics, art, in its oblique relationship to an expression of the self (or amplification in the case of reproduced artworks) always stands not to correct or duplicate, but to distort, obscure, or undermine ideology. Louis Althusser has argued in *Ideology and Ideological State Apparatuses* that the individual is produced through ideologies that interpolate subject positions through social practices. In Chantal Mouffe's agonistic approach (to the political), "critical art is art that foments dissensus, that makes visible what the dominant consensus tends to obscure and obliterate." Mouffe, "Artistic Activism and Agonistic Spaces."

63 One member of HudRada stated that a few larger panels were donated to the museum as partial payment for the use of the gallery space.

64 As noted by Mitchell, "Image, Space, Revolution," 101.

65 Ibid., 101, 112.

66 Agamben, *Homo Sacer*, 199.

67 "Brushing and Marking Actions," 2009–2012. Video. Images shared by permission of the artist Mykola Ridnyi. SOSka Group website, accessed 22 February 2018, http://www.soskagroup.com/brushing-and-marking-actions.

68 A direct reference to Komar and Melamid's work can be seen in the inclusion of one of their paintings into an earlier video project, also featuring territory and politics; see SOSka Group, Ridnyi, Kreventsova, and Popov, "Barter."

69 Malashkin, "Muskuly," poem qtd. in Naiman, *Sex in Public*, 66–7.

342 Notes to pages 234-8

70 The artist's text accompanying the video from the exhibit catalogue: "The artists spilt a red line on the ground around the Kharkiv SBU (Ukrainian Secret Service) building which then led to the zoo, and then another one from the city administration building to the circus. The lines are a critical retort aimed at organs of state power and their working principles. Using a line to make a statement gives it a visual syntactical form, expressing its actions through the language of graffiti and street art. These acts were not political protests, but rather a meditation on political art in the urban environment. Since graffiti and street art are often a way for their creators to publicise themselves in the urban realm, or just exist as decorative forms, the ephemeral nature of the red line asks a question about how far such public actions and expressions are responsible, and what their value is. Except where they were close to official institutions, the red lines enjoyed a lifespan of about a week disappearing with melting snow." Ridnyi, qtd. in HudRada, *Exhibit Catalogue*, 39.

71 Alina Kleytman, interview by author, 10 February 2018, Kyiv.

72 Anderson, *Imagined Communities*, 173.

73 *Disputed Territory/ Spirna terytoria/ Spornaya terytorya. 4th Exposition by HudRada. Kroshitsky Art Museum, Sevastopol, Crimea.* Exhibit Catalogue. Kyiv: ADEF, 2013.

74 "Untangling this knot is to inadvertently miss the point, since the key to the 'aesthetic' is the 'ability to think contradiction.' However, in this 'way' the paradox is overcome through its affirmation. 'The best art is that which effectively affirms the paradox of combining autonomous and heteronomous existence: preserving art in the face of invasion by instrumental rationality while at the same time participating in the emergence of countless communities.' (Rancière, Malaise dans l'esthetique)." Venediktova, "Homeopathic Aggravation," 19.

75 Ibid.

76 Naiman, *Sex in Public*, 45. The appearance of Mikhail Artsybashev's novel *Sanin* in 1907 exploded public controversies around the social significance of private life. The event was compared to the appearance of Turgenev's *Fathers and Sons*. The new cult of the individual evolved along the fascination with mysticism, Nietzsche, and decadence that was developing elsewhere in Europe at the time. While the young radicals of the 1860s had been anti-Romantic in their writings about the extraordinary in life, their examination of politics transgressing the personal sphere can be read in the discussions of sex in the literary and legal debates of the 1910s.

77 In *The History of Sexuality*, Michel Foucault lays out the premise that the deployment of sexuality contains within it the mechanisms of class repression in western nations: "There is little question that one of the primordial forms of class consciousness is the affirmation of the body; at least, this was the case for the bourgeoisie during the eighteenth

century ... in order for the proletariat to be granted a body and a sexuality, economic emergencies had to arise ... lastly, there had to be established a whole technology of control which made it possible to keep that body and sexuality, finally conceded to them, under surveillance" (126).

78 The dissonance in the image could be likened to Agamben's taking to task Arendt's concept of the refugee, who signals a total crisis in rights: "The separation between humanitarianism and politics that we are experiencing today is the extreme phase of the separation of the rights of man from the rights of the citizen ... A humanitarianism separated from politics cannot fail to reproduce the isolation of sacred life at the basis of sovereignty, and the camp – which is to say, the pure space of exception – is the biopolitical paradigm that it cannot master." Rejecting Arendt's thesis that the decline of human rights implies the end of the nation state, Agamben instead calls for a renewal of categories (birth-nation, man-citizen). Agamben, *Homo Sacer*, 134.

79 Scholars of gender and the nation state have pointed out how constructions of masculinity and femininity guided the state's transition to Western liberal ideologies backing the new welfare economy after the fall of socialism. See Phillips, *Women's Social Activism in the New Ukraine*; Chatterjee, *Celebrating Women*; Gal and Kligman, *Reproducing Gender*; Johnson and Robinson, *Living Gender after Communism*; and Kaganovsky, *How the Soviet Man Was Unmade*.

80 Venediktova, "Homeopathic Aggravation," 19.

81 Polish author Marek Bieńczyk includes Kundera in his metaphysical discourse on the extensiveness of transparency as a metaphor in the concept of being, the crowd, and the public developed in the nineteenth and twentieth centuries. Bieńczyk, *Transparency*, 76.

82 Venediktova, "Homeopathic Aggravation," 20.

83 Tsvetaeva, *Art in the Light of Conscience*, 150.

84 "In order to be good (not lead into temptation the little ones of this world), art would have to renounce a fair half of its whole self. The only way for art to be wittingly good is – not to be. It will end with the life of the planet." Ibid., 157.

85 Ibid., 161.

5. Bad Myth: Picturing Intergenerational Experiences of Revolution and War

1 Negative attitudes towards LGBTQ populations in Ukraine have increased in the decade since the Orange Revolution; see Martsenyuk, "Ukrainian Societal Attitudes towards the Lesbian, Gay, Bisexual and Transgender Communities."

2 For a more detailed discussion on the specific terms and impacts of these policies, see Minakov, *Development and Dystopia*.

3 The scholar Adriana Helbig contextualizes this increase in violence through the particular instance of attacks on Roma in a 2019 article drawing on her longer-term fieldwork involving the symbolic, material, and other forms of exclusion leveraged on these communities across the different regions of Ukraine since 1991. Helbig, "Morals and Money."

4 In a widely circulated 2018 report published on the Atlantic Council website, the proliferation of far-right activity is stated as partly stemming from funds bracketed for "patriotic education" by the Ministry of Youth and Sport being provided to the extremist group C-14. See Cohen, "Ukraine's Got a Real Problem with Far-Right Violence."

5 Minakov, *Development and Dystopia*.

6 For example, Mikhail Minakov's recent study of oligarchic clans shoring up power reveals the hierarchical nature of the legislation of public institutions, including museums and universities that regulate speech. Minakov, *Development and Dystopia*.

7 Vova Vorotniov, interview by author, 15 November 2017, Kyiv.

8 For a more detailed discussion on this point, see Jacques, "Interview with Jessica Zychowicz and Maria Kulikokovska."

9 Boym comments on the feminization of domestic work in communal dwellings in the Soviet era: "The burden of the communal interactions and negotiations rested entirely on women; the world of the communal kitchen has often been called matriarchal, but I would add that it has been matriarchal by necessity and not by choice." *Common Places*, 147.

10 Visual Culture Research Center website, http://vcrc.org.ua/en.

11 VCRC has received an outpouring of international support: the lists of signatories on petitions include figures such as Judith Butler and Slavoj Žižek.

12 Visual Culture Research Center website, http://vcrc.org.ua/en.

13 Mishchenko, *The Book of Kyiv*.

14 VCRC, *The Book of Kyiv*, edited by Kateryna Mishchenko, 15.

15 Ibid.

16 The School of Kyiv website, accessed 20 December 2017, http://theschoolofkyiv.org/.

17 The first biennial was held in 2012. In November 2013 two Austrian curators, Hedwig Saxenhuber and Georg Schöllhammer, had signed on to organize the second event slated for 2014. For more details on the curation and planning of the event, see Matusevich, "This Is Not a Biennale."

18 On 17 November 2017 activists gathered at the Ministry of Social Policy in Kyiv to discuss the future of architectural monuments of modernism and the steps necessary for their preservation. The meeting was initiated by activists Anton Verkhun, Kateryna Sokolova, and Viktor Gerasimenko and resulted in an official appeal to suspend the dismantling of the

"Tarilka" (UFO) building, constructed by Florian Yuriev in 1978. As with many other sites in Kyiv, the building does not have official status, which limits its legislative defence. See the article by #SaveKyivModernism, "Активісти вступилися за аркітектурний спадок модернізму в Києві" [Activists stand up for the architectural legacy of Modernism in Kyiv].

19 Cherepanyn, "What Is International?," in *Guidebook of the Kyiv International*, 15.

20 Ibid., 19.

21 BBC, "Ukraine Arrests Pilot Hero Savchenko Over 'Coup Plot.'"

22 For a detailed, comprehensive study of networks and global knowledge flows, see Kennedy, *Globalizing Knowledge.*

23 United Nations, *Humanitarianism in the Network Age.*

24 According to Ukraine expert on management, telecommunications, and information technology development, Dr. Zakhar Popovych, internet access and its diffusion throughout society has reached a maximum saturation user per provider level, contributing to a lack of incentive among providers for the transparent management of information, which is a more concerning variable than access in terms of what drives the "new" digital divide. This dynamic contributes to public educational institutes' and scientific researchers' inability to pay for subscriptions to information and research services, software, and databases, thus compelling further dependency on pirated materials to keep pace with R&D across all sectors of society. Popovych, "Ukraine on the Way from Digital Divide to Intellectual Exclusion," shared with permission from the author; and Popovych, "Novi zavdannia stratehichnoho pozytsionuvannia Ukrtelekomu na rynku komp'iuternoho zv'iazku" [New tasks in the strategic positioning of JSC Ukrtelecom on the computer communications market]. Also see Freedom House, "Freedom on the Net 2017: Ukraine."

25 Curated by Oleksandr Roytburd and Alisa Lozhkina at the National Art Museum in Kyiv from 26 April to 24 August 2014. See Lozhkina and Roytburd, "Inventory of a Dictator."

26 For more context on the role of student unions and youth activism in the protests on the Maidan 2013–14, see Channell-Justice, "Flexibility and Fragmentation."

27 Pospieszna, *Democracy Assistance from the Third Wave.*

28 Cherepanyn, "Declaration of the School of Kyiv."

29 Ibid.

30 Ibid.

31 Partners include the Polish Institute, Muzeum Sztuki Nowoczesnej; ERSTE Foundation, Goethe Institut; the Ministry of Culture of Georgia; local news outlets *Ukrainian Pravda*, *Kyiv Post*, Hromadske TV; and the UART Foundation for Cultural Diplomacy, among others.

32 The Freedom House report, "Freedom on the Net 2017," scores Ukraine as "partly free." The score reflects high levels of web access, yet massive institutional failures to reduce the financial and other burdens faced by citizens. The IATP (Internet Access and Training Program) in Eastern Europe and Central Asia is one of the key international development initiatives working to close the digital divide through education; IATP website, accessed 20 February 2018, http://www.comminit.com/global/content/internet-access-and-training-program-iatp-eastern-europe-central-asia.

33 Bociurkiw, *This Is Gay Propaganda!*

34 The painting (in chapter 4) depicted politicians and church figures falling into a nuclear reactor, and marching workers, intellectuals, and dissidents resembling members from the feminist activist groups Pussy Riot and Femen. Radio Free Europe / Radio Liberty, "Ukrainian Museum Director Destroys Critical Painting Ahead of President's Visit."

35 Freedom House, "Freedom on the Net 2017"; Amnesty International, "Ukraine: The Authorities' Inaction Emboldens Rising Violence by the Far-Right"; Human Rights Watch, "World Report 2018: Ukraine." The Human Rights Watch report states, "The government took several steps to restrict freedom of expression and media freedom, justifying them by the need to counter Russia's military aggression in eastern Ukraine and anti-Ukraine propaganda." UkraineAlert compiled the top ten globally circulated articles of 2018 into one article published by Atlantic Council under the headline, "Ukraine's Got a Problem with Far-Right Violence."

36 Anthropologist Emily S. Channell-Justice articulates the ongoing marginalization of leftists during the revolution and post-Maidan. This poses risks for further polarization of society; I hold that the situation is made more acute by the problematic outcomes of the state's passage and application of decommunization laws. I am largely in agreement with her methological position on engaged scholarship. In this particular regard, the practices and resulting texts in my own work as a founding and acquisitions editor of the *Krytyka* Forum on Race and Postcolonialism can also help to illuminate a statement by one of Channell-Justice's interlocutors: "To this activist and other leftist scholars, Ukraine's status as a post-socialist country mattered less than its similarities to other decolonized and decolonizing nations." Channell-Justice, "Thinking through Positionality in Post-Socialist Politics," 62.

37 *Maidan: Rough Cut*, directed by Roman Bondarchyk, Volodymyr Tykhy, Kateryna Gornostai, Andriy Lytvyenko, et al., 2014.

38 Tchermalykh, "We Felt That the Country Was in the Stage of a Rough Cut," shared with the author's permission.

39 Iakovlenko, "The Artist Who 'Made Donbas Human.'"

40 Kakhidze, "В 2015 году мои."

41 Kakhidze participated, along with several other artists and authors from Ukraine, in a conference in Moscow in 2013 dedicated to feminist themes, entitled Feminist Pencil II. See Plungian and Lomasko, *Feminist Pencil II*; and a review by Tchermalykh, "Vziat' na karandash."

42 Kakhidze, "В 2015 году мои."

43 Kakhidze, "Prozhyt' vojnu," 200–1.

44 Kakhidze, *Where Curating Is*, 117.

45 Nakonechna, *Where Curating Is*, 96.

46 See Kakhidze, "Muzychi Expanded History Project," accessed 13 November 2016, http://www.alevtinakakhidze.com/.

47 Ralko, *Kyivskiy Shchodenyk*.

48 Ralko, *Kyivskiy Shchodenyk*, 10.

49 Shevchenko, *Kobzar*, trans. Vera Rich, 77.

50 Ralko, *Kyivskiy Shchodenyk*, 9.

51 The four laws collectively known as "decommunization" were introduced by President Petro Poroshenko on 9 April 2015 without parliamentary or public debate. The laws are as follows: Law 2538-1, On the legal status and honoring of fighters for Ukraine's independence in the 20th century; Law 2558, On condemning the communist and National Socialist (Nazi) totalitarian regimes and prohibiting propaganda of their symbols; Law 2539, On remembering the victory over Nazism in the Second World War; Law 2540, On access to the archives of repressive bodies of the communist totalitarian regime from 1917-1991. Scholars have criticized the arbitrary interpretation and application of this legislation as retrograde. For one early critique, see political scientist Oksana Shevel, "'De-Communization Laws' Need to Be Amended to Conform to European Standards."

52 Yurii Mushketyk, "Koleso. Kilka dumok z pryvodu suchasnoho ukrainskoho postavanhardu," *Literaturna Ukraina*, 27 October 1994, as cited in Wilson, *The Ukrainians: Unexpected Nation*, 231.

53 This photograph by Dima Sergeev first appeared in *Calvert Journal*, 13 July 2016, accessed 16 April 2017, https://www.calvertjournal.com/news/show/6394/kiev-installation-lets-you-stand-in-lenins-shoes.

54 Izolyatsia has since gained wide international support and investment for their exhibits, workshops, and courses in Kyiv, with governmental and NGO partners in Europe, Canada, and the United States; https://izolyatsia.org (accessed 10 April 2018).

55 For a foundational study on the challenges and opportunities for civil society and the rule of law in emerging trends afforded by new technologies, see van Dijk, *The Network Society*.

56 Alexievich, *Secondhand Time: The Last of the Soviets*, 11. Original quote in Russian: "Встретила на улице молодых ребят в майках с серпом и молотом и портретом Ленина. Знают ли они, что такое коммунизм?," 16.

57 Alexievich, *Secondhand Time: The Last of the Soviets*, 11. Original quote in Russian: "Перед революцией семнадцатого года Александр Грин написал: 'А будущее как-то перестало стоять на своем месте.' Прошло сто лет – и будущее опять не на своем месте. Наступило время секонд хэнд," 15.

58 For an in-depth study of disability and activism in Ukraine, see Phillips, *Disability and Mobile Citizenship in Post-Socialist Ukraine* (2012), and a more recent study on Ukrainian sign language, pedagogy, and deaf cultures by Dickenson, "Deaf Identity in Post-Maidan Ukraine."

59 Kakhidze, "В 2015 году мои ..."

60 Silvia Franceschini, "Introduction: The Double Bind of History," in *Yesterday, Today, Today*, ed. Kadan, 15.

61 Riabchuk, "Eurorenovation of the Soviet Soul," in *R.E.P.: Revolutionary Experimental Space, A History*, 203.

62 V.E., "Mohyla's Horizon," *The Book of Kyiv*, 10.

Conclusion

1 The structure of governance prior to the Maidan is best described in the theory of authoritarianism evidenced by Ukraine in the study by Lucan Way and Steven Levitsky, *Competitive Authoritarianism: Hybrid Regimes after the Cold War*.

2 Pyzik, *Poor but Sexy*, 10. Pyzik's book is provocatively named after a tourism campaign slogan developed by Berlin mayor Klaus Wowereit to attract outside investment.

3 Mikhail Minakov describes the years following the Maidan Revolution, targeting oligarchy, separatism, and patronage networks as serious challenges to sustaining civil rights in Ukraine, in *Development and Dystopia* (2018).

4 There is yet research to be done on the role of the conservative youth movements before and during the Maidan protests. Emily S. Channell-Justice has conducted an in-depth study on the role of the left youth in the protests, focusing on the critical role that university students played from their gathering on the Maidan on 21 November 2013 to occupation of the ministry building from 18–20 February 2014. She traces how students "responded to shifting targets within the educational sphere and the Ukrainian political landscape," basing her conclusions on participatory observation and interviews with the Kyiv-based independent student union Priiama Dia (Direct Action) and the Studentska Koordinatsijna Rada (Student Coordinating Committee), the student governing body created to participate in the Maidan Council. See the following chapters in her Phd dissertation, "Left of Maidan": "#Leftmaidan: Self-Organization and Political Legitimacy"; "Direct Action: Education

Activism and Maidan"; "'These Aren't Your Values': Gender, Nation, and Feminist (Im)Possibilities."

5 Arseniy Yatsenyuk, Oleh Tyahnybok, and Vitali Klitschko were among the leaders they petitioned. Kratochvil, "The Writers and the Maidan."

6 Investigators would later uncover documents in Yanukovych's abandoned home implicating him in a covert plot, possibly orchestrated in cooperation with covert Russian operations, to annihilate thousands of demonstrators on the Maidan by force. The fatal clashes on 18 February appear to have been the first day of that operation.

7 A collection of essays, edited by photographer and poet Yevgenia Belorusets, provides an overview of these debates on the significance of Maidan and its risks/potentials as an instrument of ideology. Belorusets, Vakhovska, and Tchermalykh, "Documenting Maidan." Also see Belorusets, Stereoscope Ukraine Project with n-ost Berlin, 1.

8 The independent curatorial union ICTM supported the Center for Peaceful Self-Organization on the Maidan Центр мирної самоорганізації, accessed 15 March 2014, https://www.facebook.com/selfmaidan.

9 Sarah D. Phillips documents the split with reference to differing perspectives on theories and practices associated with militarism in "The Women's Squad in Ukraine's Protests."

10 Mishchenko and Zownir, Ukrainian Night.

11 Compilations of their work have been published in multiple languages. See Tchermalykh, Shifting Landscapes.

12 https://maidanmuseum.org/.

13 For a short description of the 2019 march and the dangers of rising online organizing among far-right groups in Ukraine, see my post on the Kennan Institute Blog, "Ukraine Hosts Most Successful LGBTQ Event in the Nation's History, but New Challenges Appear."

Bibliography

Ackermann, Niels, and Sébastian Gobert. *Looking for Lenin*. London: FUEL Design & Publishing, 2017.

Adorno, Theodor W., and Rolf Tiedemann. *Theory and History of Literature*. Minneapolis: University of Minnesota Press, 1997.

Agamben, Giorgio. *Homo Sacer: Sovereign Power and Bare Life*. Palo Alto: Stanford University Press, 1998.

– *Nudities*. Edited by David Kishik and Stefan Pedatella. Palo Alto: Stanford University Press, 2011.

Aheieva, V.P. *Zhinochyi prostir feministychnyi dyskurs ukrainskogo modernizmu*. Kyiv: Fakt, 2008.

Alexievich, Svetlana. "On the Battle Lost." Nobel Prize Lecture at the Swedish Academy, Stockholm, 7 December 2015.

– *Secondhand Time*. Translated by Bela Shayevich. New York: Random House, 2016.

– *Vremya sekond khend*. Moskva: Vremya, 2013.

Al-Mahadin, Salam. "Do Muslim Women Need Saving? Making (Non)sense of FEMEN's Ethico-Aesthetics in the Arab World." *Women's Studies in Communication* 38 (2015): 388–92.

Amnesty International. "Ukraine: The Authorities' Inaction Emboldens Rising Violence by the Far Right." 16 May 2018. Accessed 1 October 2018. https://www.amnesty.org/en/documents/eur50/8434/2018/en/.

Anderson, Benedict R. *Imagined Communities: Reflections on the Origin and Spread of Nationalism*. London and New York: Verso, 2006.

– *Under Three Flags: Anarchism and the Anti-Colonial Imagination*. New York: Verso, 2005.

Andryczyk, Mark. "Four Bearings of West for the Lviv Bohema." In *Over the Wall / After the Fall*, edited by Sibelan Forrester, Magdalena J. Zaborowska, and Elena Gapova, 238–50. Bloomington and Indianapolis: Indiana University Press, 2004.

Arendt, Hannah. "Civil Disobedience" and "On Violence." In *Crises of the Republic*. New York: Harcourt Brace, 1972.

– *The Human Condition*. Chicago: University of Chicago Press, 1998.

Aristarkhova, Irina. "Beyond Representation and Affiliation: Collective Action in Post-Soviet Russia." In *Collectivism after Modernism: The Art of Social Imagination after 1945*, edited by Blake Stimson, Gregory Sholette, 253–73. Minneapolis: University of Minnesota Press, 2007.

Austin, J.L. *How to Do Things with Words*. Cambridge, MA: Harvard University Press, 1962.

Azar, Ilia. "Femen: Konechno, a Kak Zhe Zh." *Colta.ru*, 4 February 2013. Accessed 5 February 2013. http://www/colta.ru/docs/12363.

Azoulay, Ariella. *Civil Imagination: A Political Ontology of Photography*. Translated by Louise Bethlehem. London and New York: Verso, 2012.

Babij, Larissa. "Fear and Hope." *Artforum International* 53 (1 September 2014): 395.

Badura-Triska, Eva, and Hubert Klocker, eds. *Vienna Actionism: Art and Upheaval in 1960s Vienna*. Vienna: Mumok Museum Moderner Kunst Siftung Ludwig Wien, 2000.

Baidyanova, Kateryna. "Atlantic Parallax." *Prostory* (Простори). Accessed 16 March 2018. http://prostory.net.ua/ua/krytyka/306-analiticheskij-paralich.

Bakhtin, Mikhail M. *The Dialogic Imagination: Four Essays*. Edited by Michael Holquist. Translated by Michael Holquist and Caryl Emerson. Austin: University of Texas Press, 1981.

– *Rabelais and His World*. Translated by Hélène Iswolsky and Michael Holquist. Bloomington: Indiana University Press, 1984.

Balmforth, Richard. "FEMEN, Topless Activists, Plan Euro 2012 Soccer Tournament Protests." *Huffingtonpost.com*, 21 May 2012. Accessed 21 June 2012. http://www.huffingtonpost.com/2012/05/21/femen-euro-2012-protest-ukraine_n_1532544.html.

Balsamo, Anne. "The Virtual Body in Cyberspace." In *Technologies of the Gendered Body: Reading Cyborg Women*, 116–32. Durham, NC: Duke University Press, 1996.

Bateson, Ian. "On Femen, Pussy Riot and Crosses." *KyivPost*, 5 October 2012. Accessed 10 November 2012. http://www.kyivpost.com/opinion/op-ed/on-femen-pussy-riot-and-crosses-313994.html.

BBC. "Femen's Inna Shevchenko Inspired France's Marianne Stamp." *BBC News Europe*, 15 July 2013. Accessed 10 January 2015. http://www.bbc.com/news/world-europe-23320741.

– "Topless Protester Inspired Marianne." *BBC News Europe*, 15 July 2013. Accessed 16 July 2013. http://www.bbc.co.uk/news/world-europe-23320741.

– "Ukraine Arrests Pilot Hero Savchenko Over 'Coup Plot.'" *BBC World News*, 22 March 2018. Accessed 2 April 2018. http://www.bbc.com/news/world-europe-43504396.

Bean, Annemarie. "Black Minstrelsy and Double Inversion, Circa 1890." In *African-American Performance and Theatre History: A Critical Reader*, edited by Harry Justin Elam and David Krasner, 171–91. Oxford: Oxford University Press, 2001.

Beauvoir, Simone de. *The Second Sex*. Edited by H.M. Parshley. New York: Vintage Books, 1989.

Belorusets, Yevgenia. "Finishing What Yanukovych Started." Stereoscope Ukraine Project with n-ost Berlin. *Transitions Online*, 6 March 2015.

– "How to Stop the War in Eastern Ukraine." Stereoscope Ukraine Project with n-ost Berlin. *Transitions Online*, 3 March 2015.

– "Observers on the Line of Death." Stereoscope Ukraine Project with n-ost Berlin. *Transitions Online*, 20 March 2015.

– "What Can Ukrainians Expect from Europe?" Stereoscope Ukraine Project with n-ost Berlin. *Transitions Online*, 13 March 2015.

– "What Remains after Maidan?" Stereoscope Ukraine Project with n-ost Berlin. *Transitions Online*, 27 February 2015.

– "Комментарии к Фотопроекту Гоголевская 32/Gogol 32." Все ж Продолжает Нерей в Аонийских Свирепствовать Водах: Повседневность Как Событие [Commentary on the photo project Gogol St. 32 / Everything follows Nereus on the raging Aonian waters: everyday life as an event], 2011. Accessed 12 November 2014. http://yevgeniabelorusets.blogspot.com/2011/03/32-i.html.

– "Международный Фестиваль Квир-культуры в Санкт-Петербурге" [International Festival of Queer Culture in Saint Petersburg]. *Queerfest*, 20–29 September 2019. Accessed October 2019. http://queerfest.ru/eugene-belorusets_en.php.

– "Стихійний ринок. Фоторепортаж" [Stykhinyi market: photo report]. Спільне: журнал соціальної критики [Spilne / Commons: a journal of social criticism], no. 1 (2010): 57–78. Accessed 16 March 2018. https://commons.com.ua/uk/.

– "Unfit for Living. 2010 Joan Wakelin Bursary Winner Yevgenia Belorusets." *RPS Journal* 151, no. 5 (June 2011), 286–9.

Belorusets, Yevgenia, Nelia Vakhovska, and Nataliya Tchermalykh, eds. "Documenting Maidan." Special issue, *Prostory Literary Journal*, no. 8 (December 2013–February 2014). Accessed 5 January 2014. www.prostory.net.ua.

Belov, Anatoly. "Eros 2012: Neimovirne pryhody shvediv u Kyivi (drawings)." *Krytyka Polityczna* 4 (2013): 79–91.

Benhabib, Seyla. "Introduction: The Democratic Moment and the Problem of Difference." In *Democracy and Difference: Contesting the Boundaries of the Political*, 3–18. Princeton, NJ: Princeton University Press, 1996.

– *Situating the Self: Gender, Community, and Postmodernism in Contemporary Ethics*. New York: Routledge, 1992.

Benjamin, Walter. "The Ruin." In *The Work of Art in the Age of Its Technological Reproducibility and Other Writings on Media*, 180–6. Edited by Michael W. Jennings, Brigid Doherty, and Thomas Y. Levin. Translated by Edmund Jephcott, Rodney Livingstone, and Howard Eiland. Cambridge, MA: Harvard University Press, 2008.

– "Theses on the Philosophy of History." In *Illuminations*, edited and with an introduction by Hannah Arendt. Translated by Harry Zohn. New York: Schocken Books, 1986.

Bennetts, Marc. *Kicking the Kremlin: Russia's New Dissidents and the Battle to Topple Putin*. London: OneWorld Publications, 2014.

Berman, Marshall. *All That Is Solid Melts into Air: The Experience of Modernity*. New York: Penguin Books, 1988.

Bernstein, Anya. "An Inadvertent Sacrifice: Body Politics and Sovereign Power in the Pussy Riot Affair." *Critical Inquiry* (University of Chicago), September (2013). Accessed 3 November 2013. http://criticalinquiry.uchicago.edu/an_inadvertent_sacrifice_body_politics_and_sovereign_power_in_the_pussy_rio/.

– "Caution, Religion! Iconoclasm, Secularism, and Ways of Seeing in Post-Soviet Art Wars." *Public Culture* 26, no. 3 (2014): 419–48.

Bertelsen, Olga, ed. *Revolution and War in Contemporary Ukraine: The Challenge of Change*. Columbia University Press, 2017.

Bhabha, Homi K. *The Location of Culture*. 2nd ed. Routledge, 2004.

Bieńczyk, Marek. *Transparency*. Translated by Benjamin Paloff. London: Dalkey Archive Press, 2012.

Biesenbach, Klaus Peter, ed. *Marina Abramović: The Artist Is Present*. New York: Museum of Modern Art, 2010.

Bilaniuk, Laada. "Race, Media, and Postcoloniality: Ukraine between Nationalism and Cosmopolitanism." *Krytyka: Thinking Ukraine* (Harvard Ukrainian Research Institute), October 2017. Accessed 29 January 2018. https://krytyka.com/en/race-and-postcolonialism-ukraine-and-north-america/articles/race-media-and-postcoloniality-ukraine.

Bilenky, Serhiy. *Imperial Urbanism in the Borderlands: Kyiv, 1800–1905*. Toronto: University of Toronto Press, 2017.

Bishop, Claire. *Artificial Hells: Participatory Art and the Politics of Spectatorship*. New York: Verso, 2012.

Bociurkiw, Marusya, dir. *This Is Gay Propaganda! LGBT Rights and the War in Ukraine*. Documentary film, 53 mins. Winds of Change Productions, 2015.

Bohachevsky-Chomiak, Martha. *Feminists Despite Themselves: Women in Ukrainian Community Life, 1884–1939*. Edmonton: University of Alberta, 1988.

Bordo, Susan. "Feminism, Postmodernism, and Gender-Scepticism." In *Feminism/Postmodernism*, edited by Linda J. Nicholson, 133–56. New York and London: Routledge, 1990.

Borenstein, Eliot. *Overkill: Sex and Violence in Contemporary Russian Popular Culture*. Ithaca and London: Cornell University Press, 2008.

Bourdieu, Pierre. "Censorship and the Imposition of Form." In *Language and Symbolic Power*, edited by John B. Thompson, translated by Gino Raymond and Matthew Adamson, 137–62. Cambridge, MA: Harvard University Press, 1991.

– "The Perception of the Social World and Political Struggle." In *Language and Symbolic Power*, 171–202.

Bouton, Éloïse. *Confession d'une Ex-Femen*. Paris: Editions du Moment, 2015.

Boym, Svetlana. *Another Freedom: The Alternative History of an Idea*. Chicago: University of Chicago Press, 2010.

– *Common Places*. Cambridge, MA: Harvard University Press, 1994.

– "From the Toilet to the Museum: Memory and Metamorphosis of Soviet Trash." In *Consuming Russia: Popular Culture, Sex, and Society since Gorbachev*, edited by Adele Marie Barker, 383–96. Durham and London: Duke University Press, 1999.

Braidotti, Rosi. *Nomadic Subjects: Embodiment and Sexual Difference in Contemporary Feminist Theory*. 2nd ed. New York: Columbia University Press, 2011.

Brik, Osip. "What the Eye Does Not See." In *Russian Art of the Avante-Garde: Theory and Criticism, 1902–1934*, edited by John E. Bowlt. New York: Thames and Hudson, 1988.

Briukhovetska, Oksana. "I Am Ukrainka." *Krytyka Polityczna*, 30 October 2018. Accessed 6 November 2018. http://politicalcritique.org/cee/2018/i-am-ukr ainka/?fbclid=IwAR3PuEFooN2e3pPKd8G6Ufqe_JzFUyRArbM86U23gFf 8m9BMJIOHYlhxPkg.

– *Motherhood*. Exhibit Catalogue, 6–19 March 2015. Kyiv: Visual Culture Research Center. Accessed January 2018. http://vcrc.org.ua/en/виставка -материнство/.

– *TEXTUS: Vyshyvka, Tekstyl, Feminizm Katalog* [TEXTUS: Embroidery, Textile, Feminism Catalogue]. Kyiv: Visual Culture Research Center, 2017.

– "What in Me Is Feminist?" *Paradoxa: International Feminist Art Journal* 38 (2016).

Briukhovetska, Oksana, Vasyl Cherepanyn, Oleksiy Radynski, Lesia Kulchinska, and Serhiy Klymko, eds. *Ukrains'ke tilo*. [*Ukrainian Body* exhibit catalogue]. Kyiv, Ukraine: Visual Culture Research Center and Heinrich Böll Siftung, 2012.

Briukhovetska, Oksana, and Lesia Kulchinska, eds. *The Right to Truth: Conversations on Art and Feminism*. Kyiv: VCRC, European Alternatives, and AVANTPOST-PRIM, 2019.

Briukhovetska, Oksana, Lesia Kulchinska, and Segolene Pruvo, eds. *Feminist Strategies: Art, Philosophy, Activism*. Kyiv: VCRC, European Alternatives, Tandem Ukraine, 2017.

Bürger, Peter. "Theory of the Avant Garde." In *Theory and History of Literature*, vol. 4. Foreword by Jochen Schulte-Sasse. Translated by Michael Shaw. Minneapolis: University of Minnesota Press, 1984.

Butler, Judith. *Frames of War: When Is Life Grievable?* London: Verso, 2009.

– *Gender Trouble: Feminism and the Subversion of Identity*. New York: Routledge, 1999.

Butler, Judith, and Athena Athanasiou. *Dispossession: The Performative in the Political*. Cambridge, UK, and Maiden, MA: Polity, 2013.

Carr-Gomm, Phillip. "Naked Rebellion." In *A Brief History of Nakedness*, 89–133. London: Reaktion Books, 2010.

Cassiday, Julie A., and Emily D. Johnson. "A Personality Cult for the Post-modern Age: Reading Vladimir Putin's Public Persona." In *Putin as Celebrity and Cultural Icon*, edited by Helena Goscilo, 37–64. London: Routledge, 2012.

de Certeau, Michel. *The Practice of Everyday Life*. Translated by Steven F. Rendall. Berkeley: University of California Press, 1984.

Channell-Justice, Emily S. "Flexibility and Fragmentation: Student Activism and Ukraine's (Euro)Maidan Protests." *Berkeley Journal of Sociology*, 20 October 2014. Accessed 10 November 2015. http://berkeleyjournal.org /2014/10/flexibility-and-fragmentation-student-activism-and-ukraines -euromaidan-protests/.

– "Is Sextremism the New Feminism? Perspectives from Pussy Riot and Femen." *Nationalities Papers* 42, no. 4 (July 2014): 611–14.

– "Left of Maidan: Self-Organizing and the Ukrainian State on the Edge of Europe." PhD dissertation, the Graduate Center, City University of New York, 2016. https://academicworks.cuny.edu/gc_etds/1403.

– "Thinking through Positionality in Post-Socialist Politics: Researching Contemporary Social Movements in Ukraine." *History and Anthropology* 30, no. 1 (2019): 47–66.

– "'We're Not Just Sandwiches': Gender, Nation and Feminist (Im)possibilities on Ukraine's Maidan." *Signs Journal of Women in Culture and Society* 42, no. 3 (2017): 717–41.

Chateauvert, Melinda. *Sex Workers Unite: A History of the Movement from Stonewall to Slutwalk*. Boston: Beacon Press, 2013.

Chatterjee, Choi. *Celebrating Women: Gender, Festival Culture, and Bolshevik Ideology, 1910–1939*. Pittsburg, PA: University of Pittsburg Press, 2002.

Cherepanyn, Vasyl. "Declaration of the School of Kyiv: Kyiv Biennial." *Krytyka Polityczna & European Alternatives*, 24 September 2015. Accessed 10 January 2017. http://politicalcritique.org/cee/ukraine/2015/declaration -of-the-school-of-kyiv-kyiv-biennial-2015/.

– "What Is International?" In *Guidebook of the Kyiv International: Kyiv Biennial 2017*, edited by Kateryna Mishchenko and Vasyl Cherepanyn. Kyiv: Medusa Books; Art Knyha, 2017.

Cherepanyn, Vasyl, Lesia Kulchinska, and Olha Papash, eds. "Nam nema shcho vytraty, krim nashchyh Maidaniv." *Krytyka Polityczna Ukraina*, no. 5 (2014).

Chernetsky, Vitaly. "From Anarchy to Connectivity to Cognitive Mapping: Contemporary Ukrainian Writers of the Younger Generation Engage with Globalization." *Canadian-American Slavic Studies* 44, no. 1–2 (1 June 2010): 102–17.

– *Mapping Postcommunist Cultures: Russia and Ukraine in the Context of Globalization*. Montreal: McGill-Queen's University Press, 2007.

Cixous, Hélène. "The Laugh of the Medusa." Translated by Keith Cohen and Paula Cohen. *Signs* (Chicago Journals) 1, no. 4 (Summer 1976): 875–93.

Clifford, Bob. *The Marketing of Rebellion: Insurgents, Media, and International Activism*. New York, NY: Cambridge University Press, 2005.

Cochrane, Kira. "Rise of the Naked Female Warriors." *The Guardian*, World News section, 20 March 2013. Accessed 10 April 2013. http://www.guardian .co.uk/world/2013/mar/20/naked-female-warrior-femen-topless-protesters.

Cohen, Josh. "Ukraine's Got a Real Problem with Far-Right Violence (And No, RT Didn't Write This Headline)." Atlantic Council website, 20 June 2018. Accessed 23 December 2018. https://www.atlanticcouncil.org/blogs /ukrainealert/ukraine-s-got-a-real-problem-with-far-right-violence-and-no -rt-didn-t-write-this-headline.

Condee, Nancy. "Body Graphics: Tatooing the Fall of Communism." In *Consuming Russia: Popular Culture, Sex, and Society Since Gorbachev*, edited by Adele Marie Barker, 339–61. London: Duke University Press, 1999.

Crimp, Douglas. "On the Museum's Ruins." In *The Anti-Aesthetic: Essays on Postmodern Culture*, 43–56. Port Townsend, WA: Bay Press, 1983.

Cybriwsky, Roman Adrian. *Kyiv, Ukraine: The City of Domes and Demons from the Collapse of Socialism to the Mass Uprising of 2013–2014*. Amsterdam: Amsterdam University Press, 2014.

Debord, Guy. *Society of the Spectacle*. Detroit: Black & Red Press, 1970. First published in French in 1967.

Deleuze, Gilles, and Félix Guattari. *Anti-Oedipus: Capitalism and Schizophrenia*. Minneapolis: University of Minnesota Press, 1983.

Delphy, Christine. *Separate and Dominate: Feminism and Racism and the War on Terror*. London and New York: Verso, 2018.

Denegri, Dobrila, and Stefania Miscetti, eds. *Marina Abramović: Performing Body*. Milan: Charta, 1998.

Der Spiegel. "International Support for Pussy Riot." *Der Spiegel Online*, 12 August 2012. Accessed 18 October 2018. http://www.spiegel.de/fotostrecke/photos -of-protests-in-solidarity-with-pussy-riot-fotostrecke-86274.html.

Dickenson, Jennifer. "Deaf Identity in Post-Maidan Ukraine." Fulbright Lecture, Kyiv, 21 February 2018.

van Dijk, Jan. *The Network Society*. 3rd ed. London: Sage Publications, 2012.

van Dijk, Jan, and Kenneth L. Hacker. *Internet and Democracy in the Network Society*. London: Routledge Studies in Global Information, Politics, and Society, 2018.

Dmytriyeva, Maria. "Femen na tli hrudei." *Krytyka* 15, no. 1–2 (2011): 20–3.

Dmytryk, Olenka. "'I'm a Feminist, Therefore ...': The Art of Gender and Sexual Dissent in 2010s Ukraine and Russia." *JSPPS: Journal of Soviet and Post-Soviet Politics and Society* 2, no. 1 (2016): 137–78.

Docudays UA International Human Rights Documentary Film Festival. Website. Accessed 16 March 2018. http://docudays.ua/eng/.

Duggan, Lisa, and Nan D. Hunter. *Sex Wars: Sexual Dissent and Political Culture*. New York: Routledge, 1995.

Dunin, Kinga. "Jak Przed Wojną" [As before the war]. *Krytyka Polityczna*. Polityka Literatury [The politics of literature]. Warsaw (2009): 216–61.

Dyczok, Marta. "Do the Media Matter? Focus on Ukraine." In *Media, Democracy, and Freedom: The Postcommunist Experience*, 17–42. Bern: Peter Lang, 2009.

Elam, Harry Justin, and David Krasner, eds. *African-American Performance and Theater History: A Critical Reader*. Oxford and New York: Oxford University Press, 2001.

Ellis-Kahana, Julia. "Transformative New Amazons or Destructive Neo-Colonialists? An Exploration of Militant Nudity as a Method of Radical Activism for Women's Rights in Ukraine and Beyond." MA thesis, Brown University, 2012.

Ellridge, Arthur. *Mucha: The Triumph of Art Nouveau*. Paris: Terrail, 1992.

Enwezor, Okwui. "The Production of Social Space as Artwork: Protocols of Community in the Work of Le Groupe Amos and Huit Facettes." In *Collectivism after Modernism: The Art of Social Imagination after 1945*, edited by Blake Stimson and Gregory Sholette, 223–52. Minneapolis: University of Minnesota Press, 2007.

Epstein, Alek D. "Arest uchastic gruppy 'Pussy Riot' kak katalizator hudozhestvenno-grazhdanskogo aktivizma izdatel'stvo." *Novoe literaturnoe obozrenie*, no. 84 (April 2012). Accessed 27 February 2013. http://www.nlobooks.ru/node/2585.

– "Ideas against Ideocracy: The Platonic Drama of Russian Thought." In *Marx's Shadow: Knowledge, Power, and Intellectuals in Eastern Europe and Russia*, 13–36. Lanham, MD: Lexington Books, 2010.

– *Iskusstvo na barrikadakh: "Pussy Riot," "Avtobusnaia vystavka," i Promestnyi art-aktivizm*. Moscow: Kolonna Publications, 2012.

Essig, Laurie, "Publicly Queer: Representations of Queer Subjects and Subjectivities in the Absence of Identity." In *Consuming Russia: Popular Culture, Sex, and Society since Gorbachev*, edited by Adele Marie Barker, 281–302. Durham: Duke University Press, 1999.

Face the Nation. "Is SlutWalks the Way to Deal with Sexual Harassment?" 2011. Accessed 10 March 2011. http://www.youtube.com/watch?v=yaZAxtw0jeU &feature=youtube_gdata_player.

Feher, Michel. *Nongovernmental Politics.* New York: Zone Books; Cambridge, MA: MIT Press, 2007.

Femen. Blog. Accessed 19 November 2012. http://femen.org/en.

– Alain Margot, dir. *I Am Femen.* Documentary film, 95 mins. Caravel Production and Filmcoopi Zürich, 2015.

– *Femen.* Ed. Galia Ackerman. Paris: Calmann-Levy, 2013.

– *Femen: Manifesto.* Cambridge: Polity Press, 2014.

– "My vyigrali World Press Photo 2012." Prishla, Razdelas', Pobedila, *Livejournal.com,* 10 February 2012. Accessed 5 March 2012. http://femen .livejournal.com/tag/world%20press%20photo.

– *Rébellion.* Paris: Des Femmes Antoinette Fouque, 2017.

Fernback, Jan. "Beyond the Diluted Community Concept: A Symbolic Interactionist Perspective on Online Social Relations." *New Media & Society* 9, no. 1 (2007): 49–69.

Film 86: Festival of Film and Urbanism. Slavutych. Website. Accessed 10 March 2015. http://www.86.org.ua/en/.

Firestone, Shulamith. *The Dialectic of Sex: The Case for Feminist Revolution.* New York: Bantam Books, 1971.

Foster, Hal. *Recodings: Art, Spectacle, Cultural Politics.* New York: New Press, 1985.

Foucault, Michel. "Body/Power." In *Power/Knowledge: Selected Interviews and Other Writings 1972–1977,* 55–62. New York: Pantheon Books, 1980.

– *The History of Sexuality.* Vol. 1, *An Introduction.* Translated by Robert Hurley. New York: Vintage Books, 1978.

Fowler, Mayhill. *Beau Monde on Empire's Edge: State and Stage in Soviet Ukraine.* Toronto: University of Toronto Press, 2017.

Fraser, Nancy. *Fortunes of Feminism: From State-Managed Capitalism to Neoliberal Crisis.* Brooklyn, NY: Verso Books, 2013.

Freedom House. "Freedom on the Net 2017: Ukraine." Accessed 14 April 2018. https://freedomhouse.org/report/freedom-net/2017/ukraine.

Gal, Susan, and Gail Kligman. *Reproducing Gender: Politics, Publics, and Everyday Life after Socialism.* Princeton, NJ: Princeton University Press, 2000.

Gapova, Elena. "Becoming Visible in the Digital Age: The Class and Media Dimensions of the Pussy Riot Affair." *Feminist Media Studies* 15, no. 1 (2015): 1–18.

– "Delo 'Pussy Riot': Feministskij Protest v Kontekste Klassovoj Borby." *Neprikosnovennyi zapas* 5 (2012).

– *Klassy natsiy: Feministskaya kritika natsiostroitelstva.* Moskva: Novoe literaturnoe obrozrenie (NLO), 2016.

Gapova, Elena, and Yulia Soroka. "Hola svoboda i tila na drabyni." *Krytyka* 15, no. 3–4 (2011): 17–18.

Gessen, Masha. *Words Will Break Cement: The Passion of Pussy Riot*. New York: Penguin Books, 2014.

Glenn, Susan A. *Female Spectacle: The Theatrical Roots of Modern Feminism*. Cambridge, MA: Harvard University Press, 2000.

González, Jennifer. "The Appended Subject: Race and Identity as Digital Assemblage." In *Race in Cyberspace*, edited by Beth K. Kolko, 27–50. New York and London: Routledge, 2000.

Gornostai, Kateryna. "Lenin's Teeth." In *Euromaidan: Rough Cut*. Directed by #Вавилон'13 / #Babylon'13, Kateryna Gornostai, Volodymyr Tykhyi, Andriy Lytvynenko, Roman Bondarchuk, Yulia Gontaruk, Andrey Kiselyov, Roman Liubyi, Oleksandr Techynskyi, Oleksiy Solodunov, and Dmitry Stoykov. Documentary. Kyiv, 2014.

Goscilo, Helena. *Dehexing Sex: Russian Womanhood during and after Glasnost*. Ann Arbor: University of Michigan Press, 1996.

Goujon, Olivier. *Femen: Histoire d'une Trahison*. Paris: Essai Graphique, 2017.

Gregos, Katerina. "On the Politics of Transformation." In *Yesterday, Today, Today*, edited by Nikita Kadan. Kyiv: Art Knyga, 2015.

Graff, Agnieszka. *Rykoszetem: Rzecz O Płci, Seksualności I Narodzie*. Warsaw: Wydawnictwo WAB, 2008.

– *Swiat Bez Kobiet: Płeć w Polskim Życiu Publicznym*. Warsaw: Wydawnictwo WAB, 2001.

Green, Kitty, dir. *Ukraine Is Not a Brothel: The Femen Story*. Film. Performed by Kitty Green, Viktor Sviatsky, Inna Shevchenko, Alexandra Shevchenko, Anna Hutsol, and Oksana Shachko. 4 September 2013. Australia: Noise & Light; Cinephil.

Greenberg, Jessica. *After the Revolution: Youth, Democracy, and the Politics of Disappointment in Serbia*. Stanford: Stanford University Press, 2014.

Grewal, Inderpal, and Caren Kaplan. *Scattered Hegemonies: Postmodernity and Transnational Feminist Practices*. Minneapolis: University of Minnesota Press, 1994.

Halberstam, Judith (Jack). *In a Queer Time and Place: Transgender Bodies, Subcultural Lives*. New York: New York University Press, 2005.

– *The Queer Art of Failure*. Durham: Duke University Press, 2011.

Halbwach, Maurice. *On Collective Memory*. Translated by Lewis A. Coser. Chicago: University of Chicago Press, 1992.

Hankivsky, Olena, and Anastasiya Salnykova, eds. *Gender, Politics, and Society in Ukraine*. Toronto: University of Toronto Press, 2012.

Haraway, Donna. "A Cyborg Manifesto: Science, Technology, and Socialist-Feminism in the Late Twentieth Century." In *Simians, Cyborgs, and Women: The Reinvention of Nature*, 149–82. London: Routledge, 1985.

Harrington, Jaime. "Culture Jamming Street Artist COMBO Stages Topless Spectacle in Paris." *Huffington Post*, 18 July 2013. Accessed 10 August 2013. http://www.huffingtonpost.com/jaime-rojo-steven-harrington/street-artist-combo_b_3614235.html.

Hartsock, Nancy. "Foucault on Power: A Theory for Women?" In *Feminism/ Postmodernism*, edited by Linda Nicholson, 157–75. New York: Routledge, 1990.

Hayles, Katherine N. "Virtual Bodies and Flickering Signifiers." *October* (MIT Press) 66 (1993): 69–91.

Hebdige, Dick. *Subculture: The Meaning of Style*. London: Methuen, 1979.

Helbig, Adriana. "Morals and Money: Economic Anxieties and Roma Realities in Post-Euromaidan Ukraine." *Krytyka*. Forum: Race and Postcolonialism in Ukraine and North America. Acquisitions editor Jessica Zychowicz; co-editors Oleh Kotsyuba and Grace Mahoney. May 2019.

Herbaut, Guillaume. "Dans L'intimité Des Amazones." *Stiletto*, December 2011.

– *The New Amazons*. World Press Photo. Accessed 5 March 2011. http://www.worldpressphoto.org/photo/2012guillaumeherbautpo-2?gallery=2634.

Hlavajova, Maria, and Jill Winder, eds. *Who If Not We Should at Least Try to Imagine the Future of All This*. Amsterdam: Artimo, 2004.

Hobsbawm, E.J. *Age of Extremes: The Short Twentieth Century, 1914–1991*. London: Michael Joseph, 1994.

– *Fractured Times: Culture and Society in the Twentieth Century*. London: Little, Brown, 2013.

Holmes, Brian. "Do-It-Yourself Goepolitics: Cartographies of Art in the World." In *Collectivism after Modernism: The Art of Social Imagination after 1945*, edited by Blake Stimson and Gregory Sholette, 273–95. Minneapolis: University of Minnesota Press, 2007.

Hrycak, Alexandra. "'The Coming of Chrysler Imperial': Ukrainian Youth and Rituals of Resistance." *Harvard Ukrainian Studies* 21, no. 1–2 (1997): 93–118.

– "Orange Harvest? Women's Activism and Civil Society in Ukraine, Belarus and Russia since 2004." *Canadian-American Slavic Studies* 44, no. 1–2 (2010): 151–77.

Hrycak, Alexandra, and Maria G. Rewakowicz. "Feminism, Intellectuals and the Formation of Micro-Publics in Postcommunist Ukraine." *Studies in East European Thought* 61, no. 4 (2009): 309–33.

Hrycak, Jarosław. "Nowhere Men, Czy Men of the Universe?" In *Ukrainia*, 24–59. Warsaw: Krytyka Polityczna, 2009.

Hryn, Halyna. "A Conversation with Oksana Zabuzhko." *Agni Online*, no. 53 (2001). Accessed 25 March 2012. http://www.bu.edu/agni/interviews/print/2001/zabuzhko-hryn.html.

HudRada. Curatorial Union website. Accessed 30 January 2018. http://hudrada.tumblr.com/.

– *Exhibit Catalogue: Spirna terytoria / Spornaya terytoria/ Disputed Territory 4th Exhibition by the Ukrainian Curatorial Collective HudRada*. Kroshitsky Art Museum. Sevastopol, Crimea: ADEF Ukraine, 2013. Accessed 10 March 2014. http://www.disputedterritory.org.ua/en/node/105.

Human Rights Watch. "World Report 2018: Ukraine." Accessed 1 October 2018. https://www.hrw.org/world-report/2018/country-chapters/ukraine.

Humesky, Assya. "Marko Vovchok vs. Turgenev: Feminism vs. Femininity." In *Vybrani Pratsi: Literaturoznavchi i ne til'ky* [Selected works: Literary studies and more], 587–611. New York and Kharkiv: Ukrainian-American Association of University Professors, 2011.

– "Zhinocha Symbolika U Shevchenka." In *Vybrani Pratsi: Literaturoznavchi i ne til'ky* [Selected works: Literary studies and more], 106–23.

Hummel, Julius, Silvia Jaklitsch, Barbara Toifl, and Karin Friesenbichler, eds. *Amor Psyche Action Vienna: The Feminine in Viennese Actionism*. Translated by Jeremy Gaines and Steve Tomlin. Prague: Dox Centre for Contemporary Art, 2012.

Husslein-Arco, Agnes, Jean Louis Gallemin, Michel Hilaire, and Christaine Lange, eds. *Alphonse Mucha*. Munich: Prestel, 2009.

Iakovlenko, Kateryna. "The Artist Who 'Made Donbas Human': Alevtina Kakhidze on Empathy and Discrimination in Eastern Ukraine." 29 July 2019. Open Democracy.net. Accessed 7 May 2020. https://www .opendemocracy.net/en/odr/alevtina-kakhidze-artist-donbas-ukraine/.

ICTM (Ініціатива Самозахисту Трудящих Мистецтва / Art Workers' Self-Defense Initiative). "Open Letter from the Art Workers' Self-Defense Initiative to the Ukrainian and International Art Community." 31 July 2014. Accessed 16 March 2018. https://istmkyiv.wordpress.com/.

Ilič, Melanie. "Lyudmila Mikhailovna Alekseeva: Interview with Melanie Ilic and Emilia Kosterina, 29 July 2011, Moscow." In *Life Stories of Soviet Women: The Interwar Generation*, 14–32. New York: Routledge, 2013.

Ilnytzkyj, Oleh S. *Ukrainian Futurism, 1914-1930: A Historical and Critical Study*. Cambridge, MA: HURI, 1997.

Imre, Anikó. *Identity Games: Globalization and the Transformation of Media Cultures in the New Europe*. Cambridge, MA: MIT Press, 2009.

Interfax-Ukraine. "FEMEN Says Their Male Activist Brutally Beaten Up by Security Services." *Kyiv Post*, 25 July 2013. Accessed 11 October 2013. http://www.kyivpost.com/content/ukraine/femen-says-their-male -activist-brutally-beaten-up-by-security-services-327494.html.

Ioffe, Julia. "Russia's Nationalist Summer Camp." *The New Yorker*, 16 August 2010. Accessed 4 November 2015. http://www.newyorker.com/news /news-desk/russias-nationalist-summer-camp.

Irigaray, Luce. *This Sex Which Is Not One*. Ithaca, NY: Cornell University Press, 1985.

Isaeiva, Tatiana. "The Truth about March 8: Exhibit." Translated by Jessica Zychowicz. *Gender Museum*, 2010. Accessed June 2011. http://www .gendermuseum.com/modules/8m_e/8m_03.html.

Izolyatsia Foundation. "Cultural Platform." Accessed 30 January 2016. https:// izolyatsia.org/ru/.

Jacques, Juliet. "Interview with Jessica Zychowicz and Maria Kulikokovska: Reimagining Utopias: Art and Politics in 21st Century Ukraine." *Suite 212*. Accessed 3 November 2018. https://soundcloud.com/suite-212 /reimagining-utopias-art-and-politics-in-21st-century-ukraine.

Jakobson, Roman. *Language in Literature*, edited by Krystyna Pomorska and Stephen Rudy. Cambridge, MA: Harvard University Press, 1987.

Janion, Maria. *Do Europy: Tak, Ale Razem Z Naszymi Umarłymi*. Warszawa: Sic!, 2000.

Jensen, Mie Birk. "The Body Theatre: An Analysis of FEMEN's Feminist Activism." MA thesis, Roskilde University Institute of Culture and Identity, Denmark, 2014.

Johnson, Janet E. "Fast-Tracked or Boxed In? Informal Politics, Gender, and Women's Representation in Putin's Russia." *Perspectives on Politics* 14, no. 3 (2016): 643–59.

– "Pussy Riot as a Feminist Project: Russia's Gendered Informal Politics." *Nationalities Papers: The Journal of Nationalism and Ethnicity* 42, no. 4 (2014): 583–90.

Jonson, Lena. *Art and Protest in Putin's Russia*. Abingdon, Oxon; New York, NY: Routledge, 2015.

Jurich, Joscelyn. "What Do Subjects Want?" *Afterimage: The Journal of Media Arts and Cultural Criticism* 40, no. 5 (March/April 2013): 6–10.

Kadan, Nikita. *Kości się przemieszały [Bones Mixed Together]*. Catalogue. Curated by Monika Szewyczk. Białystok: Arsenal Gallery, 2016.

– *Yesterday, Today, Today*. Kyiv: Art Knyga, 2015.

Kadan, Nikita, and Larissa Babij. "Blacked Out in Ukraine." *Guernica / A Magazine of Art & Politics*, 3 February 2014. Accessed 10 March 2014. http:// www.guernicamag.com/art/blacked-out-in-ukraine/.

Kaganovsky, Lilya. *How the Soviet Man Was Unmade: Cultural Fantasy and Male Subjectivity Under Stalin*. Pittsburgh: University of Pittsburgh Press, 2008.

Kakhidze, Alevtyna. "В 2015 году мои ..." [In the year 2015 we ...] *Livejournal*, 31 December 2015. Accessed 16 April 2017. https://trueAlevtyna .livejournal.com/.

– "Drawings." In "Documenting Maidan." Special issue, *Prostory Literary Journal*, no. 8 (December 2013–February 2014), edited by Yevgenia Belorusets, Nelia Vakhovska, and Nataliya Tchermalykh. Accessed 5 January 2014. www.prostory.net.ua.

– "Prozhyt' vojnu" [To live through war]. In *Henderni doslidzhennya [Gender research]*, edited by Katerina Mishchenko, 179–96. Donbas Studies Project. Kyiv: Izolyatsia, 2015.

– Essay. In *Where Curating Is: The Artist-as-Curator and the Curator-as-Artist in Ukraine from the 1980s to the 2010s*, edited by Kateryna Nosko and Valeriya Luk'yanets, translated by VERBatsiya (Tanya Rodionova, Veronika Yadukha, and Julia Didokha), 116–122. Kharkiv: IST Publishing, 2017.

Kayiatos, Anastasia. "Penile Servitude and the Police State." *NYU Jordan Center Blog*, 20 November 2013. Accessed 10 January 2014. http://jordanrussiacenter.org/news/penile-servitude-police-state/.

Kennedy, Michael D. *Cultural Formations of Postcommunism: Emancipation, Transition, Nation, and War*. Minneapolis: University of Minnesota Press, 2002.

– *Globalizing Knowledge: Intellectuals, Universities, and Publics in Transformation*. Stanford: Stanford University Press, 2014.

Kenney, Padraic. *A Carnival of Revolution: Central Europe 1989*. Princeton, NJ: Princeton University Press, 2002.

Kibler, M. Alison. *Rank Ladies: Gender and Cultural Hierarchy in American Vaudeville*. Chapel Hill: University of North Carolina Press, 1999.

Kirby, Michael, ed., and Jim Dine, Red Grooms, Allan Kaprow, Claes Oldenburg, Robert Whitman. *Happenings: An Illustrated Anthology*. New York: Dutton, 1965.

Kirshenblatt-Gimblett, Barbara. *Destination Culture: Tourism, Museums, and Heritage*. Berkeley: University of California Press, 1998.

Kis, Oksana. "Letter to an Official / Lyst posadovtsevi." ХайВей, 12 February 2009. Accessed 15 March 2013. http://h.ua/story/173353.

– "Restoring the Broken Continuity: Women's History in Post-Soviet Ukraine." *Aspasia: International Yearbook of Central, Eastern and Southern European Women's and Gender History* 6 (2011): 171–83.

– "Ukrainian Women Reclaiming the Feminist Meaning of International Women's Day: A Report about Recent Feminist Activism." *Aspasia* 6 (2012): 219–32.

Kleytman, Alina. Open Archive of Ukrainian Media Art. Website. Accessed 16 March 2018. http://www.mediaartarchive.org.ua/eng/author/alina-kleytman/.

Komar, Vitaly, and Aleksandr Melamid. *Painting by Numbers: Komar and Melamid's Scientific Guide to Art*. Edited by Joann Wypijewski. New York: Farrar Straus Giroux, 1997.

Kovrej, Vik. *Bereznevi Koty: Antolohiya Erotartfestu*. Uzhorod: Polihrafcentr Lira, 2010.

Krasner, David. "Black Salome: Exoticism, Dance, and Racial Myths." In *African-American Performance and Theatre History: A Critical Reader*, edited by Harry Justin Elam and David Krasner, 192–211. Oxford: Oxford University Press, 2001.

Kratochvil, Alexander. "The Writers and the Maidan." Edited by Carmen Scheide and Ulrich Schmid. *Euxeinos Governance and Culture in the Black Sea Region* 13 (November 2013): 32–7.

Kristeva, Julia. *Powers of Horror: An Essay on Abjection*. Translated by Leon Roudiez. New York: Columbia University Press, 1982.

– *Revolution in Poetic Language*. Translated by Margaret Waller. New York: Columbia University Press, 1984.

Krupskaya, Nadezhda. Untitled article. *Rabotnitsa* (Moscow), no. 1 (1914): 2.

Kuehnast, Kathleen R., and Carol Nechemias, eds. *Post-Soviet Women Encountering Transition: Nation Building, Economic Survival, and Civic Activism*. Washington DC: Woodrow Wilson Center Press; Baltimore: John Hopkins University Press, 2004.

Kvartyra 14 / Start up Troyeshchyna. Independent Urban Arts Initiative, Kyiv. Accessed 16 March 2018. www.facebook.com/Kvartyra14.

Kvit, Serhiy. *Personalniy Zhurnal Sergia Kvita*, 15 February 2012. Accessed 10 March 2012. http://kvit.ukma.Kyiv.ua/.

Labov, Jessie, and Friederike Kind-Kovács, eds. *Samizdat, Tamizdat and Beyond: Transnational Media During and after Socialism*. New York: Berghahn Books: 2013.

Lacy, Suzanne, and Leslie Labowicz. "Feminist Media Strategies for Political Performance." In *Cultures in Contention*, edited by Douglas Kahn and Diane Neumaier, 123–33. New York: Real Comet Press, 1985.

Łapawa, Karina. "No-Body, Notatki o kobiecym ciele i nagości: Amina Tyler, Alaia Magda Elmahdy, Boushra Almutawakel." *Artmix: Sztuka Feminizm Kultura Wizualna*, 8 October 2013. Accessed 10 November 2013. http://www.obieg.pl/artmix/30028.

Laruelle, Marlene. "Negotiating History: Memory Wars in the Near Abroad and the Pro-Kremlin Youth Movements." In *Russian Nationalism, Foreign Policy, and Identity Debates in Putin's Russia: New Ideological Patterns after the Orange Revolution*, edited by Marlene Laruelle and Andreas Umland, 75–105. Columbia University Ibidem Press, 2012.

Lasn, Kalle, and Media Foundation. *Design Anarchy*. Vancouver, BC: Adbusters, 2006.

Lassila, Jussi. "Making Sense of Nashi's Political Style: The Bronze Soldier and the Counter-Orange Community." In *Russian Nationalism, Foreign Policy, and Identity Debates in Putin's Russia: New Ideological Patterns after the Orange Revolution*, edited by Marlene Laruelle and Andreas Umland, 105–39. Columbia University Ibidem Press, 2012.

Latour, Bruno. *Reassembling the Social: An Introduction to Actor-Network-Theory*. Oxford and New York: Oxford University Press, 2005.

Lawton, Anna, and Herbert J. Eagle, eds. *Russian Futurism through Its Manifestos, 1912-1928*. Ithaca: Cornell University Press, 1988.

Lefebvre, Henri. *Critique of Everyday Life*. Vol. 2, *Foundations for a Sociology of the Everyday*. Translated by John Moore. London and New York: Verso, 2002.

Léger, Marc James. "Alter-Globalisation, Revolutionary Movement, and the State Mode of Production." In *Vanguardia: Socially Engaged Art and Theory*. Manchester: Manchester University Press, 2019.

Lemon, Alaina. *Between Two Fires: Gypsy Performance and Romani Memory from Pushkin to Postsocialism*. Durham, NC: Duke University Press, 2000.

Leturcq, Armelle. "A Meeting with Oksana Shachko." 22 Visconti Gallery. *Crash*, December 2017. Accessed 3 November 2018. https://www.crash.fr/a-meeting-with-oksana-shachko/.

Lisyutkina, Larisa. "Fenomen Femen: malyi vybukhovyi prystrii made in Ukraine." *Krytyka* 15, no. 3–4 (2011): 161–2.

– "Soviet Women at the Crossroads of Perestroika." In *Gender Politics and Post-Communism*, edited by Nanette Funk and Magda Mueller, 274–86. New York: Routledge, 1993.

Lomasko, Victoria. *Other Russias*. New York: N+1, 2017.

Lorde, Audre. *Sister Outsider: Essays and Speeches*. Trumansburg, NY: Crossing Press, 1984.

Losh, Elizabeth M. *Virtualpolitik: An Electronic History of Government Media-Making in a Time of War, Scandal, Disaster, Miscommunication, and Mistakes*. Cambridge, MA: MIT Press, 2009.

Lozhkina, Alisa, and Alexander Roytburd. "Inventory of a Dictator." *Art Ukraine.com*, 13 June 2014. Accessed 10 July 2014. http://artukraine.com.ua/eng/a/inventory-of-a-dictator/#.VoGnkhhN3Oo.

Lozynsky, Vasyl. *The Maidan After Hours*. Translated by Ostap Kin and Ali Kinsella. Manoa: University of Hawaii Review, 2017.

Lunceford, Brett. *Naked Politics: Nudity, Political Action, and the Rhetoric of the Body*. Lanham, MD: Lexington Books, 2012.

MacDonald, Kerri, and David Furst. "A Painterly World Press Photo Winner." *New York Times*, 10 February 2012. Accessed 20 May 2012. http://lens.blogs.nytimes.com/2012/02/10/a-painterly-world-press-photo-winner/.

Makaryk, Irena R., and Virlana Tkacz, eds. *Modernism in Kyiv: Jubiliant Experimentation*. Toronto: University of Toronto Press, 2010.

Makki, Hind, Fatemeh Fakhraie, and Leila Mouri. "Who Speaks for Muslim Women? Muslim Feminists Reject Femen's 'Sextremist' Brand of Protest." *Al Jazeera*, The Stream, 16 April 2013. Accessed 10 May 2013. http://stream.aljazeera.com/story/201304050033-0022659.

Manning, Paul. "Rose-Colored Glasses? Color Revolutions and Cartoon Chaos in Postsocialist Georgia." *Cultural Anthropology* 22, no. 2 (May 2007): 171–213.

Martsenyuk, Tamara. "Ukraine's Other Half." *Post-Soviet Post: Observation and Expert Analysis from Eurasia*, 27 March 2012. Accessed 15 July 2012. http://postsovietpost.stanford.edu/analysis/.

– Гендер для всіх: виклик стереотипам [Gender for all: Against stereotypes]. Kyiv: Osnovy, 2017.

- "Ukrainian Feminism in Action." *Global Dialogue: Newsletter for the International Sociological Association* 2, no. 5 (July 2012). Accessed 25 October 2013. http://www.isa-sociology.org/global-dialogue/2012/07/ukrainian -feminism-in-action/.
- "Ukrainian Societal Attitudes towards the Lesbian, Gay, Bisexual and Transgender Communities." In *Gender, Politics, and Society in Ukraine*, edited by Olena Hankivsky and Anastasiya Salnykova, 385–410. Toronto: University of Toronto Press, 2012.
- "До 8 березня / Жіноча сотня або право на смисли (Відповідь на статтю Марії Маєрчик)" [On the occaison of March 8th / The women's squad, or the right to sense (a response to Mariya Mayerchyk's article). *Krytyka*, 10 March 2014. Accessed 20 November 2014. http://krytyka.com/ua /community/blogs/do-8-bereznya-zhinocha-sotnya-abo-pravo-na-smysly -vidpovid-na-stattyu-mariyi.
Masoch, Leopold von Sacher. *Venus in Furs*. Translated by J. Neugroschel and L. Wolff. New York: Penguin, 2000.
Masyuk, Elena. "Ekaterina Samutsevich (Pussy Riot): My ne budem prosit' prezidenta nas pomilovat." *Novaya Gazeta*, 17 August 2012. Accessed 10 July 2013. http://www.novayagazeta.ru/society/53998.html.
- "Nadezhda Tolokonnikova (Pussy Riot): My posazheny po politicheskim motivam, v jetom somnevat'sja nevozmozhno." *Novaya Gazeta*, 16 August 2012. Accessed 10 July 2013. http://www.novayagazeta.ru/society/53999.html.
- "Posle prigovora." *Novaya Gazeta*, 21 August 2012. Accessed 10 July 2013. http://www.novayagazeta.ru/politics/54073.html.
Matusevich, Yan. "This Is Not a Biennale." *Medium.com*, 17 November 2015. Accessed 15 November 2015. https://medium.com/@yanmatusevich/this -is-not-a-biennale-63c20637646e#.abzudotdp.
Mayakovsky, V., Alexander Kruchenykh, D. Burliuk, and Victor Khlebnikov. *A Slap in the Face of Public Taste.* 15 December 1912. Moscow. Reprinted in Anna Lawton and Herbert J. Eagle, eds, *Russian Futurism through Its Manifestos, 1912–1928* (Washington: DC: New Academia Publishing, 2005).
Mayerchyk, Mariya, and Olga Plakhotnik. "Between the Time of Nation and Feminist Time: Genealogies of Feminist Protest in Ukraine." In *Feminist Circulations between East and West / Feministische Zirkulationen zwischen Ost und West*, edited by Annette Bühler-Dietrich, 47–70. Berlin: Frank and Timme GmbH, 2019.
- "From the Editors of Feminist Critique: On the Launch of the Journal's Website." *Krytyka.com*, 31 December 2016. Accessed 10 July 2017. https:// krytyka.com/en/community/blogs/editors-feminist-critique.
- "On the Occasion of March 8th / Recasting of Meanings." *Krytyka* (blog), 8 March 2014. Accessed 20 July 2014. http://krytyka.com/ua/community /blogs/do-8-bereznya-pro-pereplavku-smysliv.

- "Radykal'nyi Femen i novyi zhinochyi aktyvizmu." *Krytyka* 11, no. 11–12 (December 2012): 7–10.
- "Zahoplyenna logik, abo Svit bez Zhinok [Seizing the Logic, or A World without Women]." *Krytyka* (blog), 25 January 2014. Accessed 20 July 2014. https://krytyka.com/en/community/blogs/seizing-logic-world-without -women.

McFaul, Michael. "Conclusion: The Orange Revolution in a Comparative Perspective." In *Revolution in Orange: The Origins of Ukraine's Democratic Breakthrough*, edited by Anders Aslund and Michael McFaul, 165–96. Washington, DC: Carnegie Endowment for International Peace, 2006.

McLuhan, Marshall. *Understanding Media: The Extensions of Man.* Berkeley: Ginko Press, 2013.

Meskimmon, Marsha. *Women Making Art: History, Subjectivity, Aesthetics.* London and New York: Routledge, 2003.

Miks, Jason. "Naked Protest." *The Diplomat*, 23 November 2011. Accessed 12 December 2011. http://thediplomat.com/china-power/naked-protest/.

Minakov, Mikhail. *Development and Dystopia: Studies in Post-Soviet Ukraine and Eastern Europe.* Edited by Andreas Umland. SPPS: Soviet and Post-Soviet Politics and Society; New York: Columbia University Ibidem Press, 2018.

Mishchenko, Kateryna, Nadia Parfan, and Oleksiy Radynski. "Mryemo vyvesty na vulychyu tysyachi ogolenyx zhinok: Rozmova redakciyi PK z grupoyu Femen." *Krytyka Polityczna* 3 (February 2012): 49–56.

Mishchenko, Kateryna, and Miron Zownir. *Ukrainian Night.* Edited by Jana Fuchs. Translated by Jessica Zychowicz. Berlin: Spector Books, 2015.

Mitchell, W.J.T. "Image, Space, Revolution: The Arts of Occupation." In *Occupy: Three Inquiries in Disobedience*, 93–130. Chicago and London: University of Chicago Press, 2013.

- *What Do Pictures Want? The Lives and Loves of Images.* Chicago: University of Chicago Press, 2005.

Molodist' Kyiv International Film Festival. Website. Accessed January 2016. https://molodist.com/en/.

Moscow Feminist Group. Website. Accessed 10 March 2016. https://ravnopravka .wordpress.com/.

Moucha, Josef, and Jiří Řapek. *Alfons Mucha.* Prague: Torst, 2000.

Mouffe, Chantal. *Agonistics: Thinking the World Politically.* London: Verso Books, 2013.

- "Artistic Activism and Agonistic Spaces." *Art & Research: A Journal of Ideas, Contexts, and Methods* 1, no. 2 (Summer 2007). Accessed 10 March 2013. http://www.artandresearch.org.uk/v1n2/mouffe.html.

Munster, Anna. *Materializing New Media: Embodiment in Information Aesthetics.* Hanover, NH: Dartmouth University Press, 2006.

Muslim Women Against Femen. Facebook page. https://www.facebook.com /MuslimWomenAgainstFemen. Accessed October 2013.

Naiman, Eric. *Sex in Public: The Incarnation of Early Soviet Ideology*. Princeton, NJ: Princeton University Press, 1997.

Nakonechna, Lada. Essay. In *Where Curating Is: The Artist-as-Curator and the Curator-as-Artist in Ukraine from the 1980s to the 2010s*, edited by Kateryna Nosko and Valeriya Luk'yanets, translated by VERBatsiya (Tanya Rodionova, Veronika Yadukha, Julia Didokha), 92–8. Kharkiv: IST Publishing, 2017.

Namazie, Maryam. "Nude Photo Revolutionary Calendar." *Free Thought* (blog), 8 March 2012. Accessed 8 October 2012. http://freethoughtblogs.com/maryamnamazie/2012/03/08/nude-photo-revolutionary-calendar-is-here/.

Neufeld, Dialika. "Femen Activists Get Naked to Raise Political Awareness." *Spiegel Online*, 5 November 2012. Accessed 10 December 2012. http://www.spiegel.de/international/europe/femen-activists-get-naked-to-raise-political-awareness-a-832028.html.

Nietzsche, Friedrich. *Beyond Good and Evil: Prelude to a Philosophy of the Future*. Translated by Walter Kaufmann. New York: Vintage Books, 1966.

Ofenzywa, Feministychna. "Feministychna Ofenzywa Ceases to Exist / Феміністична Офензива припиняє існування." *Feminist Ofenzyva* (blog), 7 February 2014. Accessed 8 February 2014. http://ofenzyva.wordpress.com/2014/02/07/феміністична-офензива-припиняє-існу/.

– "Акція «За Рівність! Проти НЕКвізиції!" *Feminist Ofenzyva* (blog), 18 June 2012. Accessed 15 March 2013. http://ofenzyva.wordpress.com/2012/06/18/za-rivnist-proty-nekvizyci/.

– "Mission Statement." *Feminist Ofenzyva* (blog), 10 January 2012. Translated by Jessica Zychowicz. Accessed 10 February 2012. https://ofenzywa.wordpress.com/about/#_eng.

– "Ofenzywa Manifesto." *Feminist Ofenzyva* (blog). Translated by Jessica Zychowicz. Accessed 8 February 2020. http://ofenzyva.wordpress.com.

Onuch, Olga A. "The Puzzle of Mass Mobilization: Conducting Protest Research in Ukraine, 2004–2014." *CritCom*, 22 May 2014. Accessed 8 December 2014. http://councilforeuropeanstudies.org/critcom/the-puzzle-of-mass-mobilization-conducting-protest-research-in-ukraine-2004-2014/.

– "Social Networks and Social Media in Ukrainian 'Euromaidan' Protests." *The Washington Post*, 2 January 2014. Accessed 10 January 2014. http://www.washingtonpost.com/blogs/monkey-cage/wp/2014/01/02/social-networks-and-social-media-in-ukrainian-euromaidan-protests-2/.

Open Group. Yuriy Biley, Anton Varga, Pavlo Kovac, and Stas Turina. "Portfolio: Projects 2012–2013." Lviv. Shared with the author.

Ostow, Robin. *(Re)visualizing National History: Museums and National Identities in Europe in the New Millennium*. Toronto: University of Toronto Press, 2008.

Otrishchenko, Natalia. "Beyond the Square: The Real and Symbolic Landscapes of Euromaidan." In *Ukraine's Euromaidan: Analysis of a Civil*

Revolution, edited by David R. Marples and Frederic V. Mills, 147–61. New York: Columbia University Ibidem Press, 2014.

Oushakine, Serguei Alex. *The Patriotism of Despair: Nation, War, and Loss in Russia*. Ithaca: Cornell University Press, 2009.

Pavlychko, Solomea. *Dyskurs modernizmu v ukrains'kii literaturi*. 2nd ed. Kyiv: Lybid, 1999.

– "Feminism in Post-Communist Ukrainian Society." In *Women in Russia and Ukraine*, edited by Rosalind Marsh, 305–14. New York: Cambridge University Press, 1996.

– *Feminizm*. Kyiv: Osnovy, 2002.

Pavlyshyn, Marko. "Envisioning Europe: Ruslana's Rhetoric of Identity." *The Slavic and East European Journal* 50, no. 3 (October 2006): 469–85.

Phillips, Sarah D. *Disability and Mobile Citizenship in Post-Socialist Ukraine*. Bloomington: Indiana University Press, 2011.

– *Women's Social Activism in the New Ukraine*. Bloomington: Indiana University Press, 2008.

– "The Women's Squad in Ukraine's Protests: Feminism, Nationalism, and Militarism on the Maidan." *American Ethnologist* 41, no. 3 (August 2014): 414–26.

Piotrowski, Piotr. *Art and Democracy in Post-Communist Europe*. Translated by Anna Bryzski. London: Reaktion Books, 2012.

– *In the Shadow of Yalta: Art and the Avant-Garde in Eastern Europe 1945–1989*. Translated by Anna Brzyski. London: Reaktion Books, 2009.

Platt, Kevin M.F. *History in a Grotesque Key: Russian Literature and the Idea of Revolution*. Stanford: Stanford University Press, 1997.

Plungian, Nadia. "Как Выжить в Проходной Комнате" [How to survive in the hallway]. *A Room of One's Own*. Curator's notes by Nataliya Tchermalykh. August 2013. Cited with permission of the authors.

Plungian, Nadia, and Victoria Lomasko. *Feminist Pencil II: An Exhibition of Women's Socially Engaged Graphic Art*. Catelogue. 23 October–6 November 2013, Moscow. Accessed 30 June 2017. http://issuu.com/feminfoteka/docs/fk2_en.

Popova, Yuliya. "Feminine Femen Targets 'Sexpats.'" *Kyiv Post*, 25 September 2008. Accessed 10 January 2012. http://www.kyivpost.com/news/nation/detail/29898/.

Popovych, Zakhar. "Ukraine on the Way from Digital Divide to Intellectual Exclusion." 2018. Shared with permission from the author.

– "Novi zavdannia stratehichnoho pozytsionuvannia Ukrtelekomu na rynku komp'iuternoho zv'iazku" [New tasks in the strategic positioning of JSC Ukrtelecom on the computer communications market]. *Problemy nauki (Problems of Science)* 6 (2004): 40–7.

Pospieszna, Paulina. *Democracy Assistance from the Third Wave: Polish Engagement in Belarus and Ukraine*. Pittsburgh: University of Pittsburgh Press, 2014.

Prostory Magazine. Edited by Yevgenia Belorusets. Accessed 10 October 2018. https://prostory.net.ua/en/mission.

Prozorov, Sergei. "Pussy Riot and the Politics of Profanation: Parody, Performativity, Veridiction." *Political Studies*, 17 June 2013.

Pussy Riot. "An Open Letter from Pussy Riot." Edited by Marisa Mazria Katz. *CreativeTimeReports*, 6 February 2014. http://creativetimereports.org/2014/02/06/open-letter-pussy-riot/.

– *Pussy Riot! A Punk Prayer for Freedom*. New York: Feminist Press CUNY, 2013.

Pussy Riot and Maria Alyokhina. *Riot Days*. New York: Metropolitan Books, 2017.

Pyzik, Agata. *Poor but Sexy: Culture Clashes in Europe East and West*. London: Zero Books, 2014.

Rachok, Dafna. "Seks-rabota: ot abolytsionyzma k dekrymynalyzatsii." *Politychna Krytyka Ukrainy*, 28 February 2015. Accessed 30 May 2019. https://politkrytyka.org/2015/02/28/seks-rabota-ot-abolytsyonyzma-k-dekrymynalyzatsyy/.

Radio Free Europe / Radio Liberty. Ukrainian Service. "Ukrainian Museum Director Destroys Critical Painting Ahead of President's Visit," 26 July 2013. Accessed 13 October 2013. http://www.rferl.org/content/ukraine-art-destroyed-kuznetsov-Kyivan-rus-yanukovych/25058261.html.

Ralko, Vlada. *Kyivskiy Shchodenyk*. Kyiv: Chervonechorne Galeria, 2016.

Rancière, Jacques. "Ten Theses on Politics." In *Dissensus*, 35–52. New York and London: Continuum International Publishing Group, 2011.

– "The Paradoxes of Political Art." In *Dissensus*, 142–59.

Rayss, Agnieszka. "Award of Excellence for Photo 'Sascha from Femen.'" *POYi Pictures of the Year International*, March 2012. Accessed 10 April 2012. http://www.poyi.org/69/08/ae03.php.

R.E.P. Group (Revolutionary Experimental Space). *R.E.P.: Revolutionary Experimental Space: A History*. Edited by Lada Nakonechna. Translated by Larissa Babij, Mariana Matveichuk, Weronika Nowacka, Anastasiya Osipova, and Olena Sheremet. Berlin: The Green Box, 2015.

– Р.Е.П. Революційний експериментальний простір. Art collective website. Accessed 16 March 2018. http://nikitakadan.com/reprep/peprep/.

Rewakowicz, Maria G. *Ukraine's Quest for Identity: Cultural Hybridity in Literary Imagination, 1991–2011*. Lanham, MD: Lexington Books, 2018.

Riabchuk, Anastasiya. "Eurorenovation of the Soviet Soul." In *R.E.P.: Revolutionary Experimental Space: A History*, edited by Lada Nakonechna, 199–209. Berlin: The Green Box, 2015.

– "Homeless Men and the Crisis of Masculinity in Contemporary Ukraine." In *Gender, Politics, and Society in Ukraine*, edited by Olena Hankivsky and Anastasiya Salnykova, 385–410. Toronto: University of Toronto Press, 2012.

– "Криміналізація споживачів ін'єкційних наркотиків в Україні: стан справ, причини, наслідки, альтернативи." Спільне: журналь соціальної критики [Spilne / Commons: a journal of social criticism], no. 1 (2010): 33–44. Accessed 16 March 2018. https://commons.com.ua/uk/.

Ridnyi, Mykola. Essay. In *Where Curating Is: The Artist-As-Curator and the Curator-as-Artist in Ukraine from the 1980s to the 2010s*, edited by Kateryna Nosko and Valeriya Luk'yanets, translated by VERBatsiya (Tanya Rodionova, Veronika Yadukha, Julia Didokha), 74–82. Kharkiv: IST publishing, 2017.

Risch, William Jay. *The Ukrainian West: Culture and the Fate of Empire in Soviet Lviv*. Cambridge, MA: Harvard University Press, 2011.

Rodchenko, Alexander. *Aleksandr Rodchenko: Experiments for the Future: Diaries, Essays, Letters, and Other Writings*. Edited by Alexander N. Lavrentiev. Translated by Jamey Gambrell. New York: Museum of Modern Art, 2005.

– "For a Report on the Organization of a Museum of Decorative Arts." In *Experiments for the Future: Diaries, Essays, Letters and Other Writings*, edited by Alexander N. Lavrentiev, 115–23. New York: Museum of Modern Art, 2005.

– "On the Museum Bureau, Report at the Conference of Directors." In *Experiments for the Future: Diaries, Essays, Letters and Other Writings*, edited by Alexander N. Lavrentiev.

– "Report on the Factual Activities of the Museum Bureau." In *Experiments for the Future: Diaries, Essays, Letters and Other Writings*, edited by Alexander N. Lavrentiev.

Rosenberg, Tina. "Revolution U." *Foreign Policy*, 16 February 2011. Accessed 10 November 2013. http://www.foreignpolicy.com/articles/2011/02/16/revolution_u&page=full.

Rubchak, Marian J. "Seeing Pink: Searching for Gender Justice through Opposition in Ukraine." *European Journal of Women's Studies* 19, no. 1 (2 February 2012): 55–72.

– "Ukraine's Ancient Matriarch as a Topos in Constructing a Feminine Identity." *Feminist Review*, no. 92 (2009): 129–50.

Rubchak, Marian J., ed. *Mapping Difference: The Many Faces of Women in Contemporary Ukraine*. New York: Berghahn Books, 2011.

– *New Imaginaries: Youthful Reinvention of Ukraine's Cultural Paradigm*. New York: Berghahn Books, 2015.

Said, Edward W. "Opponents, Audiences, Constituencies and Community." In *The Anti-Aesthetic: Essays on Postmodern Culture*, edited by Hal Foster. Port Townsend, Washington: Bay Press, 1983.

– *Orientalism*. New York: Vintage Books, 2003.

Sacher-Masoch, Leopold von. *Venus in Furs*. Translated by J. Neugroschel and L. Wolff. New York: Penguin, 2000.

Sanborn, Joshua A, and Annette F. Timm. "Femen's Challenge to European Feminism." In *Gender, Sex, and the Shaping of Modern Europe: A History from the French Revolution to the Present Day*, 257–62. Berg Publishers, 2007.

#SaveKyivModernism. "Активісти вступилися за аркітектурний спадок модернізму в Києві" [Activists stand up for the architectural legacy of Modernism in Kyiv], *Art Ukraine*, 17 November 2017. Accessed 31 March 2018, http://artukraine.com.ua/n/aktivisti-vstupilisya-za-arkhitekturniy -spadok-modernizmu-v-kiyevi/#.Wr-wnam-nOQ.

Schechner, Richard. "Speculations on Radicalism, Sexuality, & Performance." *The Drama Review (TDR)* 13, no. 4 (1969): 89–110.

Scheide, Carmen, and Ulrich Schmid, eds. "The Writers and the Maidan." *Euxeinos Governance and Culture in the Black Sea Region* 13 (November 2013): 32–37.

Schneemann, Carolee. *Imaging Her Erotics: Essays, Interviews, Projects*. Cambridge and London: The MIT Press, 2002.

Schneider, Rebecca. *The Explicit Body in Performance*. New York: Routledge, 1997.

Scholder, Amy. *Pussy Riot, A Punk Prayer for Freedom: Letters from Prison, Songs, Poems, and Courtroom Statements Plus Tributes to the Punk Band That Shook the World*. New York: The Feminist Press at the City University of New York, 2013.

Scrimgeour, Alexander. Review. "Nikita Kadan." *Artforum International* 53, no. 7 (March 2015).

Semenova, Natalia. "A Soviet Museum Experiment." *Canadian-American Slavic Studies* 43, no. 4 (1 January 2009): 81–102.

Shevchenko, Inna. "Topless in the Country of Hijab. An Open Letter." *Huffington Post* (blog), 4 August 2013. Accessed 6 August 2013. http://www .huffingtonpost.co.uk/inna-shevchenko/femen-topless-in-the-country-of -hijab_b_3034211.html.

Shevchenko, Taras. Тарас Шевченко. *Kobzar*. Київ: Вид-во Соломії Павличко Основи, 2001.

– *Selected Works: Poetry and Prose*. Edited by John Weir. Moscow: Progress Publishers, 1960.

Shevel, Oksana. "'De-Communization Laws' Need to Be Amended to Conform to European Standards." *Vox Ukraine*, 7 May 2015. Accessed 14 April 2019. https://voxukraine.org/en/de-communization-laws-need -to-be-amended-to-conform-to-european-standards/.

Shilo Group. Vladyslav Krasnoshchok, Sergiy Lebedynskyy, and Vadym Trykoz. "Euromaidan." Website. Accessed 16 March 2018. http://cargocollective .com/shilo/about-shilo.

Shkandrij, Myroslav. "Contemporary Ukrainian Art and the Twentieth Century Avant-Garde." In *Contemporary Ukraine on the Cultural Map of Europe*, edited by Larissa Onyshkevych and Maria G. Rewakowicz, 411–31. London and New York: M.E. Sharpe and Shevchenko Scientific Society, 2009.

– *Modernists, Marxists and the Nation: The Ukrainian Literary Discussion of the 1920s*. Edmonton: Canadian Institute of Ukrainian Studies Press, 1992.

Shklovsky, Viktor, and Benjamin Sher. *Theory of Prose*. Elmwood Park, IL: Dalkey Archive Press, 1990.

Shore, Marci. *The Ukrainian Night: An Intimate History of Revolution*. New Haven, CT: Yale University Press, 2017.

Sify News. "Topless Ukrainian Feminists Protest Iranian Woman's Death Sentence." Video. 11 November 2012. Accessed 15 January 2012. http://www.kyivpost.com/news/ukraine/detail/89650/.

Skdorenko, V.D. "Postmodernists'ki tendentsii u suchasnomu vizual'nomu mystetstvi Ukrainy kinstsia 1980-pochatuk 1990." *Suchasne mystetstvo*. Kyiv: Akademiia mystestv Ukrainy Instytut problem suchasnoho mystetstva AMU, 2007.

Skuba, Viktoria. "'Madonna' ... from the Oligarch's Land." *Den'/День*, 21 February 2012. Accessed 1 February 2015. http://www.day.Kyiv.ua/en /article/time-out/madonna-oligarchs-land.

Skyba, Mykola. "Who Do Museums Belong to?" In *Exhibit Catalogue: Spirna terytoria / Spornaya terytoria / Disputed Territory 4th Exhibition by the Ukrainian Curatorial Collective HudRada*. Kroshitsky Art Museum. Sevastopol, Crimea: ADEF Ukraine, 2013.

Slaboshpytskiy, Myroslav, dir. *The Tribe*. Film. Kyiv: Harmata Film Production/Ukrainian Film Agency/Hubert Bals Fund, 2014. 35mm.

Smith-Prei, Carrie, and Maria Stehle. *Awkward Politics: Technologies of Popfeminist Activism*. London: McGill-Queen's University Press, 2016.

Soldatov, Andrei, and Irina Borogan. *The Red Web: The Struggle between Russia's Digital Dictators and the New Online Revolutionaries*. Philadelphia: Public Affairs Books, 2015.

Sontag, Susan. *On Photography*. New York: Picador USA, Farrar, Strauss and Giroux, 1977.

SOSka Group (Mykola Ridnyi, Anna Kreventsova, Sergiy Popov). *Barter*. 2007. Video. Accessed 22 February 2018. https://www.youtube.com/watch?v =72lXUiqt0TU.

– "Brushing and Marking Actions." 2009–2012. Video. Images shared by permission of the artist Mykola Ridnyi. SOSka Group website. Accessed 22 February 2018. http://www.soskagroup.com/brushing-and -marking-actions.

Sperling, Valerie. *Sex, Politics, and Putin: Political Legitimacy in Russia*. Oxford: Oxford University Press, 2015.

Spivak, Gayatri Chakravorty. *An Aesthetic Education in the Era of Globalization*. Cambridge, MA: Harvard University Press, 2012.

– *In Other Worlds: Essays in Cultural Politics*. New York: Routledge, 2006.

Splichal, Slavko. *Media beyond Socialism: Theory and Practice in East-Central Europe*. New York: Routledge, 1995.

Stange, Raimar. Review. "Yevgenia Belorusets." *Art Review* 66, no. 6 (September 2014): 137–43.

Starr, Terrell. "A Cop in Ukraine Said He Was Detaining Me Because I Was Black. I Appreciated It: Being a Black Man in Ukraine Showed Me

Everything That's Wrong with Race in the U.S." *The Washington Post*, 2 January 2015. Accessed 1 February 2015. http://www.washingtonpost.com /posteverything/wp/2015/01/02/a-cop-in-ukraine-said-he-was-detaining -me-because-i-was-black-i-appreciated-it/?hpid=z10.

– "Black Ukrainian Woman Faces Five Years in Prison after Baring Breasts during Protest." *The Root*, 28 July 2017. Accessed 30 January 2018. https:// www.theroot.com/black-ukrainian-woman-faces-5-years-in-prison-after -bar-1797329849.

– "Blacks in Ukraine." *The Crisis Magazine*, Summer 2010, 21–5.

Stojanović, Jelena. *An Aesthetic Education in the Era of Globalization.* Cambridge, MA: Harvard University Press, 2012.

– "Internationaleries: Collectivism, the Grotesque, and Cold War Functionalism." In *Collectivism after Modernism: The Art of Social Imagination after 1945*, edited by Blake Stimson and Gregory Sholette, 17–44. Minneapolis: University of Minnesota Press, 2007.

Suny, Ronald G. *The Soviet Experiment: Russia, the USSR, and the Successor States.* New York: Oxford University Press, 2011.

Syba, Hanna. "Pavel Althamer: Welcome Na Konhres Rysuvalnykiv." *Art Ukraine* 6, no. 2 (2013): 118–21.

Sywenky, Irene. "Geopoetics of the Female Body in Postcolonial Ukrainian and Polish Fiction." In *Postcolonial Europe? Essays on Post-Communist Literatures and Cultures*, edited by Dobrota A Pucherová and Róbert Gáfrik, 197–213. Lieden: Brill, 2015.

Szymborska, Wysława. "A Tale Begun." In *View with a Grain of Sand: Selected Poems*, 161–3. Translated by Stanisław Barańczak and Clare Cavanagh. New York: Harcourt Brace & Company, 1993.

Tayler, Jeffrey. "Femen, Ukraine's Topless Warriors." *The Atlantic*, 28 November 2012. Accessed 1 December 2012. http://www.theatlantic.com/international /archive/2012/11/femen-ukraines-topless-warriors/265624/.

– "Topless Jihad: Why Femen Is Right." *The Atlantic*, 1 May 2013. Accessed 9 May 2013. http://www.theatlantic.com/international/archive/2013/05 /topless-jihad-why-femen-is-right/275471/.

– *Topless Jihadis: Inside Femen, the World's Most Provocative Activist Group.* New York: Atlantic Books, 2013.

– "We're Coming for Fox News: Why America Is a Very Dangerous Land for Women, Because It Has Such a Party as the Republican Party." *Salon*, 7 December 2014. Accessed 8 December 2014. http://www.salon.com /2014/12/07/were_coming_for_fox_news_america_is_a_very_dangerous _land_for_women_because_it_has_such_a_party_as_the_republican_party /?source=newsletter.

Tchermalykh, Nataliya. "Feministychnyi analiz politychnyi amal'hamy mizh radykal'nymy i pomirkovanymy natsionalistamy ta relihiinymy pravamy: konservatyvnyi konsensus dovkola gendernykh ta minorytarnykh problematyk suchasnoï Ukraïny." In *Gender, relihiia i natsionalizm v ukraïni* [Gender, religion and nationalism in Ukraine]. Kyiv and Warsaw: Heinrich Böll Siftung, 2012.

– "Making Art, Breaking Law: Exploring Creative Dissent and Cause Lawyering in Contemporary Russia." PhD diss., Graduate Institute of International and Development Studies, Geneva, Switzerland, 2019.

– "Na xvyli Pussy Riot: Nova Xvylya Postradyans'koho Feminizmu?" *Krytyka Polityczna* 4 (2013): 38–42.

– ed. *Shifting Landscapes: Ukrainian Art between Revolution and War.* Kyiv and New York: Rodovid Books; Montreal: Galerie Pangée, 2015.

– "Temni Chasy." *Art Ukraine* 6, no. 2 (2013): 90–2.

– "Vziat' na karandash." *Korydor*, 13 November 2013. Accessed January 2014. http://old.korydor.in.ua/reviews/1507-wzyat-na-karandash.

– "'We Felt That the Country Was in the Stage of a Rough Cut ...': Virtual Emotions, Political Affects and the Ideological Functions of Technologically Mediated Catharsis." *Visual Anthropology Review* (forthcoming). Shared with permission of the author.

– "Will Pussy Riot Dance on #Euromaidan? New Dissidence, Civic Disobedience, and Cyber-Mythology in the Post-Soviet Context." *Religion & Gender* 4, no. 2 (2014): 215–20.

– "Акція «За Рівність! Проти НЕКвізиції!» *Feminist Ofenzywa* (blog). Accessed 3 October 2012. http://ofenzyva.wordpress.com/2012/06/18/za-rivnist-proty-nekvizyci/.

The Krasnals! "Diversity Parade." *Blogger*, 19 June 2012. Accessed 1 November 2013. http://thekrasnals.blogspot.com/2012/06/krasnals-contra-femen-diversity-parade.html.

– "EURO 2012. Polish Activists The Krasnals against Femen Feminists." *The Krasnals Blog*, 3 June 2012. Accessed 10 July 2012. http://thekrasnals.blogspot.com/2012/06/euro-2012-polish-activists-krasnals.html.

– "The Krasnals w Tate Modern. Dzięki Uklańskiemu." *Gazeta.pl.*, 30 November 2009. Accessed 10 June 2013. http://wiadomosci.gazeta.pl/wiadomosci/1,114873,7315003,The_Krasnals_w_Tate_Modern__Dzieki_Uklanskiemu.html.

Thomas, Tanja, and Miriam Stehling. "The Communicative Construction of Femen: Naked Protest in Self-Mediation and German Media Discourse." *Feminist Media Studies* (Routledge Journals) 16, no. 1 (2016): 86–100.

Tilly, Charles. *Democracy.* Cambridge: Cambridge University Press, 2007.

Tilly, Charles, and Sidney Tarrow. *Contentious Politics.* New York: Oxford University Press, 2015.

Tlostanova, Mladina. *Gender Epistemologies and Eurasian Borderlands.* New York: Palgrave Macmillan, 2010.

Tlostanova, Mladina, and Walter D. Mignolo. "Who Speaks for the 'Human' in Human Rights? Dispensable and Bare Lives." In *Learning to Unlearn:*

Decolonial Reflections from Eurasia and the Americas, 153–74. Columbus: Ohio State University Press, 2012.

Todorova, Maria. "Balkanism and Postcolonialism, or, On the Beauty of the Airplane View." In *Marx's Shadow: Knowledge, Power, and Intellectuals in Eastern Europe and Russia*, edited by Costica Bradatan and Serguei Alex Oushakine, 175–96. New York: Roman & Littlefield, 2010.

Tolokonnikova, Nadezhda. *Pussy Riot: Chto Eto Bylo?* Edited by E. Buzev. Moscow: Algoritim, 2012.

Trigos, Ludmilla A. "The Decembrists and Dissidence: Myth and Anti-Myth from the 1960s–1980s." In *The Decembrist Myth in Russian Culture*, 141–60. New York: Palgrave Macmillan, 2009.

– "The Decembrists' Desacralization during the *Glasnost* and Post-Soviet Eras." In *The Decembrist Myth in Russian Culture*, 161–84.

Tsvetaeva, Marina. *Art in the Light of Conscience: Eight Essays on Poetry.* Translated by Angela Livingstone. Cambridge, MA: Harvard University Press, 1992.

– "My Father and His Museum." In *A Captive Spirit: Selected Prose*, translated by Marian J. King, 179–90. Woodstock and New York: Ardis Press, 1980.

– "The Opening of the Museum." In *A Captive Spirit: Selected Prose*, 202–7.

Turgenev, Ivan. *Fathers and Sons.* New York: Oxford University Press, 2008.

United Nations. *Humanitarianism in the Network Age.* Report edited by Rahul Chandran, Andrew Thow, Daniel Gilman, and Andrea Noyes. New York: OCHA Policy and Studies Series, United Nations Publication, 2013.

Uzma, Kolsy. "Put Your Shirts Back on: Why Femen Is Wrong." *The Atlantic*, 6 May 2013. Accessed 9 May 2013. http://www.theatlantic.com/international/archive/2013/05/put-your-shirts-back-on-why-femen-is-wrong/275582/.

Vainshtein, Olga. "Female Fashion, Soviet Style: Bodies of Ideology." In *Russia, Women, Culture*, edited by Helena Goscilo and Beth Holmgren. Bloomington: Indiana University Press, 1996.

Végsö, Roland. *The Naked Communist: Cold War Modernism and the Politics of Popular Culture.* New York: Fordham University Press, 2013.

Venediktova, Larisa. "Homeopathic Aggravation. Similia Similibus Curantur." In *Spirna Teritorya / Spornaya Terytoriya / Disputed Territory 4th Exposition by HudRada. Kroshitsky Art Museum, Sevastopol, Crimea.* Exhibition catalogue. Kyiv: ADEF, 2013.

Verdery, Katherine. *What Was Socialism, and What Comes Next?* Princeton, NJ: Princeton University Press, 1996.

Vertov, Dzyga. *Kino-Eye: The Writings of Dziga Vertov.* Edited by Annette Michelson. Translated by Kevin O'Brien. Berkeley and Los Angeles: University of California Press, 1984.

Visual Culture Research Center [Науково-Дослідний Центр Візуальної Культури]. Website. Accessed 25 January 2018. http://vcrc.org.ua/en/.

– *The Book of Kyiv.* Edited by Kateryna Mishchenko. Kyiv: Medusa Books, 2015.

– *Guidebook of the Kyiv International: Kyiv Biennial 2017*. Edited by Kateryna Mishchenko and Vasyl Cherepanyn. Kyiv: Medusa Books; Art Knyha, 2017.
– The Kyiv International: Kyiv Biennial 2017. 20 October–26 November 2018. Website. Accessed December 2017. http://vcrc.org.ua/en/3497-2/.
– The School of Kyiv Biennial 2015. Website. Accessed November 2015. http://theschoolofkyiv.org/.
– *Ukrainian Body: Exhibition Forbidden*. July 2012. Accessed March 2012. http://www.youtube.com/watch?v=9Ci85aSX6QQ&feature=youtube_gdata_player.
– *Ukrainian Body: Exhibition Forbidden*. Catalogue. Kyiv: Visual Culture Research Center, 2012.
– "Ukrainian Body Petition for Support." Accessed 15 October 2012. http://vcrc.org.ua/ukrbody/.
VCRC, HudRada Curatorial Union, Center for Society Research, and tranzit. at. "Court Experiment." Kyiv. 12 October–12 November 2010. *Art Ukraine*, 10 April 2010. Accessed 31 October 2018. http://artukraine.com.ua/eng/a/proekt-quotsudebnyy-eksperimentquot/#.W9lF6DFrmJA.
Wanner, Catherine. *Burden of Dreams: History and Identity in Post-Soviet Ukraine*. University Park, PA: Pennsylvania State University Press, 1998.
Warner, Michael. "The Mass Public and the Mass Subject." In *Publics and Counterpublics*, 159–86. New York: Zone Books, 2002.
Way, Lucan. *Pluralism by Default: Weak Autocrats and the Rise of Competitive Politics*. Baltimore: Johns Hopkins University Press, 2015.
Way, Lucan, and Steven Levitsky. *Competitive Authoritarianism: Hybrid Regimes after the Cold War*. New York: Cambridge University Press, 2010.
White, Hayden. *The Content of the Form: Narrative Discourse and Historical Representation*. Baltimore: Johns Hopkins University Press, 1987.
Wilson, Andrew. *Ukraine Crisis: What It Means for the West*. New Haven, CT: Yale University Press, 2014.
– *The Ukrainians: Unexpected Nation*. New Haven, CT: Yale University Press, 2009.
Wolff, Larry. *Inventing Eastern Europe: The Map of Civilization on the Mind of the Enlightenment*. Stanford: Stanford University Press, 1994.
Yekelchyk, Serhy. "The Orange Revolution and the EuroMaidan." *The Conflict in Ukraine: What Everyone Needs to Know*. Oxford: Oxford UP, 2015: 85–114.
– *Ukraine: Birth of a Modern Nation*. Oxford and New York: Oxford University Press, 2007.
– "What Is Ukrainian about Ukraine's Pop Culture? The Strange Case of Verka Serduchka." *Canadian-American Slavic Studies* 44, no. 1 (1 June 2010): 217–32.
Yurchak, Alexei. *Everything Was Forever, Until It Was No More: The Last Soviet Generation*. Princeton, NJ: Princeton University Press, 2005.
– "Revolutions and Their Translators: Maidan, the Conflict in Ukraine, and the Russian New Left." *Cultural Anthropology*, 28 October 2014. Accessed 21

March 2015. http://www.culanth.org/fieldsights/619-revolutions-and
-their-translators-maidan-the-conflict-in-ukraine-and-the-russian-new-left.

Zabuzhko, Oksana. *Fieldwork in Ukrainan Sex*. Translated by Halyna Hryn.
AmazonCrossing, 2011.

– *Pol'ovi doslidzhennia z Ukrains'koho seksu*. Kyiv: Fakt, 2009.

Zguta, Russell. *Russian Minstrels: A History of the Skomorokhi*. Philadelphia:
University of Pennsylvania Press, 1978.

Zhurzhenko, Tatiana. "Gender, Nation, and Reproduction: Demographic
Discourses and Politics in Ukraine after the Orange Revolution." In *Gender,
Politics, and Society in Ukraine*, 131–51. Toronto: University of Toronto Press,
2012.

Žižek, Slavoj. *Tarrying with the Negative: Kant, Hegel, and the Critique of Ideology*.
Durham: Duke University Press, 1993.

Zlobina, Tamara. "Gender, Maidan, War, and That Which Will Be after the War."
In *Henderni doslidzhennya. Donbas Studies*, 138–55. Kyiv: Izolyatsia, 2015.

– "Hender, majdan i vijna, i te, shho pislya vijny." *Gendernye issledovaniia*
16 (2007).

Zubrzycki, Geneviève. "Aesthetic Revolt and the Remaking of National
Identity in Quebec, 1960–1969." *Theory and Sociology* 42 (2013): 423–75.

– "Introduction. Matter and Meaning: A Cultural Sociology of Nationalism."
In *National Matters: Materiality, Culture, and Nationalism*, edited by Geneviève
Zubrzycki, 1–20. Redwood City, CA: Stanford University Press, 2017.

Zychowicz, Jessica. "Femen, A Litmus." In *Transgressive Women in Modern
Russian and East European Cultures: From the Bad to the Blasphemous*, edited by
Beth Holmgren, Yana Hashamova, and Mark Lipovetsky, 165–81. New York:
Routledge, 2016.

– "FE/M/EN and the Avant Garde: Locating the Text." In *The Idea of the Avant
Garde – And What It Means Today*, Vol. 2, edited by Marc James Léger, 332–40.
Chicago: University of Chicago Press and Intellect Books, 2020.

– "The Global Controversy over Pussy Riot: An Anti-Putin Women's Protest
Group in Moscow." *International Institute Journal* (University of Michigan),
Fall 2012.

– "Introduction." In *Shifting Landscapes: Ukrainian Art between Revolution and
War*, edited by Nataliya Tchermalykh, translated by Jessica Zychowicz.
Originally published in Russian as Подвижный пейзаж. Translated into
French by Nataliya Tchermalykh as *Paysages instables*. Kyiv and New York:
Rodovid Books; Montreal: Galerie Pangée, 2015. English version forthcoming.

– "*My, Autsaiderky*: Virginia Woolf i feminizm u hlobal'nii perspektyvi / We,
Outsiders: Virginia Woolf and Feminism in Global Perspective." *Korydor*,
5 February 2019. Accessed 21 March 2019. http://www.korydor.in.ua/ua
/stories/mi-autsajderky-virdzhiniya-vulf-i-feminizm-u-globalnij-perspektyvi
.html.

– "Performing Protest: Femen, Nation, and the Marketing of Resistance."
  Krytyka: Journal of Ukrainian Politics and Society 1 (April 2015). Accessed
  18 May 2017. http://jups.krytyka.com/articles/performing-protest-femen
  -nation-and-marketing-resistance.

– "Reimagining Utopias: Art and Politics in 21st Century Ukraine: Interview
  with Jessica Zychowicz and Maria Kulikowska." Podcast hosted by
  Juliet Jacques. *Suite 212*, July 2018. Accessed 1 November 2018. https://
  soundcloud.com/suite-212/reimagining-utopias-art-and-politics-in-21st
  -century-ukraine.

–, trans. "Poems," by Taras Fedirko. In "Documenting Maidan." Special issue
  edited by Yevgenia Belorusets, Nelia Vakhovska, and Nataliya Tchermalykh.
  Prostory Literary Journal, no. 8 (December 2013–February 2014).

– "Pussy Riot Arrest at Sochi Reinforces Their Cult Status." *The Conversation*,
  19 February 2014. Accessed 10 November 2014. https://theconversation.
  com/pussy-riot-arrest-at-sochi-reinforces-their-cult-status-23277.

– "Two Bad Words: FEMEN and Feminism in Independent Ukraine."
  Anthropology of East Anthropology of East Europe Review 29, no. 2 (Fall 2011):
  215–27.

– "Ukraine Hosts Most Successful LGBTQ Event in the Nation's History,
  but New Challenges Appear." *Focus Ukraine: A Blog of the Kennan Institute*,
  2 August 2019. Accessed 24 March 2020. https://www.wilsoncenter.org
  /blog-post/ukraine-hosts-most-successful-lgbtq-event-the-nations-history
  -new-challenges-appear.

Zychowicz, Jessica, and Nataliya Tchermalykh. "Global Protest Movements
  in American-Ukrainian Dialogue: From Femen to Occupy / Погляд на
  глобальні протестні рухи з Американсько-Української перспективи: від
  Femen до Occupy." *Krona* 33 (October 2013).

– "Asymptotes: Pussy Riot and FEMEN's Global Trajectories in Law,
  Society, and Culture." In *The Routledge International Handbook to Gender in
  Central-Eastern Europe and Eurasia*, edited by Mara I. Lazda, Katalin Fabian,
  and Janet E. Johnson. Forthcoming.

Index

abortion, 135, 194, 280; and proposed ban, 89, 185, 244

Abramović, Marina, 111–12, 321

Actionists, Viennese, 88–9, 111

activism, 74, 143, 189, 320n78, 348n57; locally scaled definitions of need, 26; new media technologies and the sex wars of the 1970s, 77; transatlantic contexts of the 1990s and 1920s, 24, 141; women's, 128, 133

Adorno, Teodor, 31, 109, 254; opposition between art and reality, 109; representation, 111

aesthetics, 11, 119, 131, 194, 219, 237, 315n1, 331n89, 342n74; anarchism-as-aesthetics, 224, 336n15, 341n61; Ariella Azoulay and affective qualities of an image, 169; digital surfaces and real-time contexts, 93; in early Soviet filmmaking, 145; materialist, 144, 206; modernism and Ukrainians in the early avant-garde, 203; Soviet propaganda aesthetics, 246–7, 252; subversive, 39, 78, 115, 145, 300; of survival and post-Soviet life, 155; traditional folk, 52, 196;

and Walter Benjamin, 11. *See also* performance; protest

Agamben, Giorgio, 231, 343n78

agora: agoraphilia, 97, 199, 217; museum, 236

allegory, 11, 18, 210, 238, 280; of collective subjugation/emancipation, 47, 58; for the exchange of women in economic relations, 74; geopolitical, 47, 212, 279; national, 40, 62, 71, 195, 205, 210; production of space, 192, 265; and Walter Benjamin, 161

Althamer, Pawel, 215

Althusser, Louis, 341n62

Alyokhina, Maria, 83–4; of Pussy Riot, 22

Amazon figure: as allegory, 56, 66, 309n69 (*see also* archetype and myth); New Amazons, 32, 79; as site for power relations in Western myths of East, 47–9, 74; and Voltaire, 50

anachronism, 49, 55, 195, 216; of the female body and nation in modernity, 49; and political subjectivity, 129; in public narratives in the 2000s, 62

proliferation of mass culture and pop culture, 14, 306n37

glass house: as symbol of surveillance and crowds, 240; as symbol of utopia, 239; as trope in fin-de-siècle literature, 138, 140

globalization, cultural, 143–4, 341n61

Gogol Street 32 Project, 18, 147, 159, 161–2, 169–74, 192, 331n82

Great Patriotic War, 310n77; memorial museum to, 309; myth, 248; socialist-realist depictions of, 55

Green, Kitty, 71

Habermas, Jürgen, 31, 63, 307n42, 318n45

Halberstam, Judith (Jack), 181, 185, 333n113, 334n122

happenings, 40; antipolitical, 106; end of the Polish People's Republic, 13; Femen, 73, 109; genre, 30, 38, 306n39; Major Frydrych, 39–40. See also performance

Haraway, Donna J., 96,

Heavenly Hundred (Heroyiv Nebesnoyi Sotni), 36, 252–3, 294

Hebdige, Dick, 116

hegemonic masculinity, 175

heroes: heroes/villains, 294; heroines, 49, 55, 318n48; heroism, 161, 199; Slavic, 52; superfluous, 6, 198; unsung, 284

heteronormative privilege, 181–3

Hnylytska, Ksenia, 336n16

homophobia, 177, 183–6

homosexuality, 185; decriminalize, 177, 282

Hrushevsky Street, 36, 193–5, 252. See also Heavenly Hundred (Heroyiv Nebesnoyi Sotni)

HudRada, 192–3, 228–30, 236, 240–2, 246, 260, 290–1; censorship case, 294; and counternarratives to national museum system, 206, 214; Disputed Territory exhibit, 194–5, 215; and "the political," 198. See also REP Group (Revolutionary Experimental Space); VCRC (Visual Culture Research Center)

human rights, 5, 282, 296, 308n58; Human Rights Watch, 245, 259, 346n35; and Hannah Arendt, 340n57, 343n78

Hutsol, Anna, 106, 317n35, 323n109; and changing climate for protest in Ukraine, 27, 40, 64, 86, 101; leadership critique of, 123; on the Orange Revolution, 33; and Slutwalks in 2012, 315n3; stance on sex work, 321n88; and transnational feminism, 5, 100. See also Femen

ICTM Art Workers Self-Defense Initiative, 328n47; formation of new cultural policy principles, 211, 336n16; international open letter on censorship, 208, 338n33; Maidan, 217, 349n7

International Women's Day, 9, 17, 123, 128, 132–5, 142, 150

internet, 20, 24, 71; and the body as function of ideology and politics, 213; censorship from Google, 108; censorship laws, 187; generation, 223; globalized Ukraine, 48, 63, 254; media culture, 34, 221; meme culture, 34, 113, 221. See also Maidan Revolution

internet access, 345n24, 346n32

interrevolutionary, 17, 19, 295

against unfair elections, 28, 32, 127, 185; as site for nonviolent civil demonstrations, 13, 20, 134; as site of police violence against civil demonstrations, 188, 237, 296; as site of protest performance parodies, 31, 34, 48, 74, 205. *See also* Maidan Revolution of Dignity; Orange Revolution

Maidan Revolution of Dignity, 8, 32, 293, 308n54, 340n57; and the church, 338n28; depiction in film, 261–4, 278; and differing concepts of freedom and independence, 18–22, 221; and emancipatory rhetoric surrounding, 11, 193, 214, 253, 284; feminism post-revolution, 117, 122–3, 128, 175; impacts on cultural institutions post-revolution, 243–6, 251–2, 285, 296, 339n39, 340n51; oligarchy and separatism, 348n1–4; and Putin during Sochi Olympics, 73; and removal of Lenin statues, 85, 132, 262, 279; and the shift of generations, 221, 248; women demonstrators in, 136, 188, 192. *See also* Orange Revolution; Russia-Ukraine conflict

Malashkin, Sergei, 232

Malevich, Kazimir, 206, 209–10

Martsenyuk, Tamara: and critiques of International Women's Day, 309n66; decreasing social tolerance towards gender minorities in Ukraine, 122; gender inequality in employment, 327n37; and NGOs analyses of, 182

Marx, Karl, 144, 187, 326n25

Marxism: Marxist-oriented theorists, 10, 114, 149, 310n78, 317n36; Marxist traditionalists, 149,

211; and notion of international friendship, 132

Masoch, Leopold Von Sacher, 51

Mayerchyk, Mariya, 81; connotations of feminism and its Soviet connections, 12, 29, 30; and critique of Femen, 303n5, 312n102, 319n52, 322n97, 324n110; gender in Ukrainian public speech, 185–6; and journal *Krytyka*, 189. *See also* Ofenzywa Feministychna

media activism: body message, 114; internet culture, 79

Method Fund, 268; relations with cultural institutions, 208, 268

Minakov, Mikhail, 246, 344n6, 348n3

Mishchenko, Kateryna, 24, 194, 334n1, 336n13; creative ethnographic essays of everyday life in Ukraine, 293

modernism: and origins in masculinist notions of linear progress, 56; post-Soviet modernism, 199; Soviet modernism, 213; themes of expansion, building, and invention, 219

Mohanty, Chandra, 331n88

Monumentalism, 213

monuments, 186–7, 248–50, 274, 277, 309n71; and #SaveKyivModernism, 251, 344n18; cross-cutting, 83–9; and decommunization laws, 245, 276; national, 59

Mouffe, Chantal, 323n103; agonistics and concept of "the political," 130, 325n13–16, 341n62; articulation among public spaces, 37; dissensus and critical art, 122, 332; participatory publics and the culture market, 31

Plungian, Nadiya, 176, 179–80,
347n40; feminist debates in art,
332n104
Poland, 30, 61, 82, 107, 180,
241, 257, 289, 306n37; Polska
Rzeczpospolita Ludowa (PRL),
13; National Museum in Warsaw
and censorship in newly elected
government, 111
Poland and Ukraine: avant-garde
art in 1980s, 30, 39, 218, 306;
exchanges between, 39, 72, 117;
events of 1989 and demonstrations
on Maidan, 289, 301n26; histories
of occupation and foreign rule,
37, 61, 216; as hooligan twins, 73,
107, 115; mainstream audiences
in, 117; and Russia and art under
authoritarianism, 241; strong
desire for change over stagnation,
37. See also Krasnals
police state, 32–4, 38, 185, 193–5, 234,
262, 266, 290
"the political": in Nancy Fraser's
critique of the roles of culture
and economics in second-wave
feminism, 315n6, 320n75; in
ideas of good and bad feminism,
322n97; and question of the role of
art in politics, 198; search for more
critical model of the contemporary
public sphere, 110; versus the
aesthetic, 331n89
politics, 10, 144–5, 179, 204, 343n78;
aesthetics and art-activism, 78,
109, 315n1, 329n59, 331n89;
and claims-making, 38; and
the configuration of space, 69,
222–3, 226–7; of detachment, 204;
of everyday life and gender in
late-Soviet culture, 18; of female
subjectivity, 11, 187, 300n9, 346n36;

of feminism(s) in Eastern Europe,
108, 134; of gender difference, 222;
and the internet, 213, 323n98–9;
of memory, 261; oppositional, 110,
223; performative notion of, 11,
206; and public relations with the
church, 338n28; relationship to art,
22, 176, 241–2, 320n75, 331n89; of
the self and censorship, 213, 227;
of self-expression, censorship,
and protest in civic vocabularies,
21, 39, 97, 114, 160, 288, 325n13,
326n25, 337n18; transnational, 252.
See also feminism
pop culture, 65, 306n37–40;
idiomatic, 30–1, 68, 74
PORA, 256, 308n59
pornography, 98, 257, 323n109;
Catharine MacKinnon and
debates about, 78
postcolonial, 31, 317n41, 328;
feminism as a cultural axis,
99; and former "Second
World," 42, 62; Homi Bhabha
and postmodernism, 206;
intersectional feminist critiques
and theory, 99–100; national
autonomy and feminism, 12,
312n102; production of the citizen-
subject, 238, 331n88; Rosi Bradiotti
and nomadic feminism, 311n90
postcommunism, 4, 10; cultural
myths about poverty and, 175;
intersecting with globalization,
24, 108, 196; local women's
own experiences, 119, 227;
as a nonclassical instance of
postcoloniality, 12, 224, 317n41;
Western receptions of post-Soviet
feminism, 25, 38, 185, 288, 315n7
post-Maidan, 32, 44; civic
vocabulary for, 270; creative

of issues in Ukraine, 9, 25. *See also* body language; race

Riabchuk, Anastasia, 285; gender marginalization, 175; socioeconomic inequality, 174

Ridnyi, Mykola, 205, 232–4, 341n68, 342n70; the invisibility of the experiences of people, 233; the journal *Prostory*, 276; and SOSka Group, 231

rights, 6, 42, 78, 148, 303n4; conflicts around gender equality and the Soviet past, 186; designation of in the production of citizen-subjects by the state, 238; emerging links between citizenship and electronic media in national imaginaries, 20, 38, 122; failure to sign the Anti-Discrimination Law, 242–4; and the question of the role of the artist in society, 204; radical critique of democratic ethos in a receding public sphere, 239; women's in transatlantic history of activism between Washington and Kyiv, 141–2

Rodchenko, Alexander, 162–4, 172, 190; constructivism, 153; contrast to the laws of Soviet photography, 17–18, 130, 152, 166; representations of daily life, 175; social transformation, 146, 172–3

ruin, 20, 147, 152; documented as modern life, 149, 161; ideological meanings that pervade common language, 164; of institutions, 258; Soviet, 261, 276

Rukh, political youth group, 44

Ruslana, 307n51; erotic fantasy of Ukraine, 68; and ideological design of the Colour Revolutions, 30, 49, 66–71

Russian Futurism, 56, 327n40

Russia-Ukraine conflict, 276–8; and cultural production, 25, 131; memory politics, 204, 245–8, 280–4; museum, 246. *See also* war

samizdat, 43; nonconformist strategies, 20, 339n39

Samutsevich, Yekaterina, 84

satire: and cultural rhetoric of the Orange Revolution, 16; and feminist deconstruction of national canons, 61; on the global sex industry, 102; and mass-media logics of erotic identification, alienation, and consumption, 125; self-deprecatory, 66; on Ukraine's relationship with Europe, 69; and Western hegemony, 95, 106–7

Schechner, Richard, 38

Schneeman, Carolee, 88

School of Kyiv, First Biennial, 251, 286; panel titles and events, 255, 259, 285; role of art in public life, 257. *See also* VCRC (Visual Culture Research Center)

Second World War, 95, 347n50; myth, 248; Soviet mythology, 134; Stalinism and fascism, 149, 254, 301n27, 329n59. See also *war*

self-education and social organizing, 259, 348n4; in securing freer spaces for education and open debate, 295; in struggle for fair labour practices in cultural institutions, 204; in women's groups and the question of violence on Maidan, 142, 189; women's rights and legacy of International Women's Day, 133

Symbolism: dissolution of the movement at the turn-of-the-century, 219; high modernism in the 1920s, 203; universalization of the body in public rhetoric, 10, 238

Tchermalykh, Nataliya, 124, 327n34; curator of *A Room of One's Own* series, 137, 146, 176, 180–1; divisions between private/public and social stigmas, 176; feminist debates around Femen, 121, 322n98; feminist debates around Pussy Riot, 316n19; Feminist Pencil II Moscow, 347n41; film screening of *Maidan: Rough Cut*, 264; *Prostory Magazine*, 328n47, 334n1, 339n41; *Ukrainian Body Exhibit*, 137, 323n108. *See also* Ofenzywa

Tolokonnikova, Nadezhda, 83, 189, 222; court case and trial, 84
totalitarianism, 88, 205, 285
The Tribe (Plemya) 2014 film, 277, 281, 326n26
tropes, 21, 276–9, 326; of the dissident, 222; feminism as ideal, 7, 125; for imperialism, 201, 216; information commoditization, 98; "nomadic subjectivity," 187; racial, 103; of violence, 91
Tsvetaeva, Marina, 240–1; museum and women's limited access to, 201–2
Turgenev, Ivan, 4, 57
Tyler, Amina, 93
Tymoshenko, Yulia, 9, 32, 68, 287, 308n58

Ukrainian Body Exhibit, 146, 326n26; closed and banned from Kyiv-Mohyla Academy, 137, 205–7,

249, 332n102; and "homosexual propaganda," 236; and the marginalization of different minorities, 18, 177, 183, 206, 213; petition to reinstate the centre in the university, 378
Ukrainka, Lesia, 117, 186–7
utopia, 16, 31, 66–8, 72; and anarchism, 224; in artistic innovation v. conformism, 212; critiques of society during the interrevolutionary period in 2000s Ukraine, 17; grand narratives of capitalism and socialism, 280–8; illusions of permanence in Russia's imperial nineteenth century, 200; in imagined modernities, 288; in modern life, 140, 318n48; in modernism, 145; Milan Kundera, 140, 239; NEP era, 88–9; suspended timeframes of revolution, 192; Ukraine's state-museum complex, 230; visual language in counterimages, 118

VALIE EXPORT, 88–9, 114
VCRC (Visual Culture Research Center), 118, 137, 176, 205, 215; autonomy and rhetoric of dissidence, 248–9, 257–9; censorship and decommunization, 252, 260, 285; and October Cinema, 294; and Ofenzywa feminist workshop, 136–7; and Oksana Briukhovetska, 118–19, 146; shutdown over *Ukrainian Body* exhibit, 183, 332n102, 337n23. *See also* Briukhovetska, Oksana; Cherepanyn, Vasyl
Vertov, Dzyga, 145–9, 167, 329n55
Vorotniov, Vova, 136, 246–8, 277, 326n26